JUNK

—RECORD OF THE LAST HERO—

KIA ASAMIYA PRESENTS

5

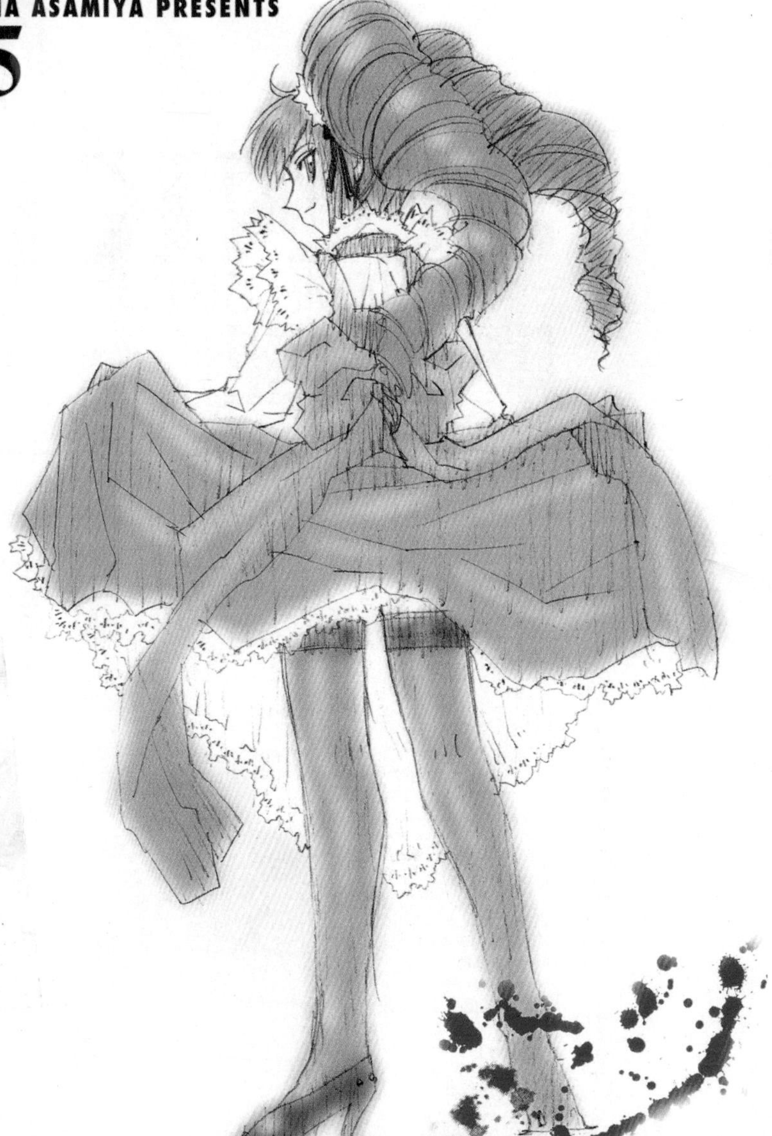

JUNK
—RECORD OF THE LAST HERO—
麻宮騎亜
KIA ASAMIYA PRESENTS

Author / Kia Asamiya
Translator / Kenji Komiya
Production / Bryce Gunkel
English Adaptation / Ailen Lujo
Editor / Benjamin Stone
Supervising Editor / Matthew Scrivner
V.P. of Operations / Yuki Chung
President / Jennifer Chen

JUNK - RECORD OF THE LAST HERO - volume 5
© STUDIO TRON 2006
Originally published in Japan in 2006 by Akita Publishing Co.,Ltd.
English translation rights arranged with Akita Publishing Co.,Ltd.
through TOHAN CORPORATION, Tokyo.

JUNK - RECORD OF THE LAST HERO - volume 5
English translation © 2007 DrMaster Publications Inc.

Publisher
DrMaster Publications Inc.
4044 Clipper Ct.
Fremont, CA 94538
www.DrMasterpublications.com

First Edition: December 2007

ISBN 13: 978-1-59796-135-6

JUNK
— RECORD OF THE LAST HERO —

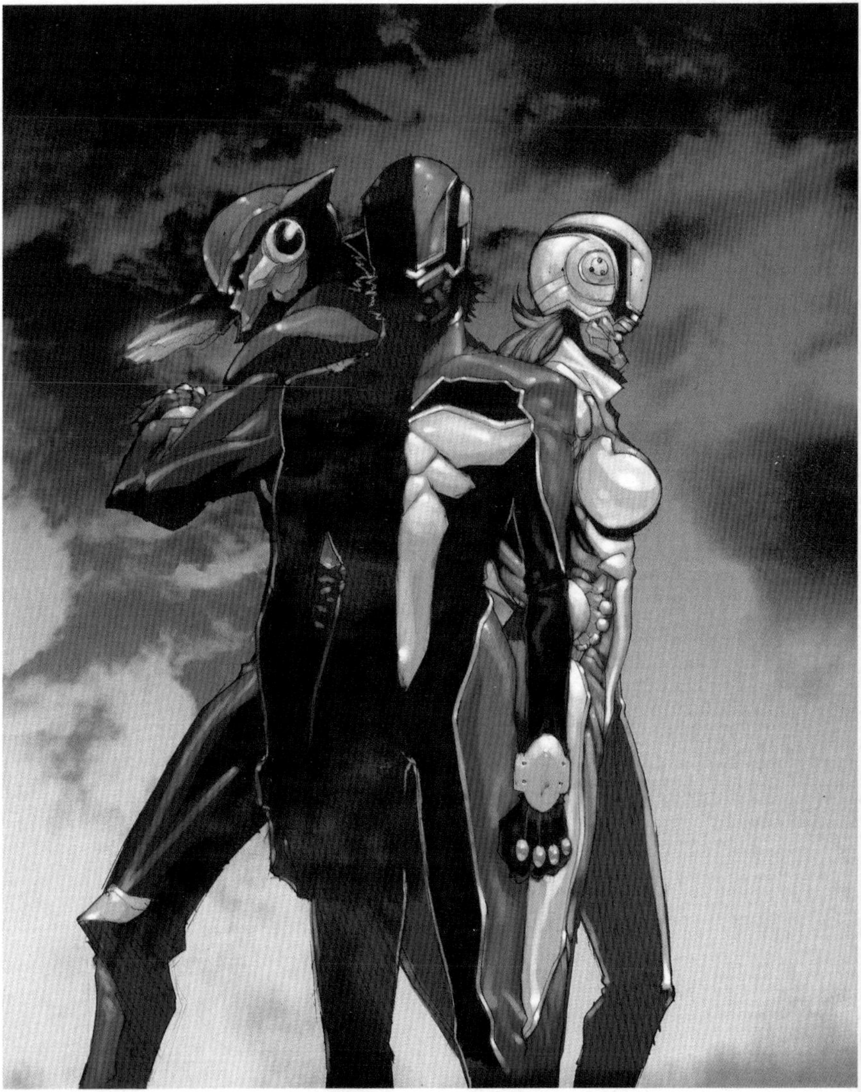

KIA ASAMIYA

JUNK
—RECORD OF THE LAST HERO—
KIA ASAMIYA PRESENTS

5
CONTENTS

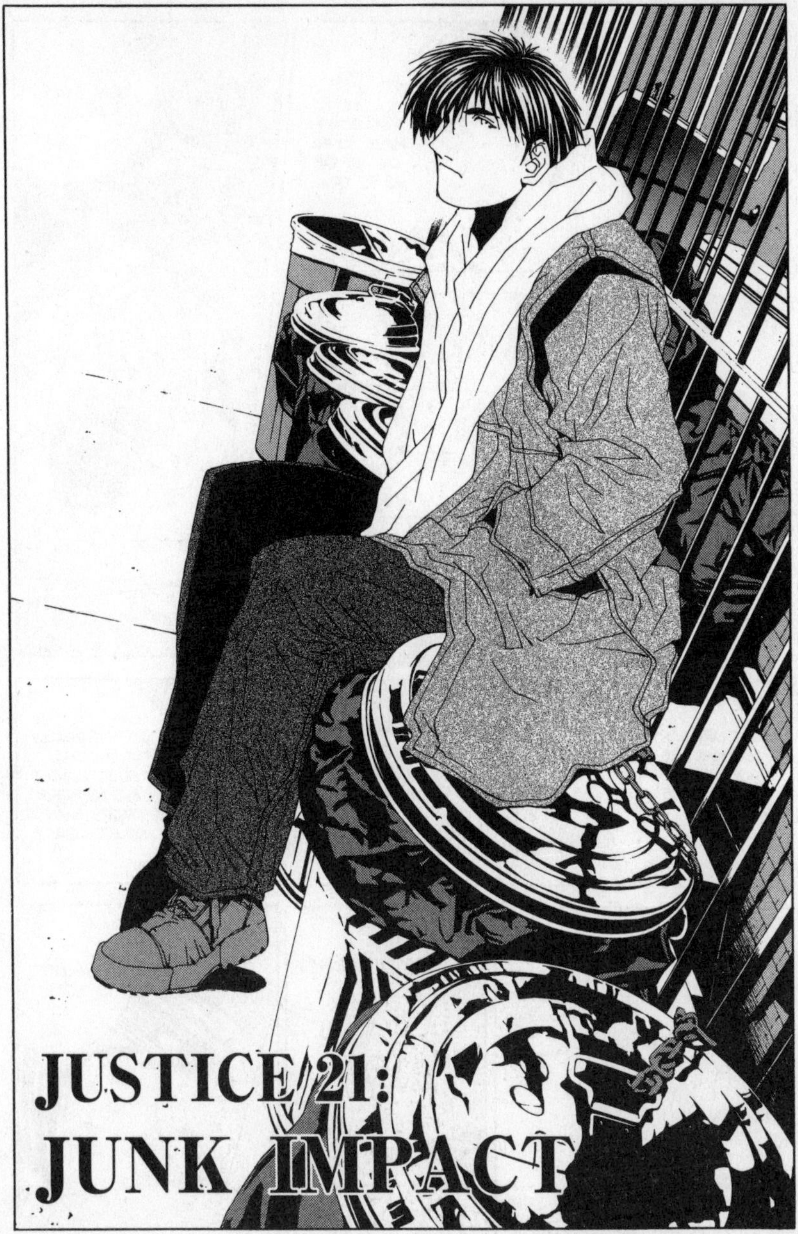
JUSTICE 21:
JUNK IMPACT

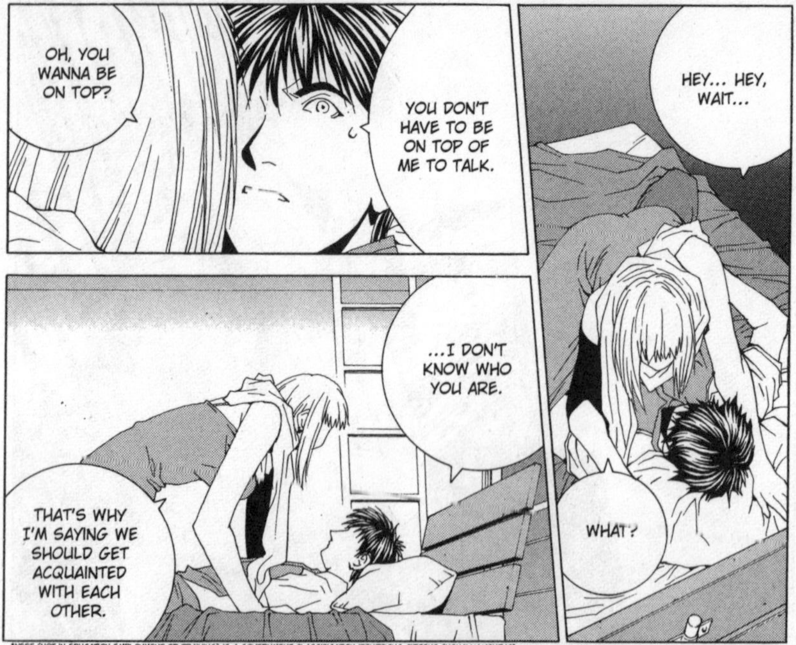
HEY... HEY, WAIT...
WHAT?
YOU DON'T HAVE TO BE ON TOP OF ME TO TALK.
OH, YOU WANNA BE ON TOP?
...I DON'T KNOW WHO YOU ARE.
THAT'S WHY I'M SAYING WE SHOULD GET ACQUAINTED WITH EACH OTHER.

*NEET (NOT IN EDUCATION EMPLOYMENT OR TRAINING) IS A GOVERNMENT CLASSIFICATION IDENTIFYING CITIZENS (USUALLY YOUTHS) WHO ARE NEITHER IN SCHOOL NOR ACTIVELY PURSUING WORK OR JOB TRAINING.

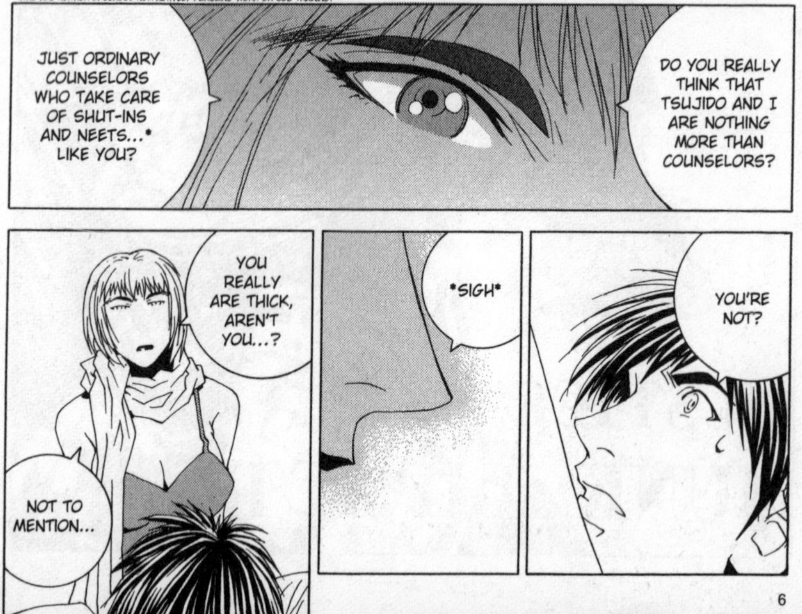
DO YOU REALLY THINK THAT TSUJIDO AND I ARE NOTHING MORE THAN COUNSELORS?
JUST ORDINARY COUNSELORS WHO TAKE CARE OF SHUT-INS AND NEETS...* LIKE YOU?
YOU'RE NOT?
SIGH
YOU REALLY ARE THICK, AREN'T YOU...?
NOT TO MENTION...

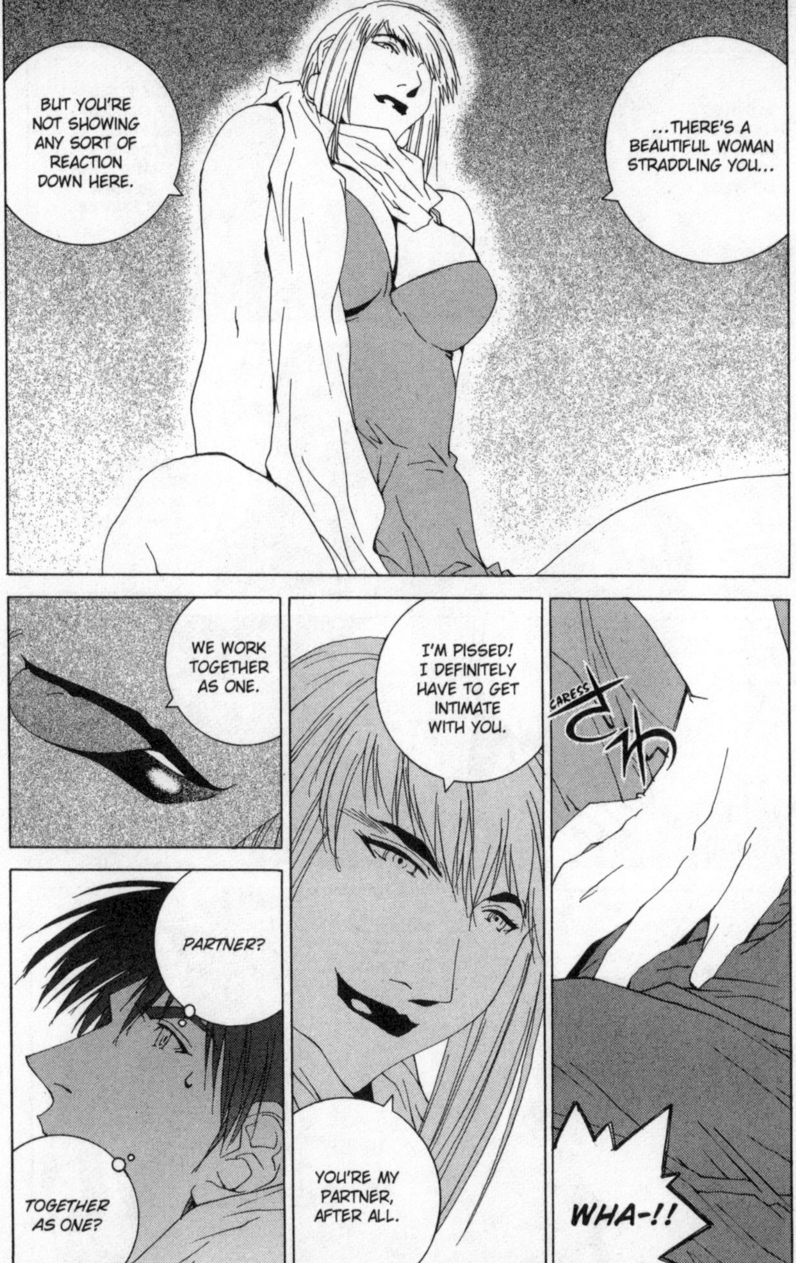
...THERE'S A BEAUTIFUL WOMAN STRADDLING YOU...
BUT YOU'RE NOT SHOWING ANY SORT OF REACTION DOWN HERE.
CARESS
WHA-!!
I'M PISSED! I DEFINITELY HAVE TO GET INTIMATE WITH YOU.
YOU'RE MY PARTNER, AFTER ALL.
WE WORK TOGETHER AS ONE.
PARTNER?
TOGETHER AS ONE?

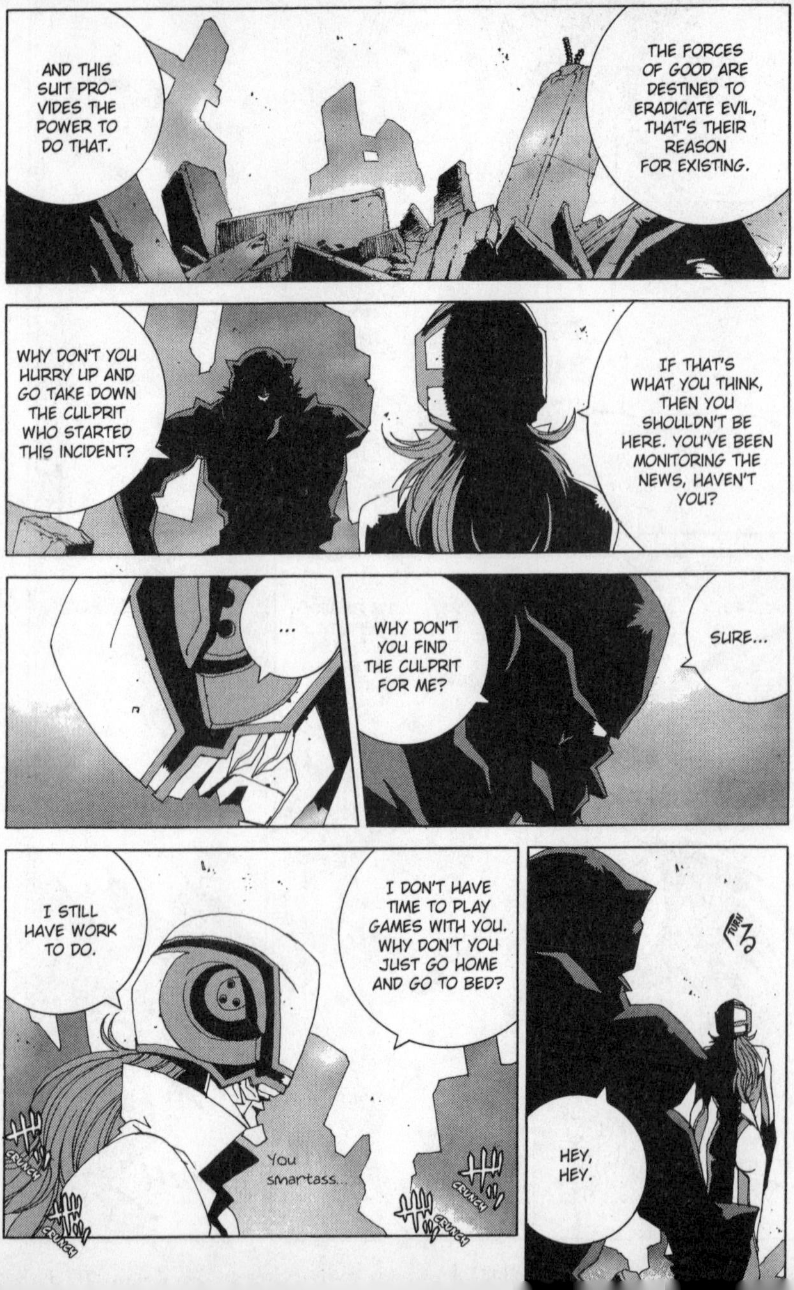
THE FORCES OF GOOD ARE DESTINED TO ERADICATE EVIL, THAT'S THEIR REASON FOR EXISTING.
AND THIS SUIT PRO-VIDES THE POWER TO DO THAT.
IF THAT'S WHAT YOU THINK, THEN YOU SHOULDN'T BE HERE. YOU'VE BEEN MONITORING THE NEWS, HAVEN'T YOU?
WHY DON'T YOU HURRY UP AND GO TAKE DOWN THE CULPRIT WHO STARTED THIS INCIDENT?
SURE...
WHY DON'T YOU FIND THE CULPRIT FOR ME?
...
TURN
HEY, HEY.
I DON'T HAVE TIME TO PLAY GAMES WITH YOU. WHY DON'T YOU JUST GO HOME AND GO TO BED?
I STILL HAVE WORK TO DO.
CRUNCH
CRUNCH
You smartass...
CRUNCH
CRUNCH

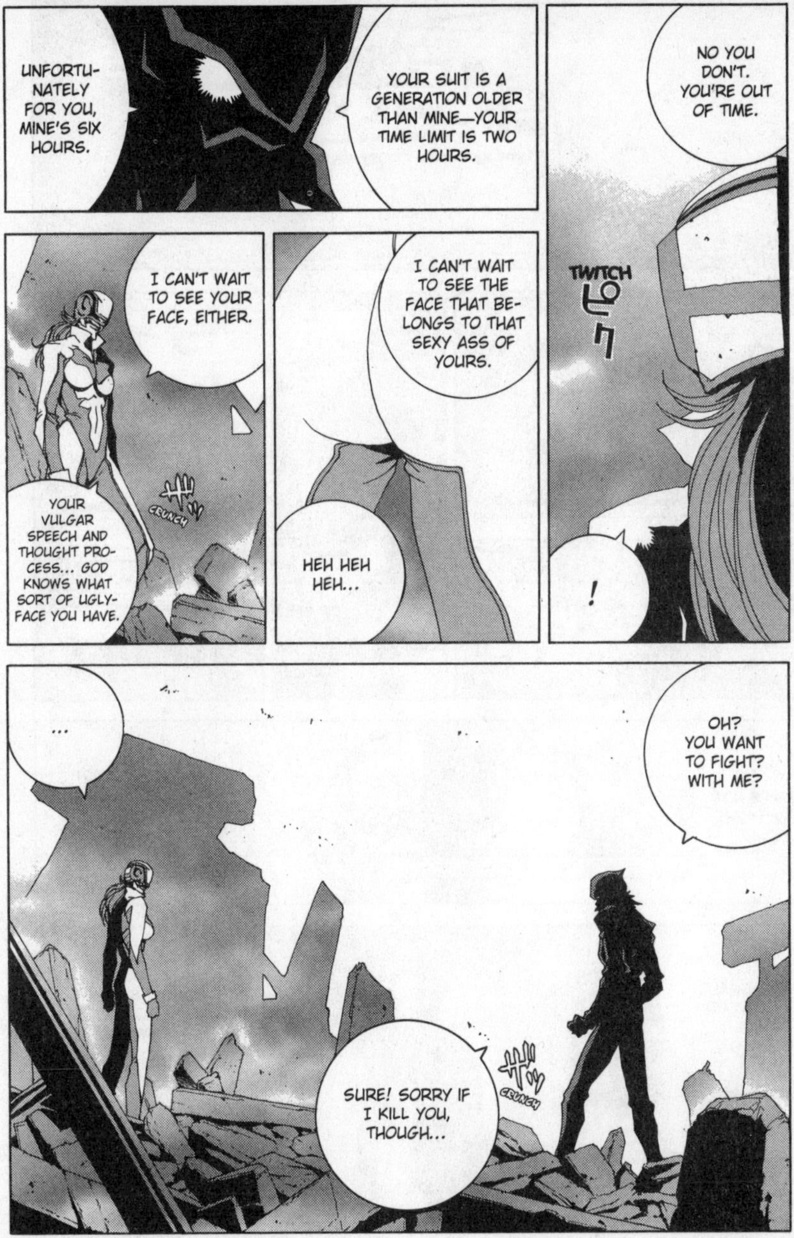
NO YOU DON'T. YOU'RE OUT OF TIME.
TWITCH
ピク
!
YOUR SUIT IS A GENERATION OLDER THAN MINE—YOUR TIME LIMIT IS TWO HOURS.
UNFORTUNATELY FOR YOU, MINE'S SIX HOURS.
I CAN'T WAIT TO SEE THE FACE THAT BELONGS TO THAT SEXY ASS OF YOURS.
HEH HEH HEH...
I CAN'T WAIT TO SEE YOUR FACE, EITHER.
CRUNCH
YOUR VULGAR SPEECH AND THOUGHT PROCESS... GOD KNOWS WHAT SORT OF UGLY-FACE YOU HAVE.
OH? YOU WANT TO FIGHT? WITH ME?
...
CRUNCH
SURE! SORRY IF I KILL YOU, THOUGH...

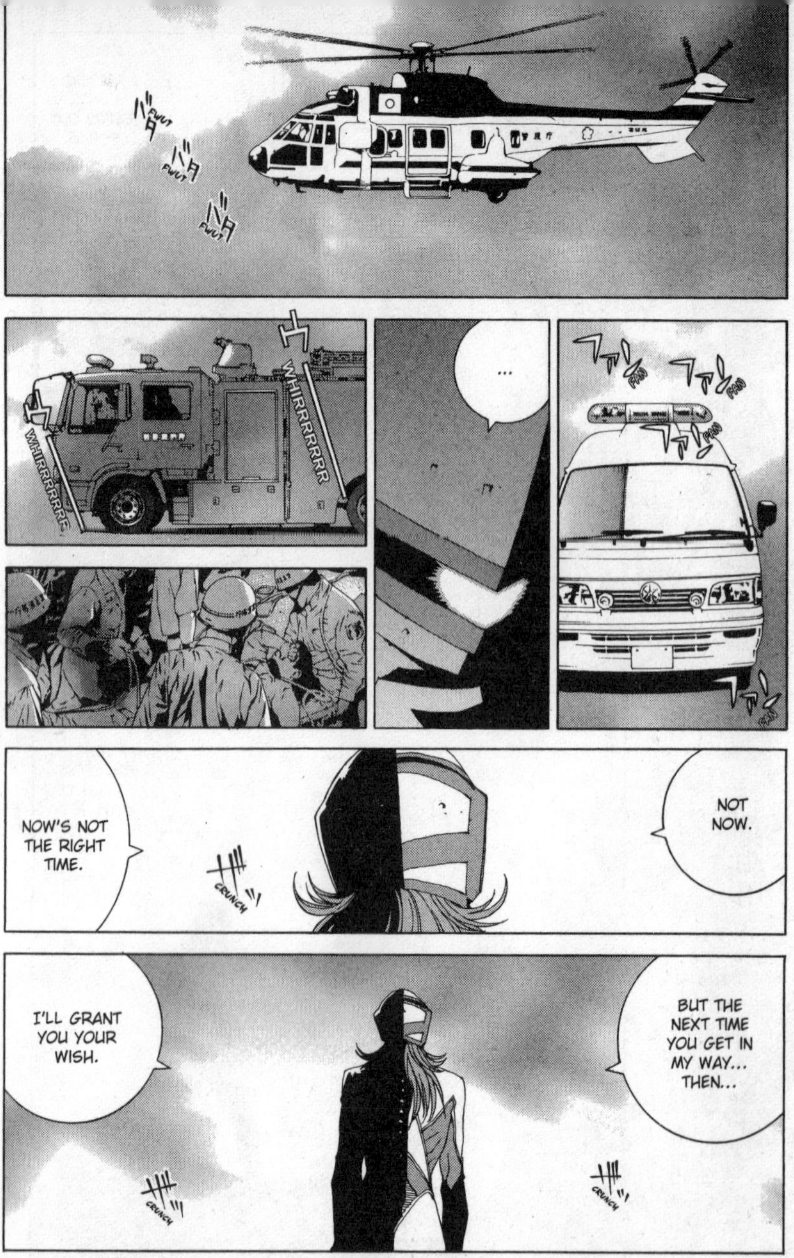
FWUT
FWUT
FWUT
FAN
FAN
FAN
FAN
...
WHIRRRRRRR
WHIRRRRRRR
NOT NOW.
NOW'S NOT THE RIGHT TIME.
CRUNCH
BUT THE NEXT TIME YOU GET IN MY WAY... THEN...
I'LL GRANT YOU YOUR WISH.
CRUNCH
CRUNCH

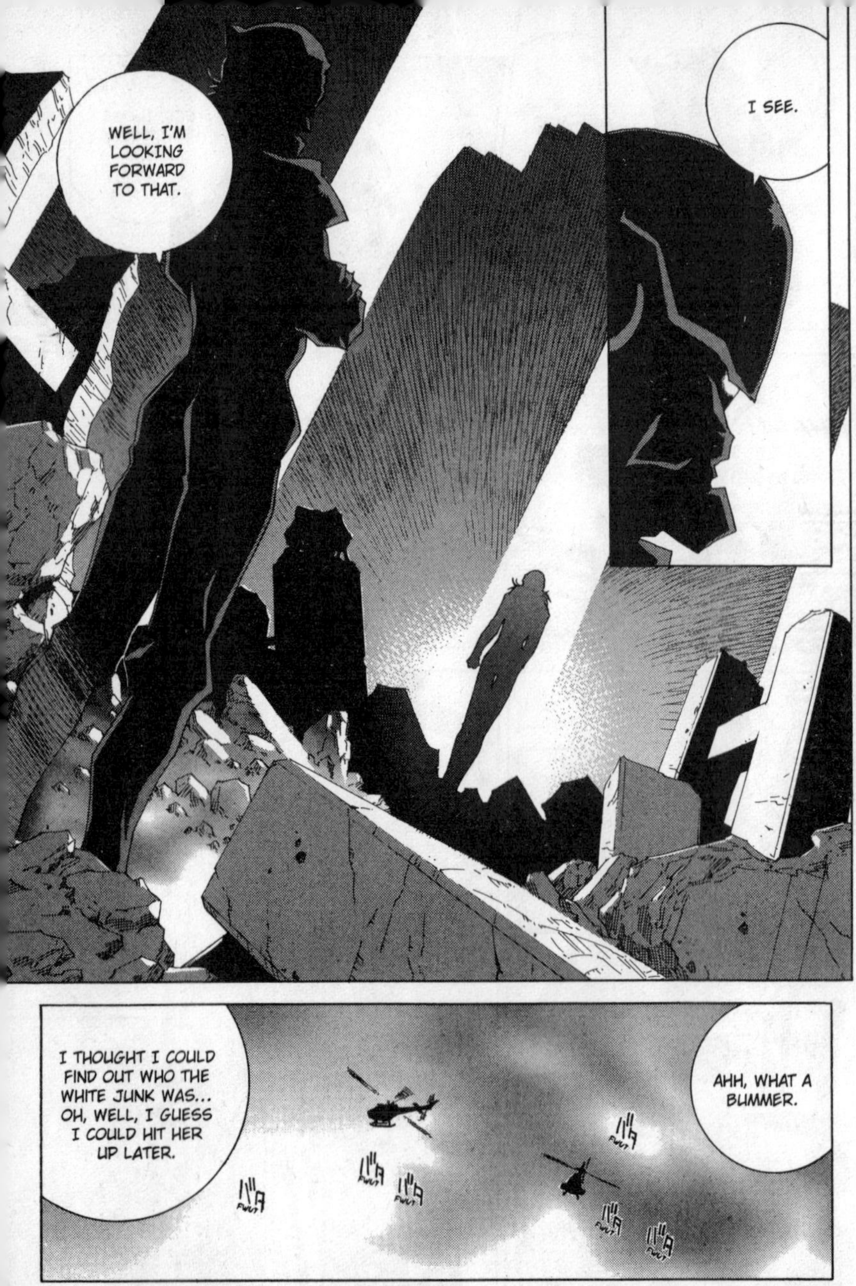
I SEE.
WELL, I'M LOOKING FORWARD TO THAT.
AHH, WHAT A BUMMER.
I THOUGHT I COULD FIND OUT WHO THE WHITE JUNK WAS... OH, WELL, I GUESS I COULD HIT HER UP LATER.

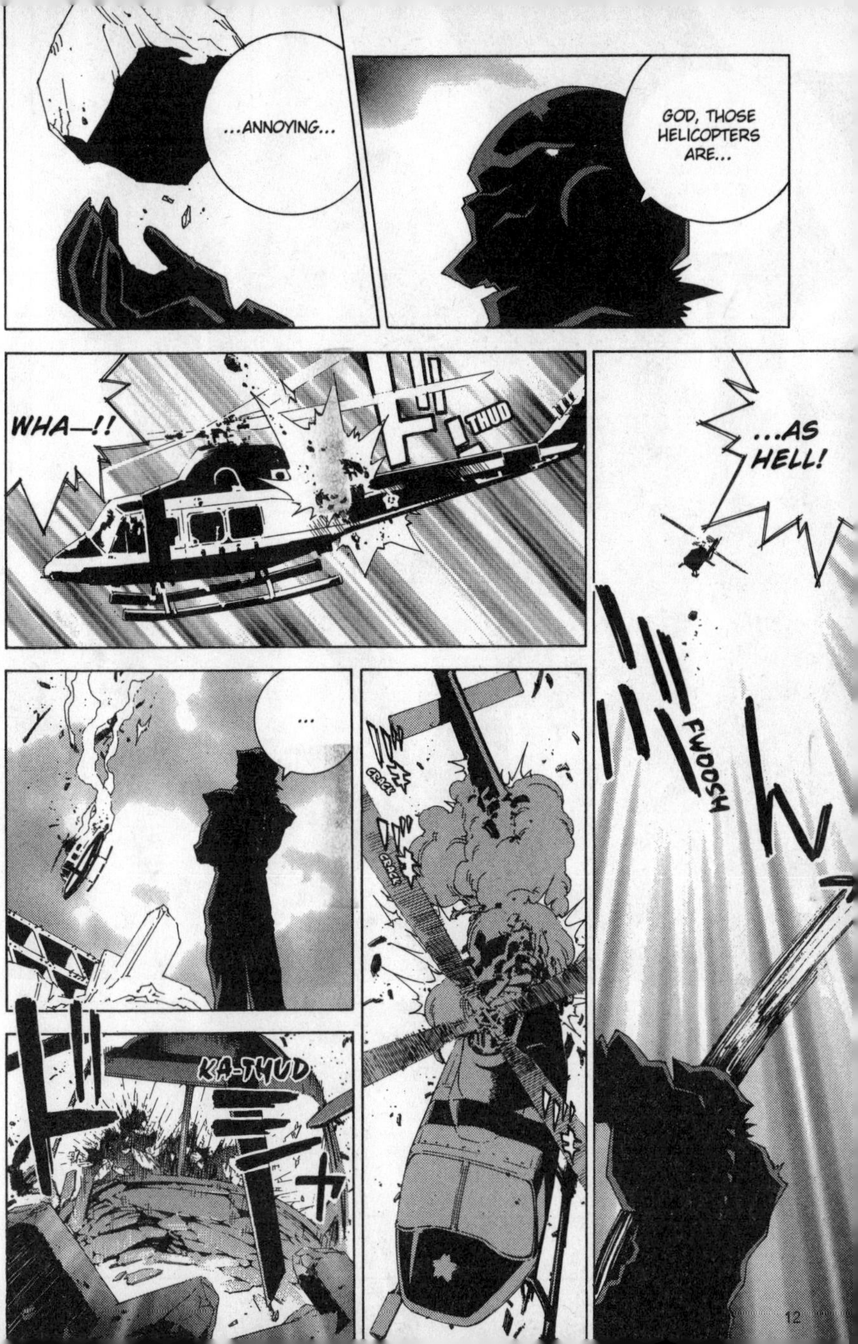
GOD, THOSE HELICOPTERS ARE...
...ANNOYING...
...AS HELL!
FWOOSH
WHA—!!
THUD
CRACK
CRACK
...
KA-THUD

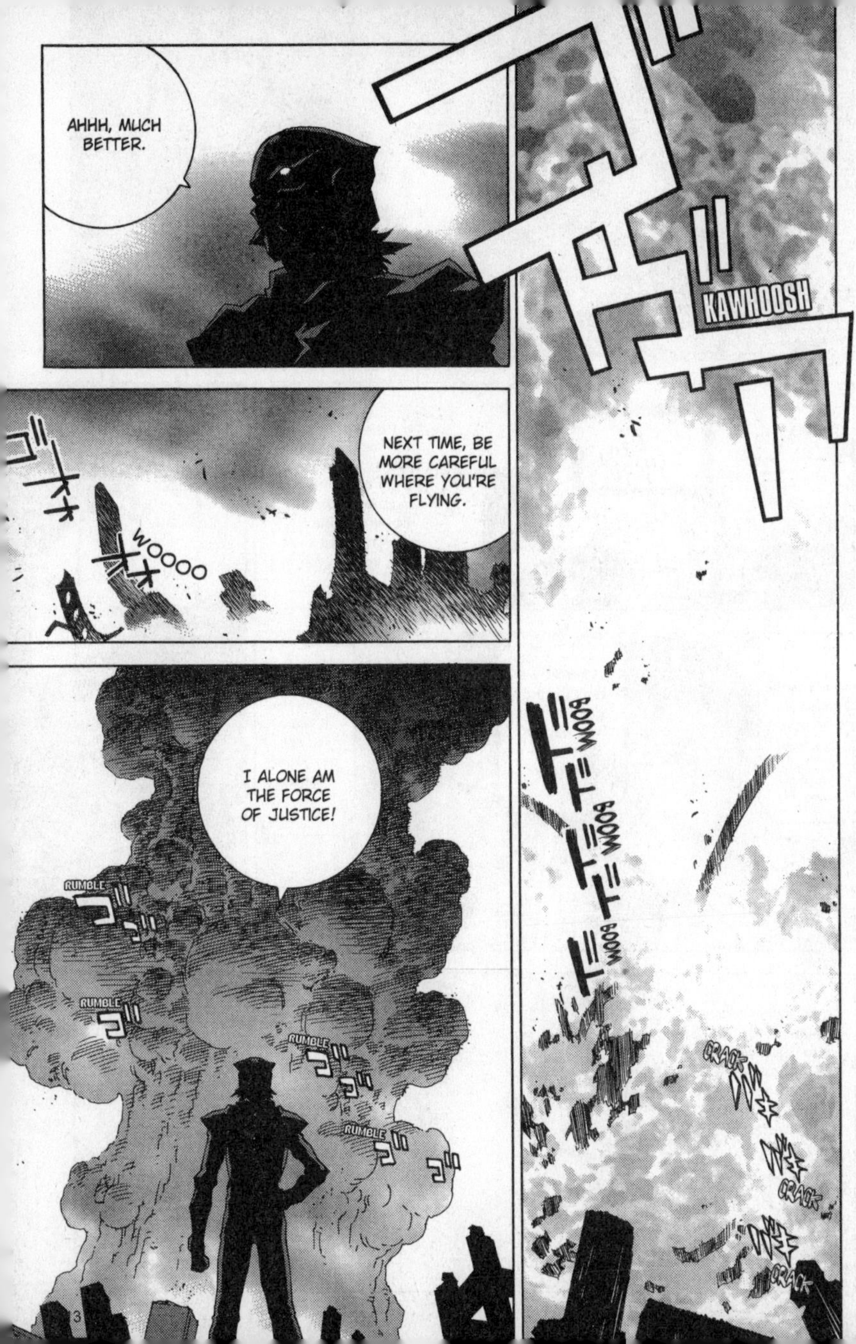
KAWHOOSH
BOOM BOOM BOOM
CRACK
CRACK
CRACK
AHHH, MUCH BETTER.
NEXT TIME, BE MORE CAREFUL WHERE YOU'RE FLYING.
WOOOO
I ALONE AM THE FORCE OF JUSTICE!
RUMBLE
RUMBLE
RUMBLE
RUMBLE

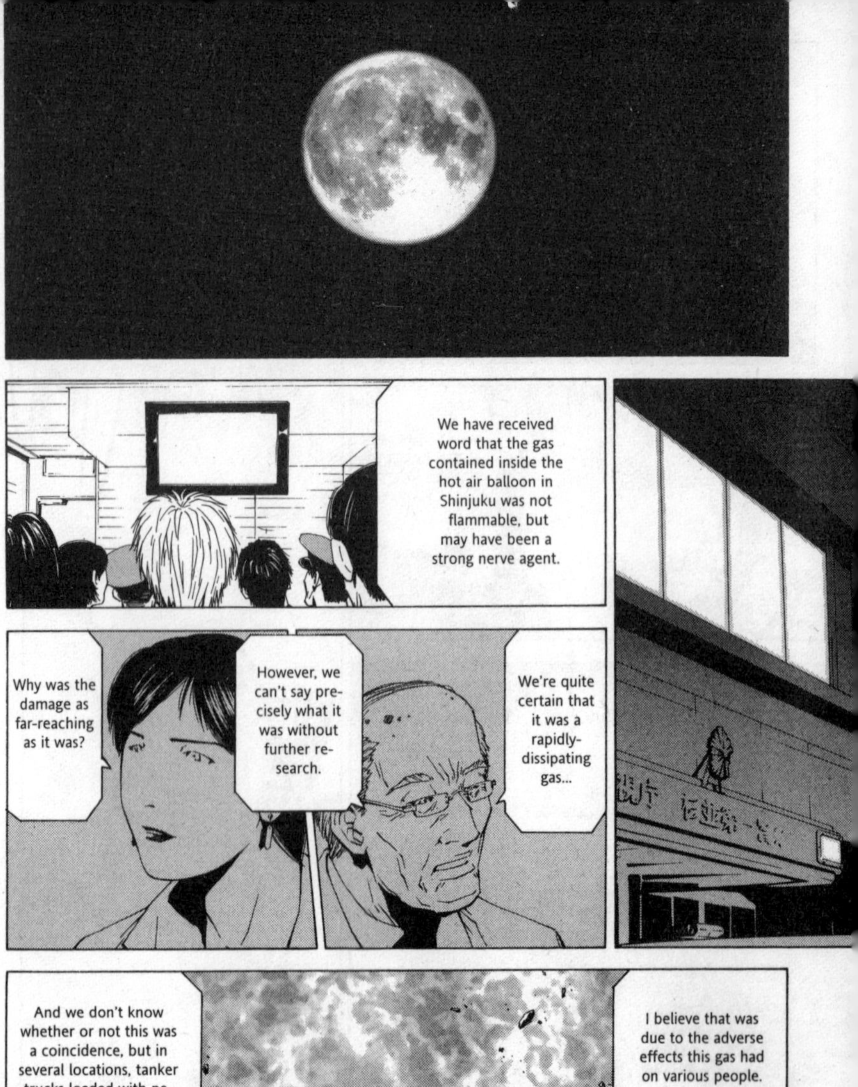
We have received word that the gas contained inside the hot air balloon in Shinjuku was not flammable, but may have been a strong nerve agent.
We're quite certain that it was a rapidly-dissipating gas...
However, we can't say precisely what it was without further research.
Why was the damage as far-reaching as it was?
I believe that was due to the adverse effects this gas had on various people.
Also, restaurants and bars in the Kabukicho district were just opening up and the gas usage was high, so that may have been a factor in how quickly the flames spread.
And we don't know whether or not this was a coincidence, but in several locations, tanker trucks loaded with petroleum crashed into storefronts.

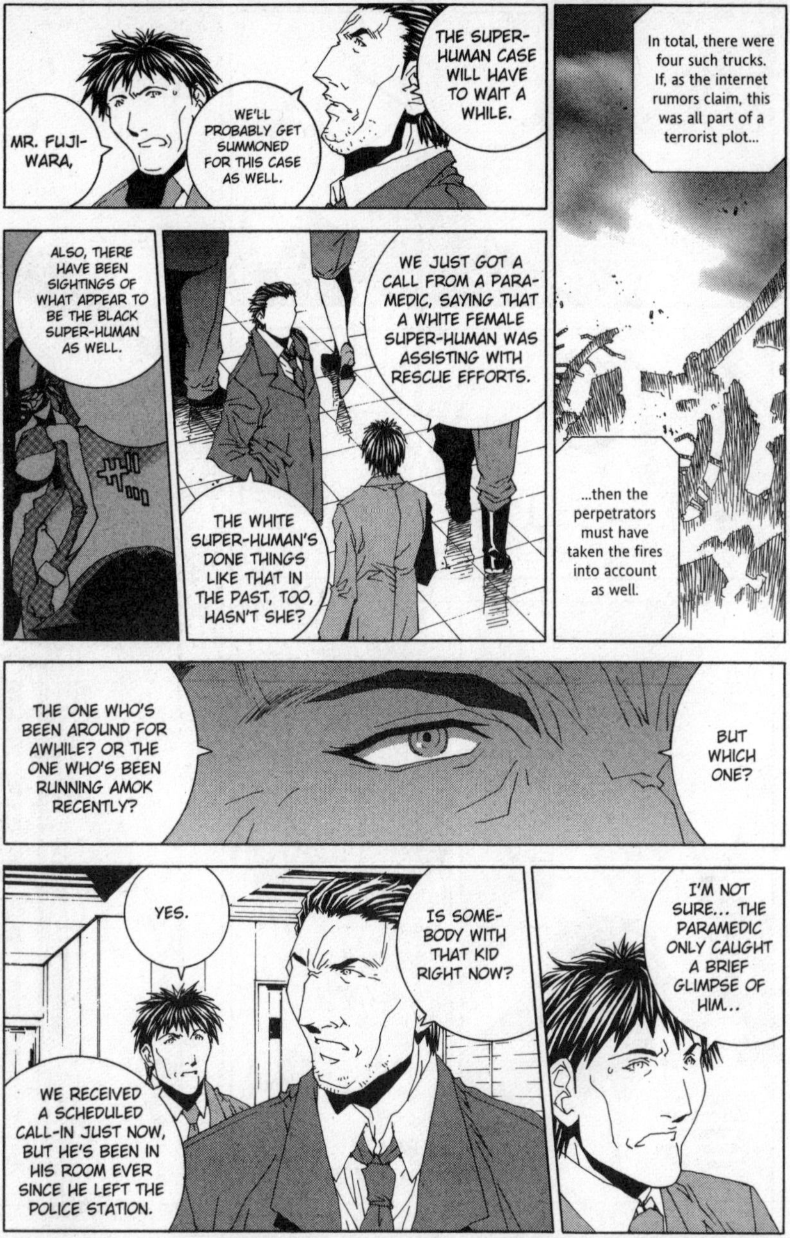

In total, there were four such trucks. If, as the internet rumors claim, this was all part of a terrorist plot...
...then the perpetrators must have taken the fires into account as well.
THE SUPER-HUMAN CASE WILL HAVE TO WAIT A WHILE.
WE'LL PROBABLY GET SUMMONED FOR THIS CASE AS WELL.
MR. FUJI-WARA,
WE JUST GOT A CALL FROM A PARA-MEDIC, SAYING THAT A WHITE FEMALE SUPER-HUMAN WAS ASSISTING WITH RESCUE EFFORTS.
THE WHITE SUPER-HUMAN'S DONE THINGS LIKE THAT IN THE PAST, TOO, HASN'T SHE?
ALSO, THERE HAVE BEEN SIGHTINGS OF WHAT APPEAR TO BE THE BLACK SUPER-HUMAN AS WELL.
BUT WHICH ONE?
THE ONE WHO'S BEEN AROUND FOR AWHILE? OR THE ONE WHO'S BEEN RUNNING AMOK RECENTLY?
I'M NOT SURE... THE PARAMEDIC ONLY CAUGHT A BRIEF GLIMPSE OF HIM...
IS SOME-BODY WITH THAT KID RIGHT NOW?
YES.
WE RECEIVED A SCHEDULED CALL-IN JUST NOW, BUT HE'S BEEN IN HIS ROOM EVER SINCE HE LEFT THE POLICE STATION.

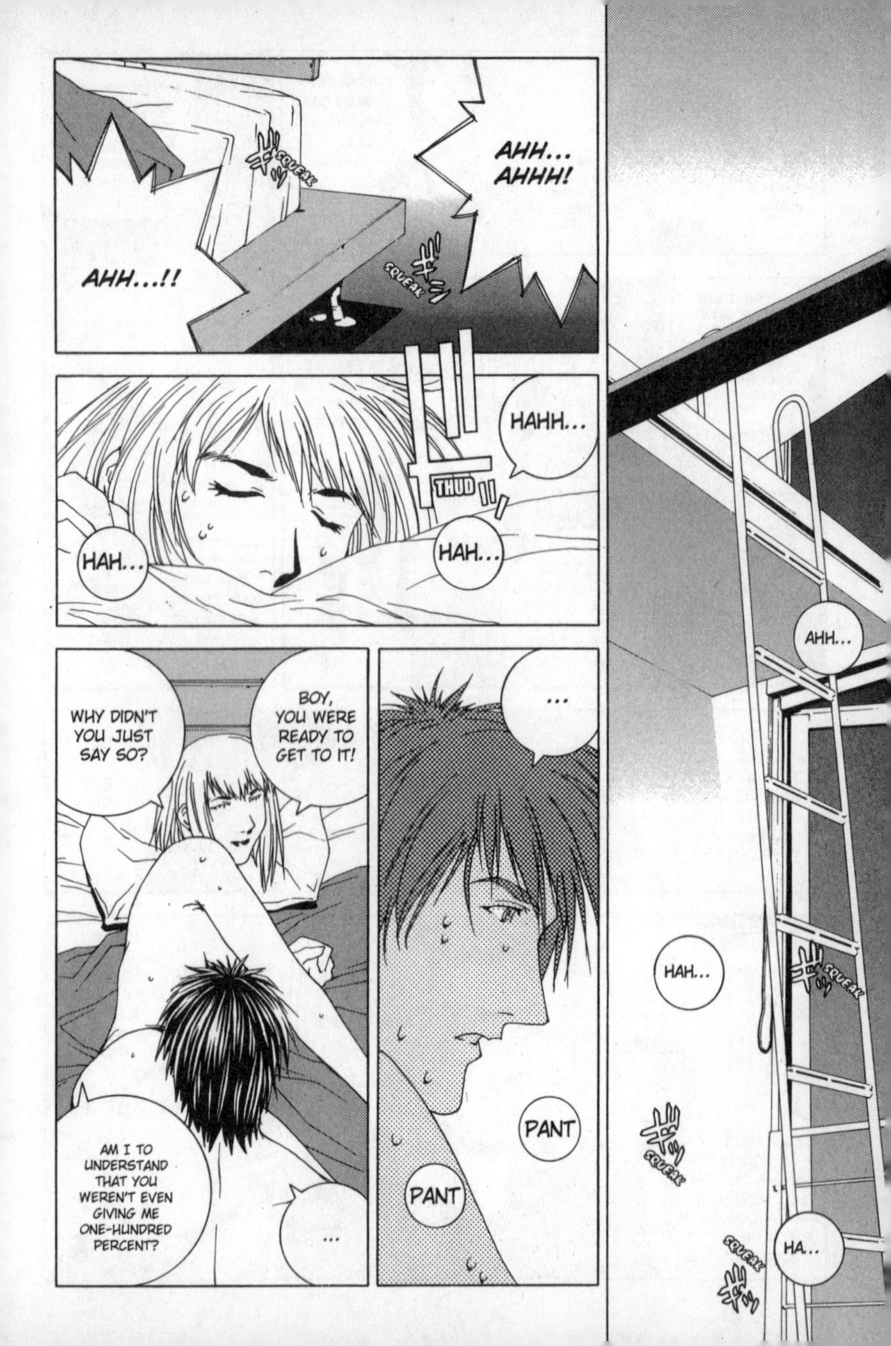
AHH...
SQUEAK
HAH...
SQUEAK
HA...
SQUEAK
AHH... AHHH!
SQUEAK
SQUEAK
AHH...!!
THUD
HAHH...
HAH...
HAH...
...
PANT
PANT
BOY, YOU WERE READY TO GET TO IT!
WHY DIDN'T YOU JUST SAY SO?
AM I TO UNDERSTAND THAT YOU WEREN'T EVEN GIVING ME ONE-HUNDRED PERCENT?
...

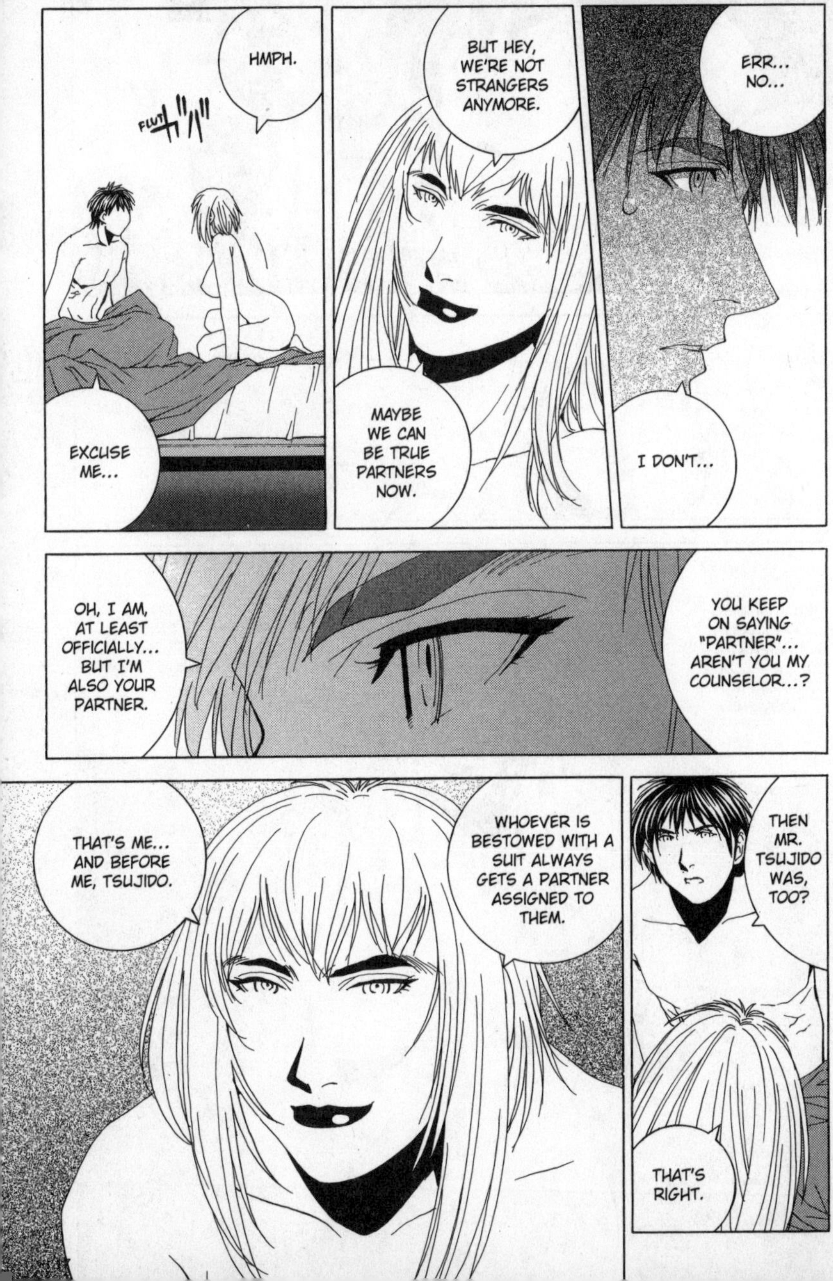
ERR... NO...
I DON'T...
BUT HEY, WE'RE NOT STRANGERS ANYMORE.
MAYBE WE CAN BE TRUE PARTNERS NOW.
HMPH.
FLUT
EXCUSE ME...
YOU KEEP ON SAYING "PARTNER"... AREN'T YOU MY COUNSELOR...?
OH, I AM, AT LEAST OFFICIALLY... BUT I'M ALSO YOUR PARTNER.
THEN MR. TSUJIDO WAS, TOO?
THAT'S RIGHT.
WHOEVER IS BESTOWED WITH A SUIT ALWAYS GETS A PARTNER ASSIGNED TO THEM.
THAT'S ME... AND BEFORE ME, TSUJIDO.

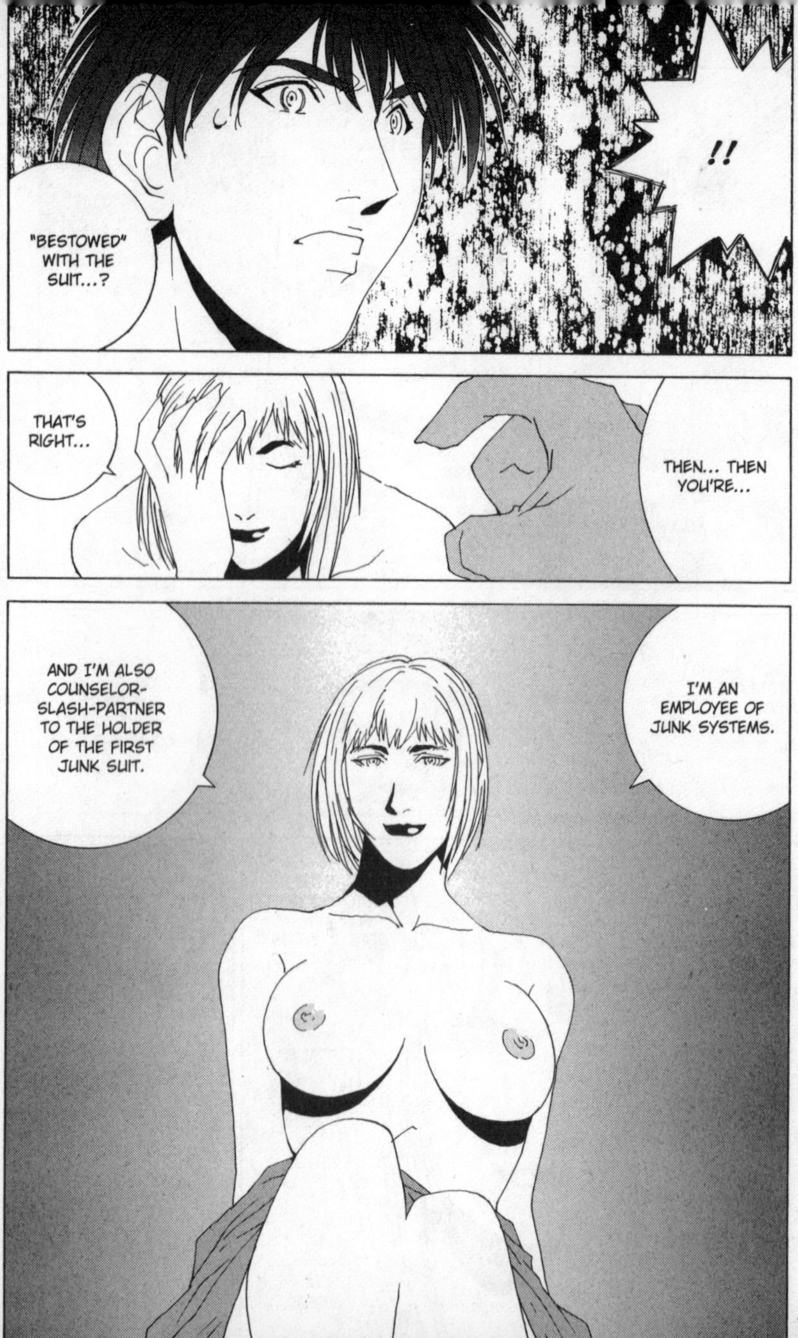
!!
"BESTOWED" WITH THE SUIT...?
THEN... THEN YOU'RE...
THAT'S RIGHT...
I'M AN EMPLOYEE OF JUNK SYSTEMS.
AND I'M ALSO COUNSELOR-SLASH-PARTNER TO THE HOLDER OF THE FIRST JUNK SUIT.

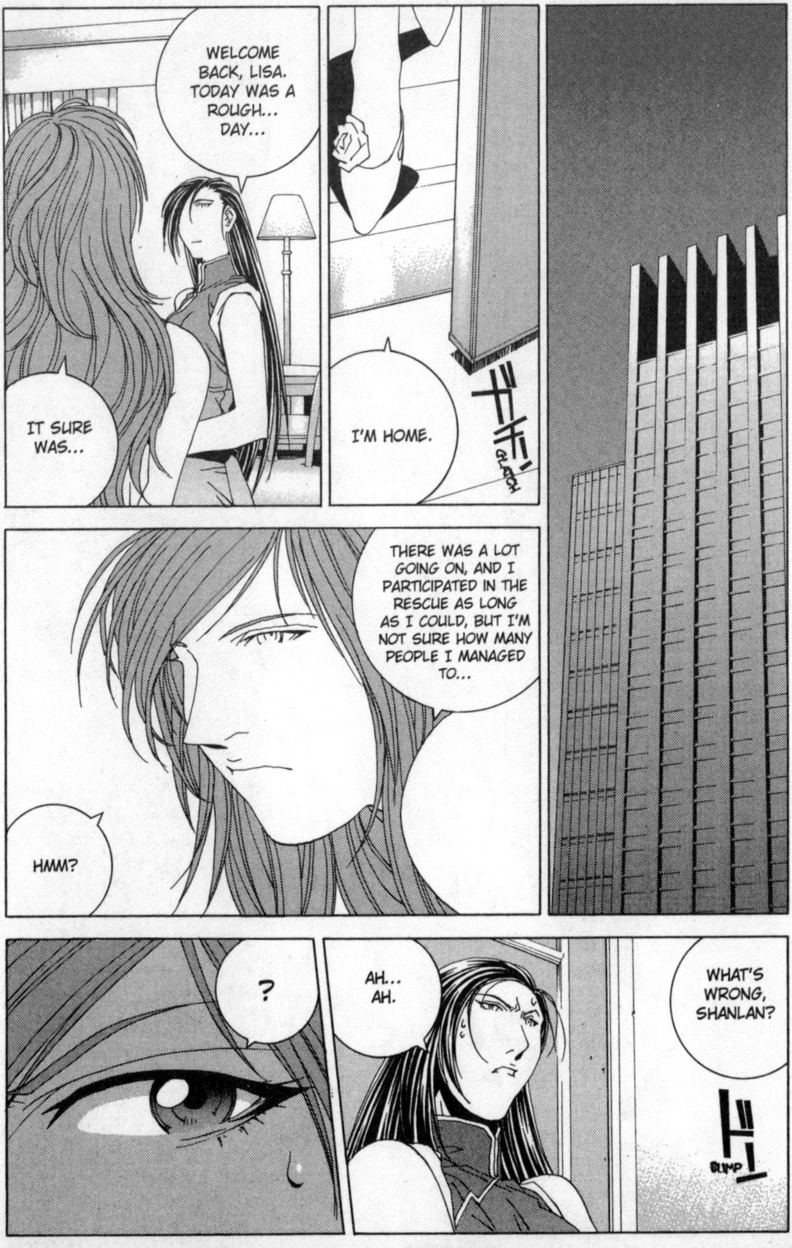
I'M HOME.
GLATCH
WELCOME BACK, LISA. TODAY WAS A ROUGH... DAY...
IT SURE WAS...
THERE WAS A LOT GOING ON, AND I PARTICIPATED IN THE RESCUE AS LONG AS I COULD, BUT I'M NOT SURE HOW MANY PEOPLE I MANAGED TO...
HMM?
WHAT'S WRONG, SHANLAN?
AH... AH.
?

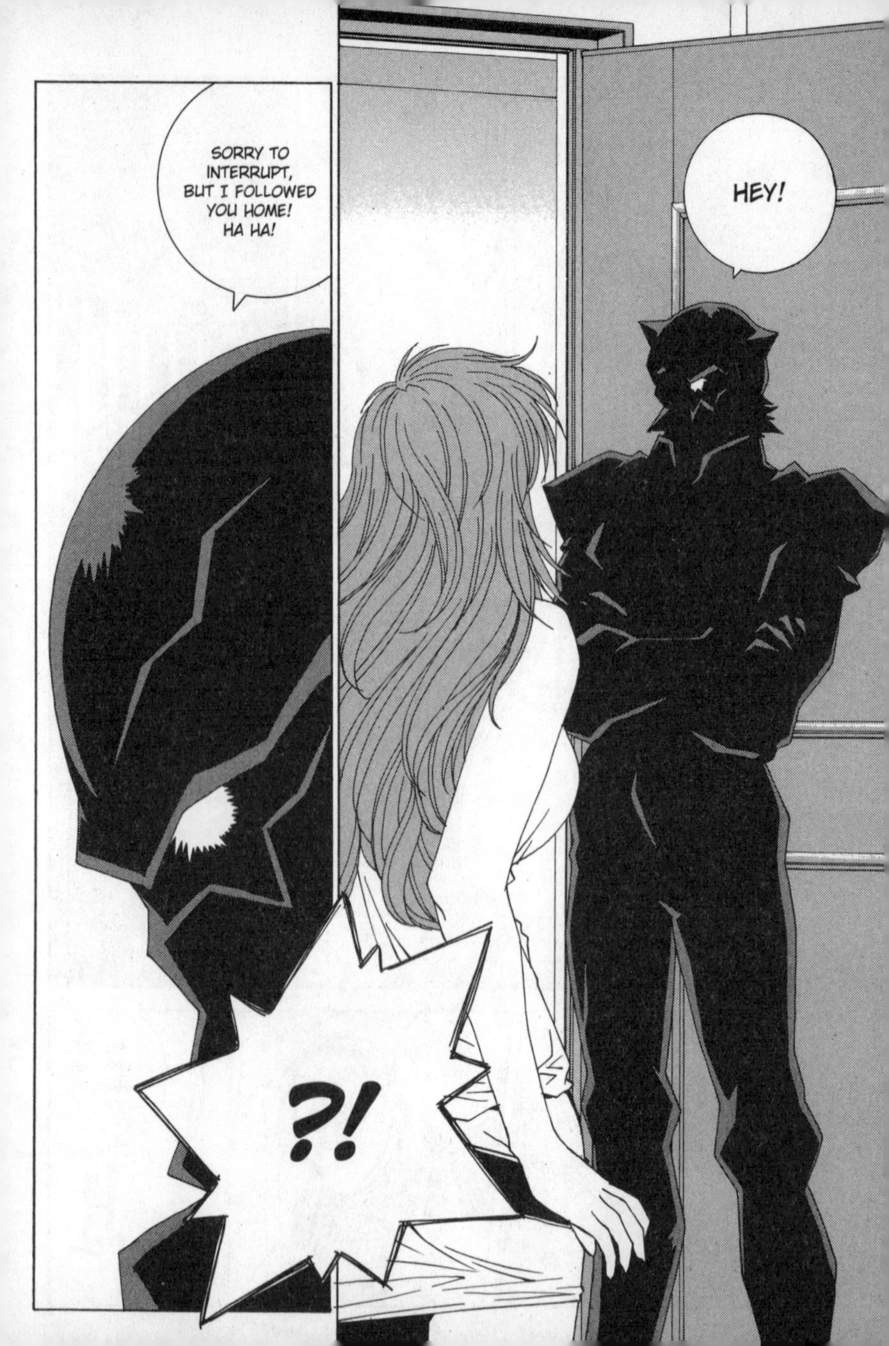
HEY!
SORRY TO INTERRUPT, BUT I FOLLOWED YOU HOME! HA HA!
?!

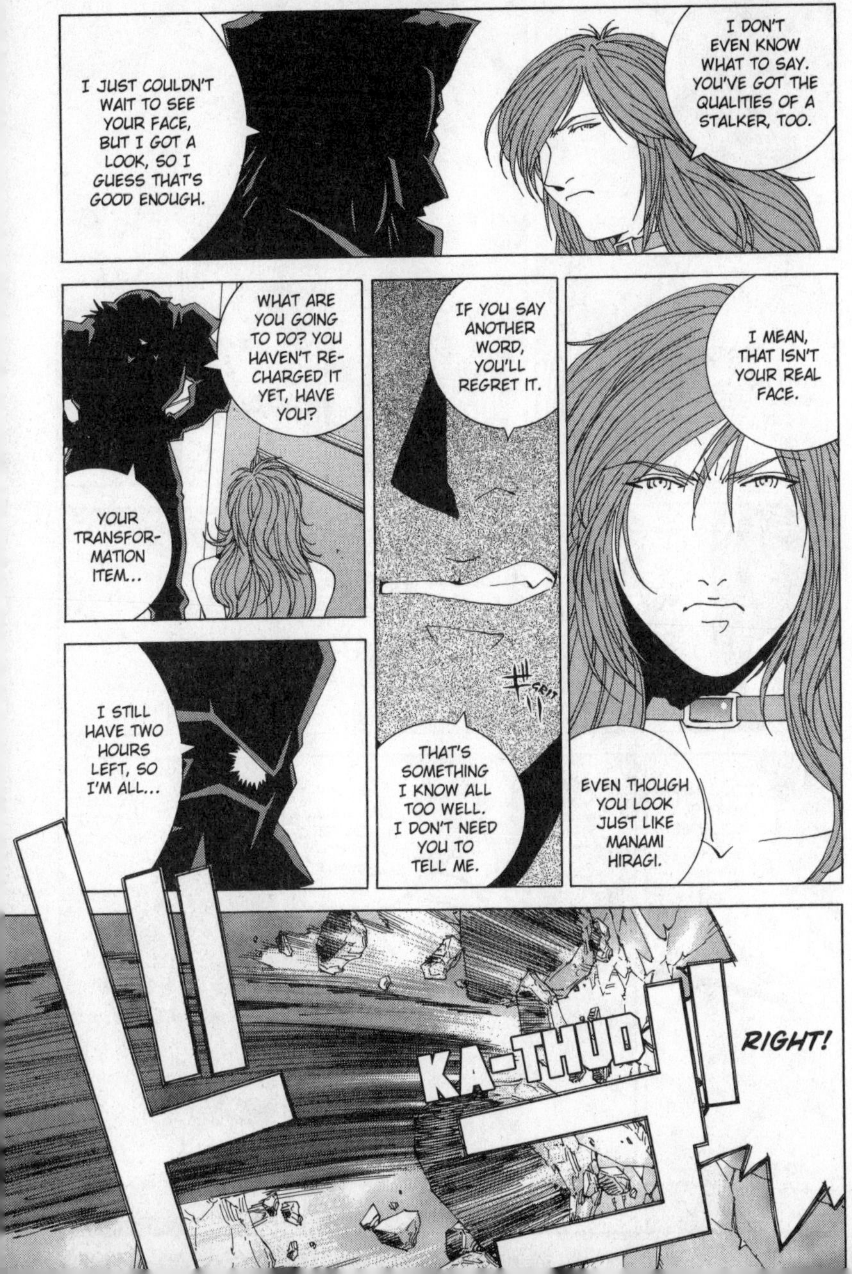
I DON'T EVEN KNOW WHAT TO SAY. YOU'VE GOT THE QUALITIES OF A STALKER, TOO.
I JUST COULDN'T WAIT TO SEE YOUR FACE, BUT I GOT A LOOK, SO I GUESS THAT'S GOOD ENOUGH.
I MEAN, THAT ISN'T YOUR REAL FACE.
EVEN THOUGH YOU LOOK JUST LIKE MANAMI HIRAGI.
IF YOU SAY ANOTHER WORD, YOU'LL REGRET IT.
GRIT
THAT'S SOMETHING I KNOW ALL TOO WELL. I DON'T NEED YOU TO TELL ME.
WHAT ARE YOU GOING TO DO? YOU HAVEN'T RE-CHARGED IT YET, HAVE YOU?
YOUR TRANSFORMATION ITEM...
I STILL HAVE TWO HOURS LEFT, SO I'M ALL...
RIGHT!
KA-THUD

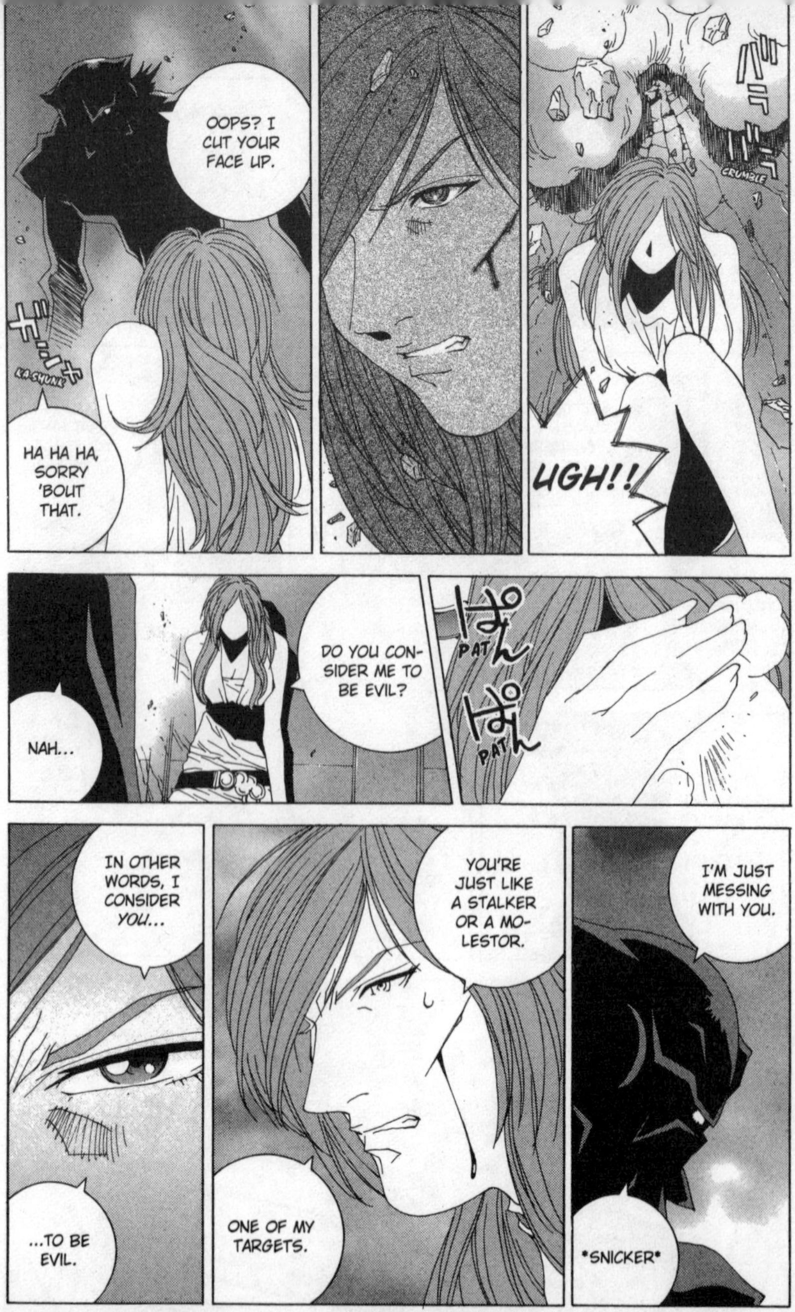
CRUMBLE
UGH!!
OOPS? I CUT YOUR FACE UP.
KA-SHUNK
HA HA HA, SORRY 'BOUT THAT.
ぱん
PAT
ぱん
PAT
DO YOU CON-SIDER ME TO BE EVIL?
NAH...
I'M JUST MESSING WITH YOU.
SNICKER
YOU'RE JUST LIKE A STALKER OR A MO-LESTOR.
ONE OF MY TARGETS.
IN OTHER WORDS, I CONSIDER YOU...
...TO BE EVIL.

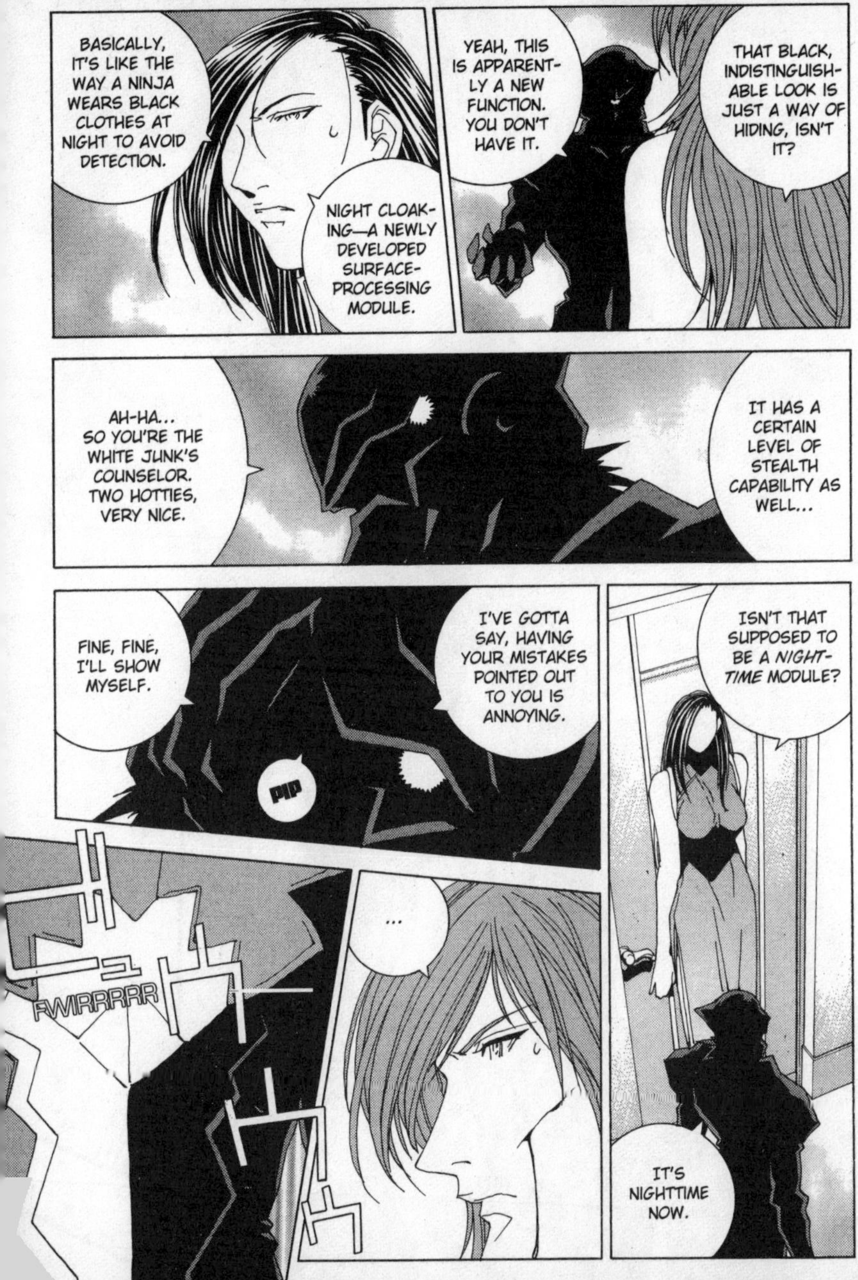
THAT BLACK, INDISTINGUISHABLE LOOK IS JUST A WAY OF HIDING, ISN'T IT?
YEAH, THIS IS APPARENTLY A NEW FUNCTION. YOU DON'T HAVE IT.
NIGHT CLOAKING—A NEWLY DEVELOPED SURFACE-PROCESSING MODULE.
BASICALLY, IT'S LIKE THE WAY A NINJA WEARS BLACK CLOTHES AT NIGHT TO AVOID DETECTION.
IT HAS A CERTAIN LEVEL OF STEALTH CAPABILITY AS WELL...
AH-HA... SO YOU'RE THE WHITE JUNK'S COUNSELOR. TWO HOTTIES, VERY NICE.
ISN'T THAT SUPPOSED TO BE A *NIGHT-TIME* MODULE?
IT'S NIGHTTIME NOW.
I'VE GOTTA SAY, HAVING YOUR MISTAKES POINTED OUT TO YOU IS ANNOYING.
FINE, FINE, I'LL SHOW MYSELF.
PIP
...
FWIRRRRR

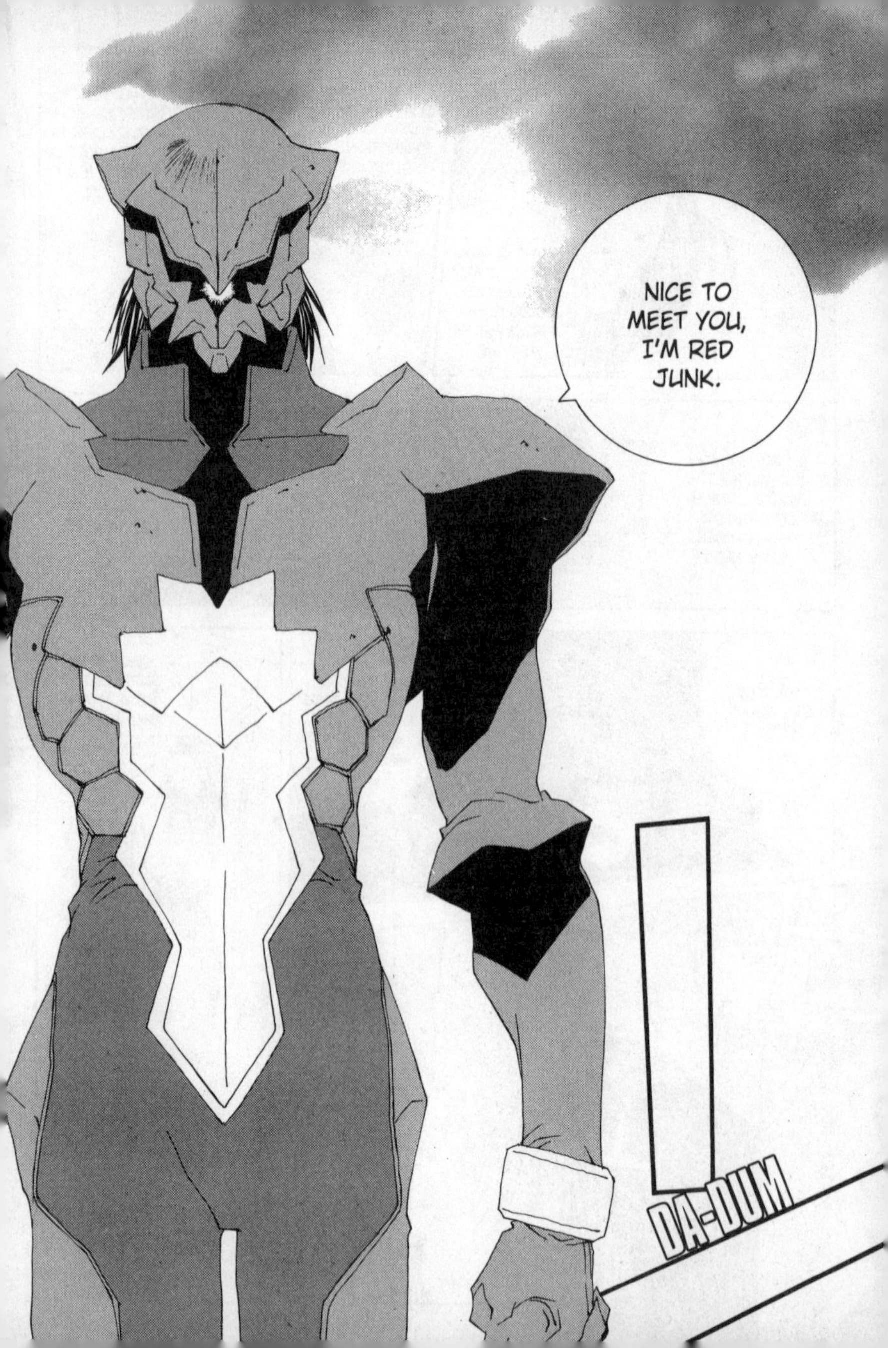
NICE TO MEET YOU, I'M RED JUNK.
DA-DUM

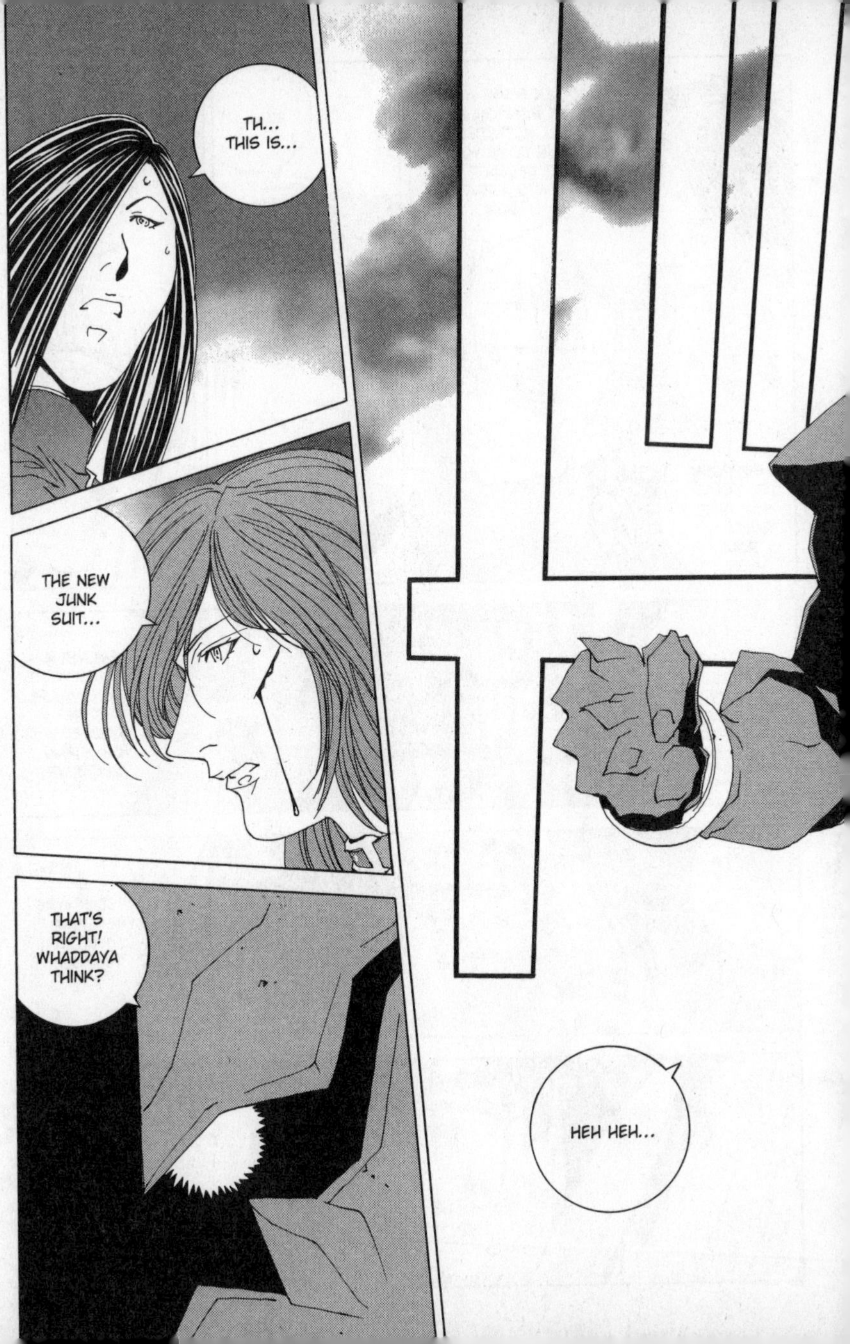
HEH HEH...
TH... THIS IS...
THE NEW JUNK SUIT...
THAT'S RIGHT! WHADDAYA THINK?

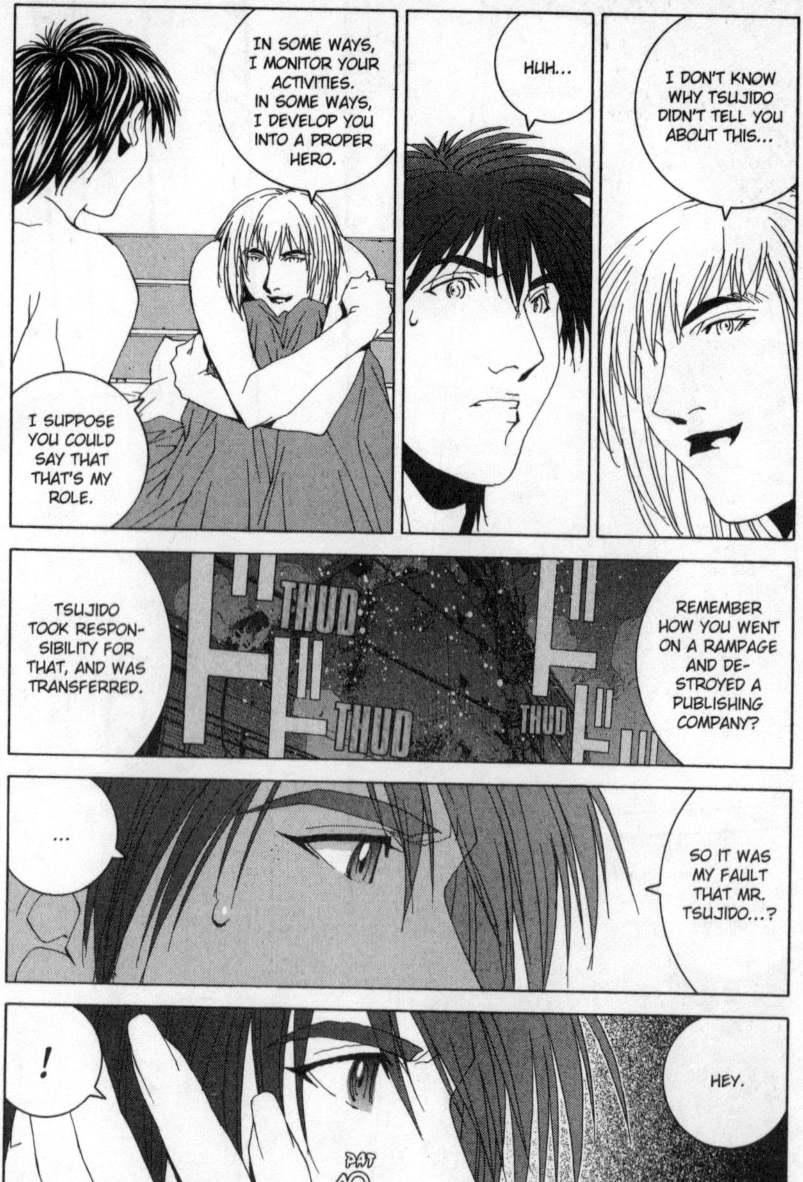

I DON'T KNOW WHY TSUJIDO DIDN'T TELL YOU ABOUT THIS...
HUH...
IN SOME WAYS, I MONITOR YOUR ACTIVITIES. IN SOME WAYS, I DEVELOP YOU INTO A PROPER HERO.
I SUPPOSE YOU COULD SAY THAT THAT'S MY ROLE.
REMEMBER HOW YOU WENT ON A RAMPAGE AND DE-STROYED A PUBLISHING COMPANY?
THUD
THUD
THUD
TSUJIDO TOOK RESPON-SIBILITY FOR THAT, AND WAS TRANSFERRED.
SO IT WAS MY FAULT THAT MR. TSUJIDO...?
...
HEY.
PAT
!

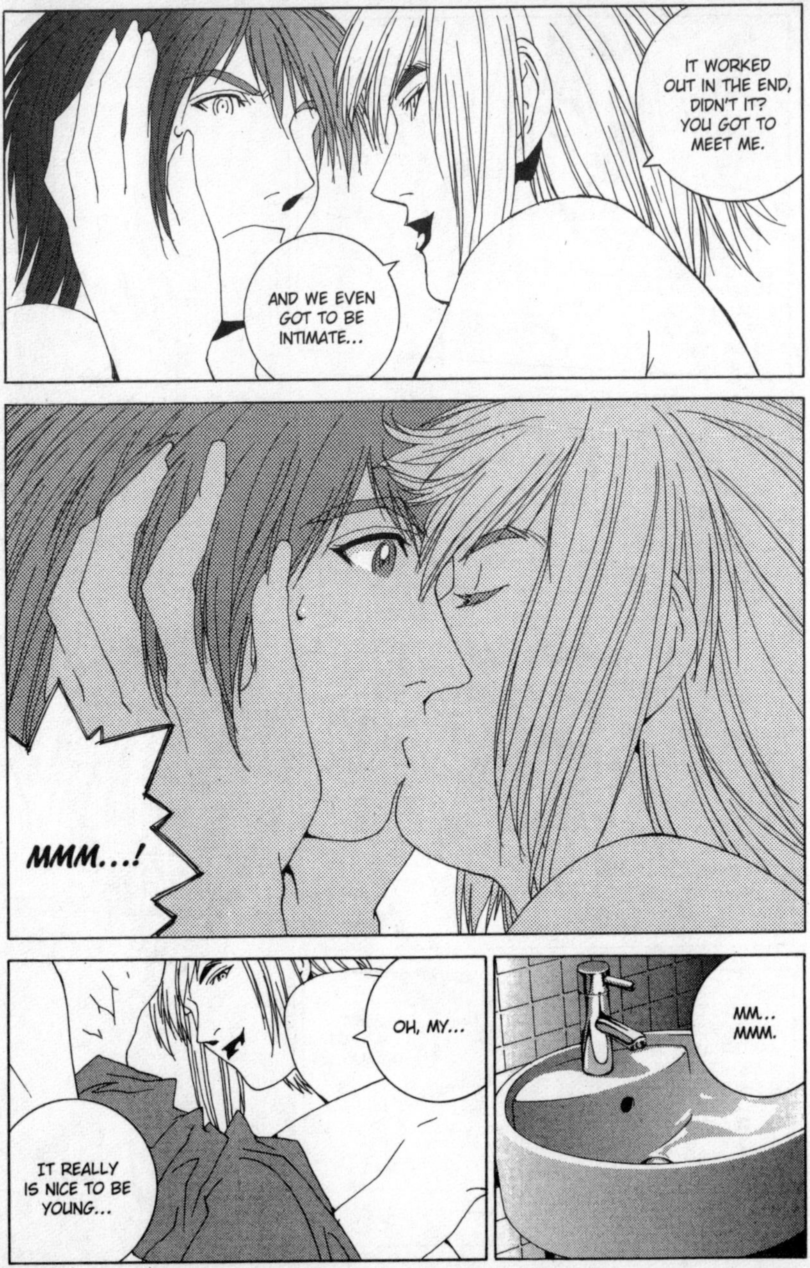
IT WORKED OUT IN THE END, DIDN'T IT? YOU GOT TO MEET ME.
AND WE EVEN GOT TO BE INTIMATE...
MMM...!
MM... MMM.
OH, MY...
IT REALLY IS NICE TO BE YOUNG...

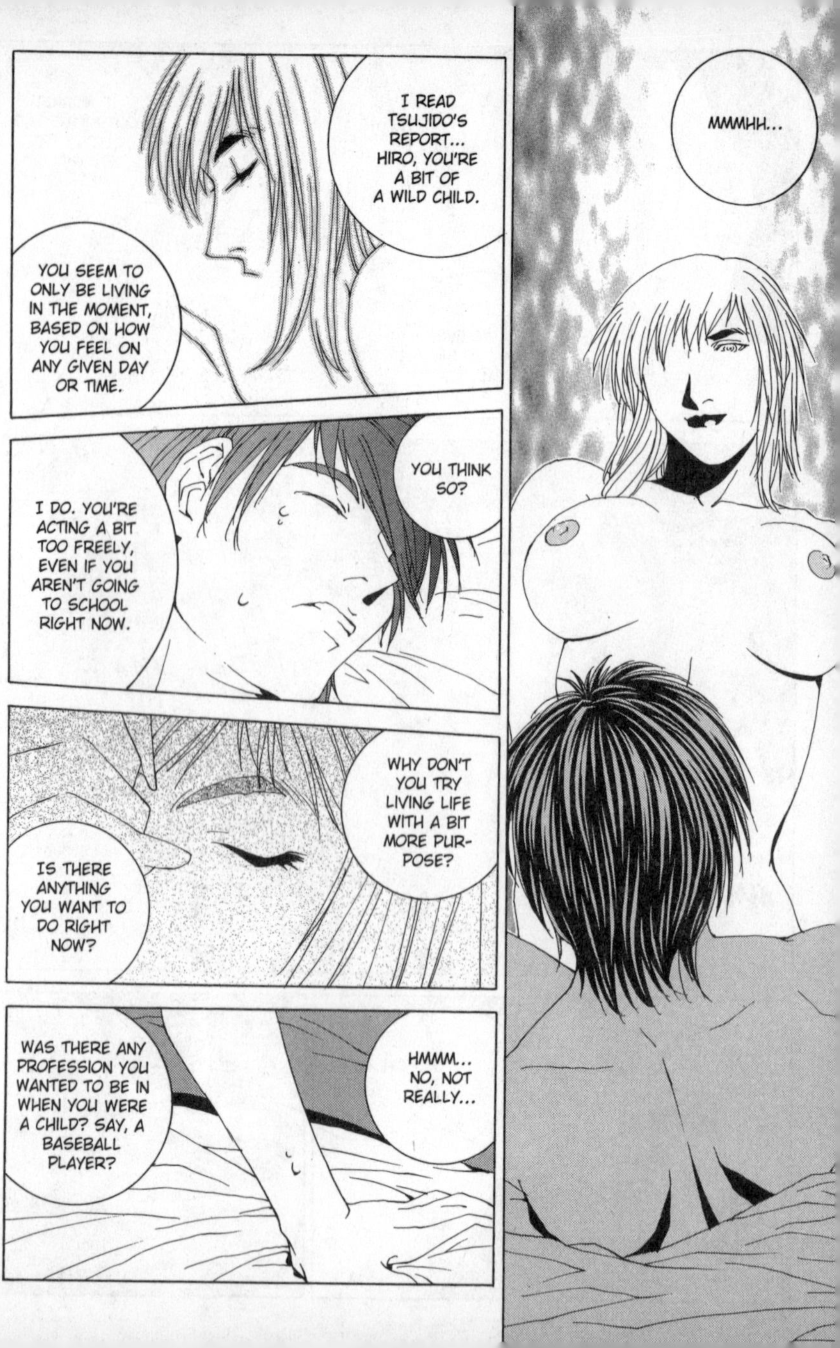
MMMHH...
I READ TSUJIDO'S REPORT... HIRO, YOU'RE A BIT OF A WILD CHILD.
YOU SEEM TO ONLY BE LIVING IN THE MOMENT, BASED ON HOW YOU FEEL ON ANY GIVEN DAY OR TIME.
YOU THINK SO?
I DO. YOU'RE ACTING A BIT TOO FREELY, EVEN IF YOU AREN'T GOING TO SCHOOL RIGHT NOW.
WHY DON'T YOU TRY LIVING LIFE WITH A BIT MORE PUR-POSE?
IS THERE ANYTHING YOU WANT TO DO RIGHT NOW?
HMMM... NO, NOT REALLY...
WAS THERE ANY PROFESSION YOU WANTED TO BE IN WHEN YOU WERE A CHILD? SAY, A BASEBALL PLAYER?

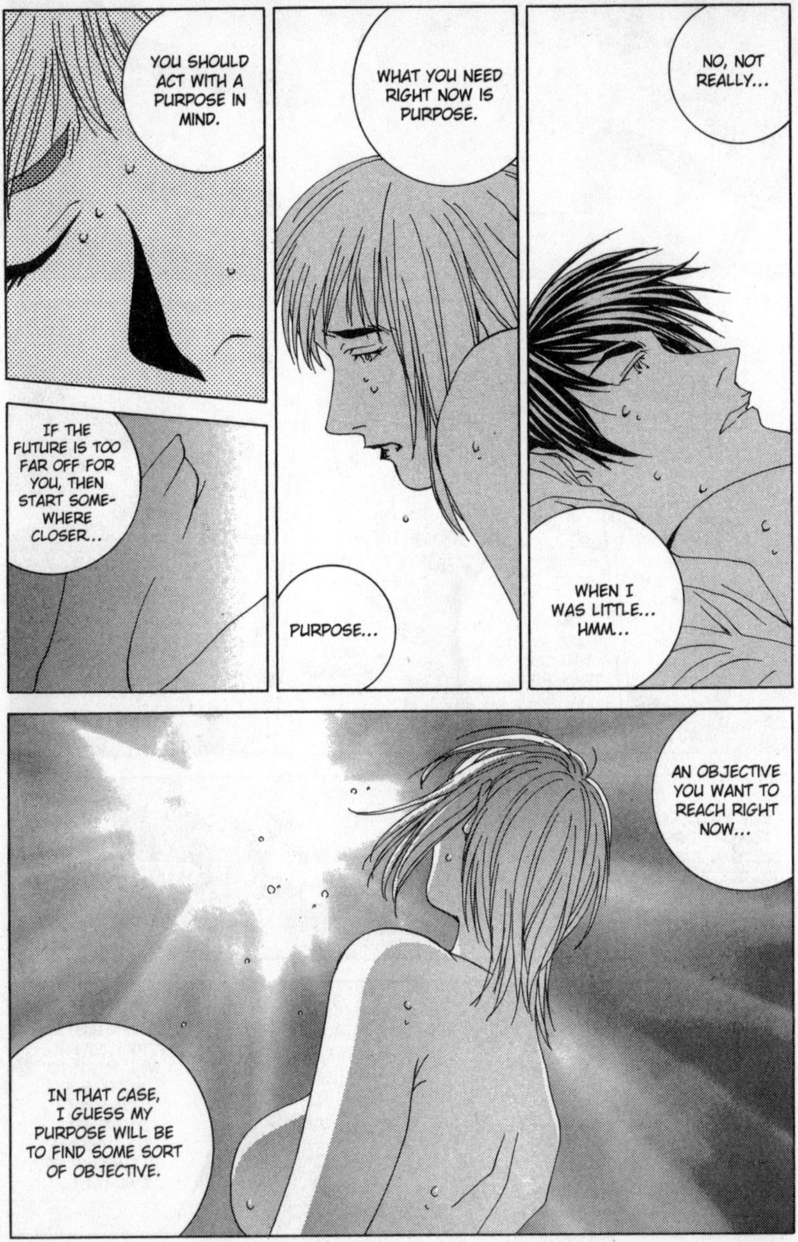
NO, NOT REALLY...
WHEN I WAS LITTLE... HMM...
WHAT YOU NEED RIGHT NOW IS PURPOSE.
PURPOSE...
YOU SHOULD ACT WITH A PURPOSE IN MIND.
IF THE FUTURE IS TOO FAR OFF FOR YOU, THEN START SOME-WHERE CLOSER...
AN OBJECTIVE YOU WANT TO REACH RIGHT NOW...
IN THAT CASE, I GUESS MY PURPOSE WILL BE TO FIND SOME SORT OF OBJECTIVE.

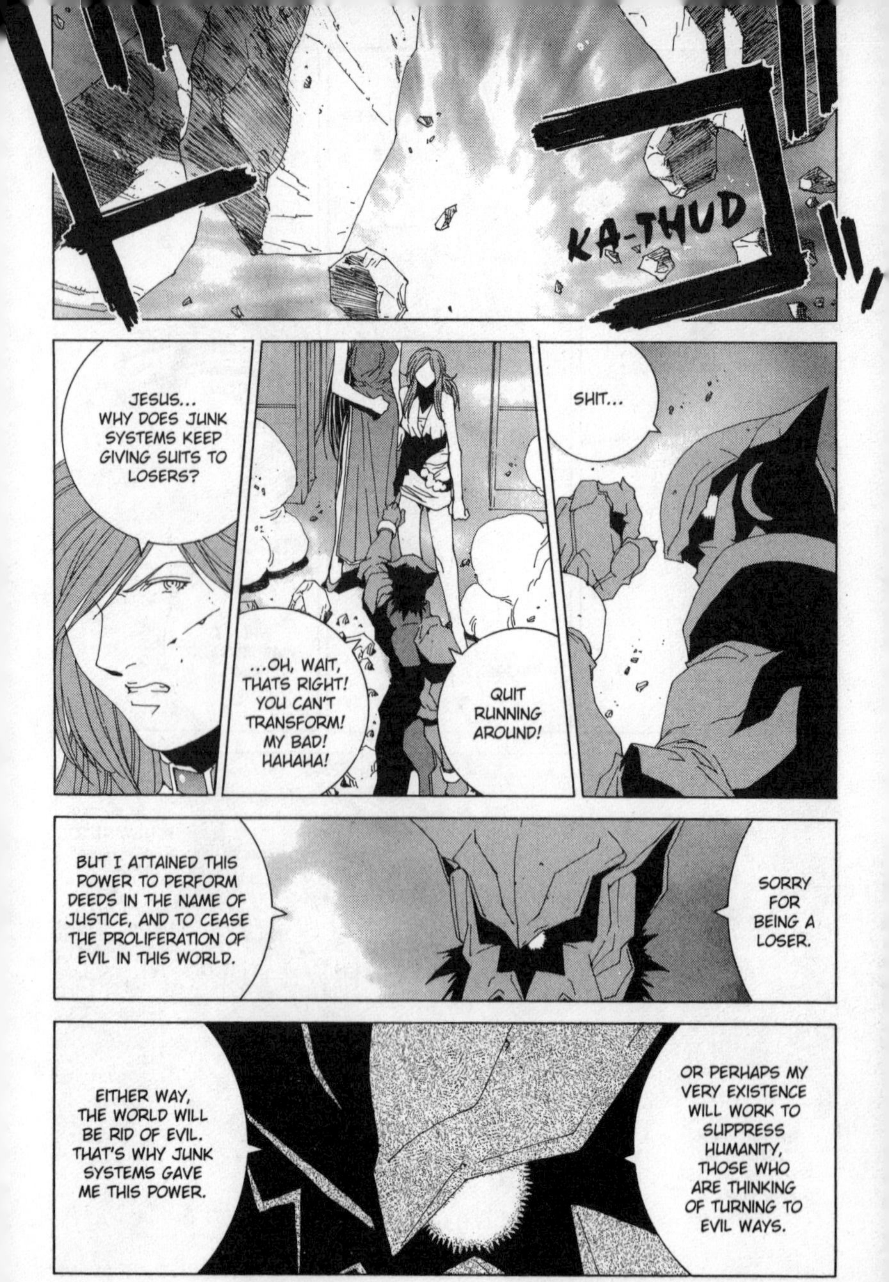
KA-THUD
SHIT...
QUIT RUNNING AROUND!
...OH, WAIT, THATS RIGHT! YOU CAN'T TRANSFORM! MY BAD! HAHAHA!
JESUS... WHY DOES JUNK SYSTEMS KEEP GIVING SUITS TO LOSERS?
SORRY FOR BEING A LOSER.
BUT I ATTAINED THIS POWER TO PERFORM DEEDS IN THE NAME OF JUSTICE, AND TO CEASE THE PROLIFERATION OF EVIL IN THIS WORLD.
OR PERHAPS MY VERY EXISTENCE WILL WORK TO SUPPRESS HUMANITY, THOSE WHO ARE THINKING OF TURNING TO EVIL WAYS.
EITHER WAY, THE WORLD WILL BE RID OF EVIL. THAT'S WHY JUNK SYSTEMS GAVE ME THIS POWER.

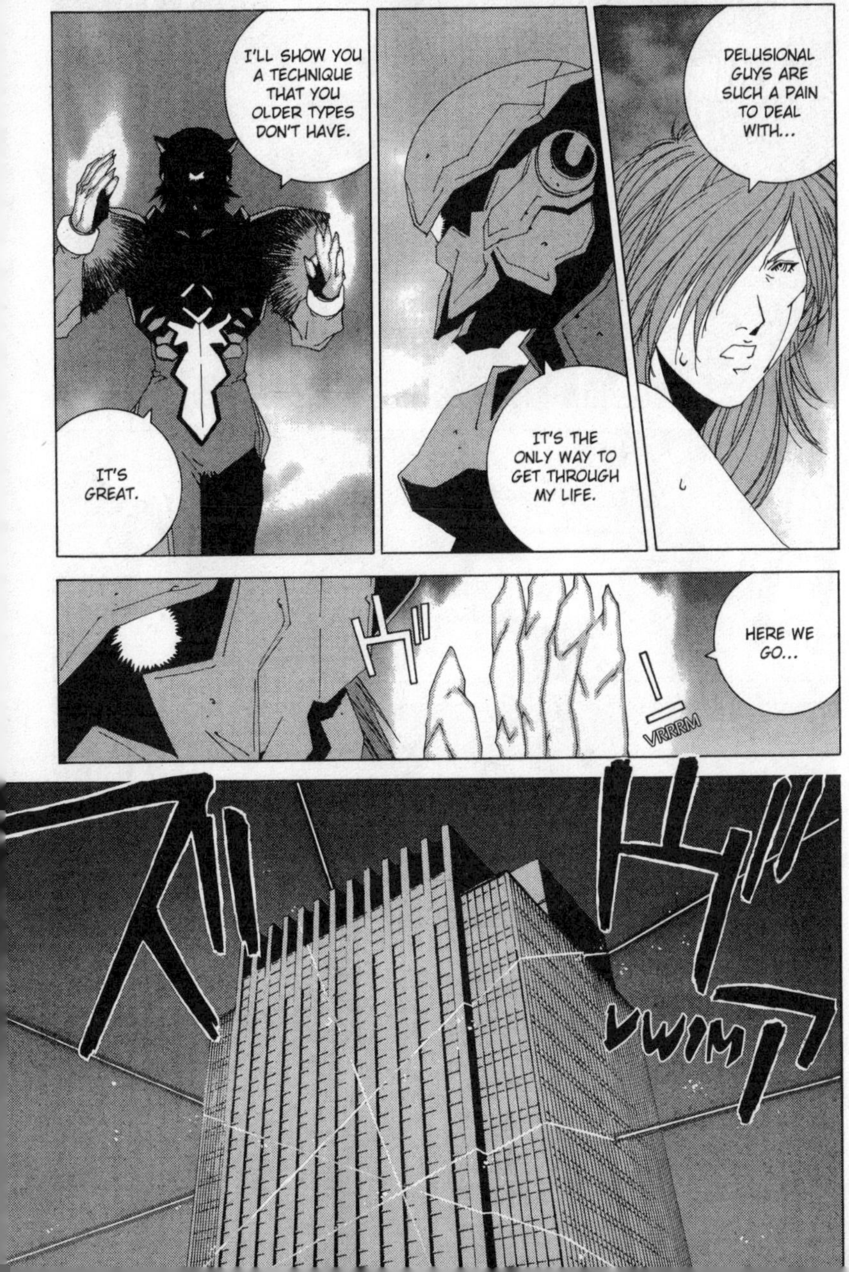
DELUSIONAL GUYS ARE SUCH A PAIN TO DEAL WITH...
IT'S THE ONLY WAY TO GET THROUGH MY LIFE.
I'LL SHOW YOU A TECHNIQUE THAT YOU OLDER TYPES DON'T HAVE.
IT'S GREAT.
HERE WE GO...
VRRRM
VWIM

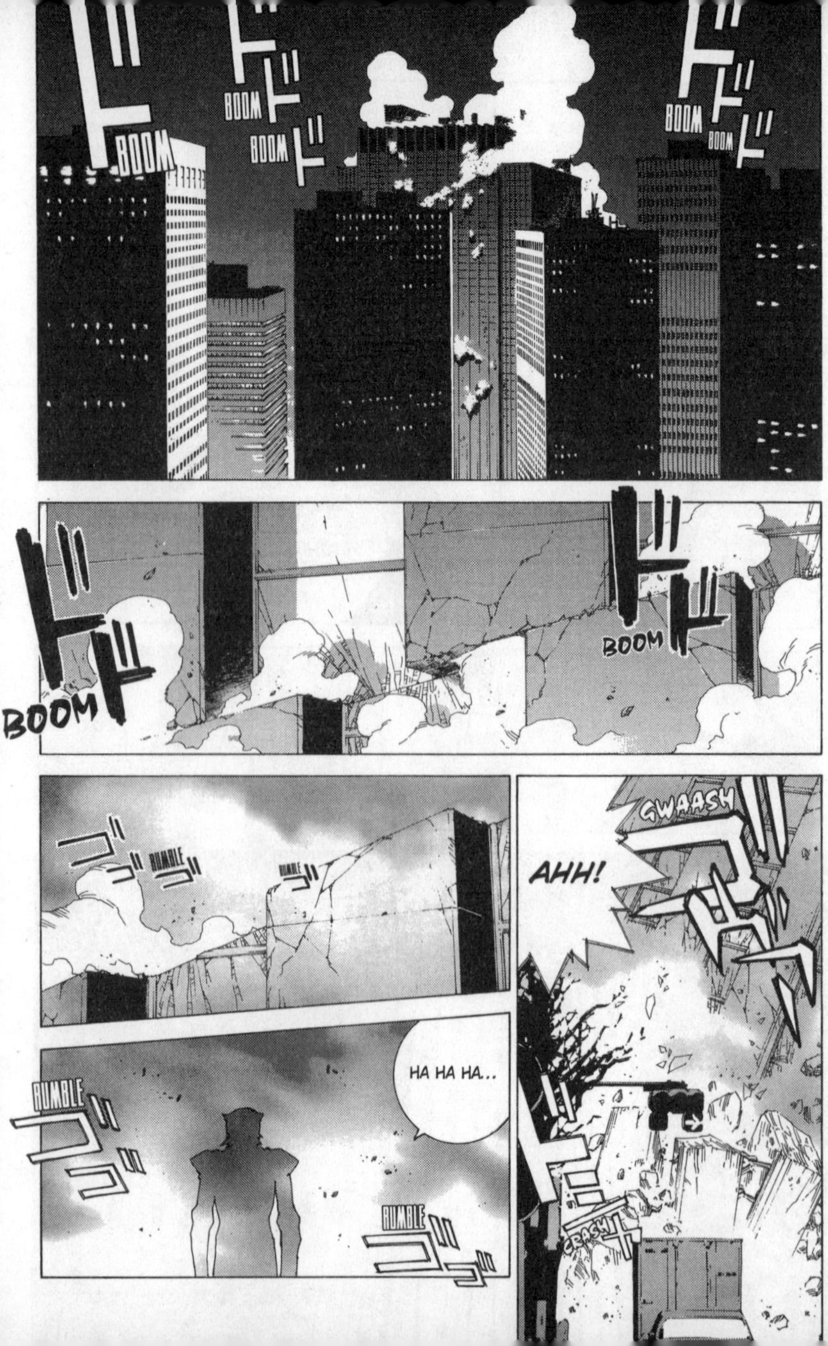
BOOM
BOOM
BOOM
BOOM
BOOM
BOOM
BOOM
GWAASH
AHH!
CRASH
RUMBLE
RUMBLE
HA HA HA...
RUMBLE
RUMBLE

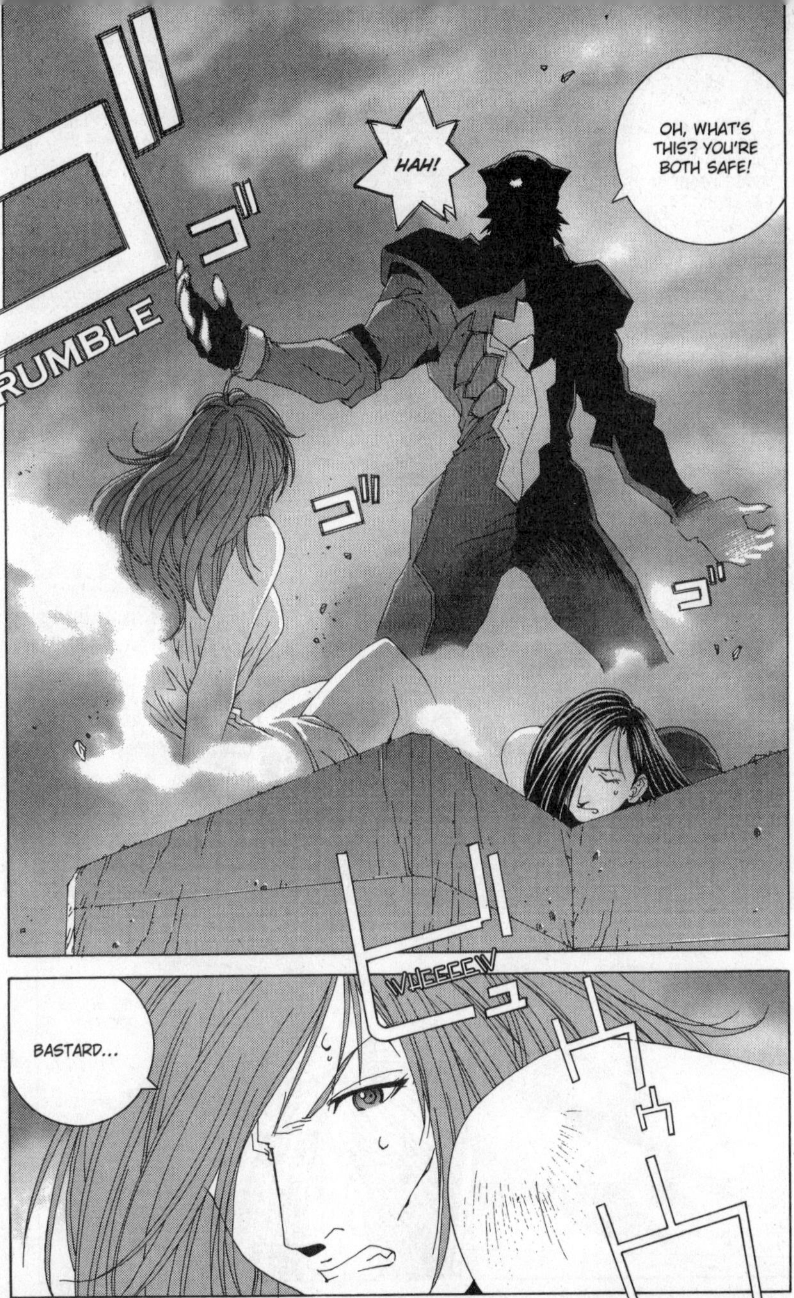
OH, WHAT'S THIS? YOU'RE BOTH SAFE!
HAH!
RUMBLE
WHEEEEW
BASTARD...

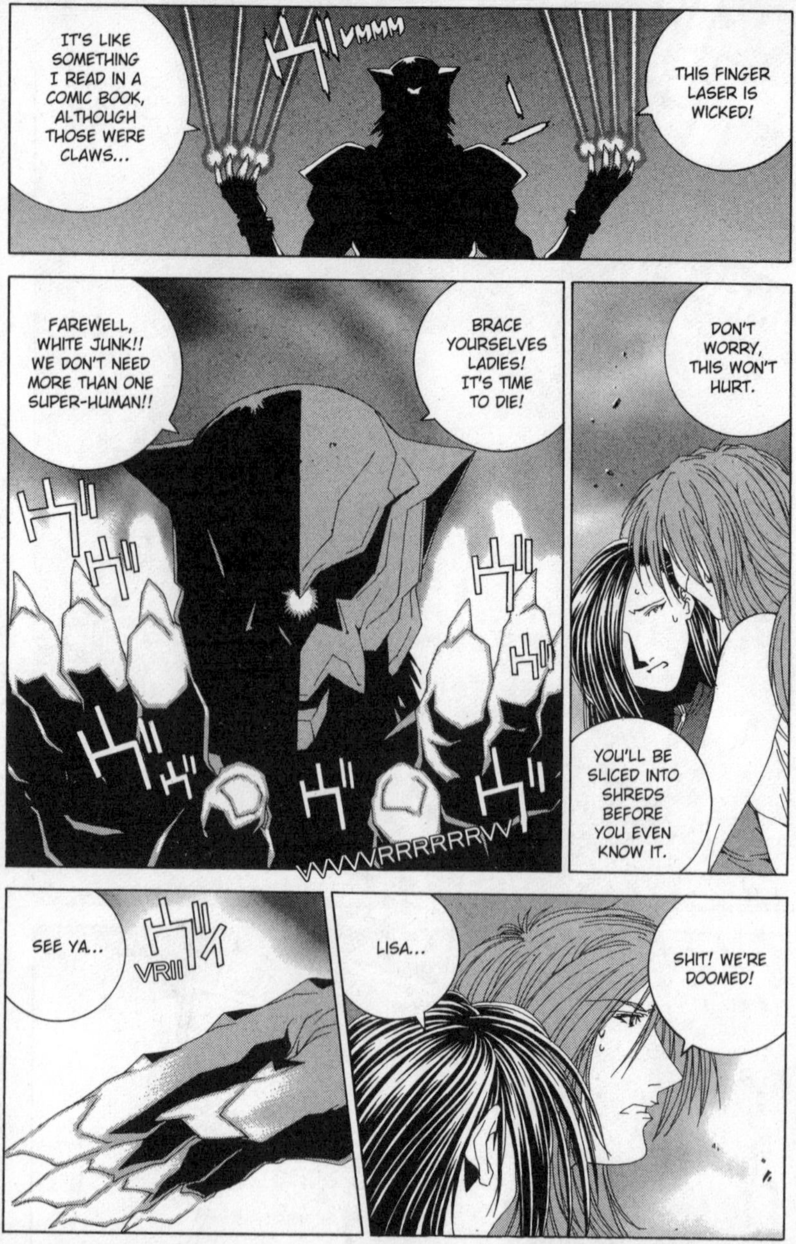
VMMM
THIS FINGER LASER IS WICKED!
IT'S LIKE SOMETHING I READ IN A COMIC BOOK, ALTHOUGH THOSE WERE CLAWS...
DON'T WORRY, THIS WON'T HURT.
YOU'LL BE SLICED INTO SHREDS BEFORE YOU EVEN KNOW IT.
BRACE YOURSELVES LADIES! IT'S TIME TO DIE!
FAREWELL, WHITE JUNK!! WE DON'T NEED MORE THAN ONE SUPER-HUMAN!!
VVVVVRRRRRRVV
SHIT! WE'RE DOOMED!
LISA...
VRII
SEE YA...

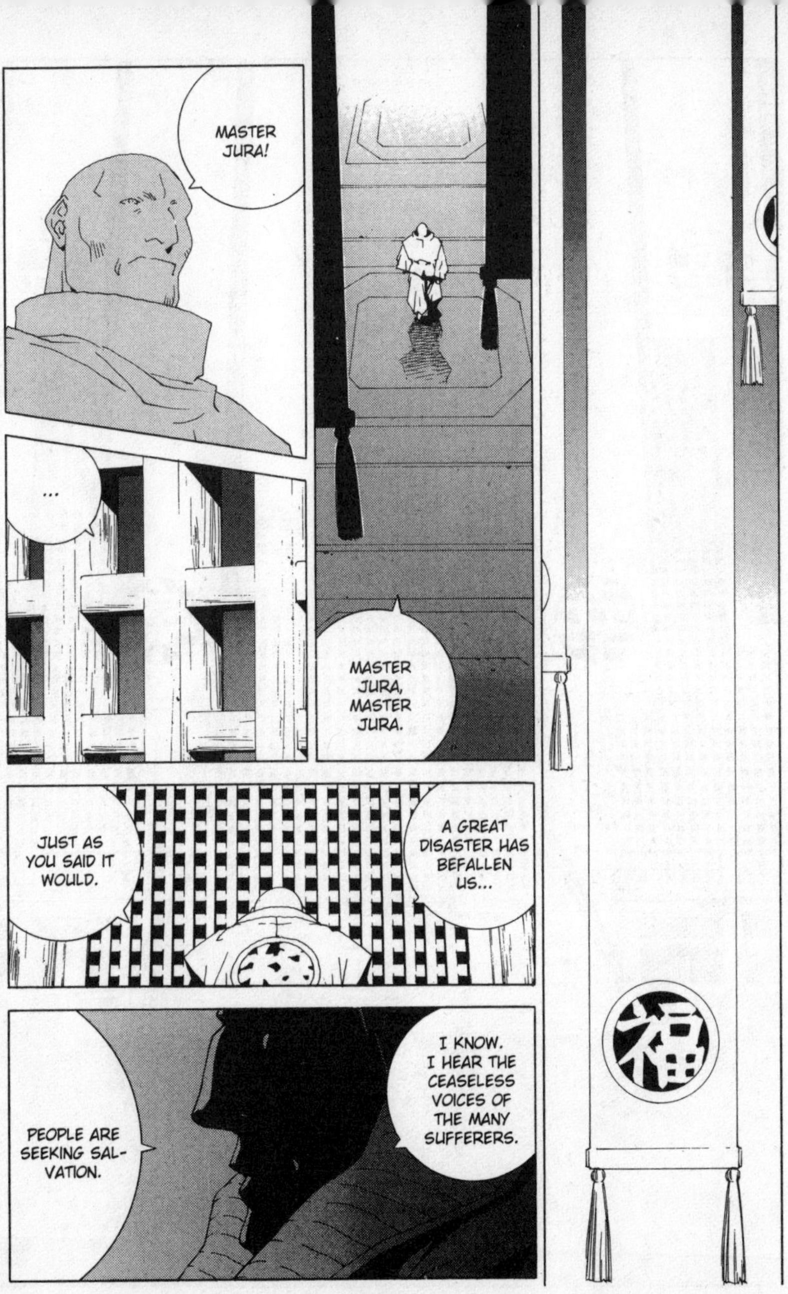
MASTER JURA, MASTER JURA.
MASTER JURA!
...
A GREAT DISASTER HAS BEFALLEN US...
JUST AS YOU SAID IT WOULD.
I KNOW. I HEAR THE CEASELESS VOICES OF THE MANY SUFFERERS.
PEOPLE ARE SEEKING SAL-VATION.

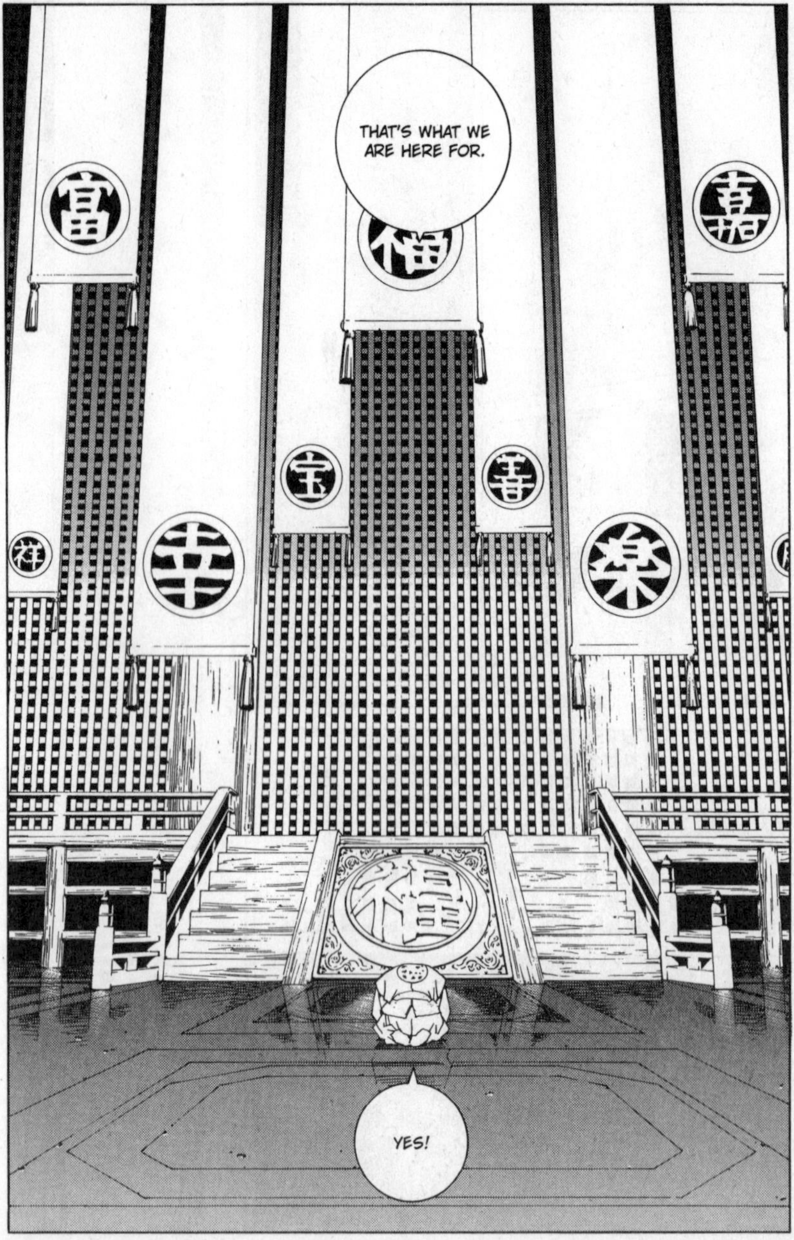
THAT'S WHAT WE ARE HERE FOR.
YES!

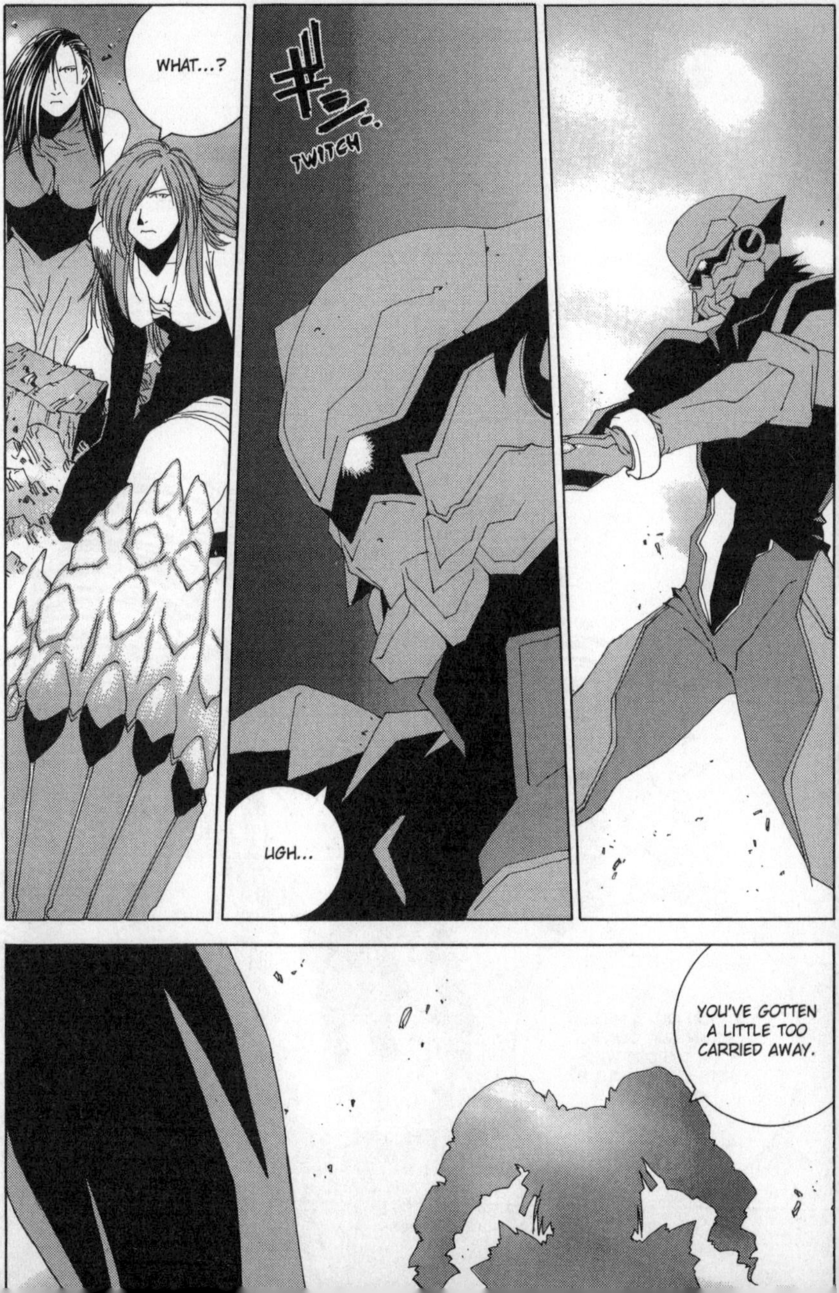
TWITCH
UGH...
WHAT...?
YOU'VE GOTTEN A LITTLE TOO CARRIED AWAY.

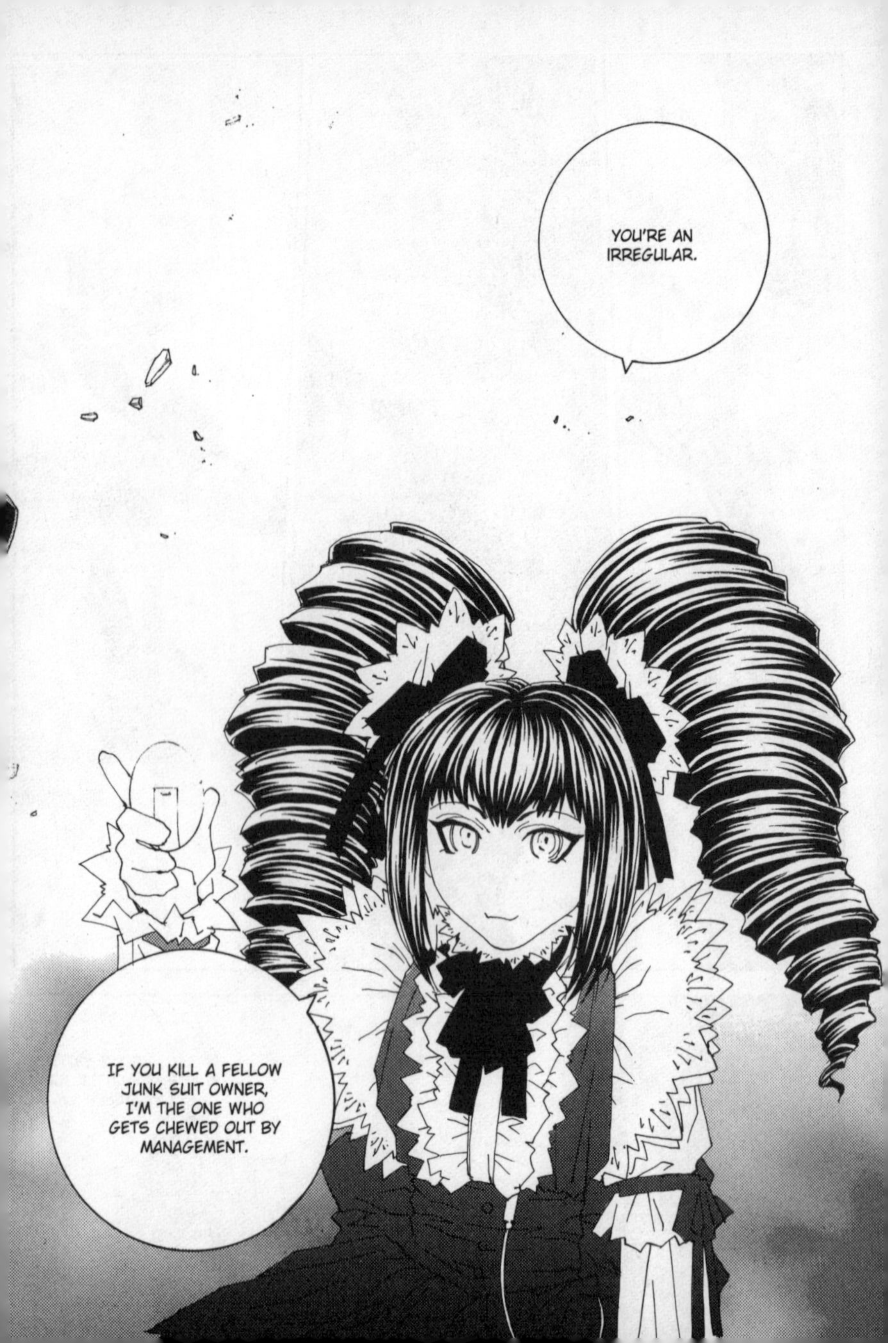
YOU'RE AN IRREGULAR.
IF YOU KILL A FELLOW JUNK SUIT OWNER, I'M THE ONE WHO GETS CHEWED OUT BY MANAGEMENT.

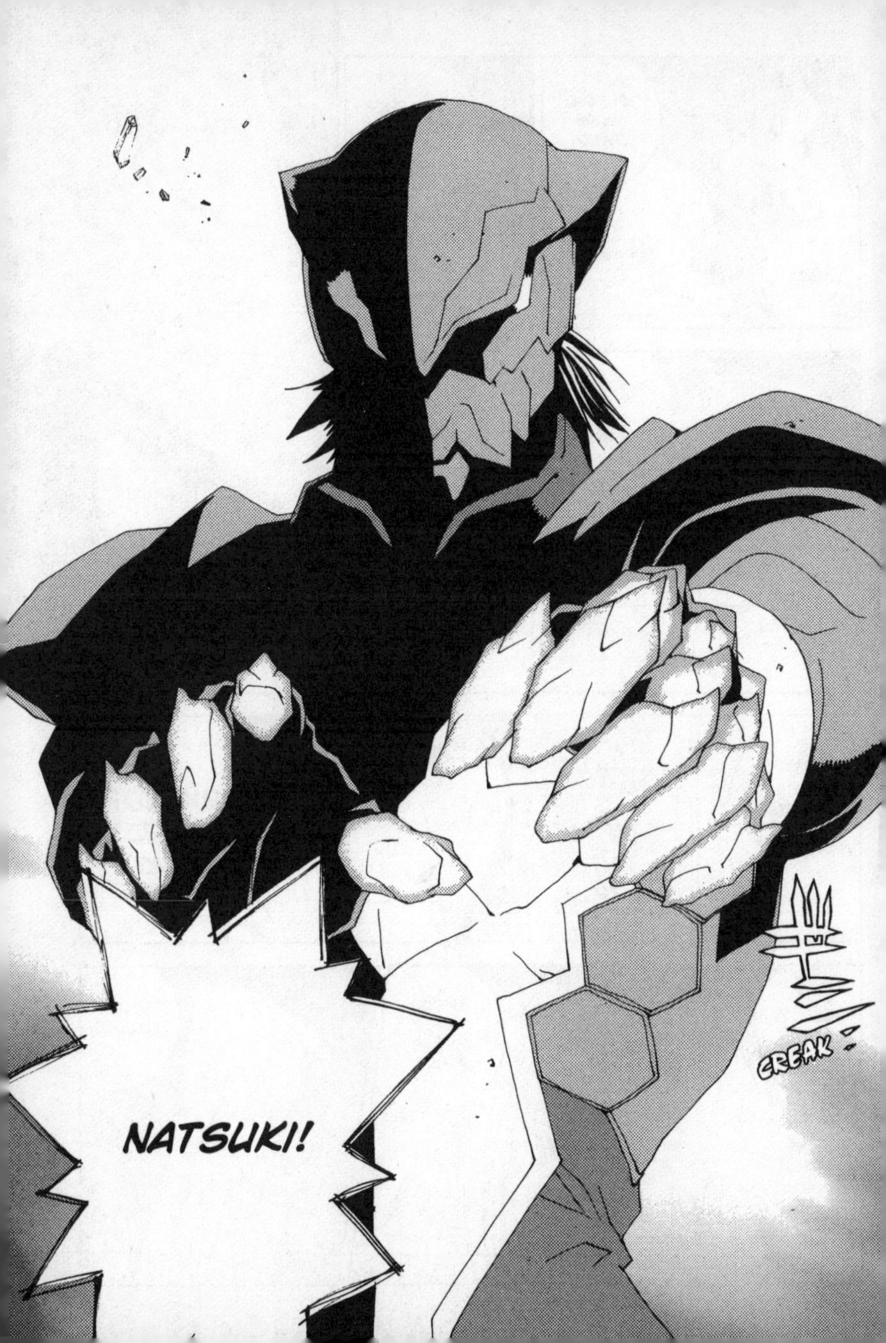
CREAK
NATSUKI!

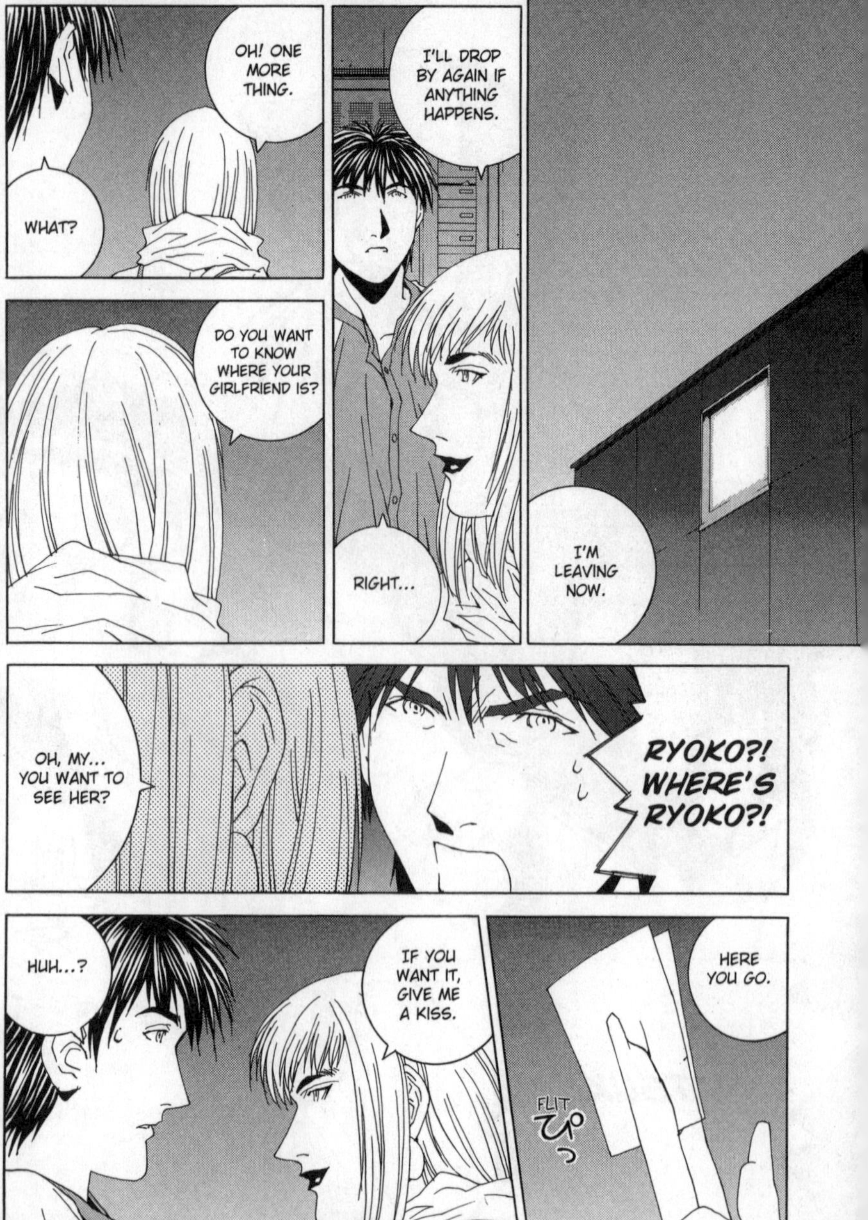
I'M LEAVING NOW.
I'LL DROP BY AGAIN IF ANYTHING HAPPENS.
RIGHT...
OH! ONE MORE THING.
WHAT?
DO YOU WANT TO KNOW WHERE YOUR GIRLFRIEND IS?
RYOKO?! WHERE'S RYOKO?!
OH, MY... YOU WANT TO SEE HER?
HERE YOU GO.
FLIT
IF YOU WANT IT, GIVE ME A KISS.
HUH...?

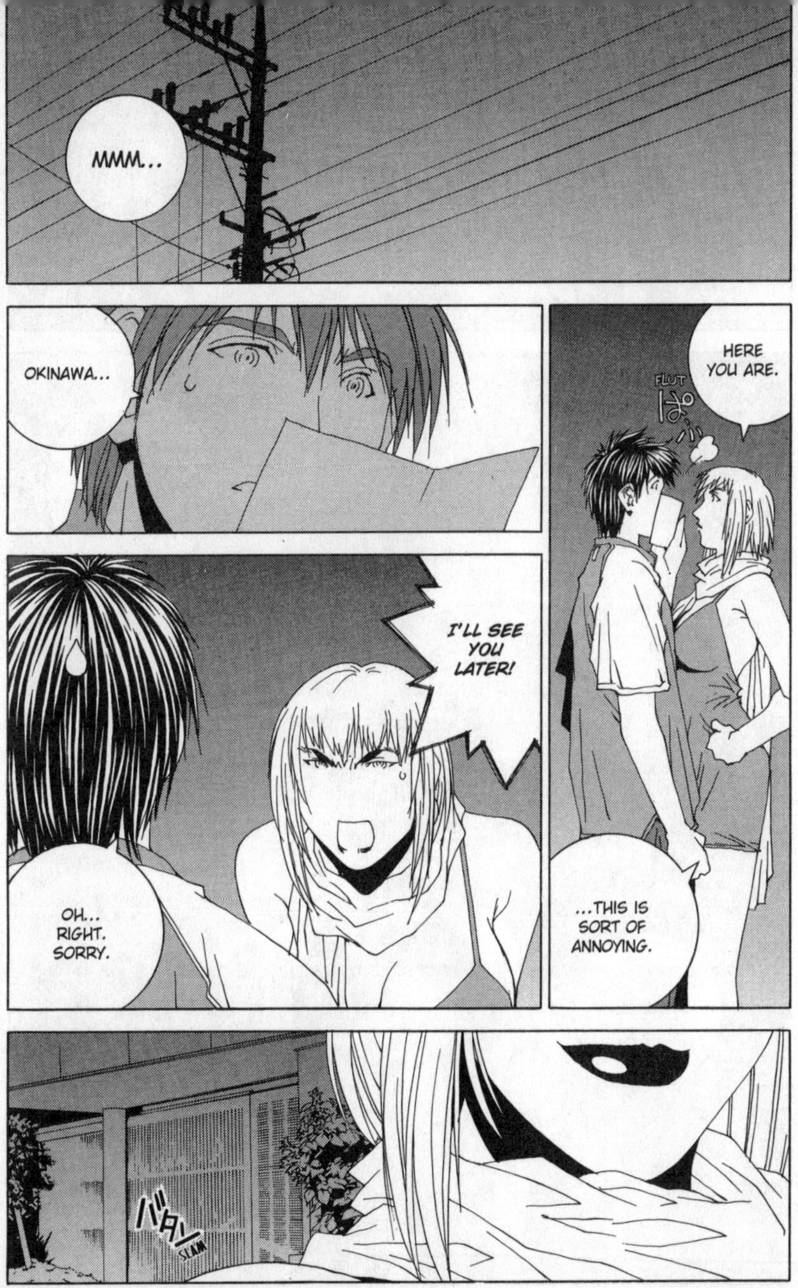
MMM...
HERE YOU ARE.
FLUT
ぱっ
...THIS IS SORT OF ANNOYING.
OKINAWA...
I'LL SEE YOU LATER!
OH... RIGHT. SORRY.
バタン
SLAM

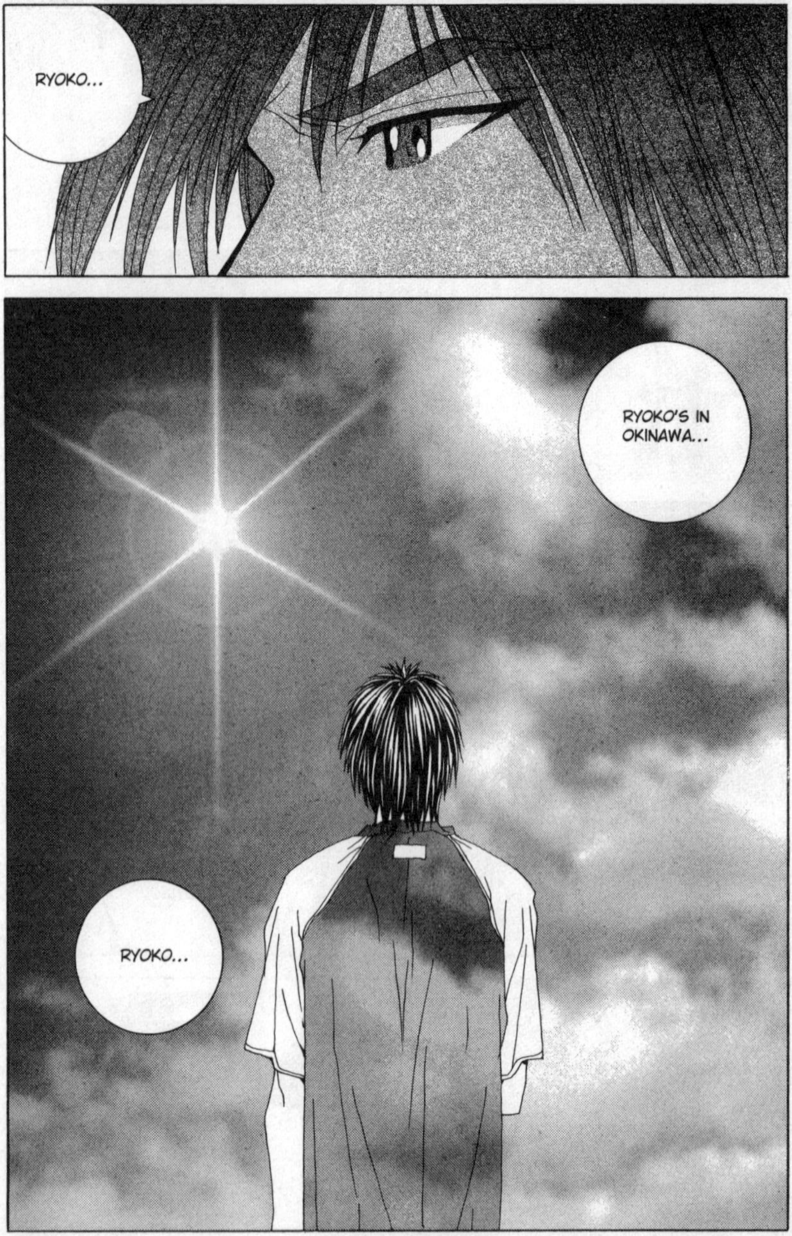
RYOKO...
RYOKO'S IN OKINAWA...
RYOKO...

JUSTICE:22 JUNK DIVERGENCE

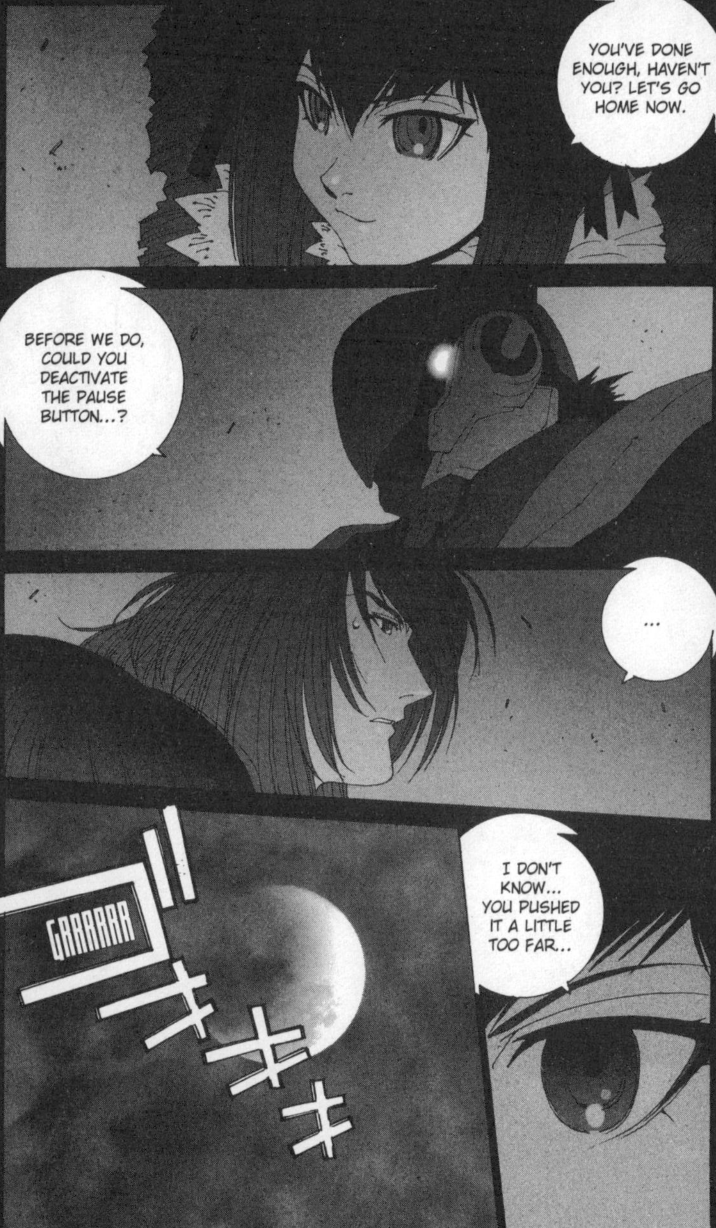
YOU'VE DONE ENOUGH, HAVEN'T YOU? LET'S GO HOME NOW.
BEFORE WE DO, COULD YOU DEACTIVATE THE PAUSE BUTTON...?
...
I DON'T KNOW... YOU PUSHED IT A LITTLE TOO FAR...
GRRRRR

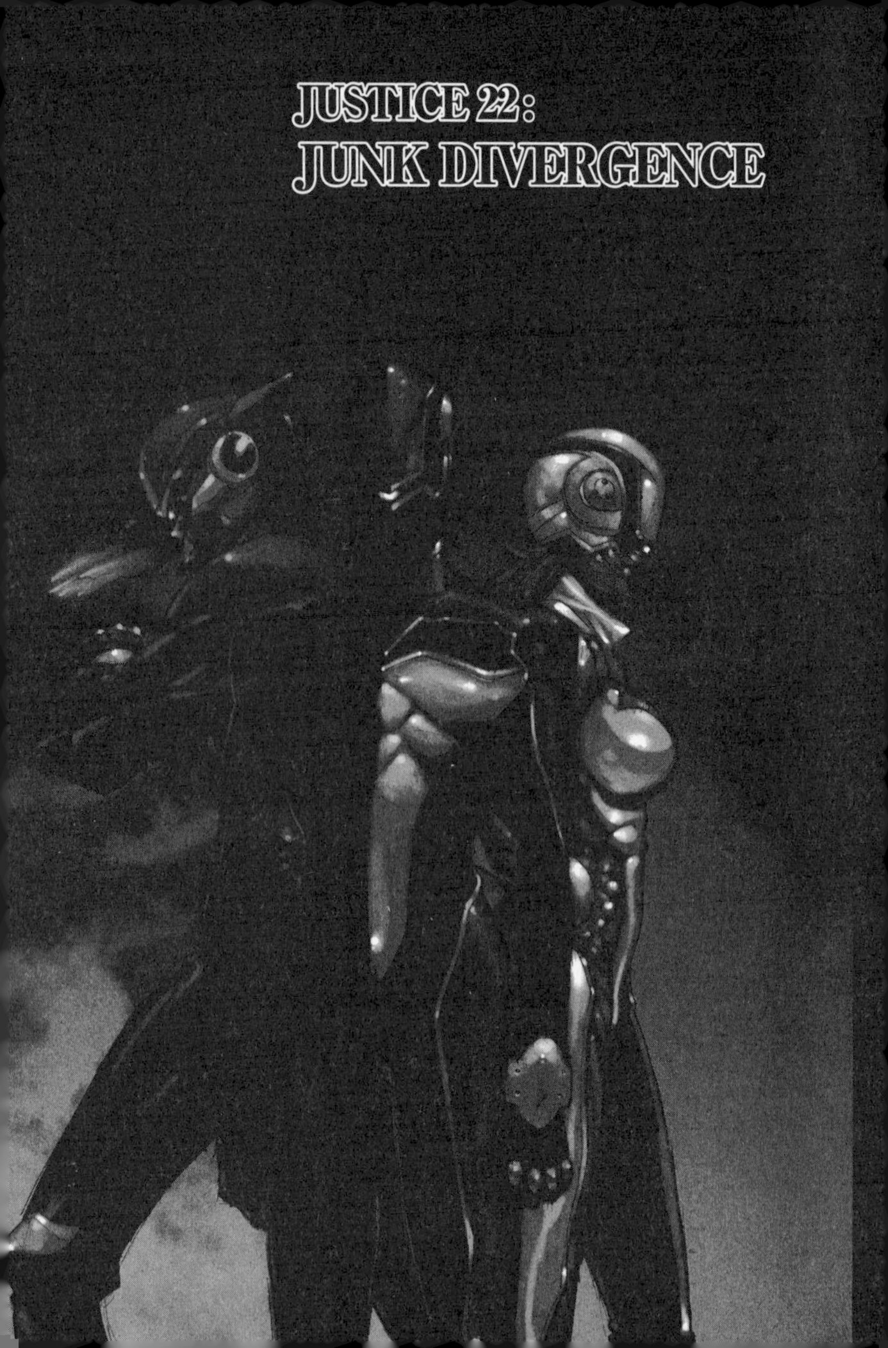
JUSTICE 22:
JUNK DIVERGENCE

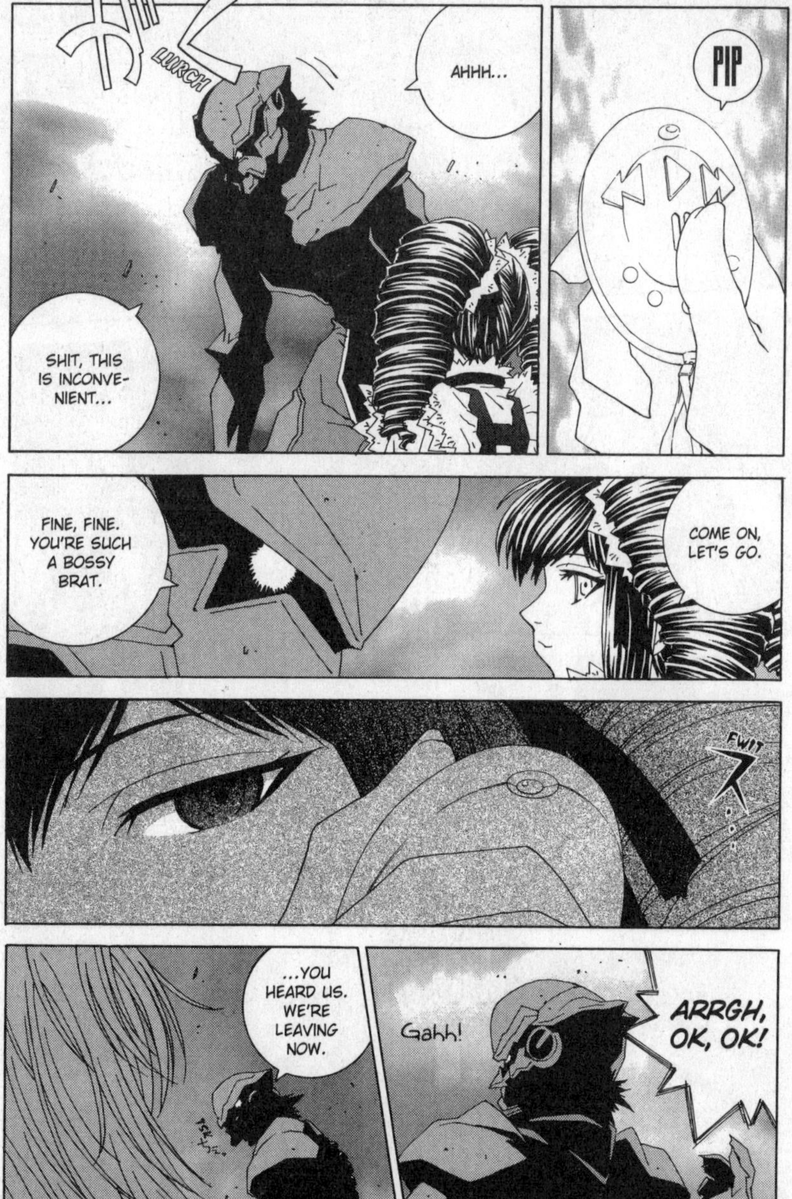
PIP
AHHH...
LURCH
SHIT, THIS IS INCONVENIENT...
COME ON, LET'S GO.
FINE, FINE. YOU'RE SUCH A BOSSY BRAT.
FWIT
ARRGH, OK, OK!
Gahh!
...YOU HEARD US. WE'RE LEAVING NOW.

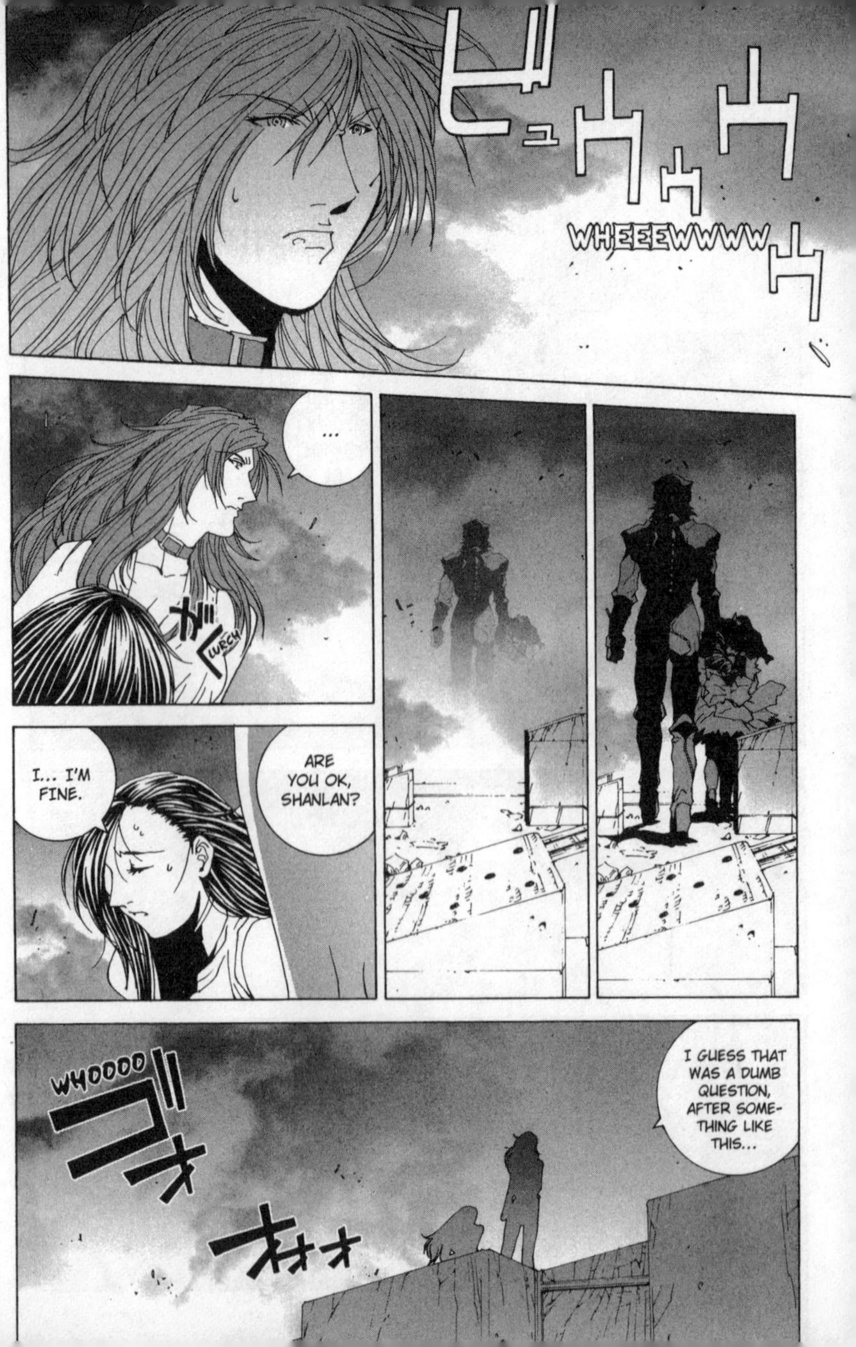
WHEEEWWWW
...
LURCH
ARE YOU OK, SHANLAN?
I... I'M FINE.
I GUESS THAT WAS A DUMB QUESTION, AFTER SOME-THING LIKE THIS...
WHOOOO

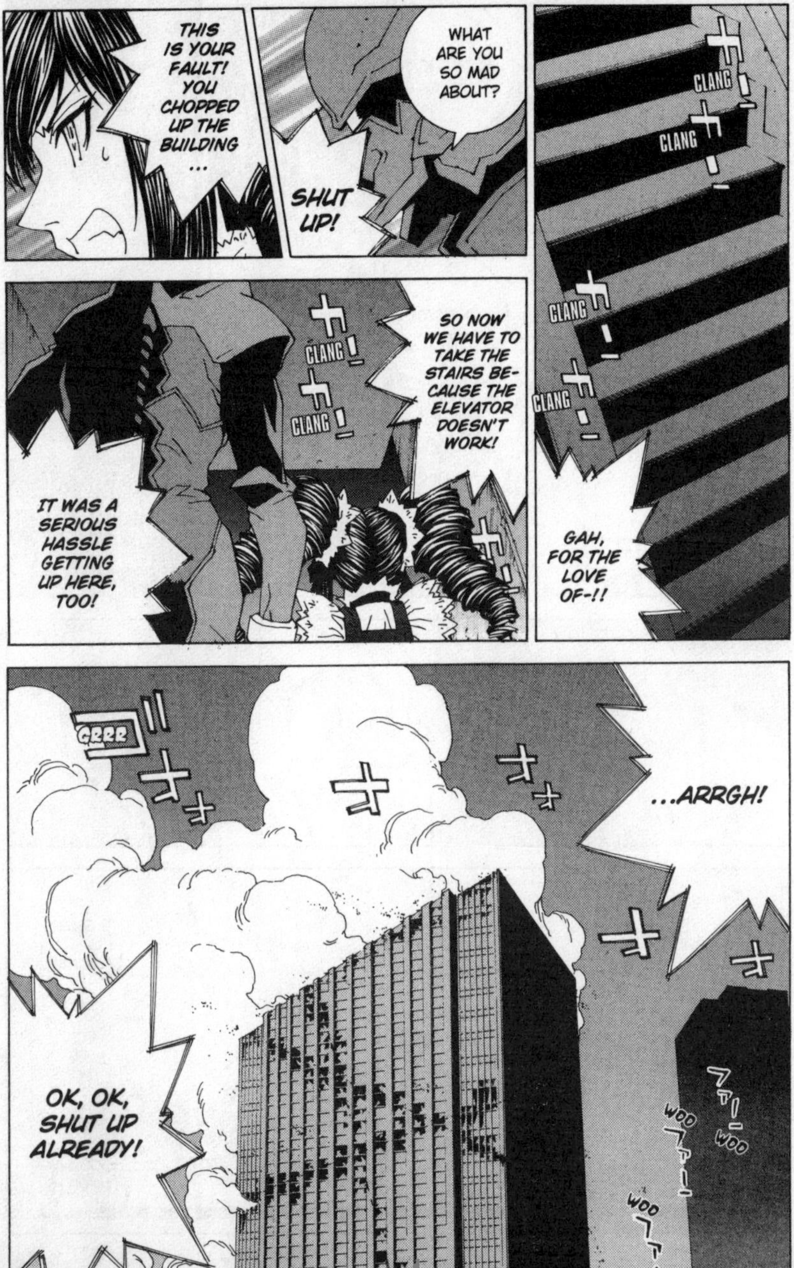
CLANG
CLANG
CLANG
CLANG
GAH, FOR THE LOVE OF-!!
WHAT ARE YOU SO MAD ABOUT?
SHUT UP!
THIS IS YOUR FAULT! YOU CHOPPED UP THE BUILDING ...
SO NOW WE HAVE TO TAKE THE STAIRS BE-CAUSE THE ELEVATOR DOESN'T WORK!
CLANG
CLANG
IT WAS A SERIOUS HASSLE GETTING UP HERE, TOO!
...ARRGH!
GRRR
OK, OK, SHUT UP ALREADY!
WOO
WOO
WOO

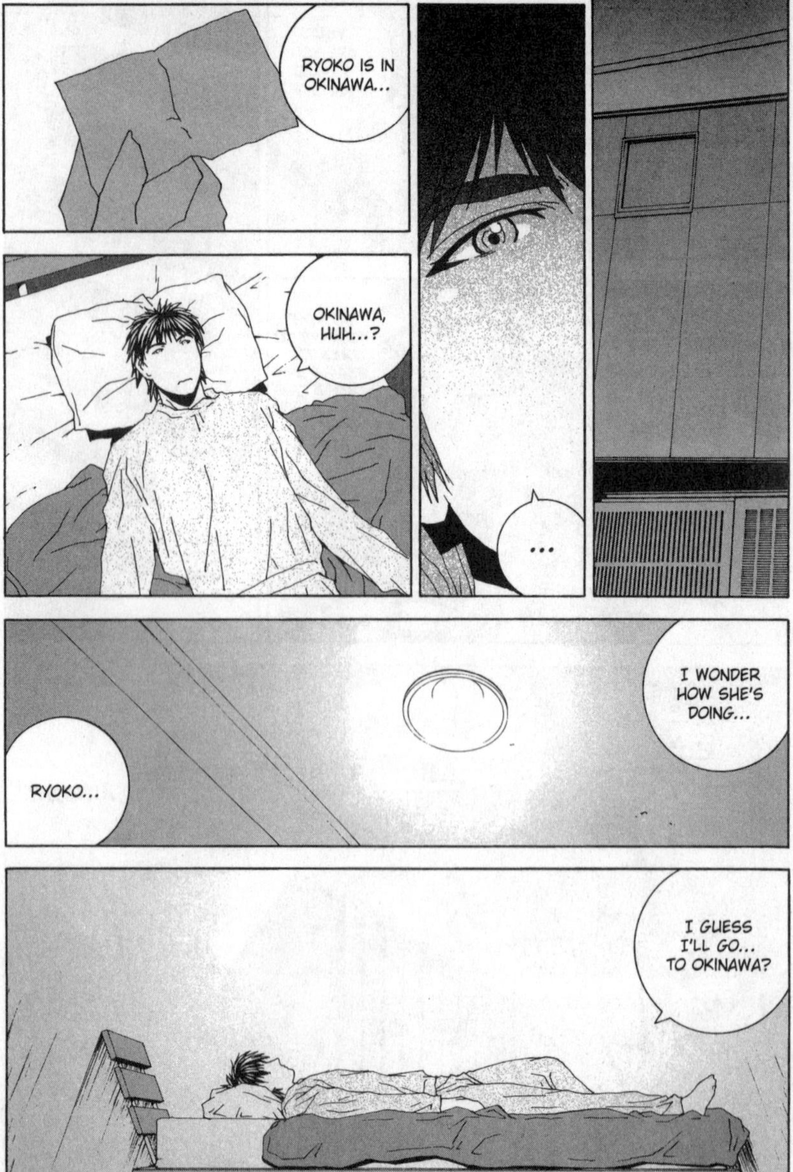
...
RYOKO IS IN OKINAWA...
OKINAWA, HUH...?
I WONDER HOW SHE'S DOING...
RYOKO...
I GUESS I'LL GO... TO OKINAWA?

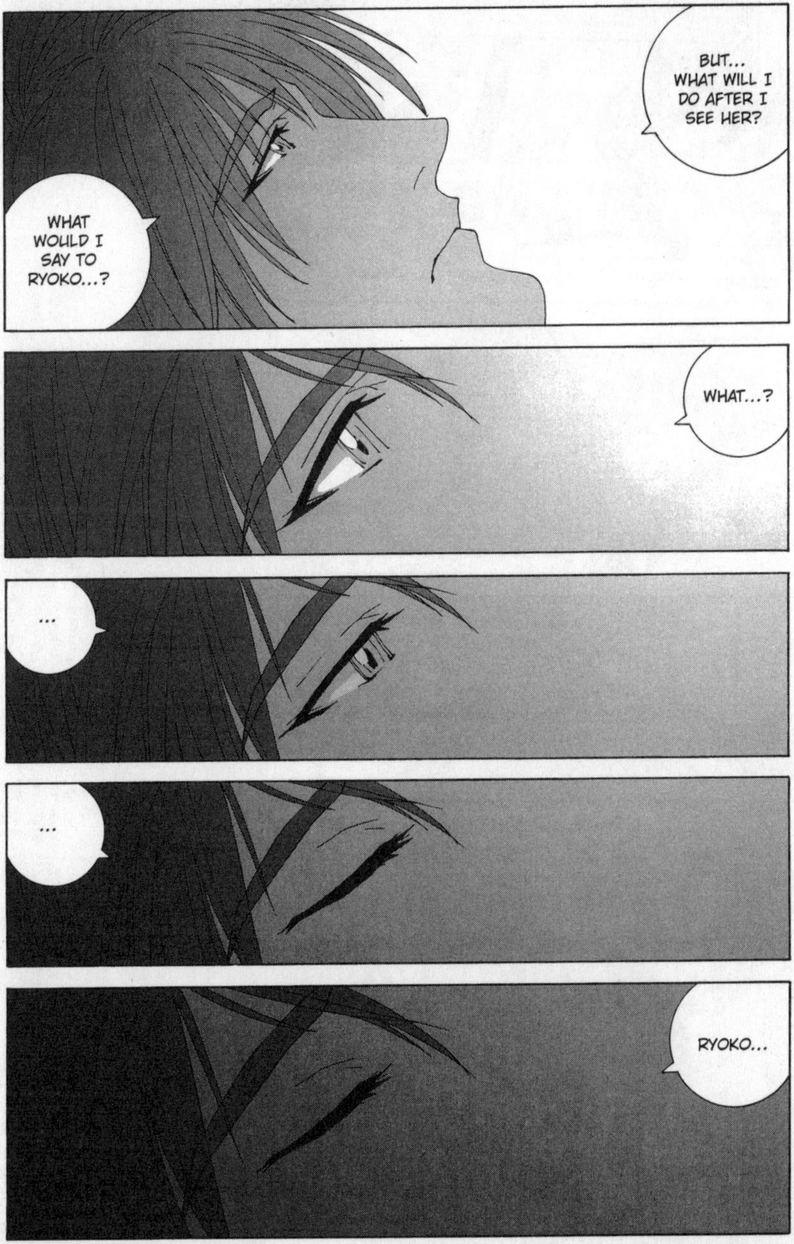
BUT... WHAT WILL I DO AFTER I SEE HER?
WHAT WOULD I SAY TO RYOKO...?
WHAT...?
...
...
RYOKO...

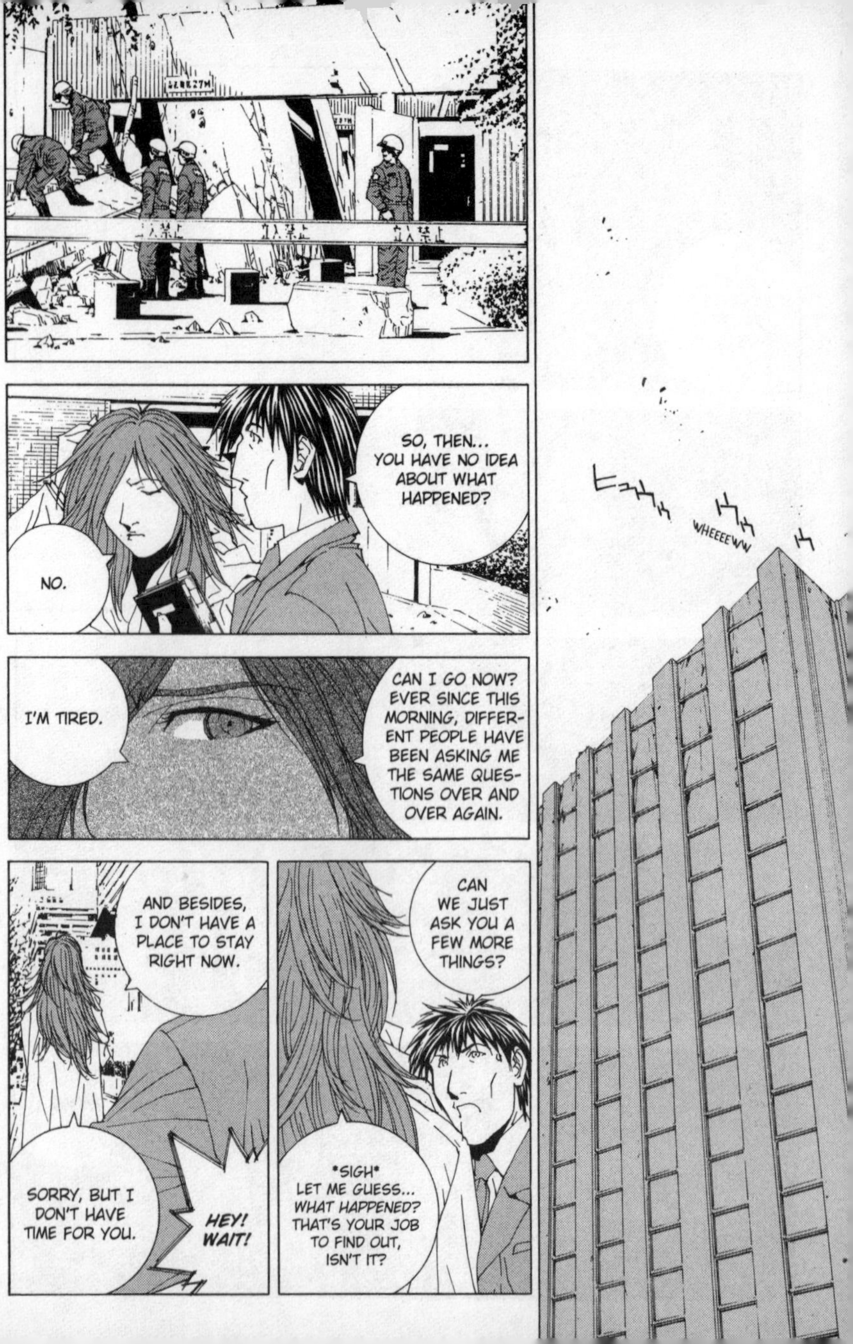
WHEEEEWW
SO, THEN... YOU HAVE NO IDEA ABOUT WHAT HAPPENED?
NO.
CAN I GO NOW? EVER SINCE THIS MORNING, DIFFERENT PEOPLE HAVE BEEN ASKING ME THE SAME QUESTIONS OVER AND OVER AGAIN.
I'M TIRED.
CAN WE JUST ASK YOU A FEW MORE THINGS?
SIGH LET ME GUESS... WHAT HAPPENED? THAT'S YOUR JOB TO FIND OUT, ISN'T IT?
AND BESIDES, I DON'T HAVE A PLACE TO STAY RIGHT NOW.
HEY! WAIT!
SORRY, BUT I DON'T HAVE TIME FOR YOU.

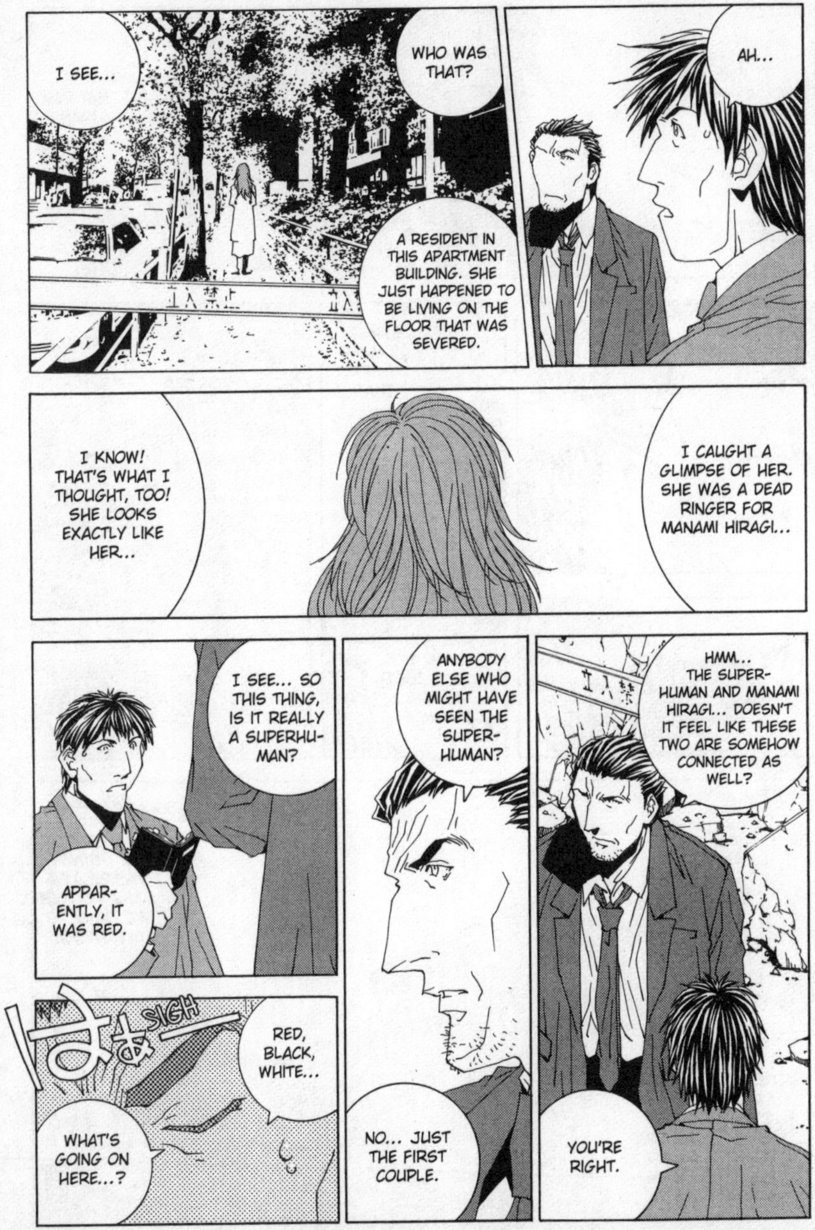
AH...
WHO WAS THAT?
I SEE...
A RESIDENT IN THIS APARTMENT BUILDING. SHE JUST HAPPENED TO BE LIVING ON THE FLOOR THAT WAS SEVERED.
立入禁止
I CAUGHT A GLIMPSE OF HER. SHE WAS A DEAD RINGER FOR MANAMI HIRAGI...
I KNOW! THAT'S WHAT I THOUGHT, TOO! SHE LOOKS EXACTLY LIKE HER...
HMM... THE SUPER-HUMAN AND MANAMI HIRAGI... DOESN'T IT FEEL LIKE THESE TWO ARE SOMEHOW CONNECTED AS WELL?
YOU'RE RIGHT.
ANYBODY ELSE WHO MIGHT HAVE SEEN THE SUPER-HUMAN?
NO... JUST THE FIRST COUPLE.
I SEE... SO THIS THING, IS IT REALLY A SUPERHU-MAN?
APPAR-ENTLY, IT WAS RED.
はぁ SIGH
RED, BLACK, WHITE...
WHAT'S GOING ON HERE...?

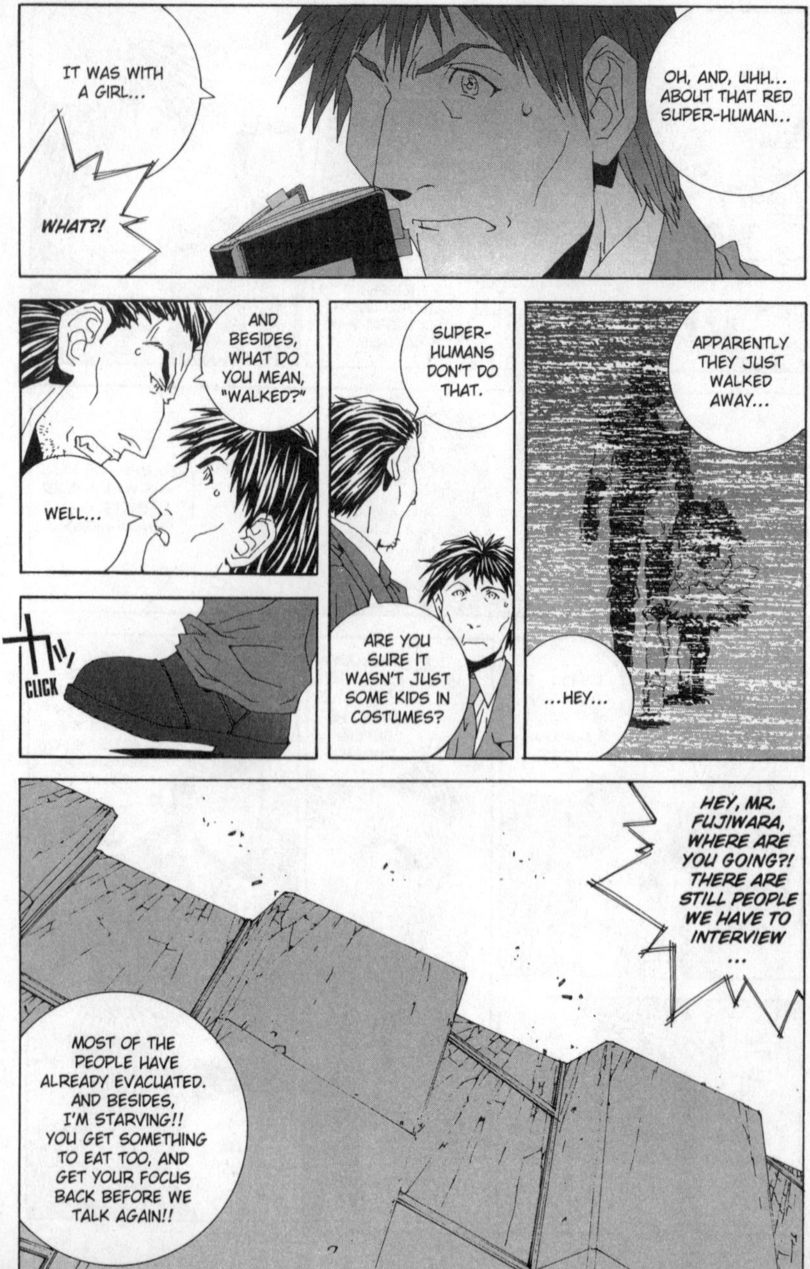

OH, AND, UHH... ABOUT THAT RED SUPER-HUMAN...
IT WAS WITH A GIRL...
WHAT?!
APPARENTLY THEY JUST WALKED AWAY...
...HEY...
SUPER-HUMANS DON'T DO THAT.
ARE YOU SURE IT WASN'T JUST SOME KIDS IN COSTUMES?
AND BESIDES, WHAT DO YOU MEAN, "WALKED?"
WELL...
CLICK
HEY, MR. FUJIWARA, WHERE ARE YOU GOING?! THERE ARE STILL PEOPLE WE HAVE TO INTERVIEW...
MOST OF THE PEOPLE HAVE ALREADY EVACUATED. AND BESIDES, I'M STARVING!! YOU GET SOMETHING TO EAT TOO, AND GET YOUR FOCUS BACK BEFORE WE TALK AGAIN!!

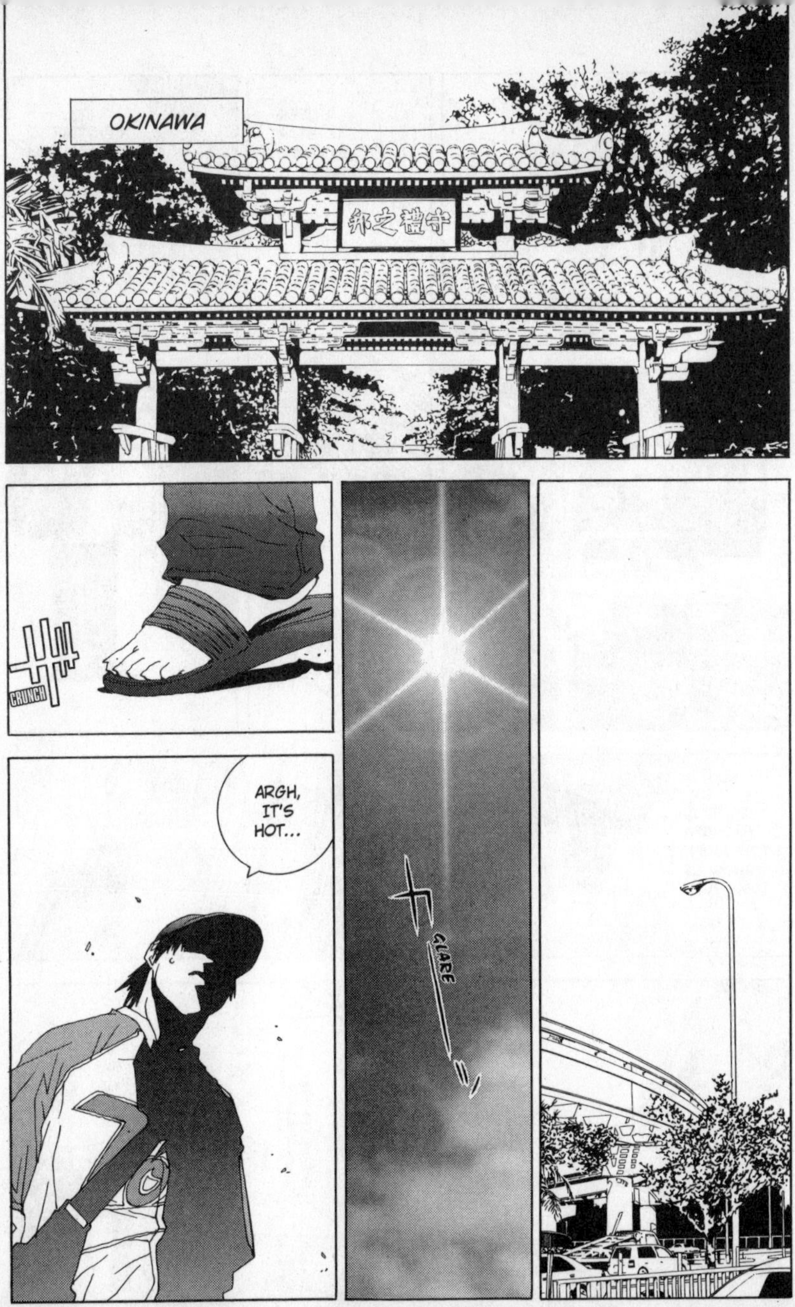
OKINAWA
守禮之邦
GLARE
CRUNCH
ARGH, IT'S HOT...

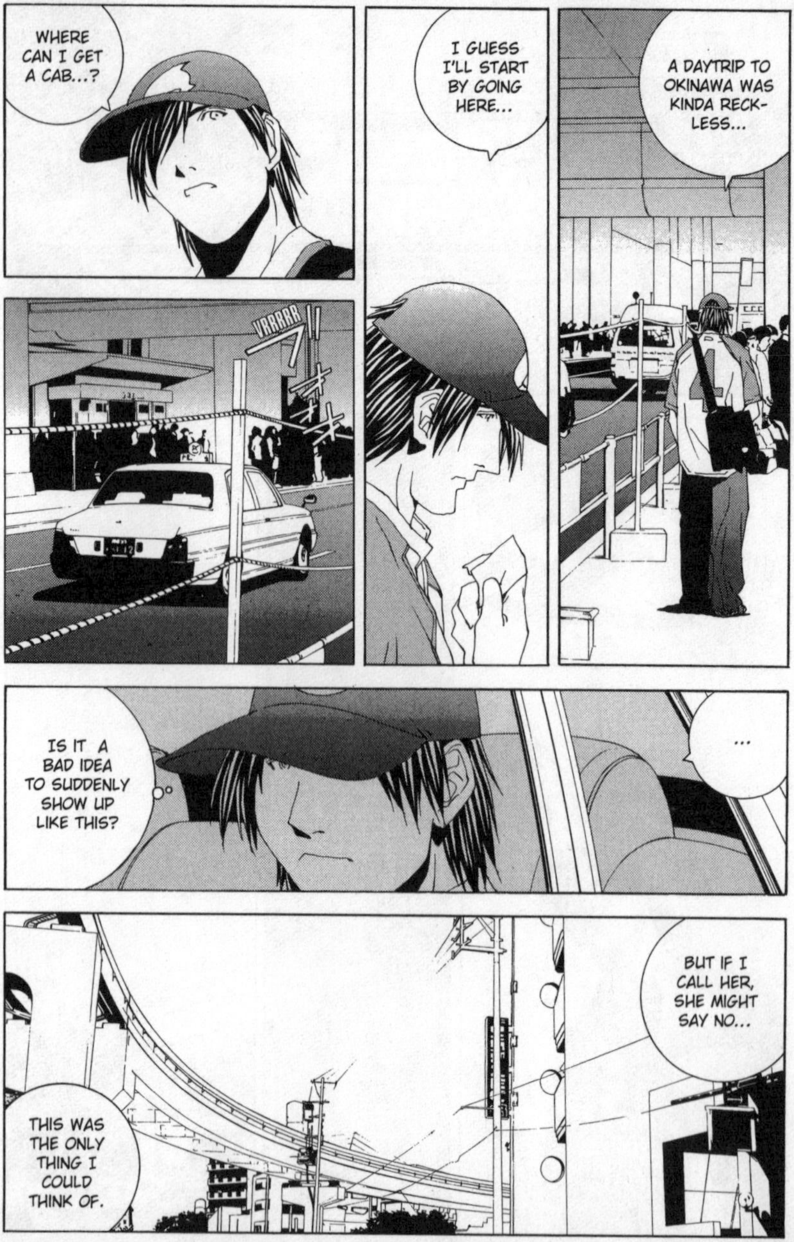
A DAYTRIP TO OKINAWA WAS KINDA RECK-LESS...
I GUESS I'LL START BY GOING HERE...
WHERE CAN I GET A CAB...?
VRRRRR
...
IS IT A BAD IDEA TO SUDDENLY SHOW UP LIKE THIS?
BUT IF I CALL HER, SHE MIGHT SAY NO...
THIS WAS THE ONLY THING I COULD THINK OF.

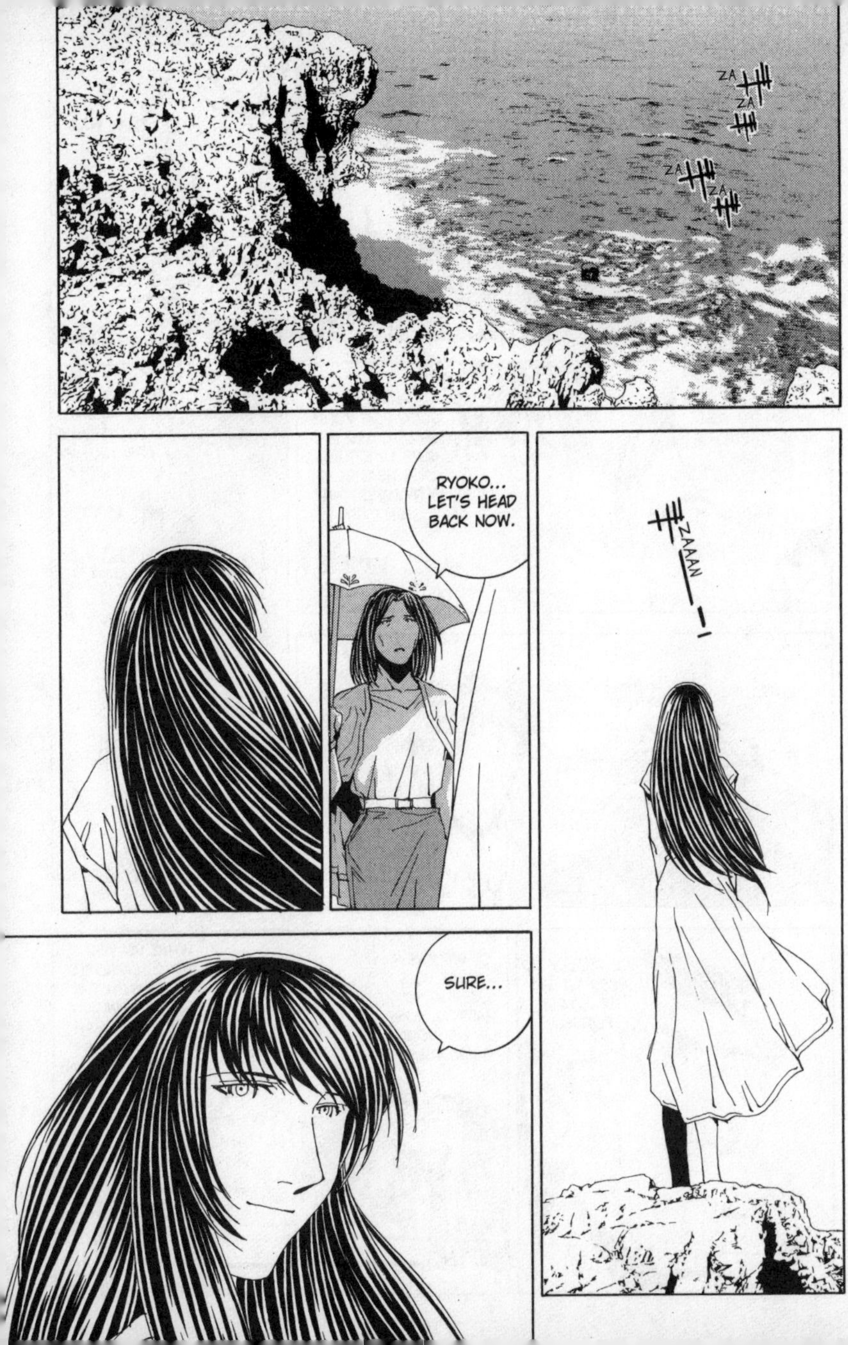
ZA ZA ZA ZA
ZAAAN
RYOKO... LET'S HEAD BACK NOW.
SURE...

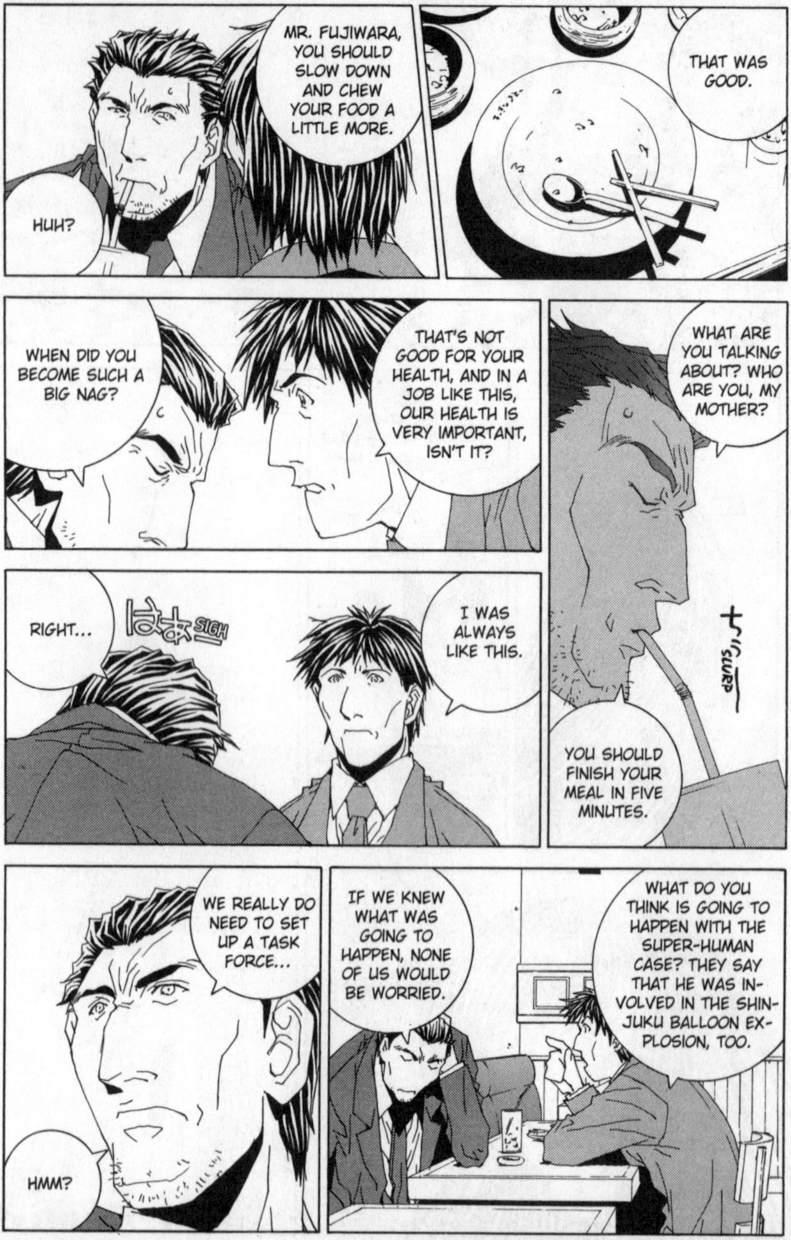
THAT WAS GOOD.
MR. FUJIWARA, YOU SHOULD SLOW DOWN AND CHEW YOUR FOOD A LITTLE MORE.
HUH?
WHAT ARE YOU TALKING ABOUT? WHO ARE YOU, MY MOTHER?
SLURP
YOU SHOULD FINISH YOUR MEAL IN FIVE MINUTES.
THAT'S NOT GOOD FOR YOUR HEALTH, AND IN A JOB LIKE THIS, OUR HEALTH IS VERY IMPORTANT, ISN'T IT?
WHEN DID YOU BECOME SUCH A BIG NAG?
I WAS ALWAYS LIKE THIS.
はぁー SIGH
RIGHT...
WHAT DO YOU THINK IS GOING TO HAPPEN WITH THE SUPER-HUMAN CASE? THEY SAY THAT HE WAS INVOLVED IN THE SHINJUKU BALLOON EXPLOSION, TOO.
IF WE KNEW WHAT WAS GOING TO HAPPEN, NONE OF US WOULD BE WORRIED.
WE REALLY DO NEED TO SET UP A TASK FORCE...
HMM?

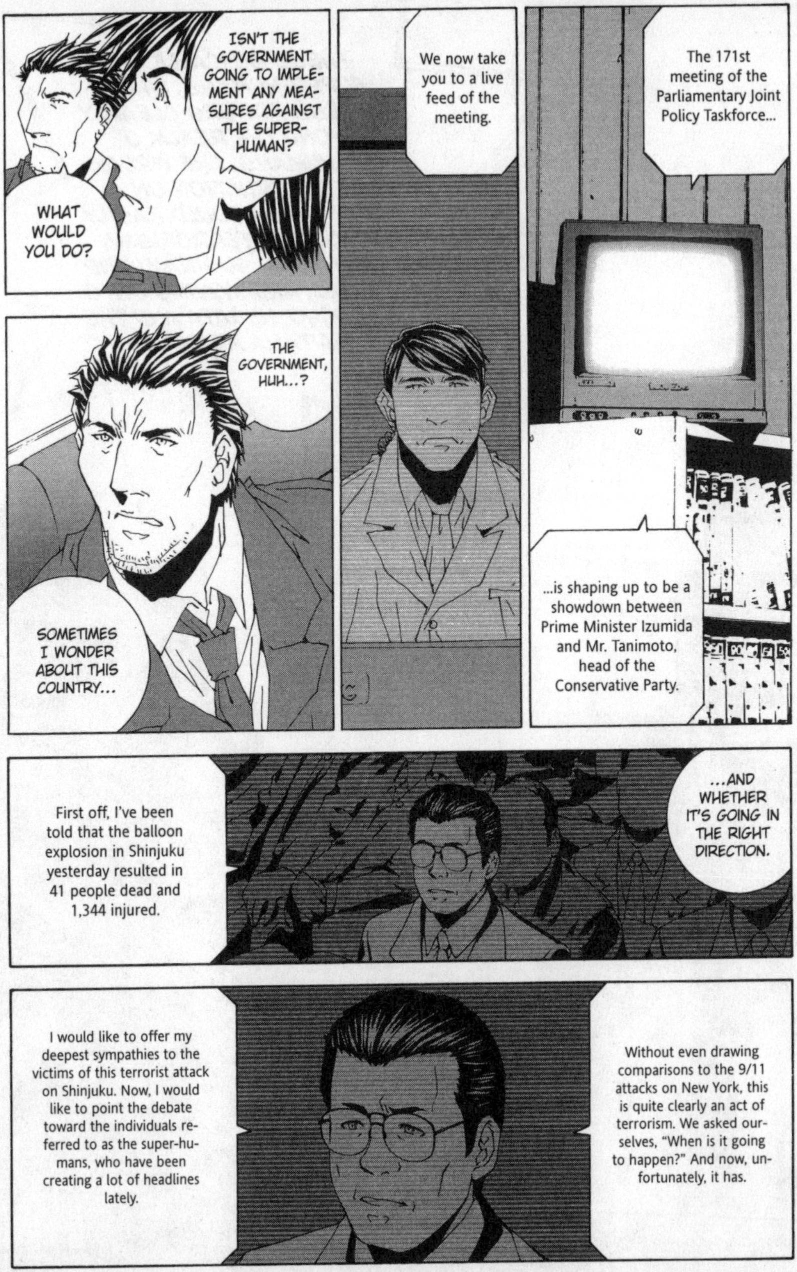
The 171st meeting of the Parliamentary Joint Policy Taskforce...
...is shaping up to be a showdown between Prime Minister Izumida and Mr. Tanimoto, head of the Conservative Party.
We now take you to a live feed of the meeting.
ISN'T THE GOVERNMENT GOING TO IMPLEMENT ANY MEASURES AGAINST THE SUPER-HUMAN?
WHAT WOULD YOU DO?
THE GOVERNMENT, HUH...?
SOMETIMES I WONDER ABOUT THIS COUNTRY...
...AND WHETHER IT'S GOING IN THE RIGHT DIRECTION.
First off, I've been told that the balloon explosion in Shinjuku yesterday resulted in 41 people dead and 1,344 injured.
Without even drawing comparisons to the 9/11 attacks on New York, this is quite clearly an act of terrorism. We asked ourselves, "When is it going to happen?" And now, unfortunately, it has.
I would like to offer my deepest sympathies to the victims of this terrorist attack on Shinjuku. Now, I would like to point the debate toward the individuals referred to as the super-humans, who have been creating a lot of headlines lately.

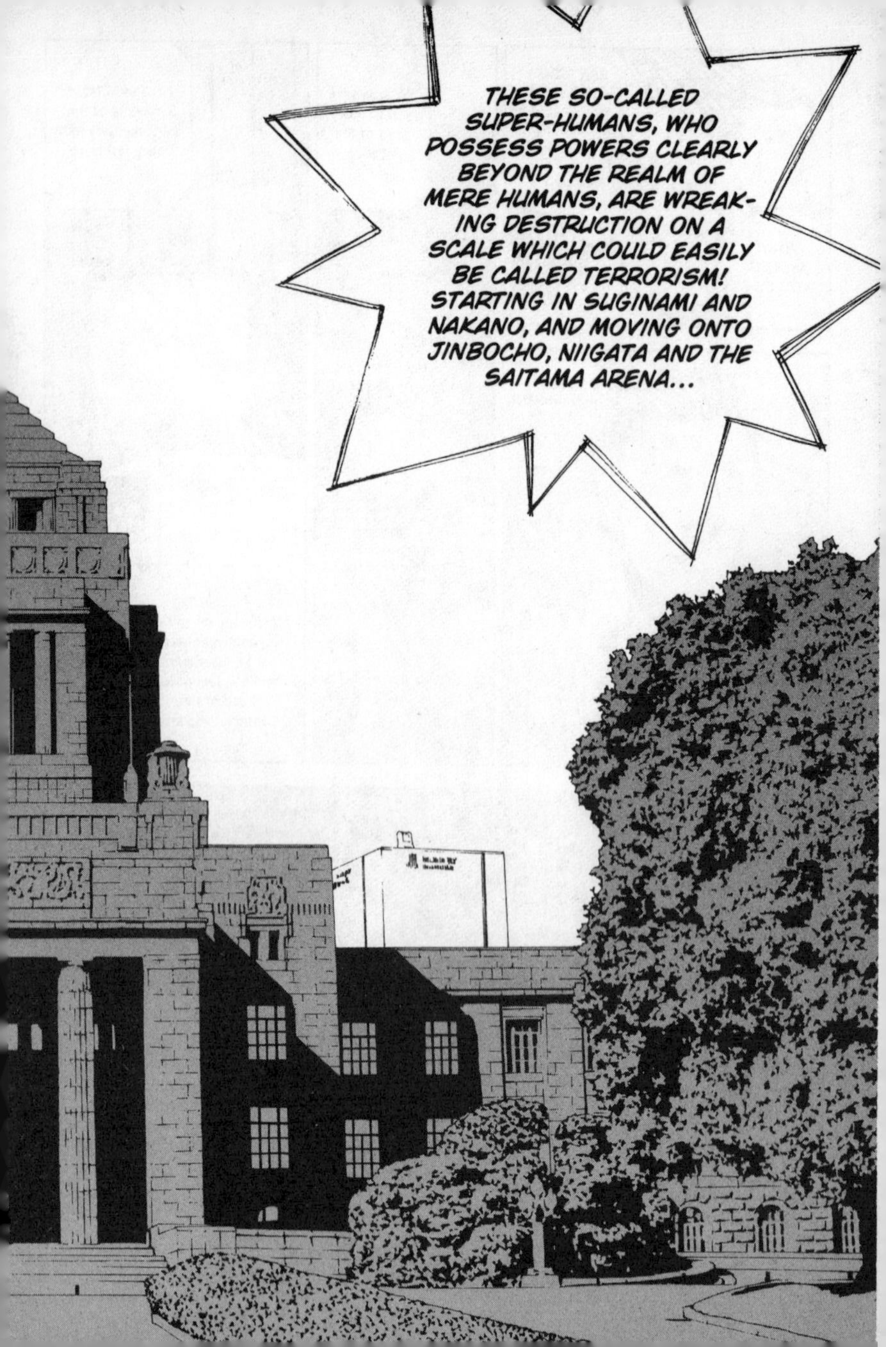
THESE SO-CALLED SUPER-HUMANS, WHO POSSESS POWERS CLEARLY BEYOND THE REALM OF MERE HUMANS, ARE WREAK-ING DESTRUCTION ON A SCALE WHICH COULD EASILY BE CALLED TERRORISM! STARTING IN SUGINAMI AND NAKANO, AND MOVING ONTO JINBOCHO, NIIGATA AND THE SAITAMA ARENA...

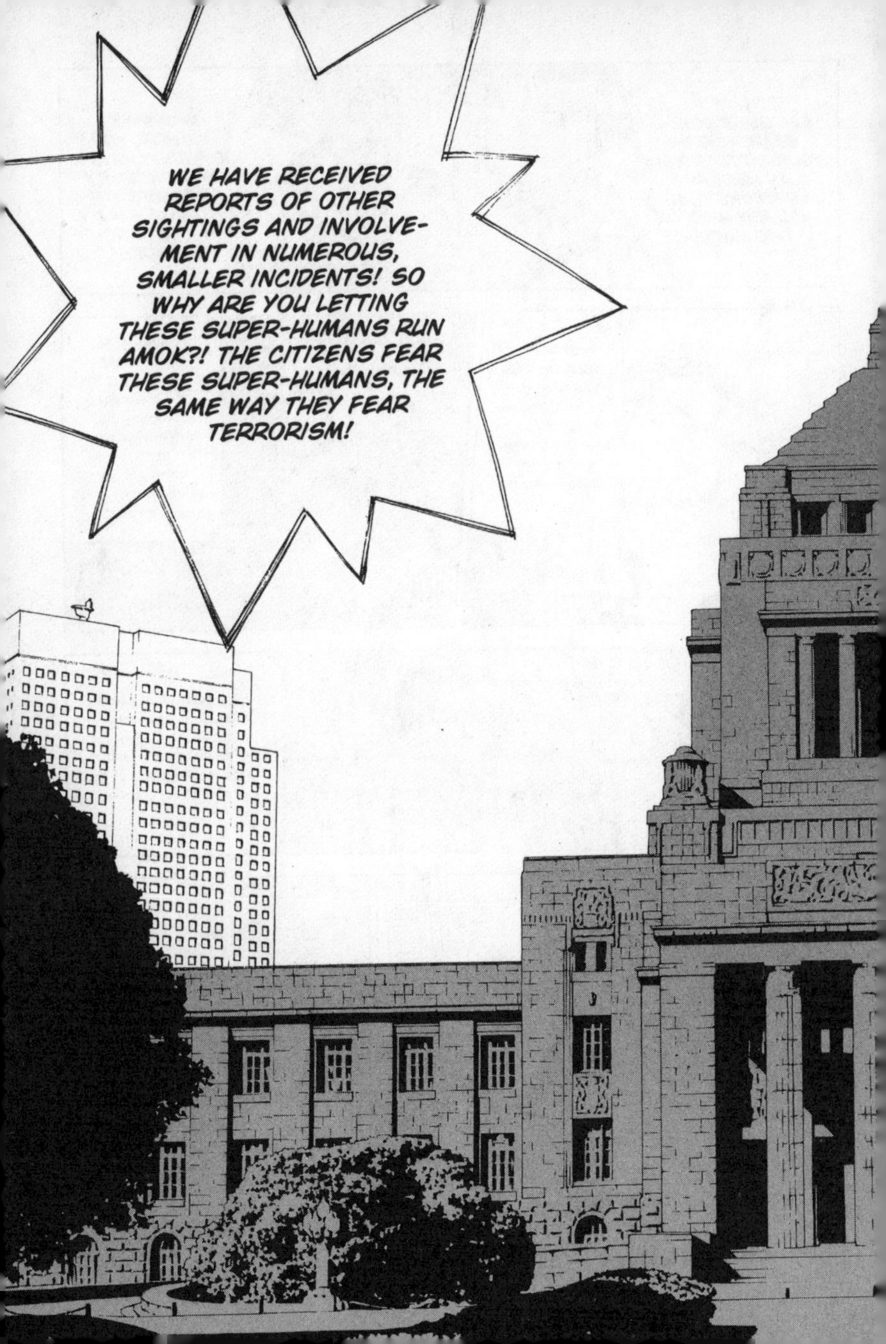
WE HAVE RECEIVED REPORTS OF OTHER SIGHTINGS AND INVOLVEMENT IN NUMEROUS, SMALLER INCIDENTS! SO WHY ARE YOU LETTING THESE SUPER-HUMANS RUN AMOK?! THE CITIZENS FEAR THESE SUPER-HUMANS, THE SAME WAY THEY FEAR TERRORISM!

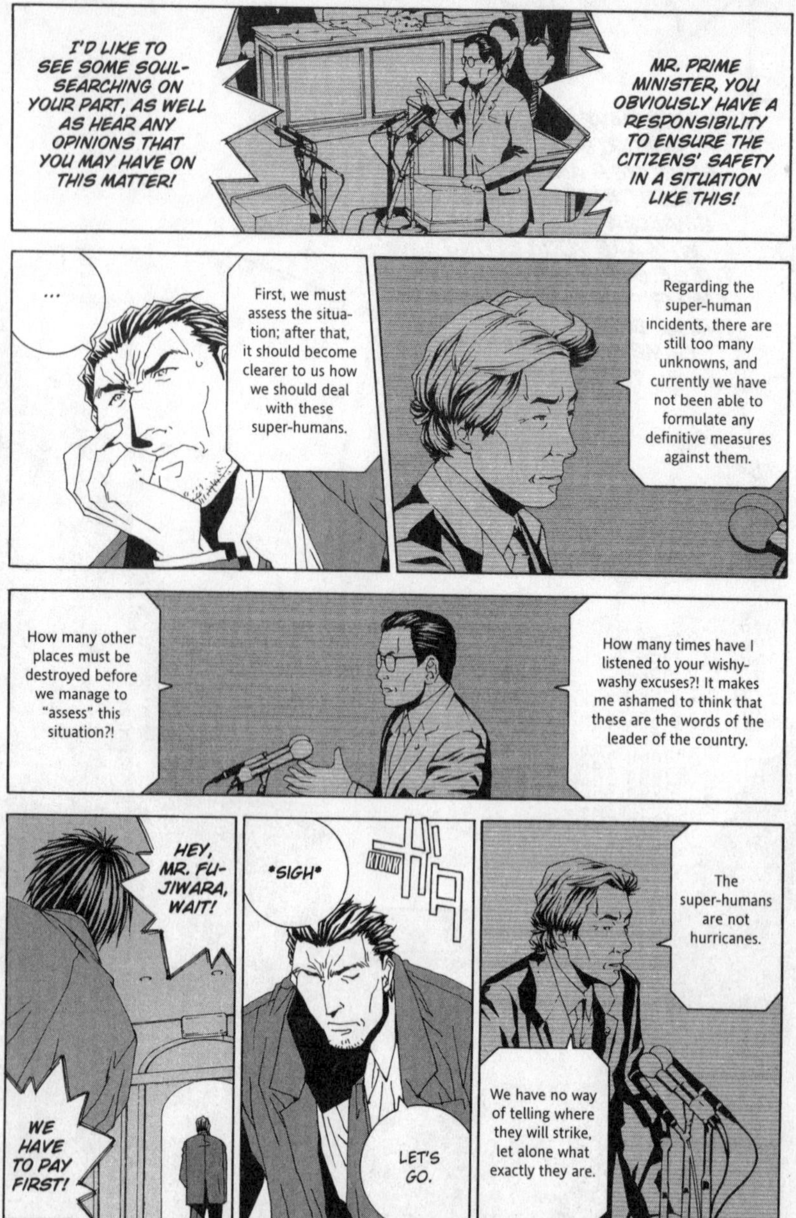
MR. PRIME MINISTER, YOU OBVIOUSLY HAVE A RESPONSIBILITY TO ENSURE THE CITIZENS' SAFETY IN A SITUATION LIKE THIS!
I'D LIKE TO SEE SOME SOUL-SEARCHING ON YOUR PART, AS WELL AS HEAR ANY OPINIONS THAT YOU MAY HAVE ON THIS MATTER!
Regarding the super-human incidents, there are still too many unknowns, and currently we have not been able to formulate any definitive measures against them.
First, we must assess the situation; after that, it should become clearer to us how we should deal with these super-humans.
...
How many times have I listened to your wishy-washy excuses?! It makes me ashamed to think that these are the words of the leader of the country.
How many other places must be destroyed before we manage to "assess" this situation?!
The super-humans are not hurricanes.
We have no way of telling where they will strike, let alone what exactly they are.
KTONK
SIGH
LET'S GO.
HEY, MR. FU-JIWARA, WAIT!
WE HAVE TO PAY FIRST!

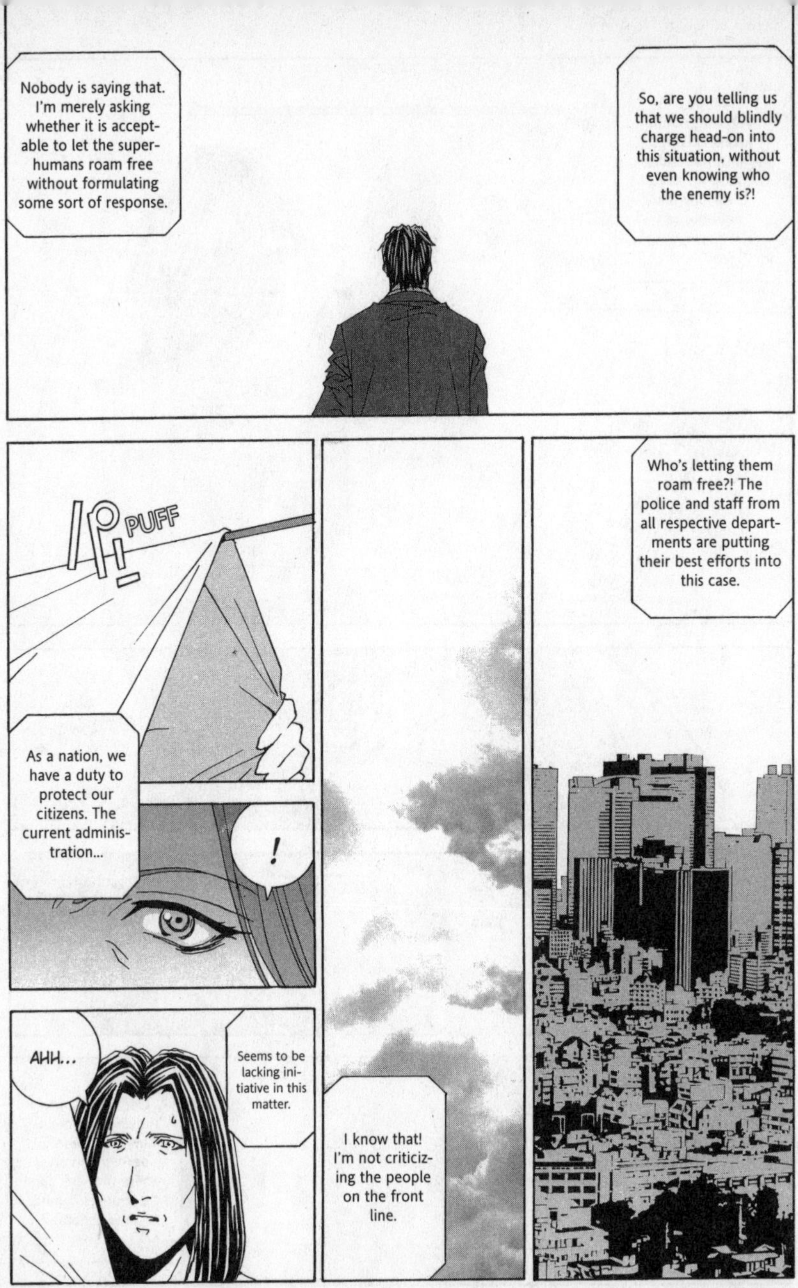

So, are you telling us that we should blindly charge head-on into this situation, without even knowing who the enemy is?!
Nobody is saying that. I'm merely asking whether it is acceptable to let the superhumans roam free without formulating some sort of response.
Who's letting them roam free?! The police and staff from all respective departments are putting their best efforts into this case.
I know that! I'm not criticizing the people on the front line.
PUFF
As a nation, we have a duty to protect our citizens. The current administration...
!
Seems to be lacking initiative in this matter.
AHH...

It's strange to be talking about taking initiative against something we have no way of predicting the activities of.

RUSTLE

RUSTLE

HIRO... HOW DID YOU...?

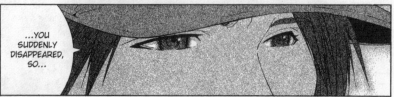

...YOU SUDDENLY DISAPPEARED, SO...

Our first priority should be to determine who these super-humans are, where they are, and the motives behind their actions.

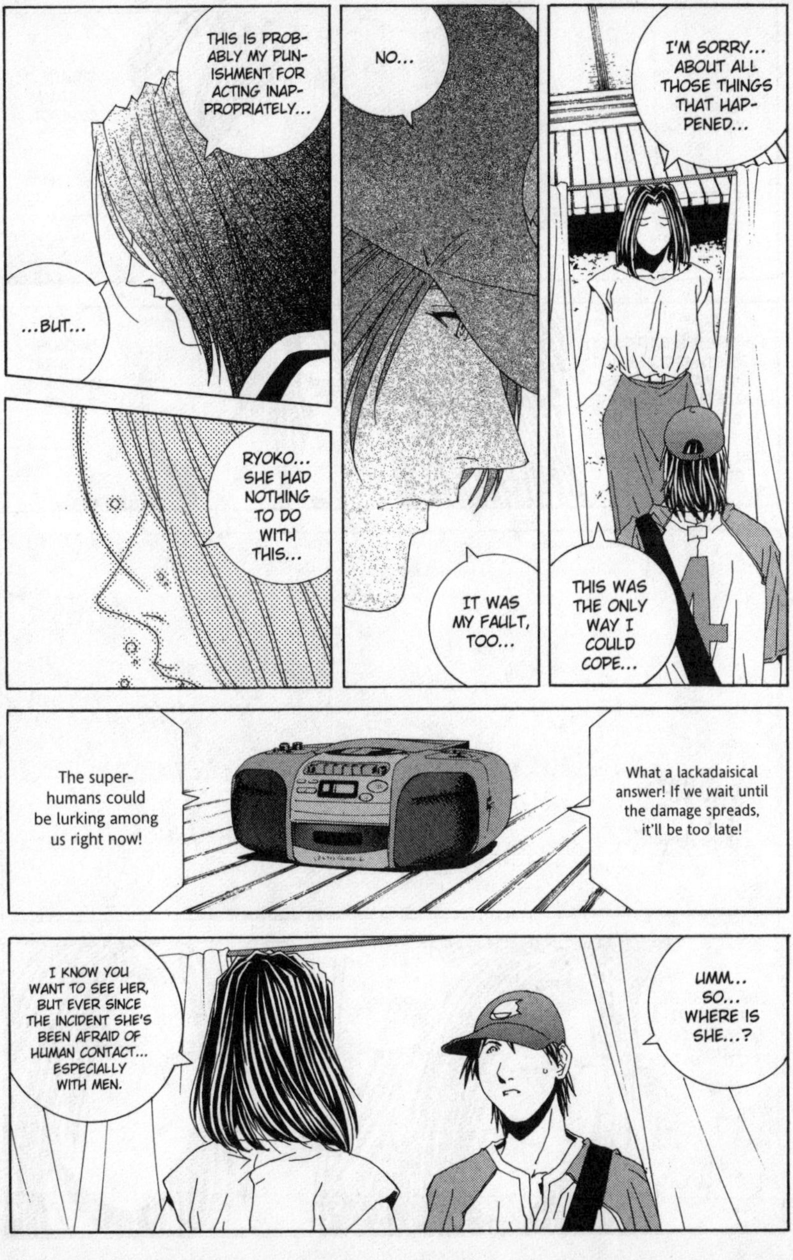
I'M SORRY... ABOUT ALL THOSE THINGS THAT HAPPENED...
THIS WAS THE ONLY WAY I COULD COPE...
NO...
IT WAS MY FAULT, TOO...
THIS IS PROBABLY MY PUNISHMENT FOR ACTING INAPPROPRIATELY...
...BUT...
RYOKO... SHE HAD NOTHING TO DO WITH THIS...
What a lackadaisical answer! If we wait until the damage spreads, it'll be too late!
The super-humans could be lurking among us right now!
UMM... SO... WHERE IS SHE...?
I KNOW YOU WANT TO SEE HER, BUT EVER SINCE THE INCIDENT SHE'S BEEN AFRAID OF HUMAN CONTACT... ESPECIALLY WITH MEN.

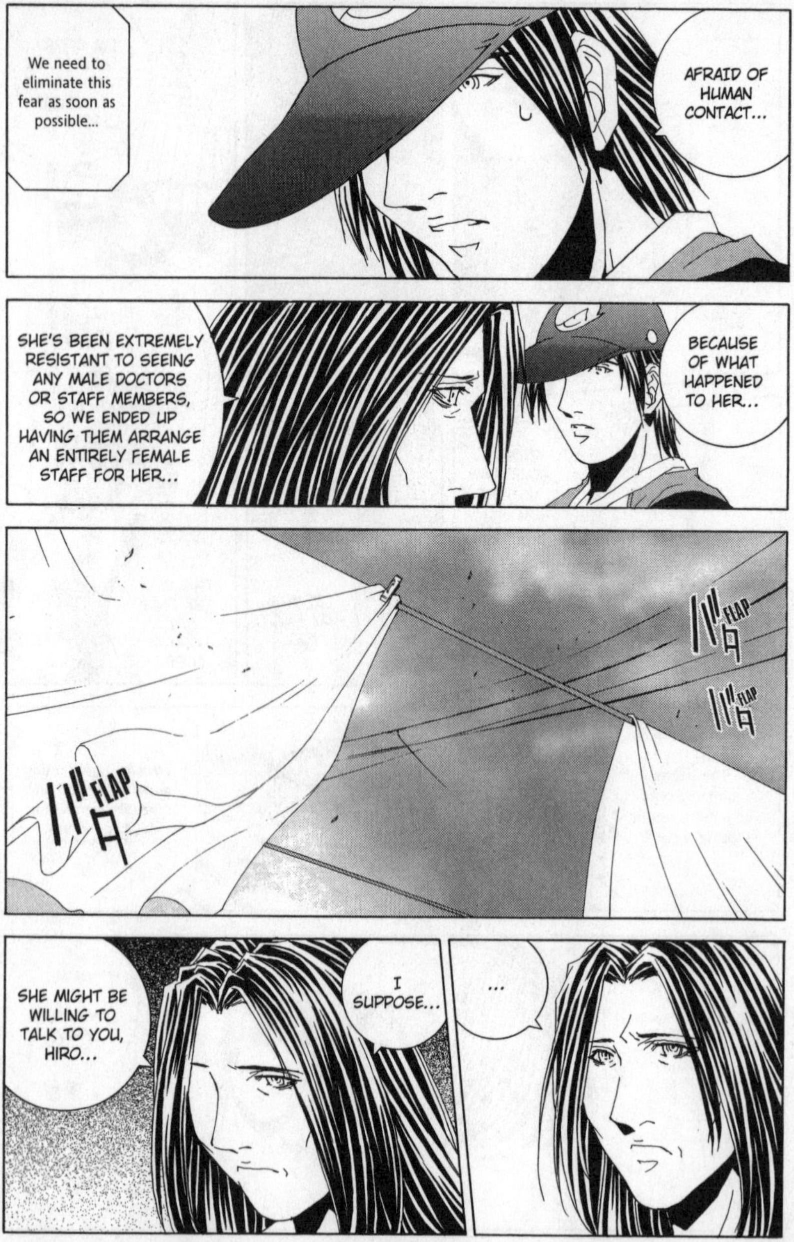
AFRAID OF HUMAN CONTACT...
We need to eliminate this fear as soon as possible...
BECAUSE OF WHAT HAPPENED TO HER...
SHE'S BEEN EXTREMELY RESISTANT TO SEEING ANY MALE DOCTORS OR STAFF MEMBERS, SO WE ENDED UP HAVING THEM ARRANGE AN ENTIRELY FEMALE STAFF FOR HER...
FLAP
FLAP
FLAP
...
I SUPPOSE...
SHE MIGHT BE WILLING TO TALK TO YOU, HIRO...

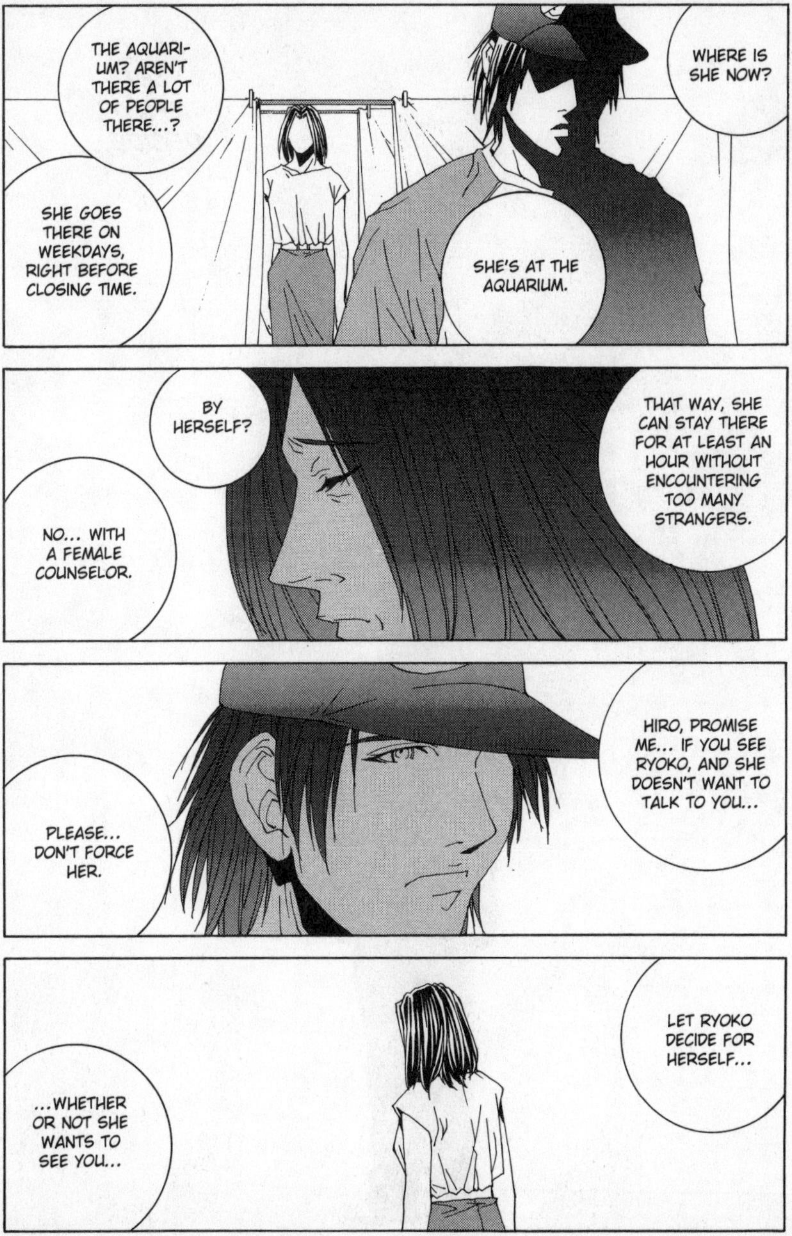
WHERE IS SHE NOW?
SHE'S AT THE AQUARIUM.
THE AQUARIUM? AREN'T THERE A LOT OF PEOPLE THERE...?
SHE GOES THERE ON WEEKDAYS, RIGHT BEFORE CLOSING TIME.
THAT WAY, SHE CAN STAY THERE FOR AT LEAST AN HOUR WITHOUT ENCOUNTERING TOO MANY STRANGERS.
BY HERSELF?
NO... WITH A FEMALE COUNSELOR.
HIRO, PROMISE ME... IF YOU SEE RYOKO, AND SHE DOESN'T WANT TO TALK TO YOU...
PLEASE... DON'T FORCE HER.
LET RYOKO DECIDE FOR HERSELF...
...WHETHER OR NOT SHE WANTS TO SEE YOU...

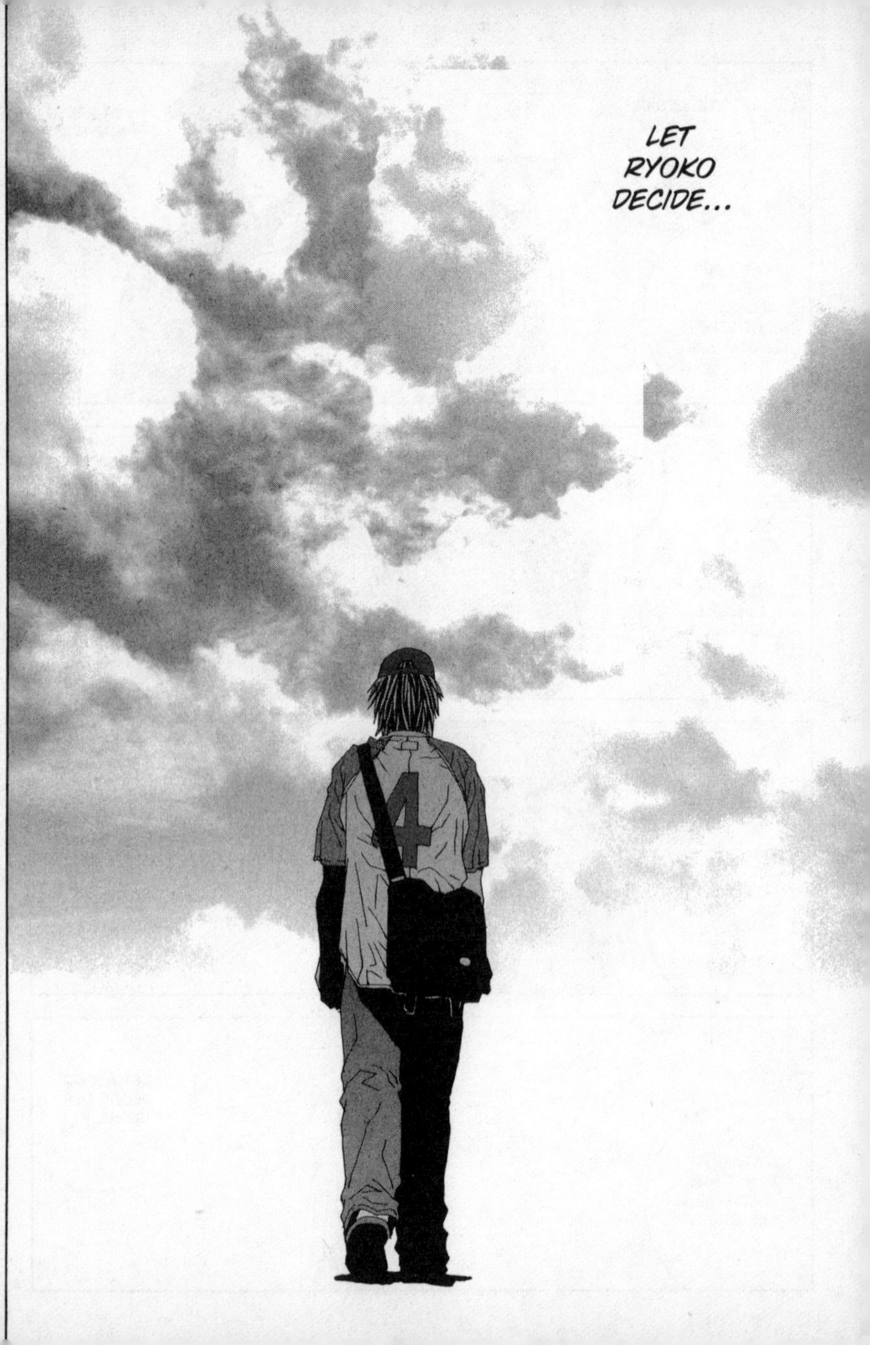
LET RYOKO DECIDE...

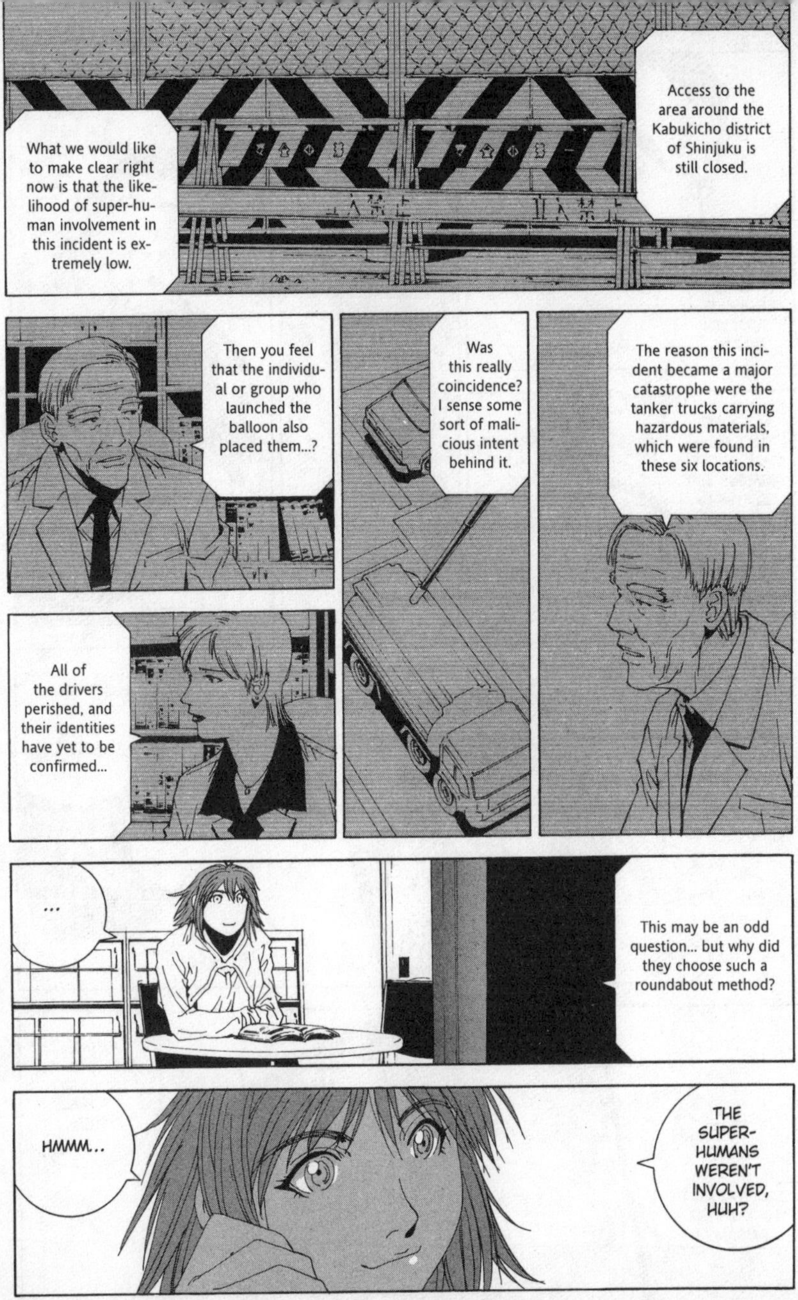
Access to the area around the Kabukicho district of Shinjuku is still closed.
What we would like to make clear right now is that the likelihood of super-human involvement in this incident is extremely low.
The reason this incident became a major catastrophe were the tanker trucks carrying hazardous materials, which were found in these six locations.
Was this really coincidence? I sense some sort of malicious intent behind it.
Then you feel that the individual or group who launched the balloon also placed them...?
All of the drivers perished, and their identities have yet to be confirmed...
This may be an odd question... but why did they choose such a roundabout method?
...
THE SUPER-HUMANS WEREN'T INVOLVED, HUH?
HMMM...

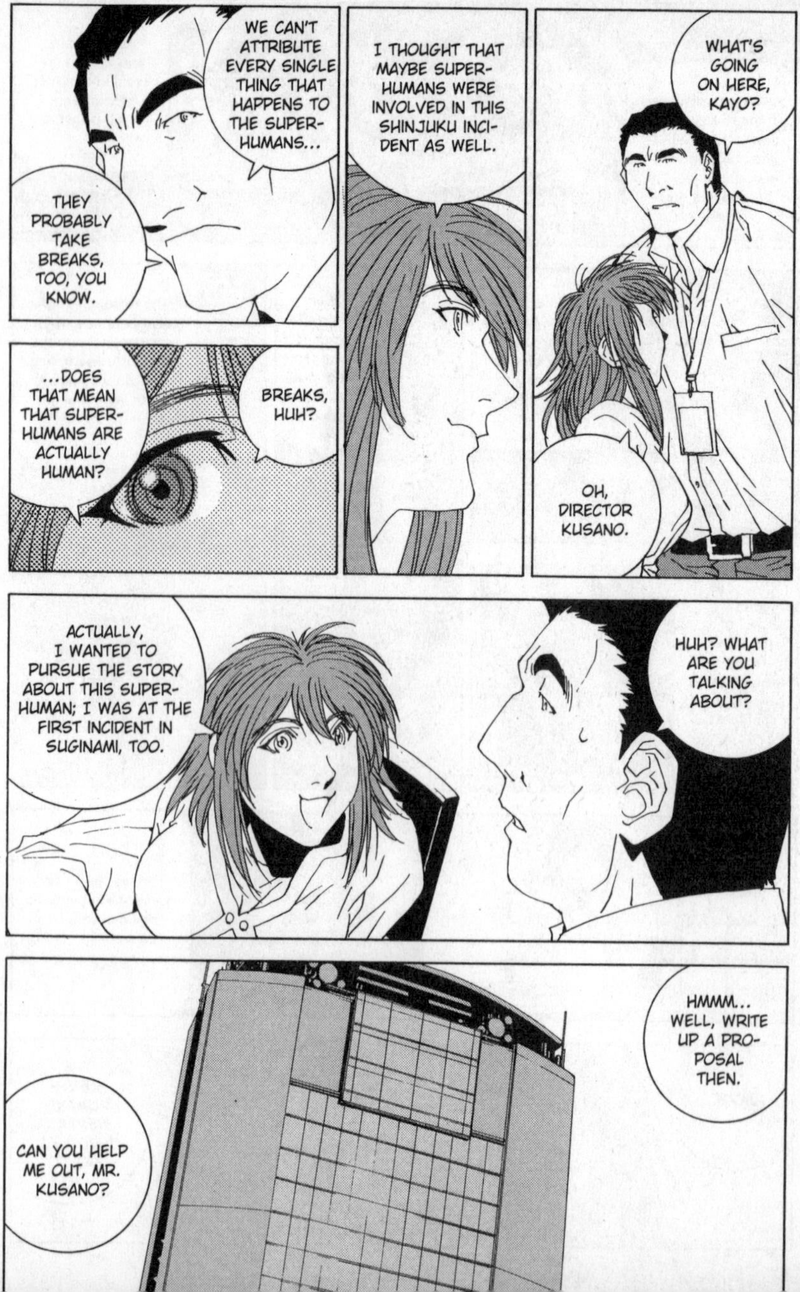
WE CAN'T ATTRIBUTE EVERY SINGLE THING THAT HAPPENS TO THE SUPER-HUMANS...
THEY PROBABLY TAKE BREAKS, TOO, YOU KNOW.
BREAKS, HUH?
...DOES THAT MEAN THAT SUPER-HUMANS ARE ACTUALLY HUMAN?
I THOUGHT THAT MAYBE SUPER-HUMANS WERE INVOLVED IN THIS SHINJUKU INCI-DENT AS WELL.
WHAT'S GOING ON HERE, KAYO?
OH, DIRECTOR KUSANO.
ACTUALLY, I WANTED TO PURSUE THE STORY ABOUT THIS SUPER-HUMAN; I WAS AT THE FIRST INCIDENT IN SUGINAMI, TOO.
HUH? WHAT ARE YOU TALKING ABOUT?
CAN YOU HELP ME OUT, MR. KUSANO?
HMMM... WELL, WRITE UP A PRO-POSAL THEN.

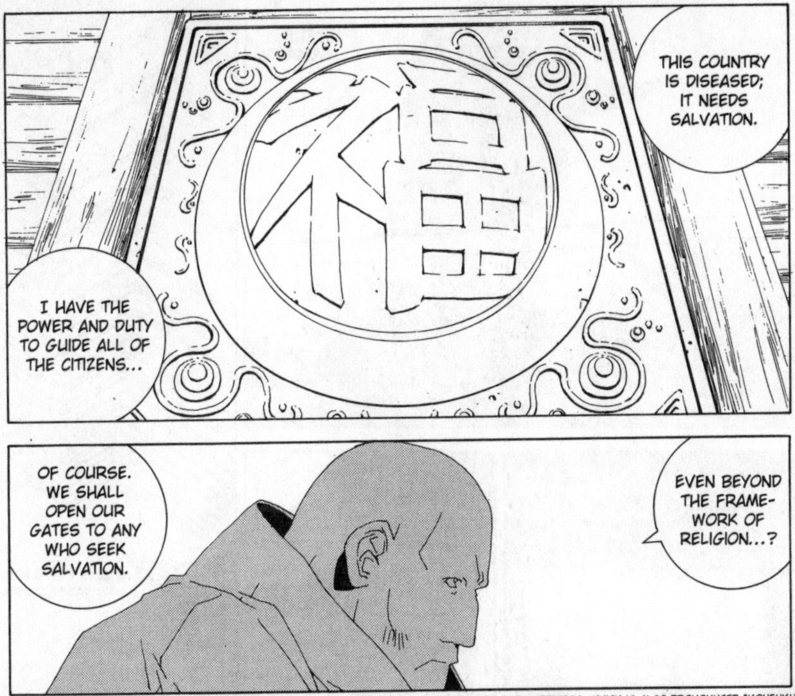
THIS COUNTRY IS DISEASED; IT NEEDS SALVATION.
I HAVE THE POWER AND DUTY TO GUIDE ALL OF THE CITIZENS...
EVEN BEYOND THE FRAME-WORK OF RELIGION...?
OF COURSE. WE SHALL OPEN OUR GATES TO ANY WHO SEEK SALVATION.

*LITERALLY SPELLED "RED FORTUNE" IN JAPANESE, THIS IS ALSO A PLAY ON THE JAPANESE WORD FOR HAPPINESS, WHICH IS ALSO PRONOUNCED "KOUFUKU."

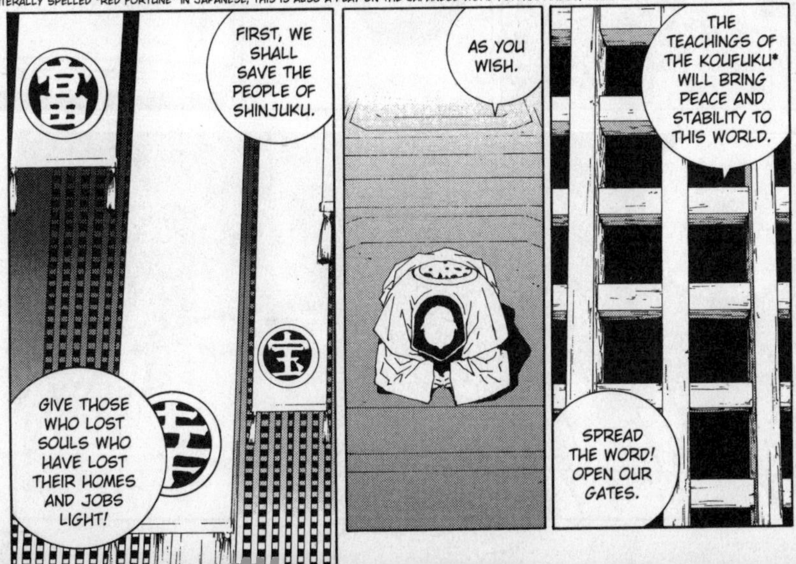
THE TEACHINGS OF THE KOUFUKU* WILL BRING PEACE AND STABILITY TO THIS WORLD.
SPREAD THE WORD! OPEN OUR GATES.
AS YOU WISH.
FIRST, WE SHALL SAVE THE PEOPLE OF SHINJUKU.
GIVE THOSE WHO LOST SOULS WHO HAVE LOST THEIR HOMES AND JOBS LIGHT!

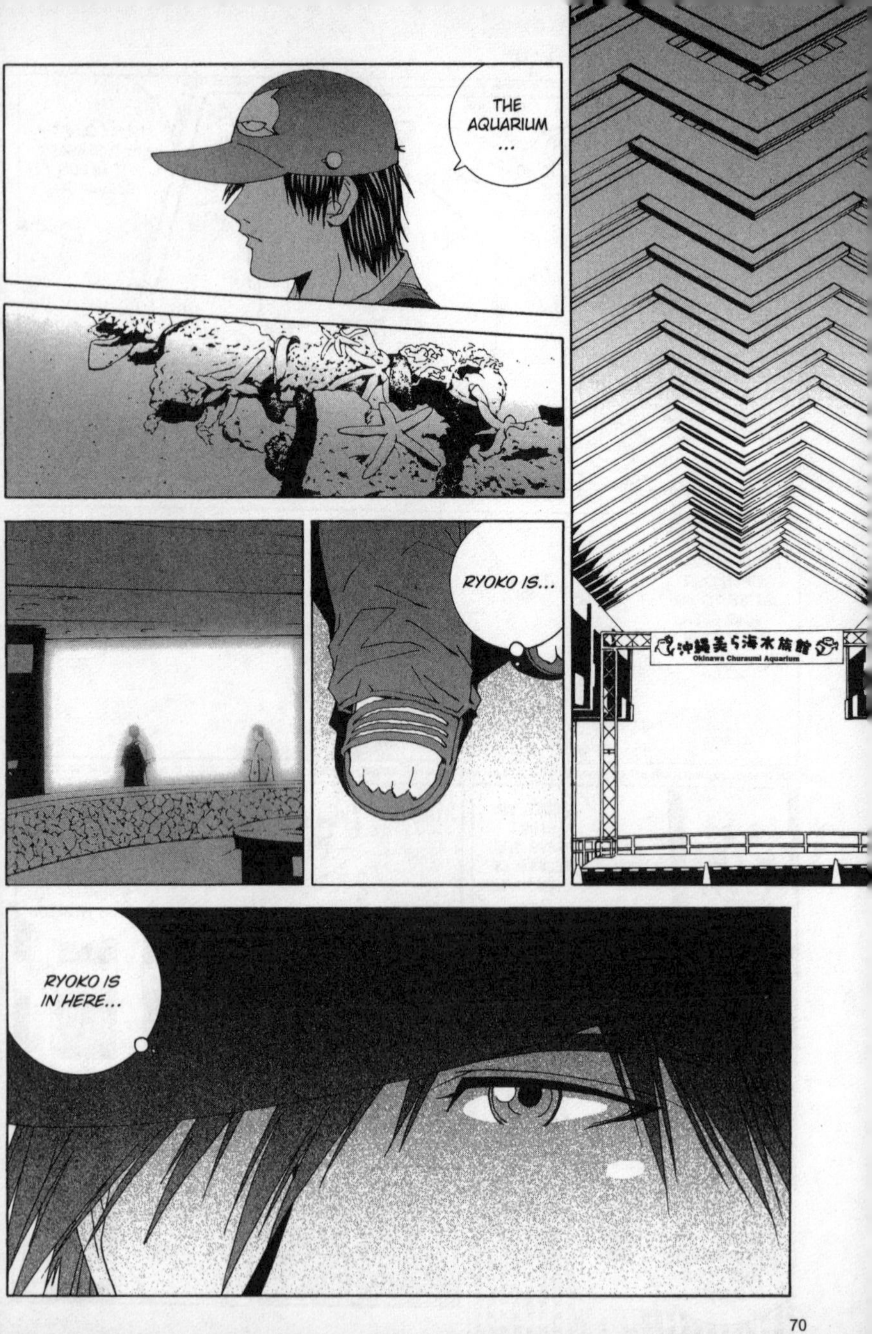
沖縄美ら海水族館
Okinawa Churaumi Aquarium
THE AQUARIUM ...
RYOKO IS...
RYOKO IS IN HERE...

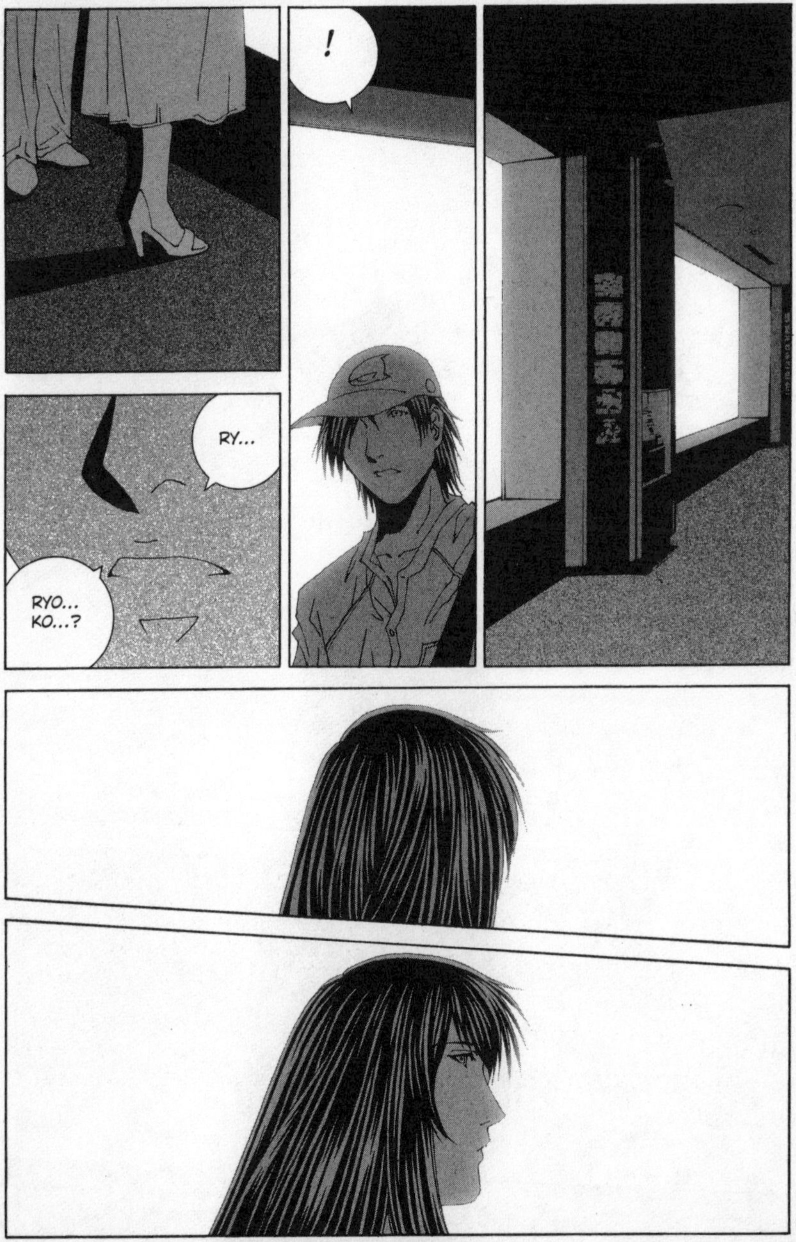
!
RY...
RYO... KO...?

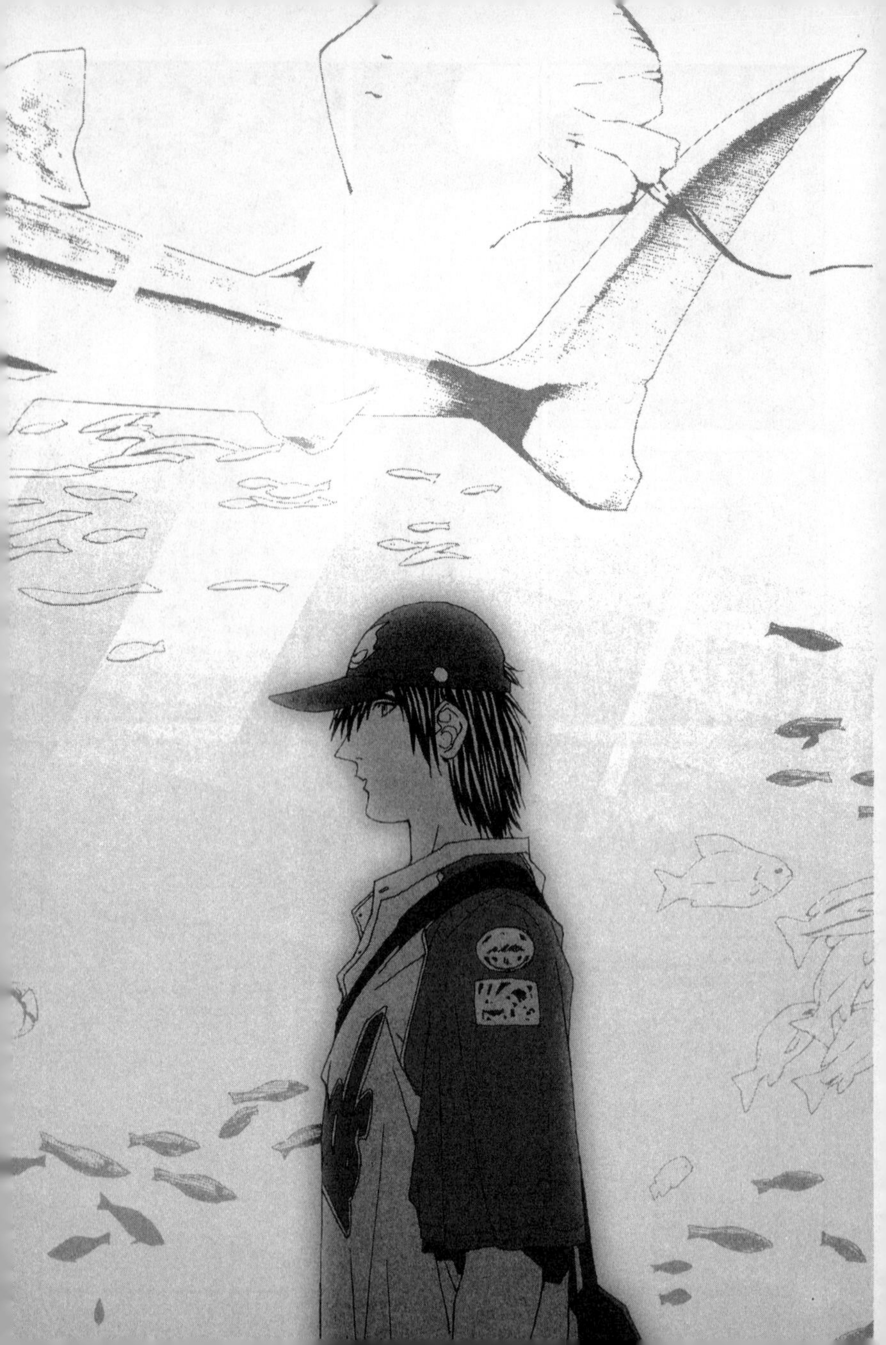

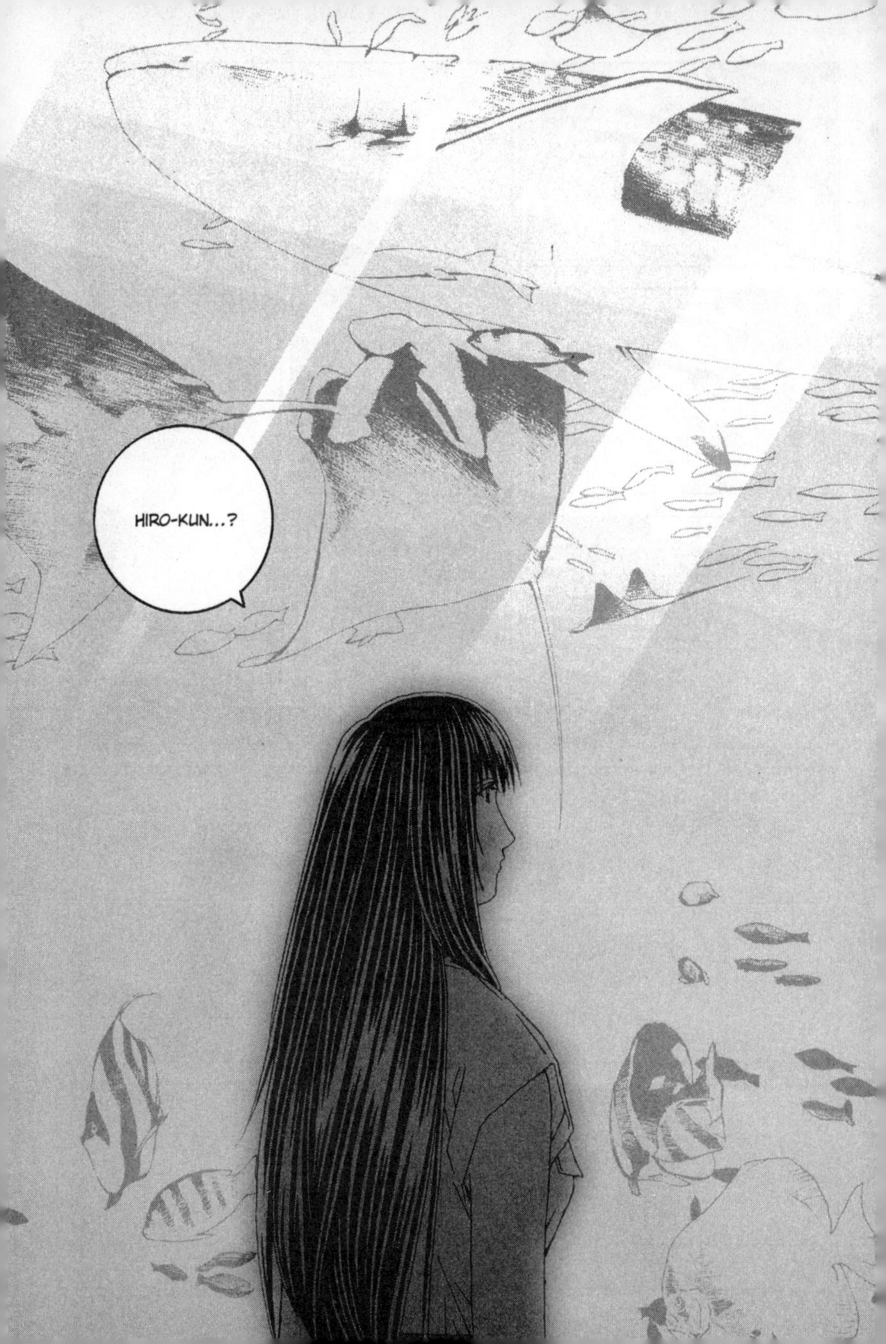
HIRO-KUN...?

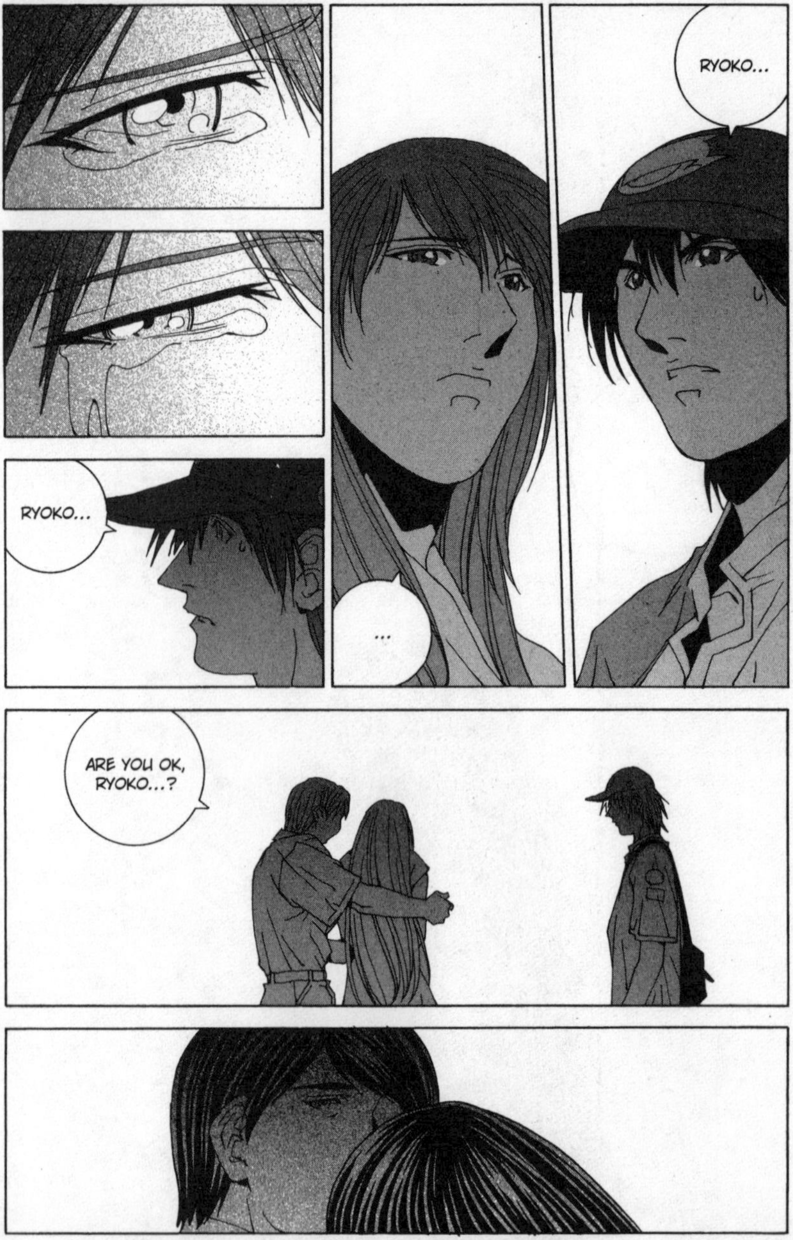
RYOKO...
...
RYOKO...
ARE YOU OK, RYOKO...?

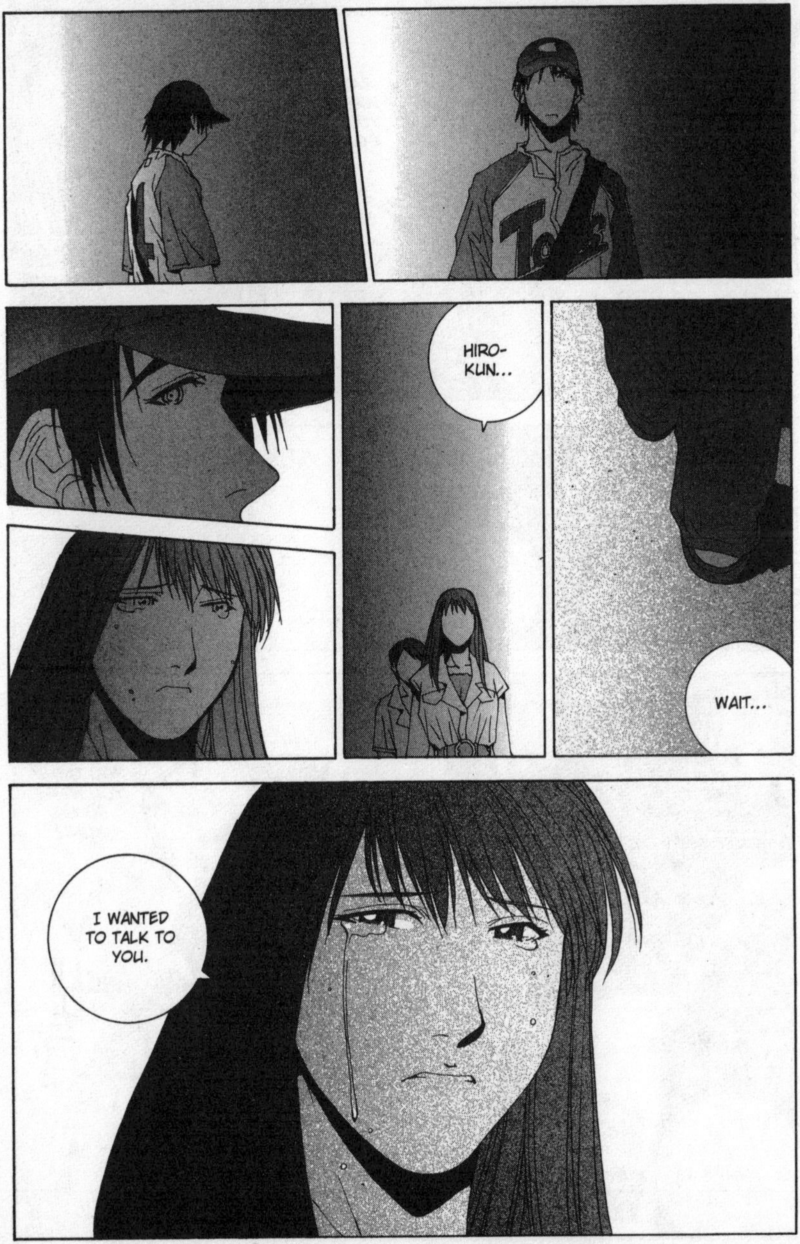
WAIT...
HIRO-KUN...
I WANTED TO TALK TO YOU.

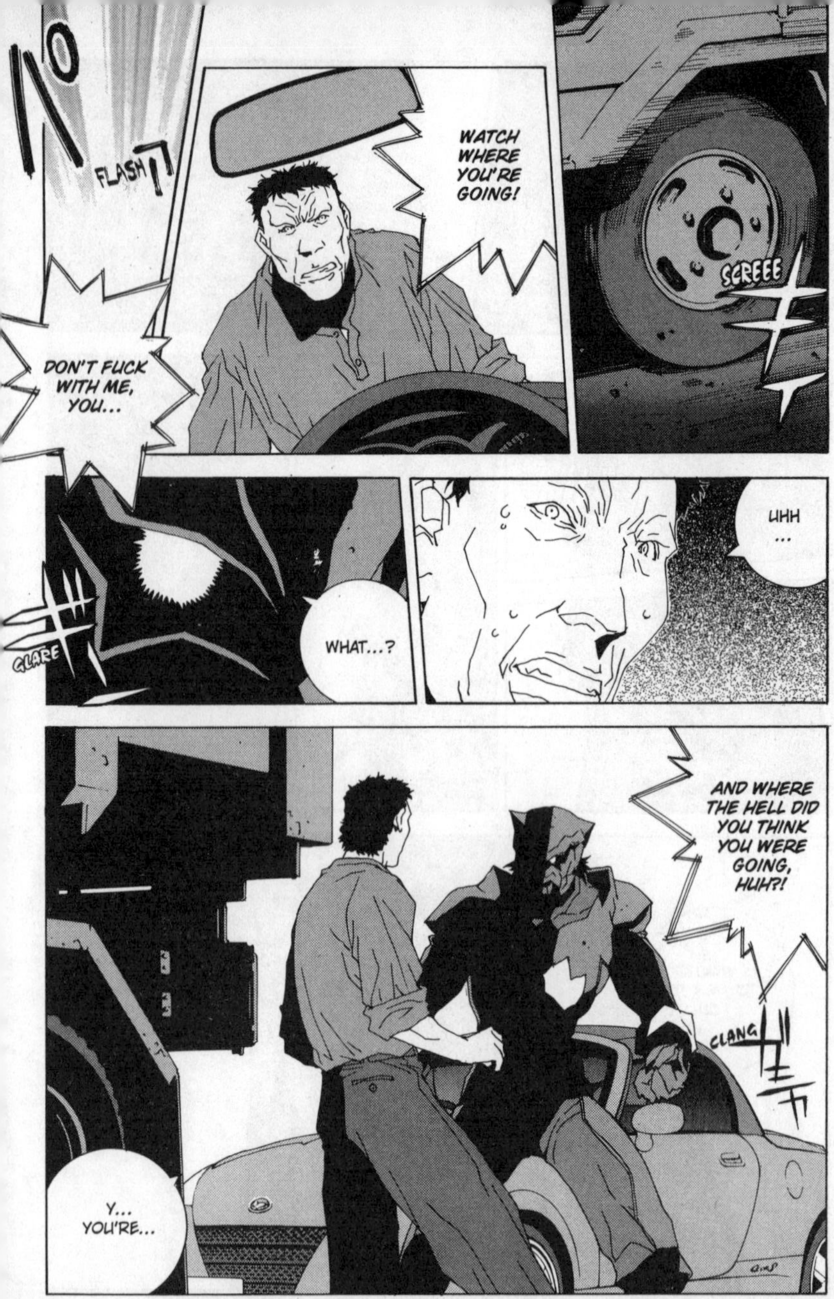
SCREEE
WATCH WHERE YOU'RE GOING!
FLASH
DON'T FUCK WITH ME, YOU...
UHH...
WHAT...?
GLARE
AND WHERE THE HELL DID YOU THINK YOU WERE GOING, HUH?!
CLANG
Y... YOU'RE...

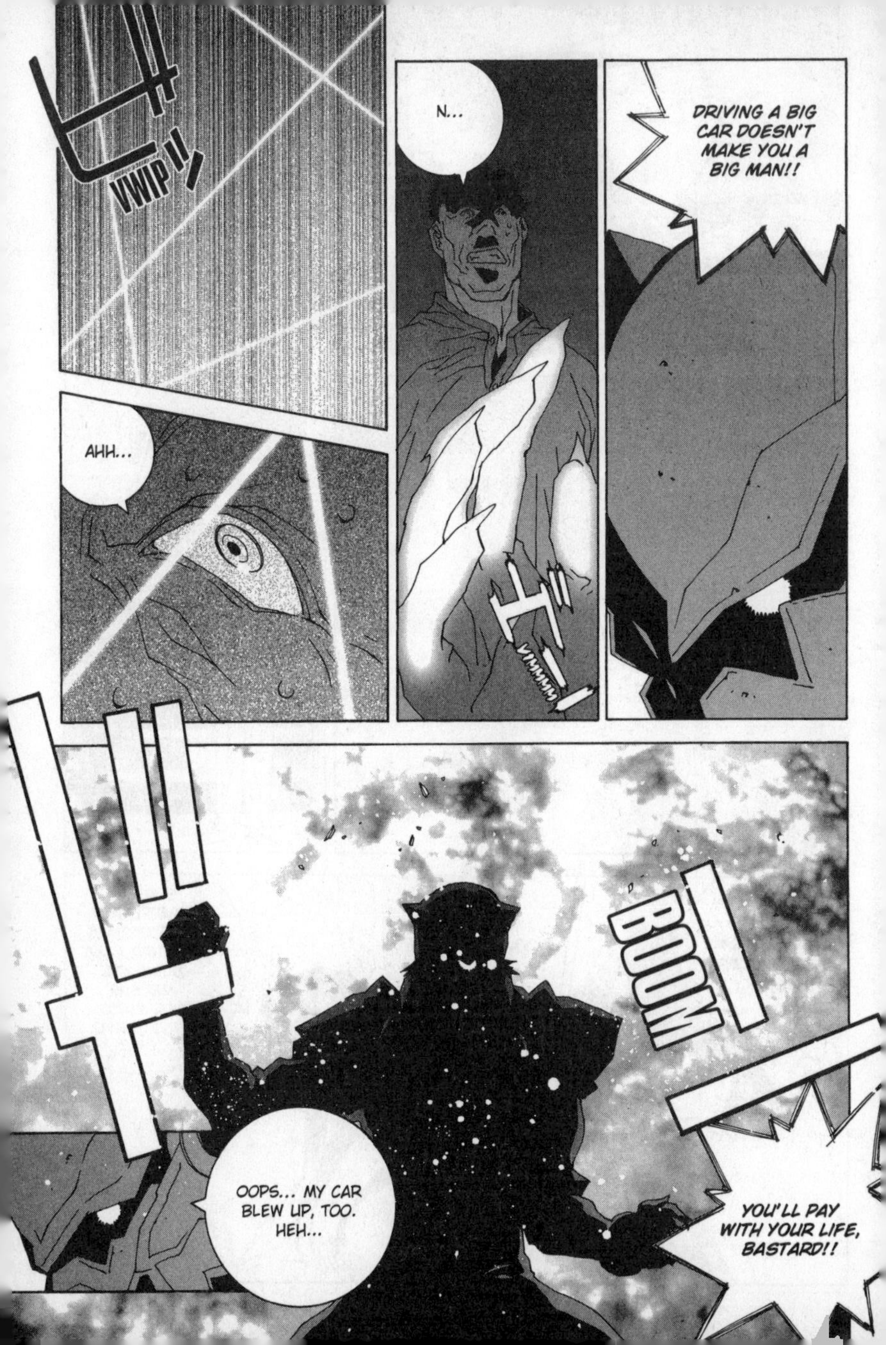
DRIVING A BIG CAR DOESN'T MAKE YOU A BIG MAN!!
N...
VIMMMM
VWIP!!
AHH...
BOOM
YOU'LL PAY WITH YOUR LIFE, BASTARD!!
OOPS... MY CAR BLEW UP, TOO. HEH...

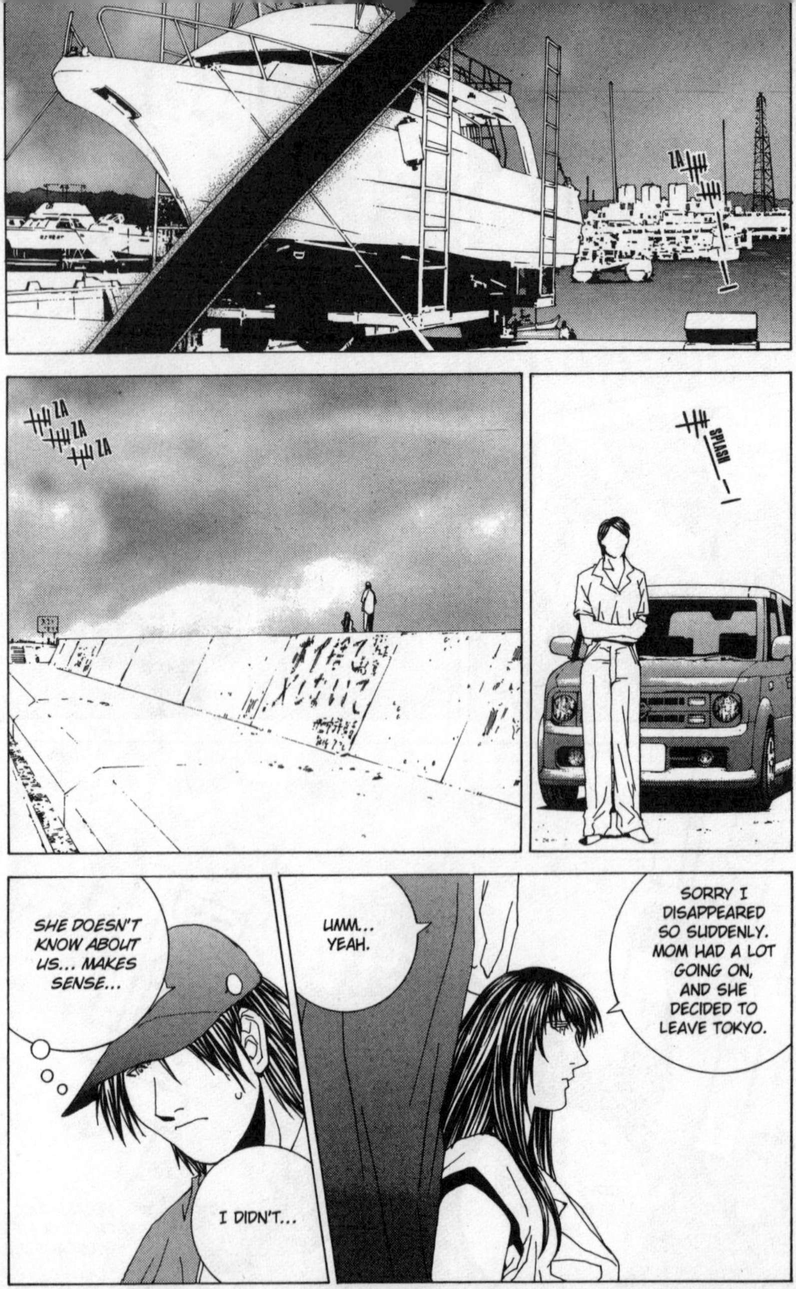
ZA
SPLASH
ZA ZA ZA
SORRY I DISAPPEARED SO SUDDENLY. MOM HAD A LOT GOING ON, AND SHE DECIDED TO LEAVE TOKYO.
UMM... YEAH.
SHE DOESN'T KNOW ABOUT US... MAKES SENSE...
I DIDN'T...

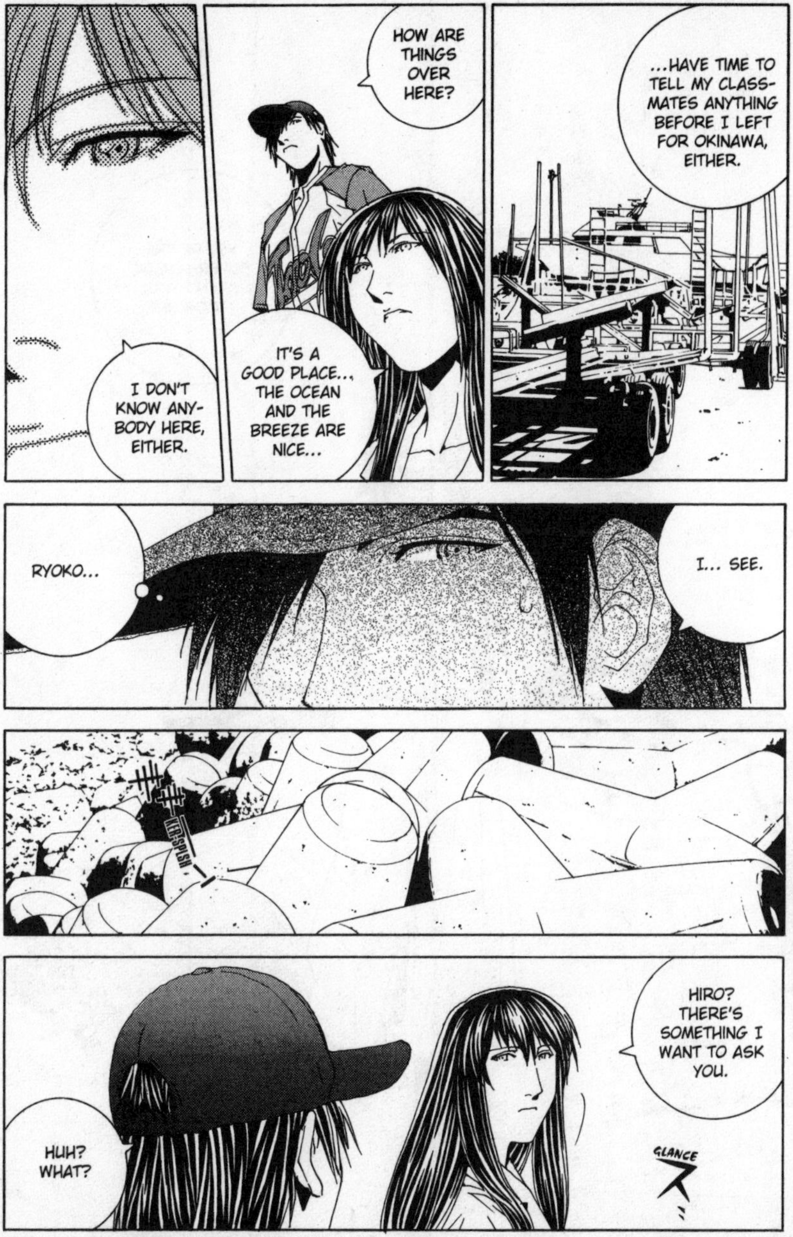
...HAVE TIME TO TELL MY CLASS-MATES ANYTHING BEFORE I LEFT FOR OKINAWA, EITHER.
HOW ARE THINGS OVER HERE?
IT'S A GOOD PLACE... THE OCEAN AND THE BREEZE ARE NICE...
I DON'T KNOW ANY-BODY HERE, EITHER.
I... SEE.
RYOKO...
KER-SPLSH
HIRO? THERE'S SOMETHING I WANT TO ASK YOU.
GLANCE
HUH? WHAT?

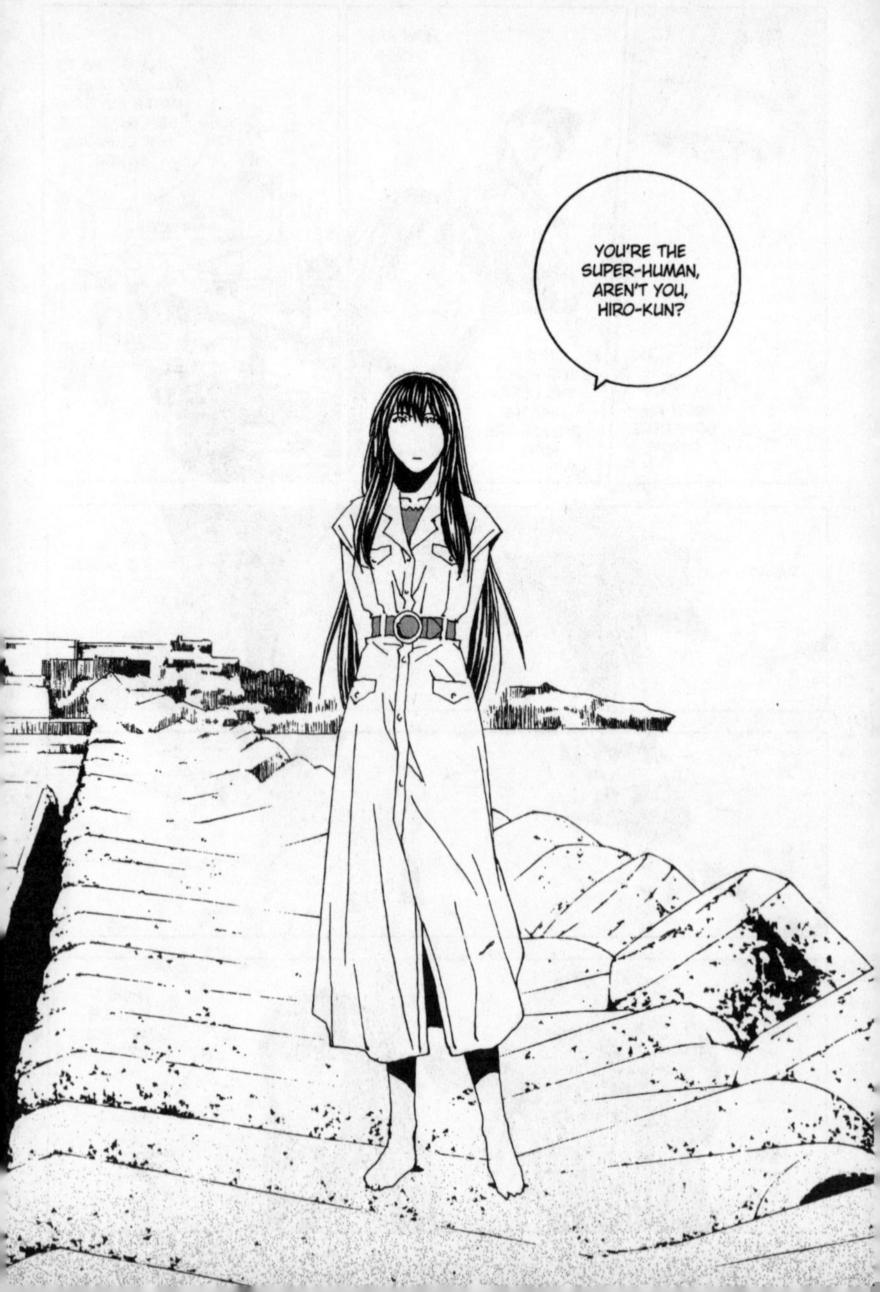
YOU'RE THE SUPER-HUMAN, AREN'T YOU, HIRO-KUN?

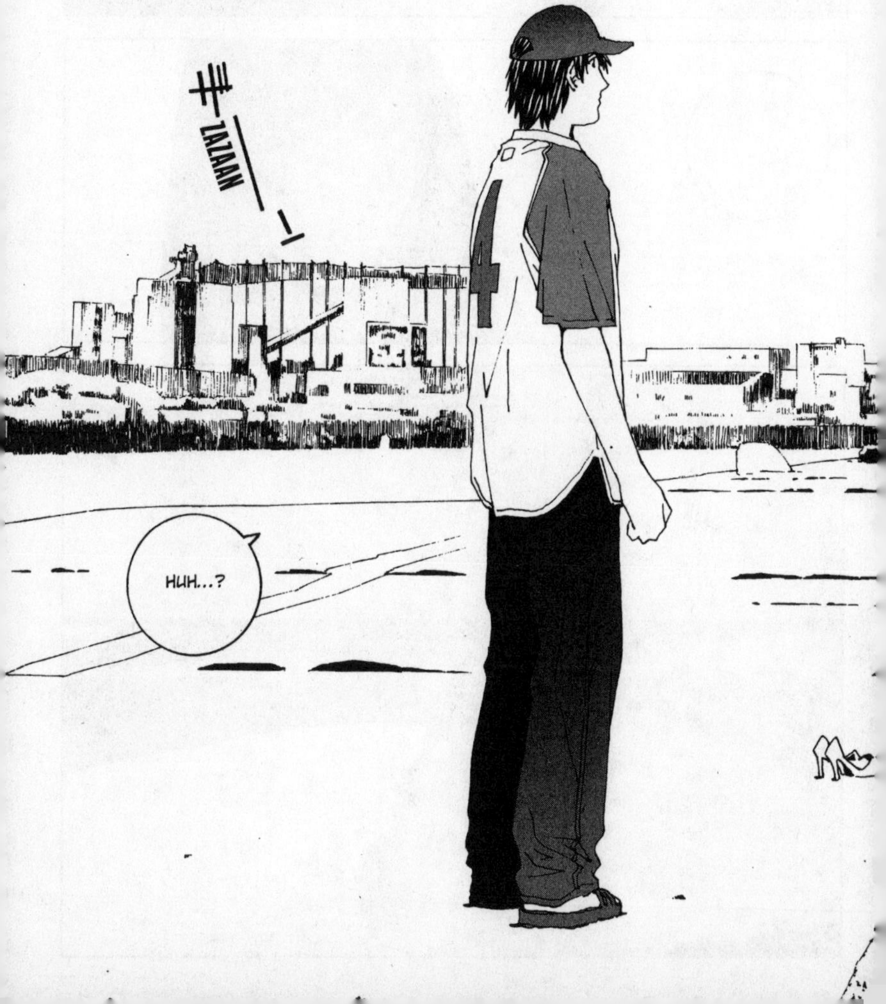
ZAZAAN
HUH...?

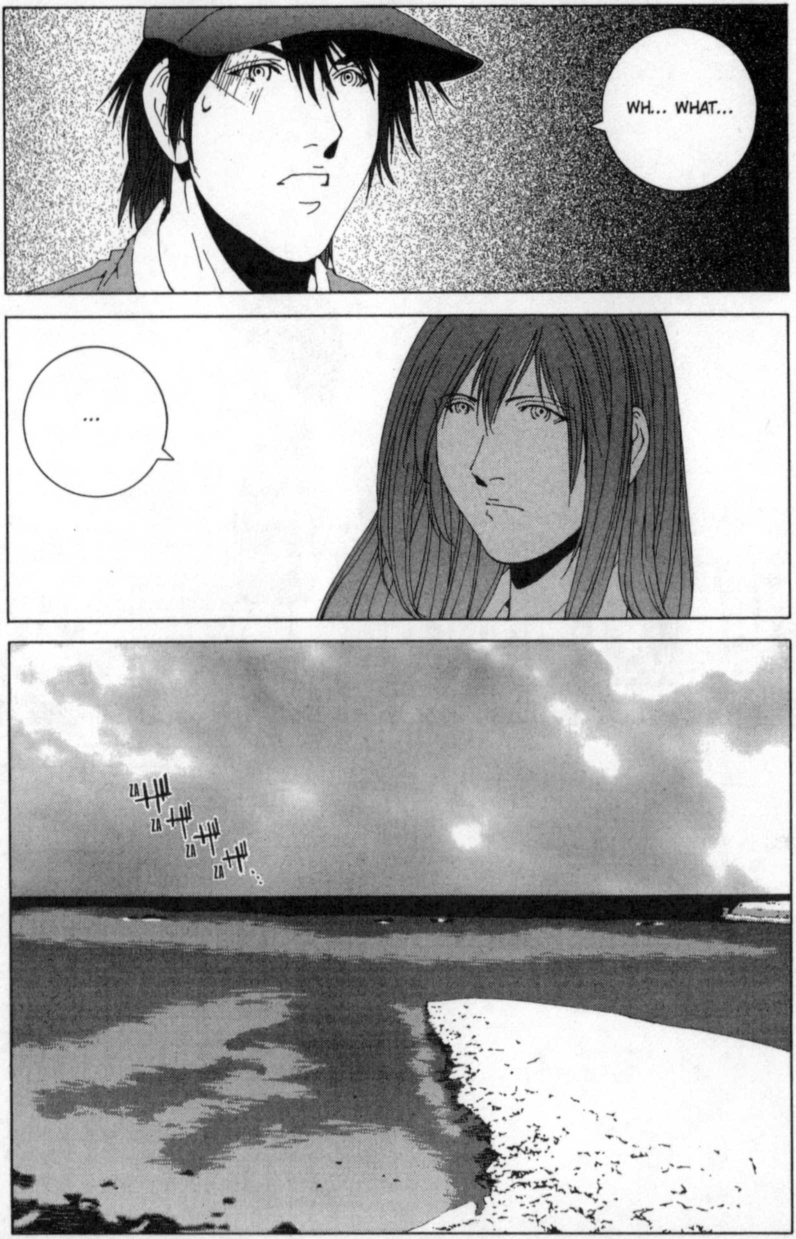

WH... WHAT...
...
ZA ZA ZA ZA...

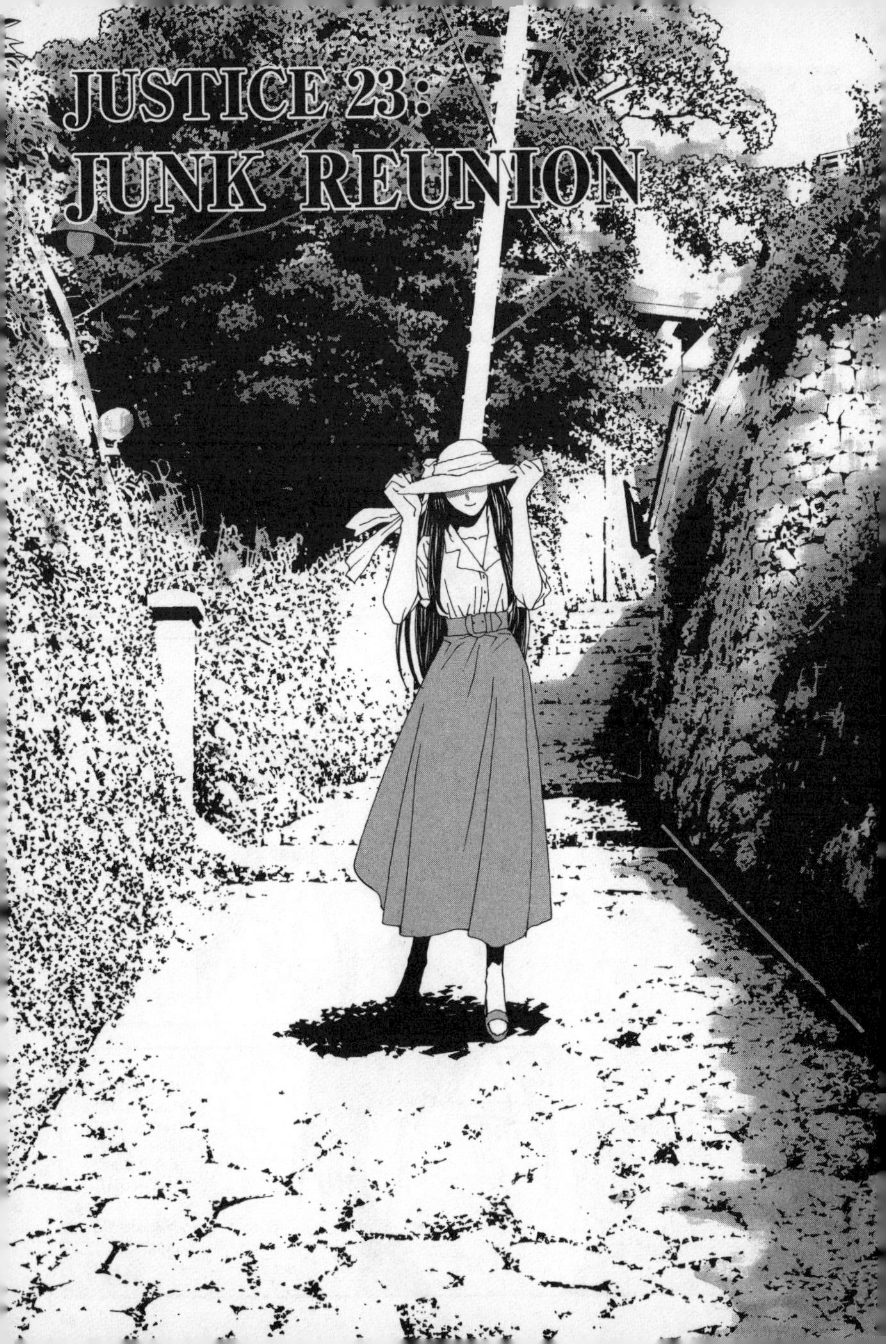
JUSTICE 23:
JUNK REUNION

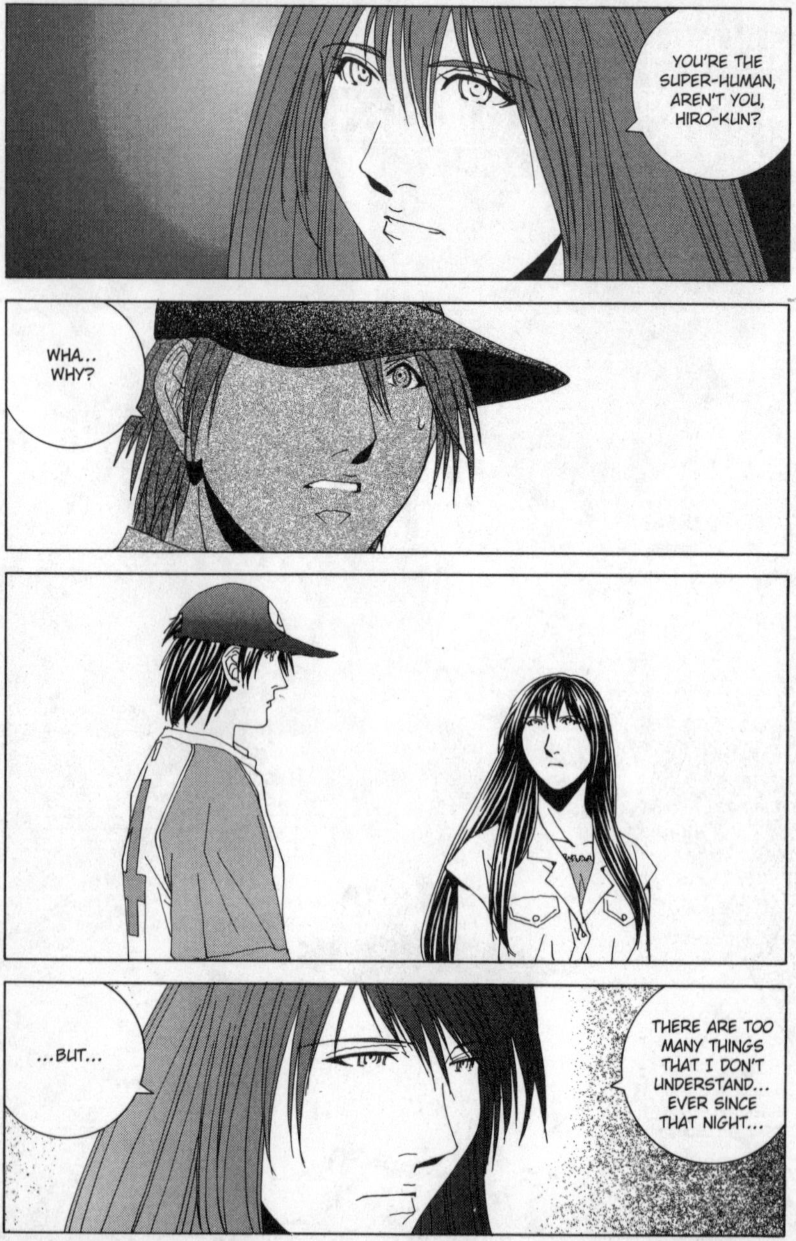
YOU'RE THE SUPER-HUMAN, AREN'T YOU, HIRO-KUN?
WHA.. WHY?
THERE ARE TOO MANY THINGS THAT I DON'T UNDERSTAND... EVER SINCE THAT NIGHT...
...BUT...

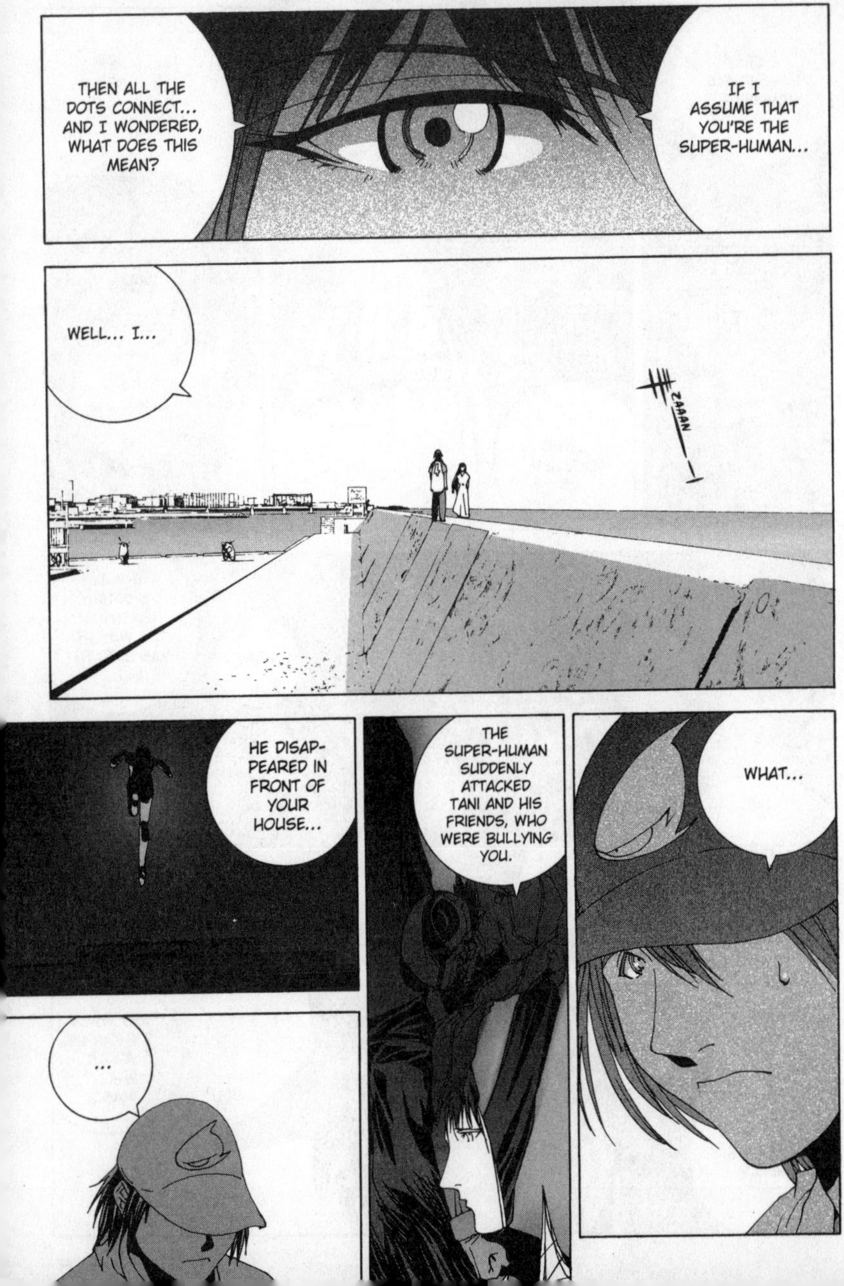
IF I ASSUME THAT YOU'RE THE SUPER-HUMAN...
THEN ALL THE DOTS CONNECT... AND I WONDERED, WHAT DOES THIS MEAN?
ZAAAN
WELL... I...
WHAT...
THE SUPER-HUMAN SUDDENLY ATTACKED TANI AND HIS FRIENDS, WHO WERE BULLYING YOU.
HE DISAPPEARED IN FRONT OF YOUR HOUSE...
...

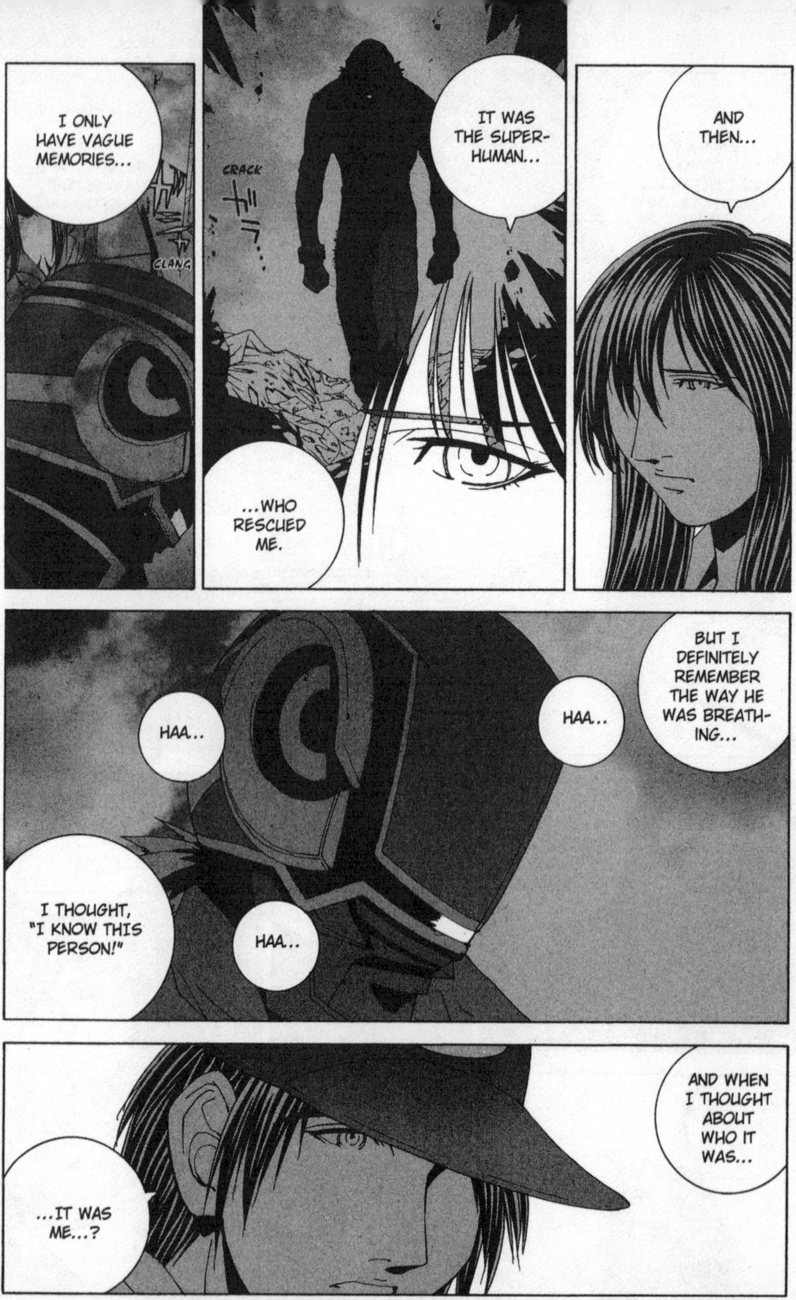
AND THEN...
IT WAS THE SUPER-HUMAN...
CRACK
...WHO RESCUED ME.
I ONLY HAVE VAGUE MEMORIES...
CLANG
BUT I DEFINITELY REMEMBER THE WAY HE WAS BREATH-ING...
HAA...
HAA...
HAA...
I THOUGHT, "I KNOW THIS PERSON!"
AND WHEN I THOUGHT ABOUT WHO IT WAS...
...IT WAS ME...?

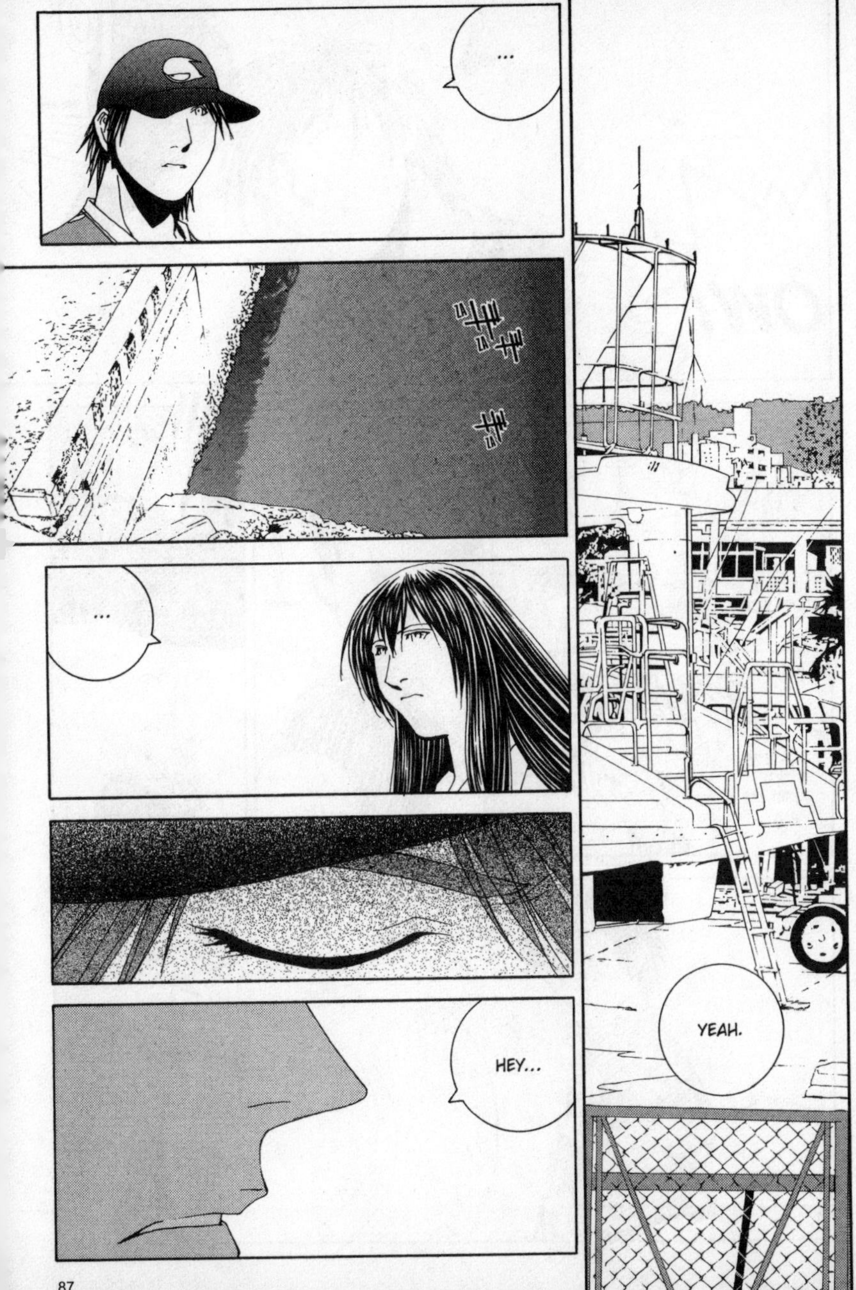
YEAH.
...
ZA
ZA
ZA
...
HEY...

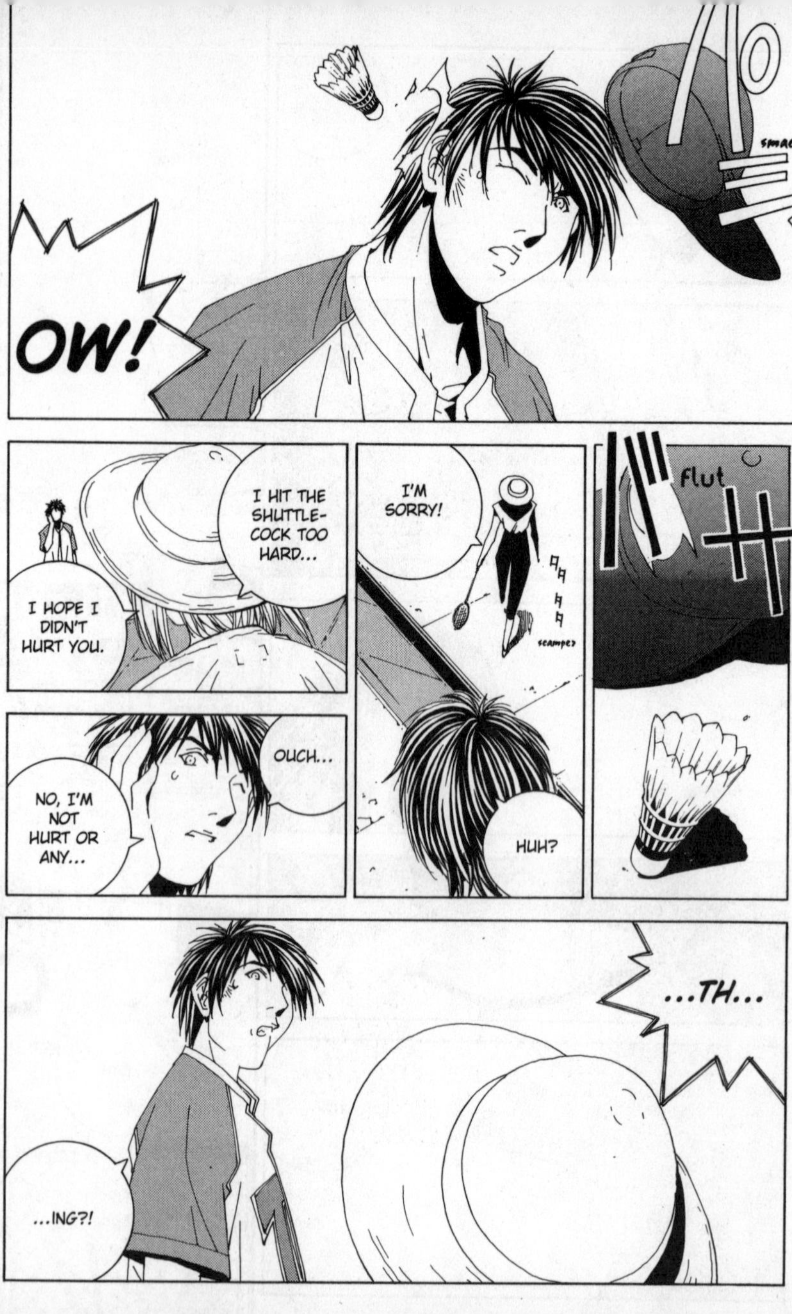

smack
OW!
flut
I'M SORRY!
scamper
HUH?
I HIT THE SHUTTLE-COCK TOO HARD...
I HOPE I DIDN'T HURT YOU.
OUCH...
NO, I'M NOT HURT OR ANY...
...TH...
...ING?!

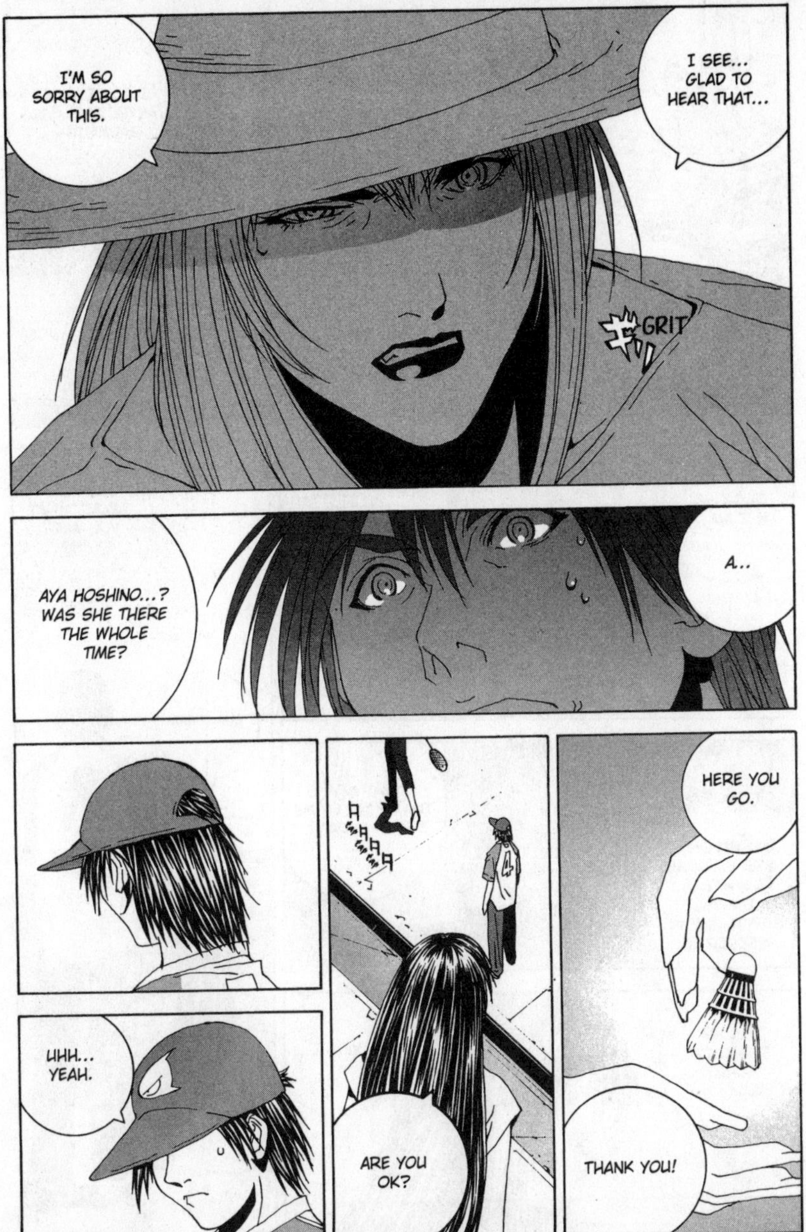
I SEE... GLAD TO HEAR THAT...
I'M SO SORRY ABOUT THIS.
GRIT
A...
AYA HOSHINO...? WAS SHE THERE THE WHOLE TIME?
HERE YOU GO.
THANK YOU!
ARE YOU OK?
UHH... YEAH.

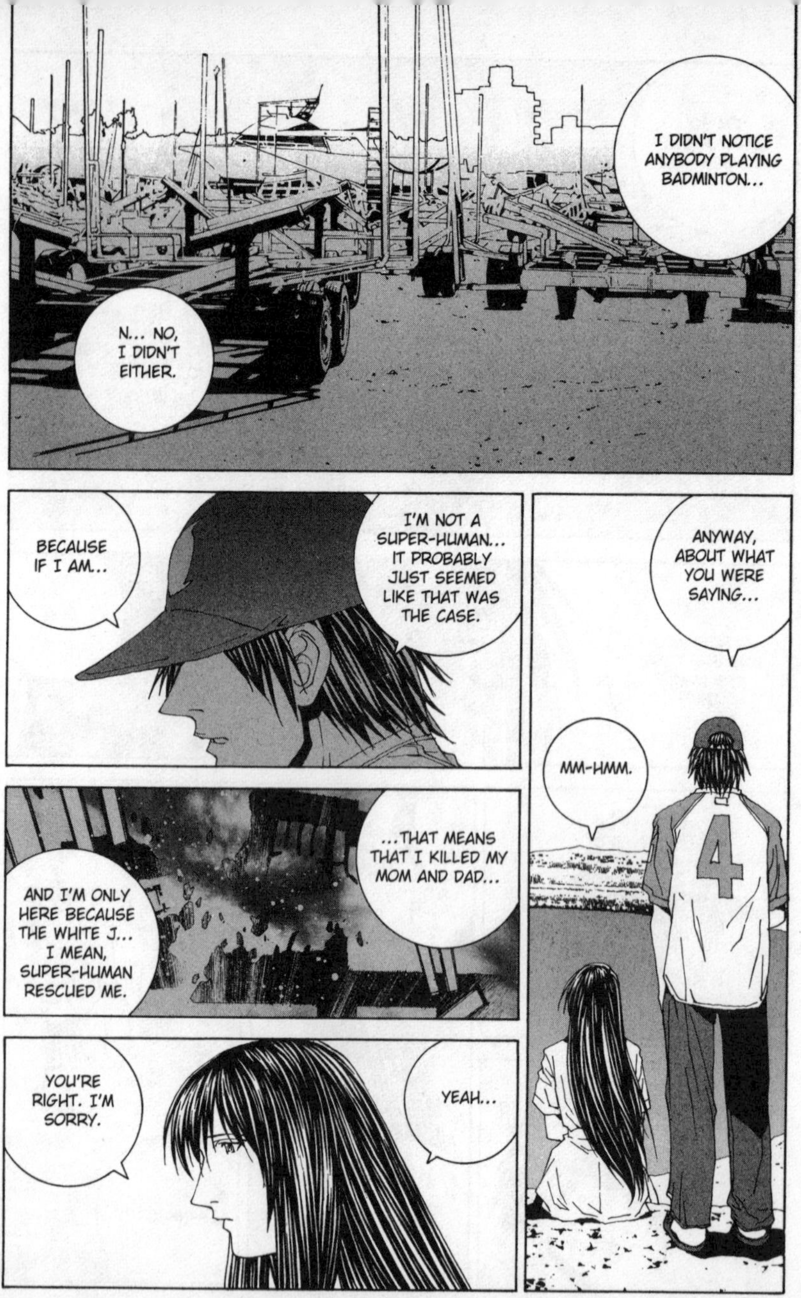
I DIDN'T NOTICE ANYBODY PLAYING BADMINTON...
N... NO, I DIDN'T EITHER.
ANYWAY, ABOUT WHAT YOU WERE SAYING...
MM-HMM.
I'M NOT A SUPER-HUMAN... IT PROBABLY JUST SEEMED LIKE THAT WAS THE CASE.
BECAUSE IF I AM...
...THAT MEANS THAT I KILLED MY MOM AND DAD...
AND I'M ONLY HERE BECAUSE THE WHITE J... I MEAN, SUPER-HUMAN RESCUED ME.
YEAH...
YOU'RE RIGHT. I'M SORRY.

YOU LOST YOUR PARENTS, DIDN'T YOU...?

YEAH...

I DID...

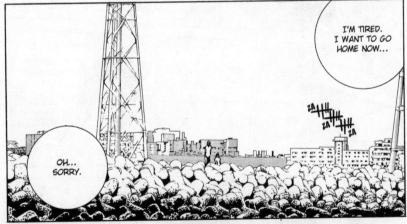

I'M TIRED. I WANT TO GO HOME NOW...

OH... SORRY.

HOW LONG ARE YOU STAYING IN OKINAWA?

I HAVEN'T REALLY THOUGHT ABOUT IT.

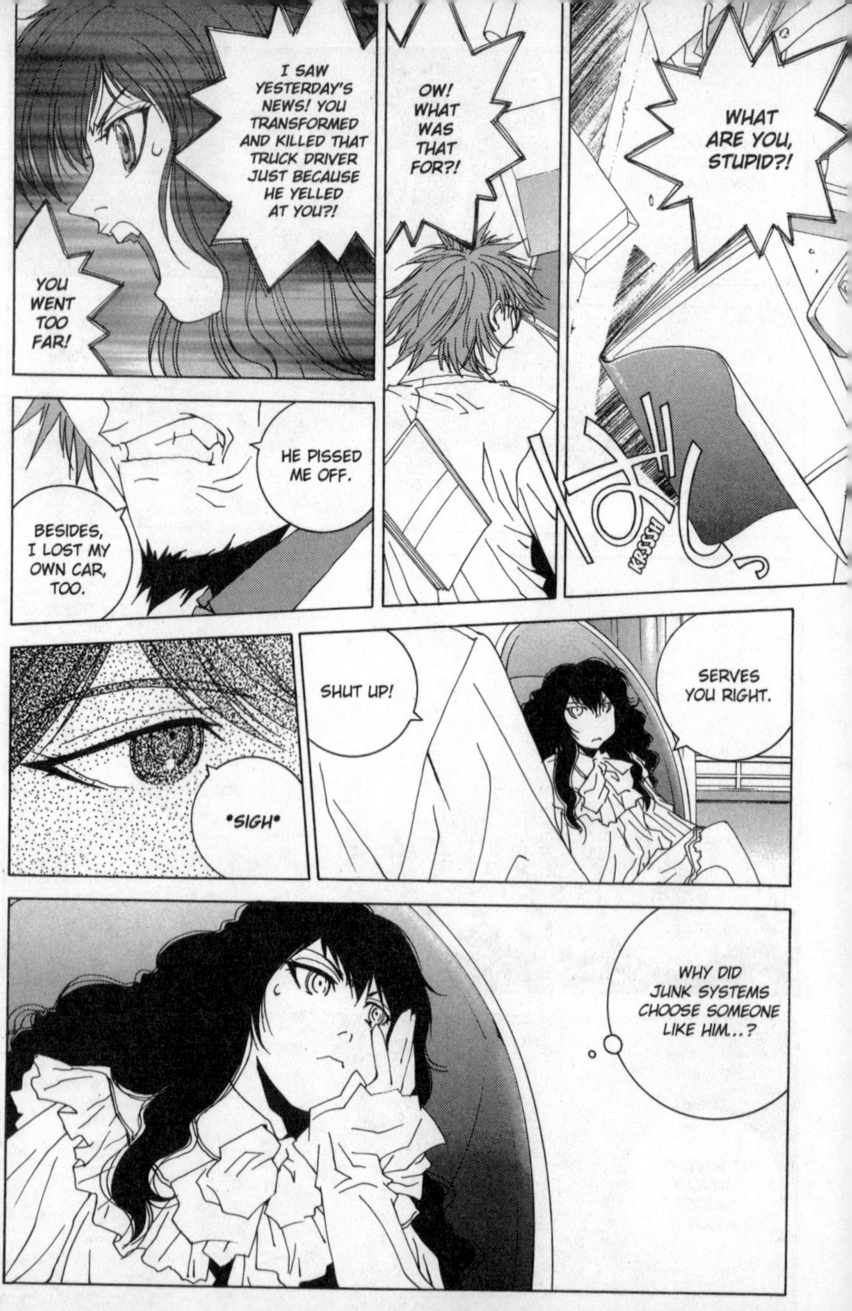
WHAT ARE YOU, STUPID?!
KRSSSH
OW! WHAT WAS THAT FOR?!
I SAW YESTERDAY'S NEWS! YOU TRANSFORMED AND KILLED THAT TRUCK DRIVER JUST BECAUSE HE YELLED AT YOU?!
YOU WENT TOO FAR!
HE PISSED ME OFF.
BESIDES, I LOST MY OWN CAR, TOO.
SERVES YOU RIGHT.
SHUT UP!
SIGH
WHY DID JUNK SYSTEMS CHOOSE SOMEONE LIKE HIM...?

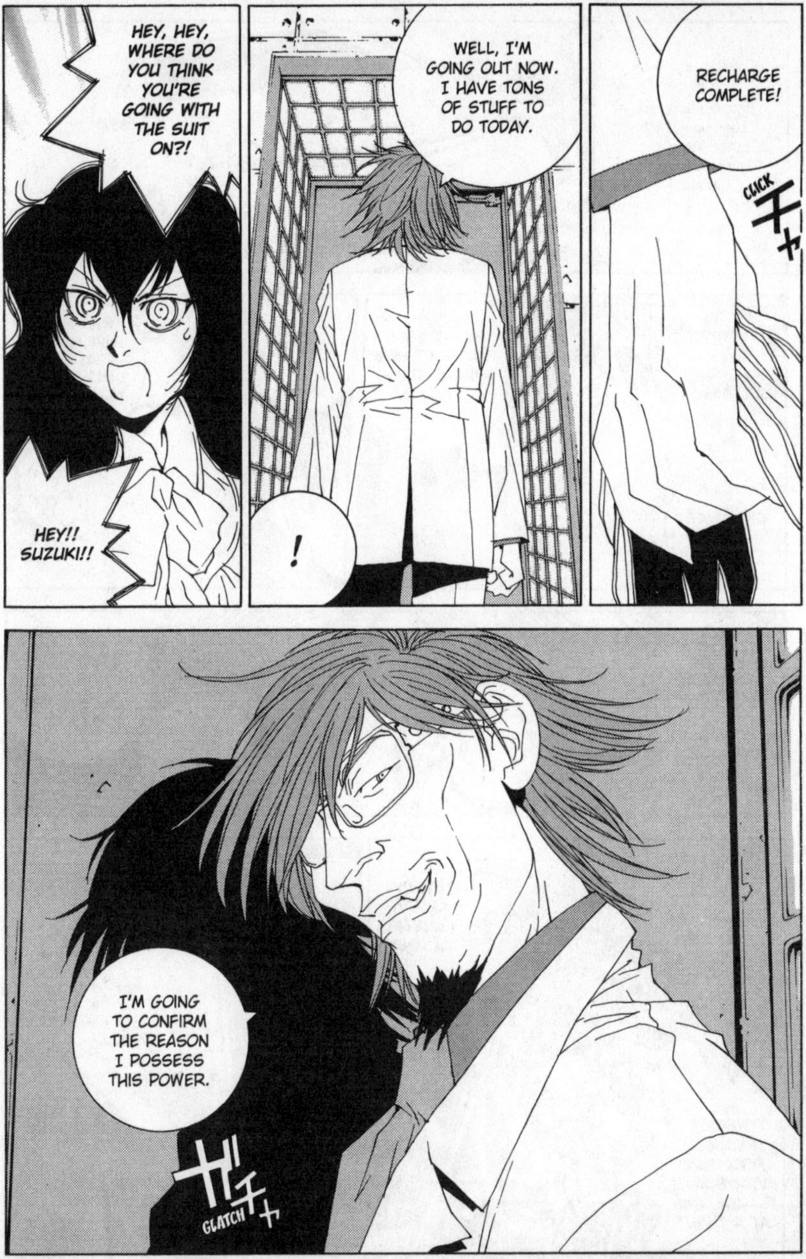

RECHARGE COMPLETE!
CLICK
WELL, I'M GOING OUT NOW. I HAVE TONS OF STUFF TO DO TODAY.
!
HEY, HEY, WHERE DO YOU THINK YOU'RE GOING WITH THE SUIT ON?!
HEY!! SUZUKI!!
I'M GOING TO CONFIRM THE REASON I POSSESS THIS POWER.
GLATCH

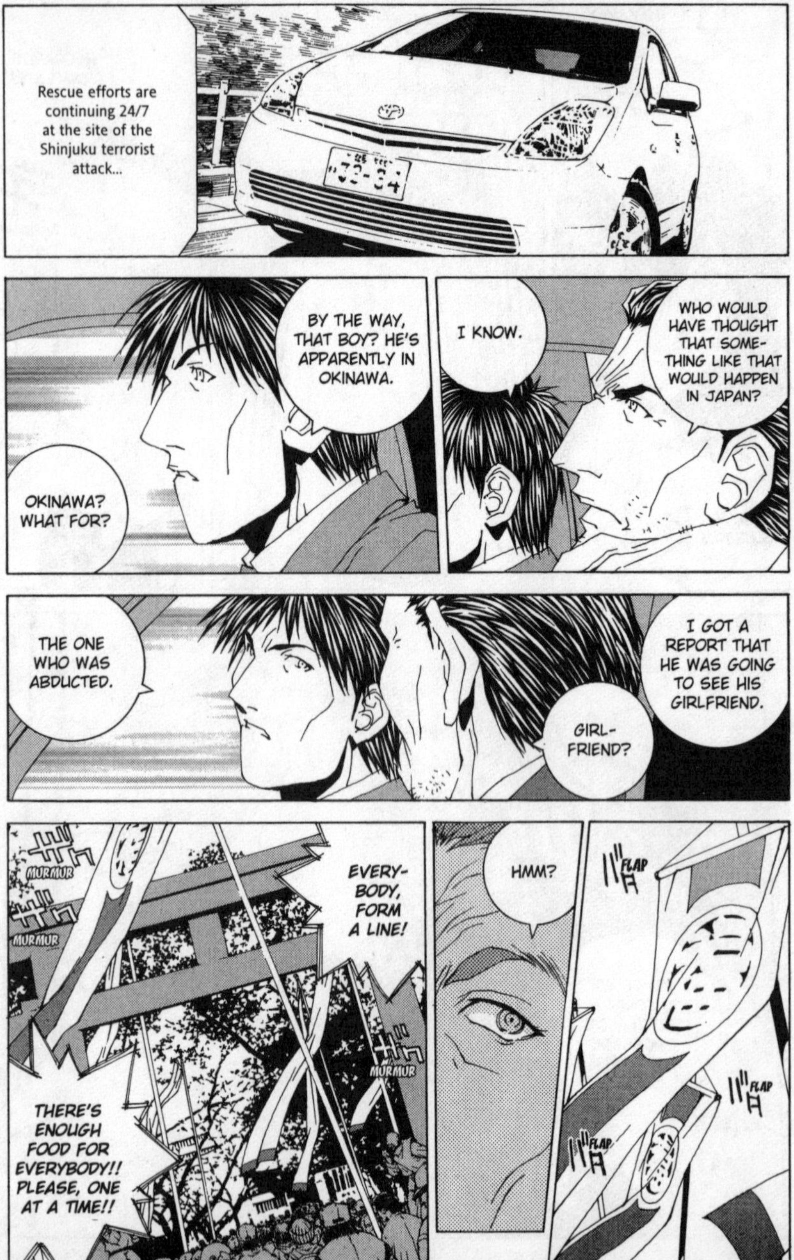

Rescue efforts are continuing 24/7 at the site of the Shinjuku terrorist attack...
WHO WOULD HAVE THOUGHT THAT SOME-THING LIKE THAT WOULD HAPPEN IN JAPAN?
I KNOW.
BY THE WAY, THAT BOY? HE'S APPARENTLY IN OKINAWA.
OKINAWA? WHAT FOR?
I GOT A REPORT THAT HE WAS GOING TO SEE HIS GIRLFRIEND.
GIRL-FRIEND?
THE ONE WHO WAS ABDUCTED.
FLAP
HMM?
FLAP
FLAP
EVERY-BODY, FORM A LINE!
MURMUR
MURMUR
MURMUR
THERE'S ENOUGH FOOD FOR EVERYBODY!! PLEASE, ONE AT A TIME!!

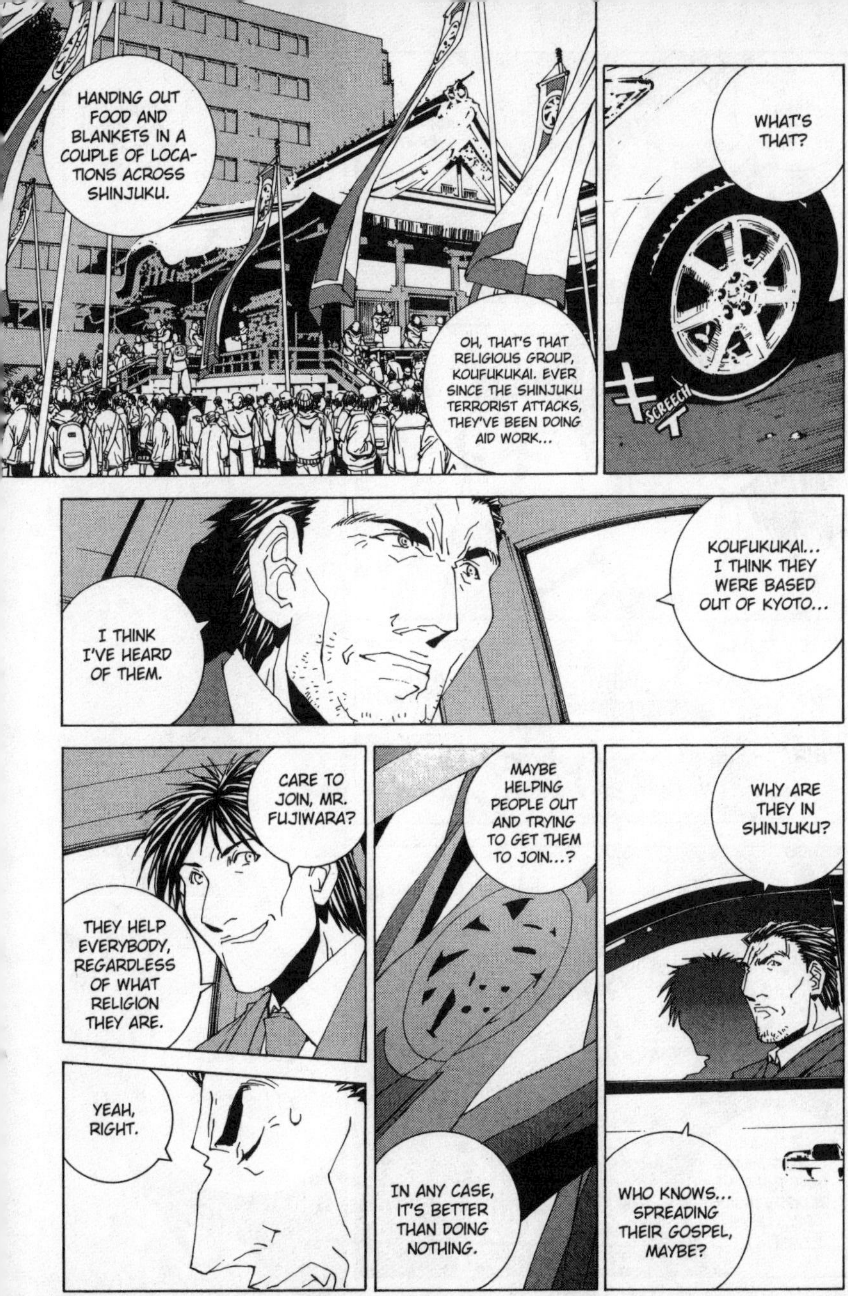
WHAT'S THAT?
SCREECH
OH, THAT'S THAT RELIGIOUS GROUP, KOUFUKUKAI. EVER SINCE THE SHINJUKU TERRORIST ATTACKS, THEY'VE BEEN DOING AID WORK...
HANDING OUT FOOD AND BLANKETS IN A COUPLE OF LOCA-TIONS ACROSS SHINJUKU.
KOUFUKUKAI... I THINK THEY WERE BASED OUT OF KYOTO...
I THINK I'VE HEARD OF THEM.
WHY ARE THEY IN SHINJUKU?
WHO KNOWS... SPREADING THEIR GOSPEL, MAYBE?
MAYBE HELPING PEOPLE OUT AND TRYING TO GET THEM TO JOIN...?
IN ANY CASE, IT'S BETTER THAN DOING NOTHING.
CARE TO JOIN, MR. FUJIWARA?
THEY HELP EVERYBODY, REGARDLESS OF WHAT RELIGION THEY ARE.
YEAH, RIGHT.

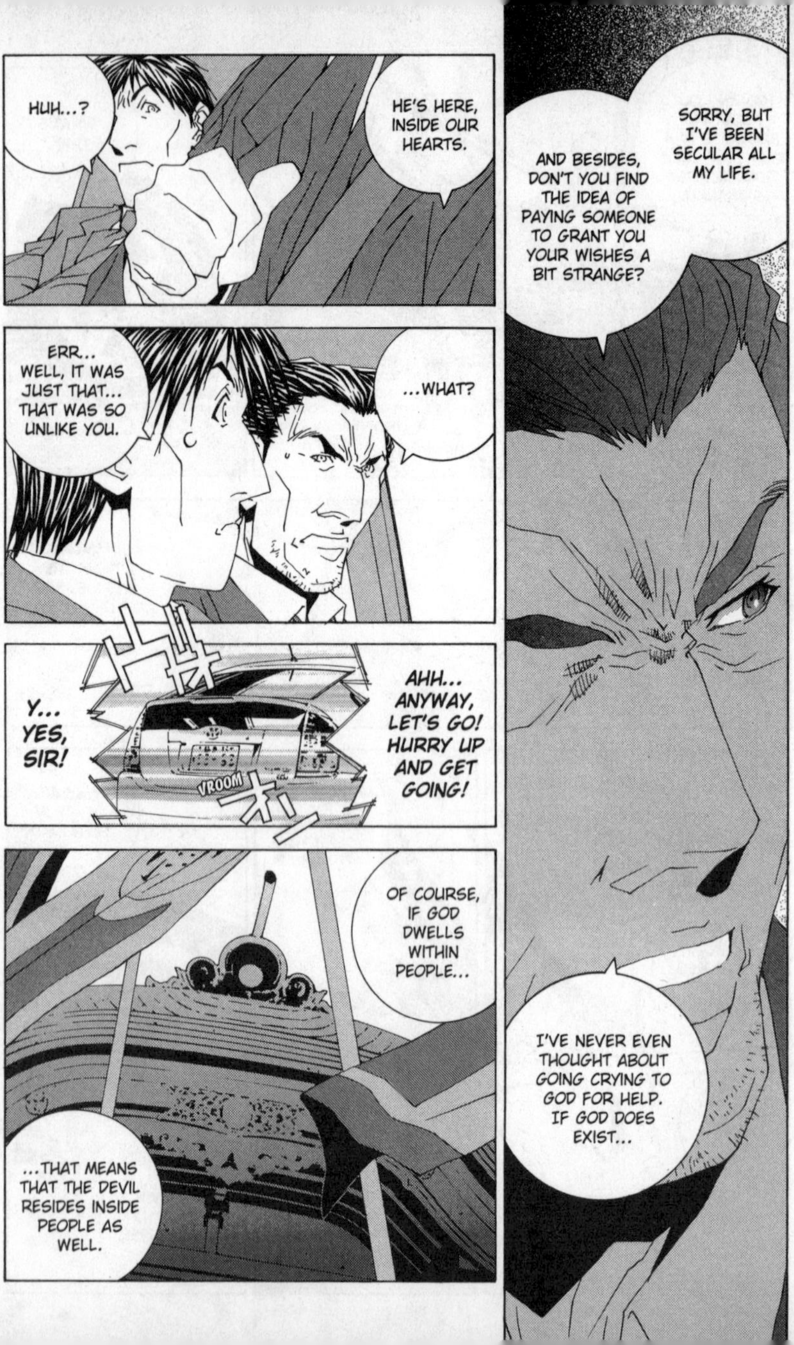
SORRY, BUT I'VE BEEN SECULAR ALL MY LIFE.
AND BESIDES, DON'T YOU FIND THE IDEA OF PAYING SOMEONE TO GRANT YOU YOUR WISHES A BIT STRANGE?
I'VE NEVER EVEN THOUGHT ABOUT GOING CRYING TO GOD FOR HELP. IF GOD DOES EXIST...
HE'S HERE, INSIDE OUR HEARTS.
HUH...?
...WHAT?
ERR... WELL, IT WAS JUST THAT... THAT WAS SO UNLIKE YOU.
AHH... ANYWAY, LET'S GO! HURRY UP AND GET GOING!
VROOM
Y... YES, SIR!
OF COURSE, IF GOD DWELLS WITHIN PEOPLE...
...THAT MEANS THAT THE DEVIL RESIDES INSIDE PEOPLE AS WELL.

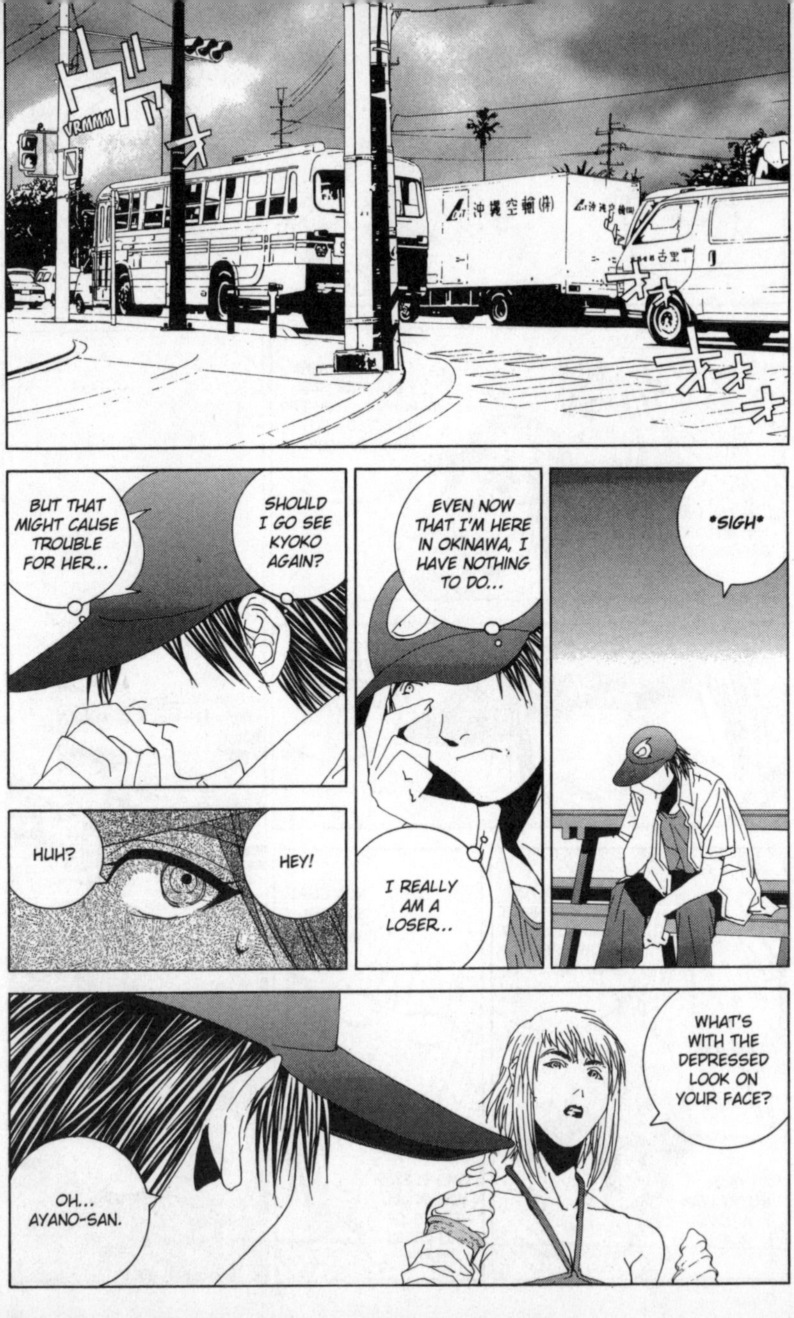
VRMMM
沖縄空輸(株)
SIGH
EVEN NOW THAT I'M HERE IN OKINAWA, I HAVE NOTHING TO DO...
I REALLY AM A LOSER...
SHOULD I GO SEE KYOKO AGAIN?
BUT THAT MIGHT CAUSE TROUBLE FOR HER...
HEY!
HUH?
WHAT'S WITH THE DEPRESSED LOOK ON YOUR FACE?
OH... AYANO-SAN.

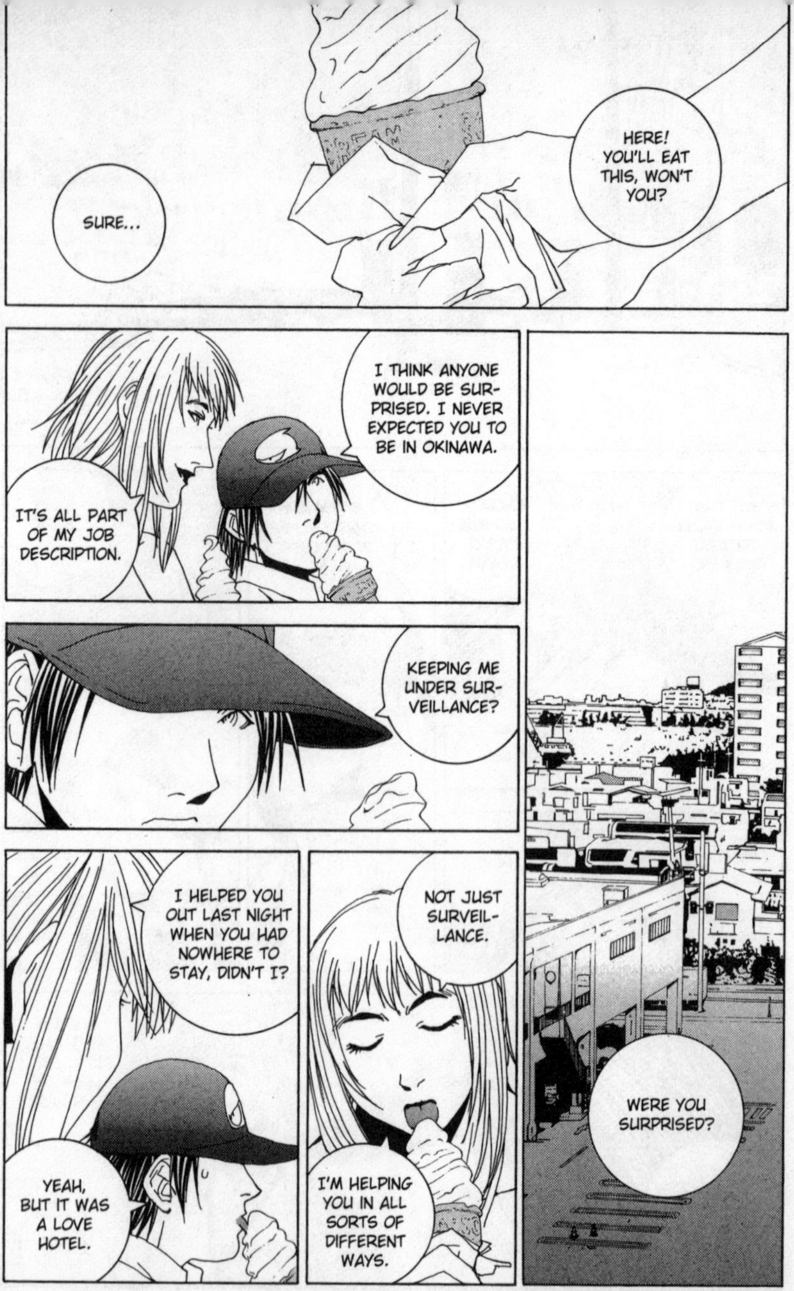
HERE! YOU'LL EAT THIS, WON'T YOU?
SURE...
WERE YOU SURPRISED?
I THINK ANYONE WOULD BE SURPRISED. I NEVER EXPECTED YOU TO BE IN OKINAWA.
IT'S ALL PART OF MY JOB DESCRIPTION.
KEEPING ME UNDER SURVEILLANCE?
NOT JUST SURVEILLANCE.
I'M HELPING YOU IN ALL SORTS OF DIFFERENT WAYS.
I HELPED YOU OUT LAST NIGHT WHEN YOU HAD NOWHERE TO STAY, DIDN'T I?
YEAH, BUT IT WAS A LOVE HOTEL.

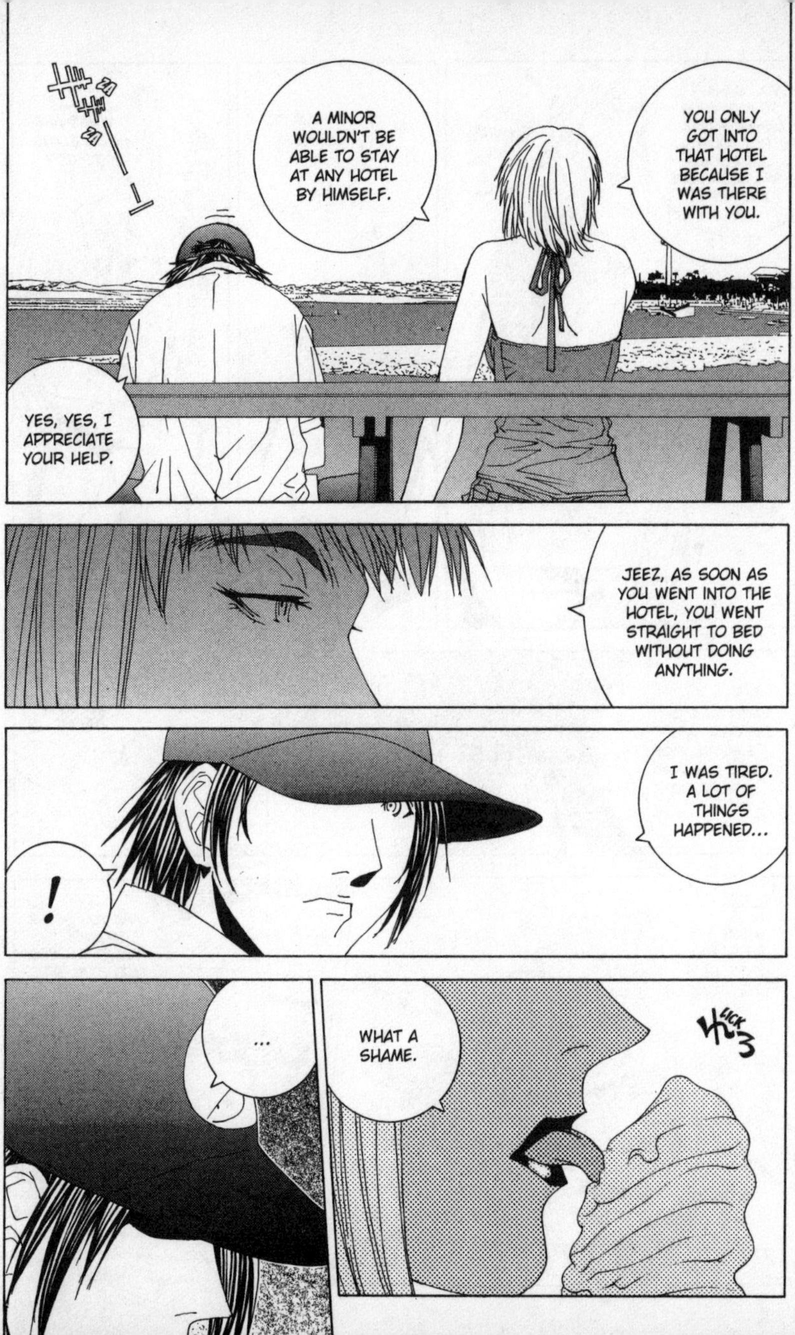
YOU ONLY GOT INTO THAT HOTEL BECAUSE I WAS THERE WITH YOU.
A MINOR WOULDN'T BE ABLE TO STAY AT ANY HOTEL BY HIMSELF.
YES, YES, I APPRECIATE YOUR HELP.
JEEZ, AS SOON AS YOU WENT INTO THE HOTEL, YOU WENT STRAIGHT TO BED WITHOUT DOING ANYTHING.
I WAS TIRED. A LOT OF THINGS HAPPENED...
!
LICK
WHAT A SHAME.
...

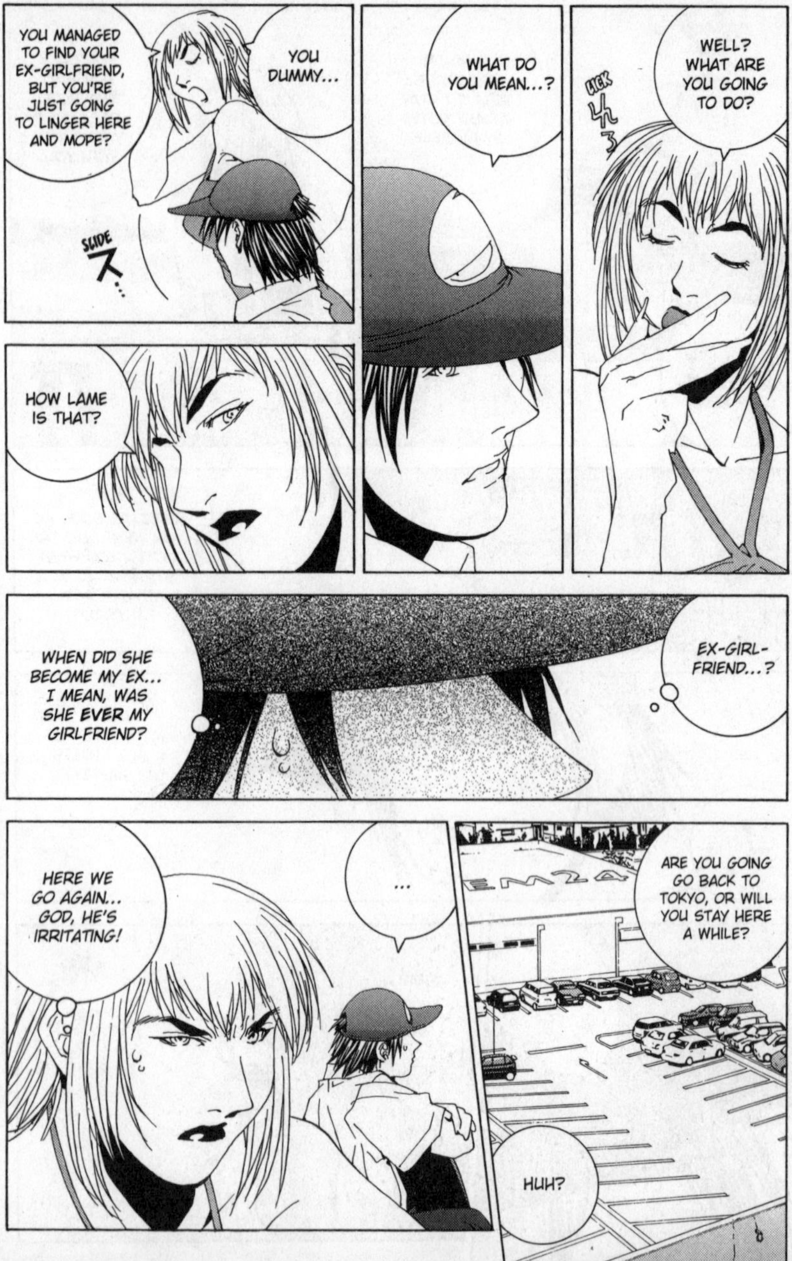
UCK
WELL? WHAT ARE YOU GOING TO DO?
WHAT DO YOU MEAN...?
YOU MANAGED TO FIND YOUR EX-GIRLFRIEND, BUT YOU'RE JUST GOING TO LINGER HERE AND MOPE?
YOU DUMMY...
SLIDE
HOW LAME IS THAT?
EX-GIRL-FRIEND...?
WHEN DID SHE BECOME MY EX... I MEAN, WAS SHE EVER MY GIRLFRIEND?
ARE YOU GOING GO BACK TO TOKYO, OR WILL YOU STAY HERE A WHILE?
HUH?
...
HERE WE GO AGAIN... GOD, HE'S IRRITATING!

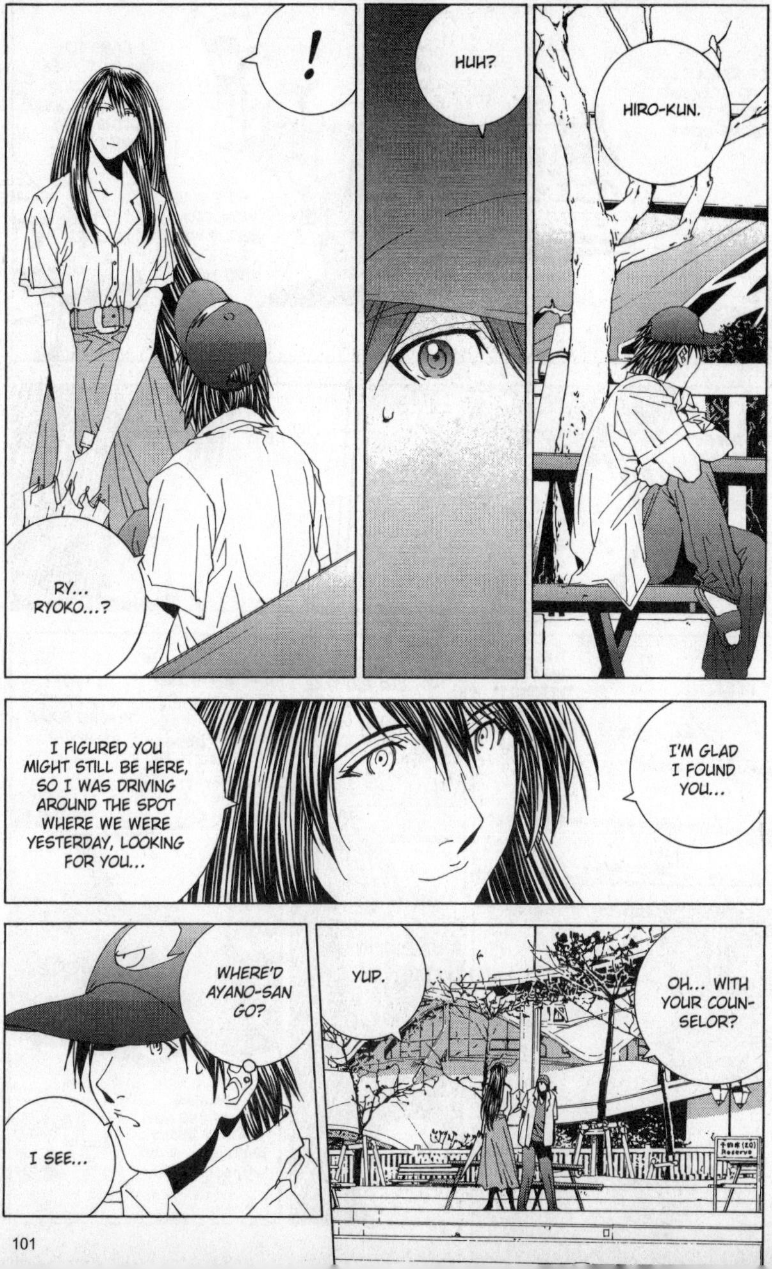
HIRO-KUN.
HUH?
!
RY... RYOKO...?
I'M GLAD I FOUND YOU...
I FIGURED YOU MIGHT STILL BE HERE, SO I WAS DRIVING AROUND THE SPOT WHERE WE WERE YESTERDAY, LOOKING FOR YOU...
OH... WITH YOUR COUN-SELOR?
YUP.
WHERE'D AYANO-SAN GO?
I SEE...

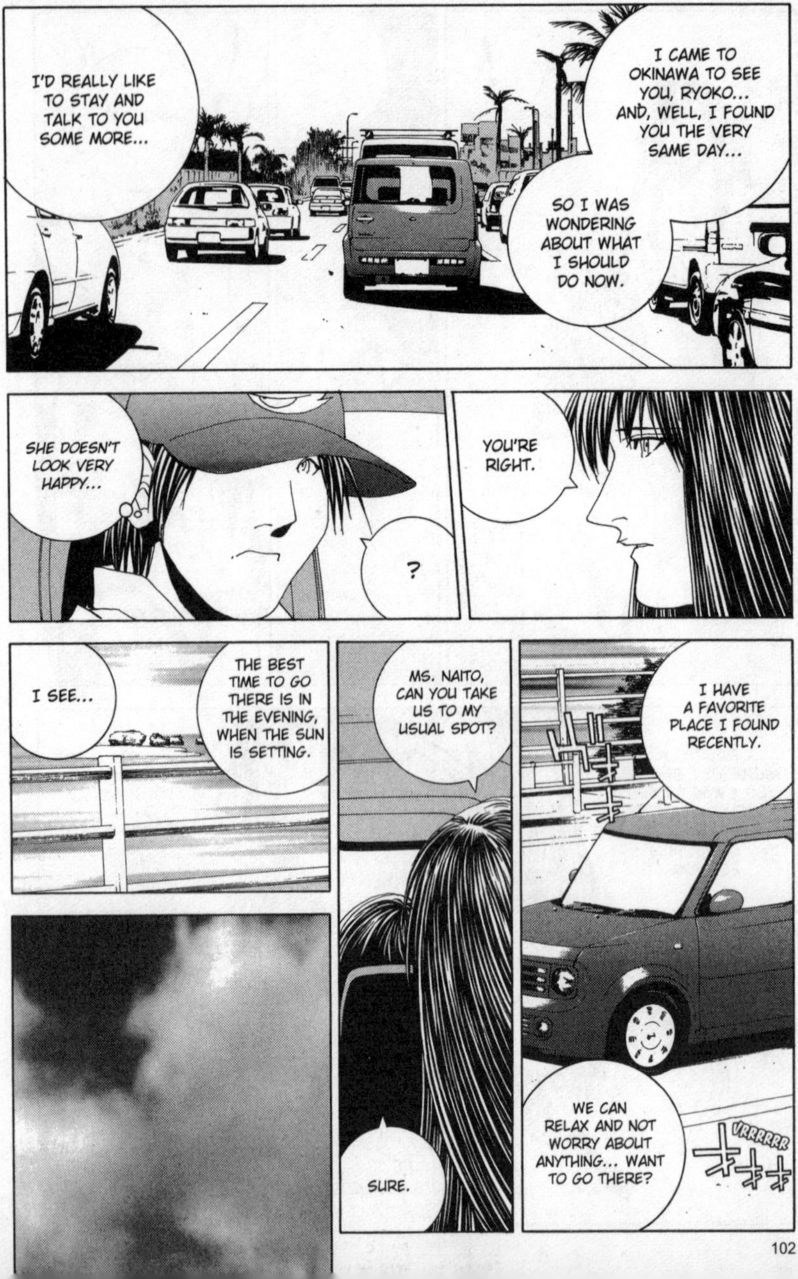
I CAME TO OKINAWA TO SEE YOU, RYOKO... AND, WELL, I FOUND YOU THE VERY SAME DAY...
SO I WAS WONDERING ABOUT WHAT I SHOULD DO NOW.
I'D REALLY LIKE TO STAY AND TALK TO YOU SOME MORE...
YOU'RE RIGHT.
SHE DOESN'T LOOK VERY HAPPY...
?
I HAVE A FAVORITE PLACE I FOUND RECENTLY.
WE CAN RELAX AND NOT WORRY ABOUT ANYTHING... WANT TO GO THERE?
VRRRRRR
MS. NAITO, CAN YOU TAKE US TO MY USUAL SPOT?
SURE.
THE BEST TIME TO GO THERE IS IN THE EVENING, WHEN THE SUN IS SETTING.
I SEE...

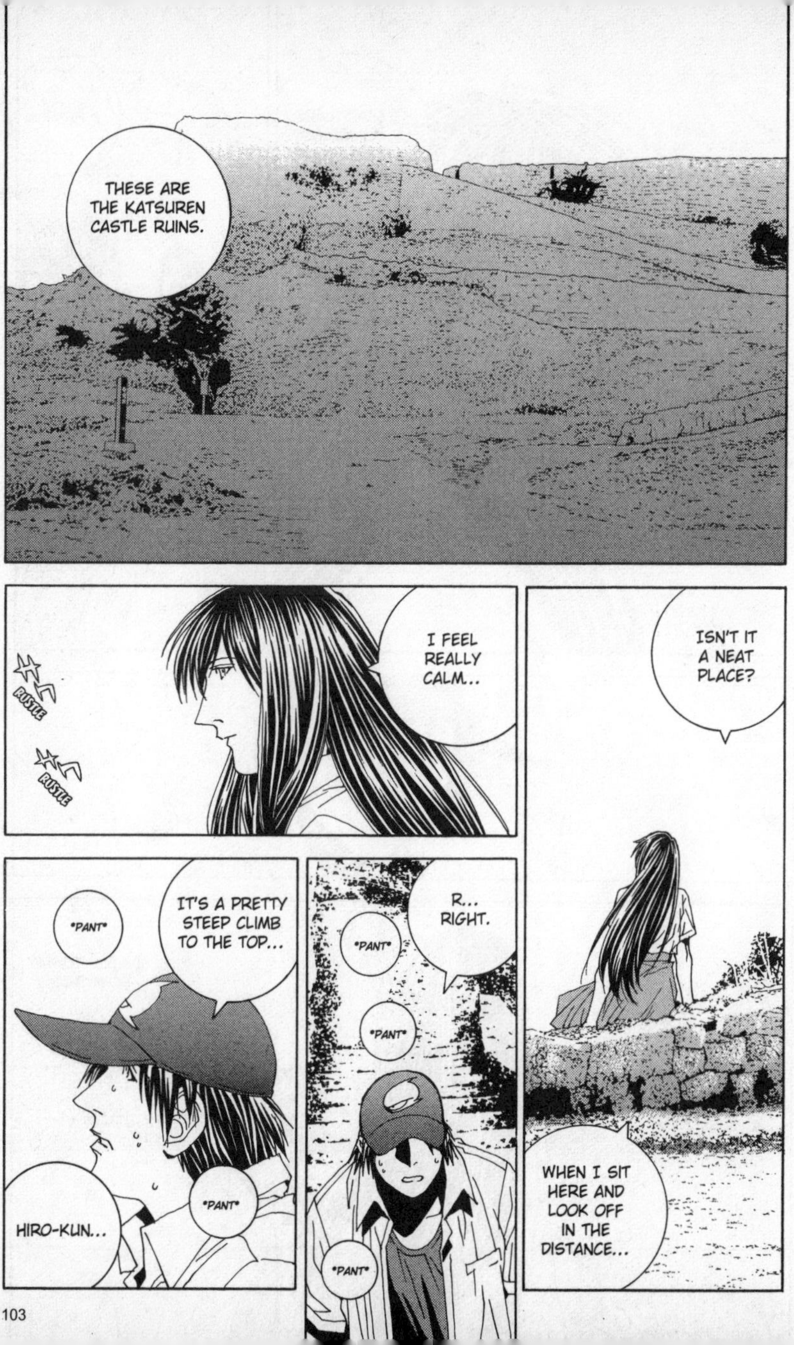
THESE ARE THE KATSUREN CASTLE RUINS.
ISN'T IT A NEAT PLACE?
WHEN I SIT HERE AND LOOK OFF IN THE DISTANCE...
I FEEL REALLY CALM...
RUSTLE
RUSTLE
R... RIGHT.
PANT
PANT
PANT
IT'S A PRETTY STEEP CLIMB TO THE TOP...
PANT
PANT
HIRO-KUN...

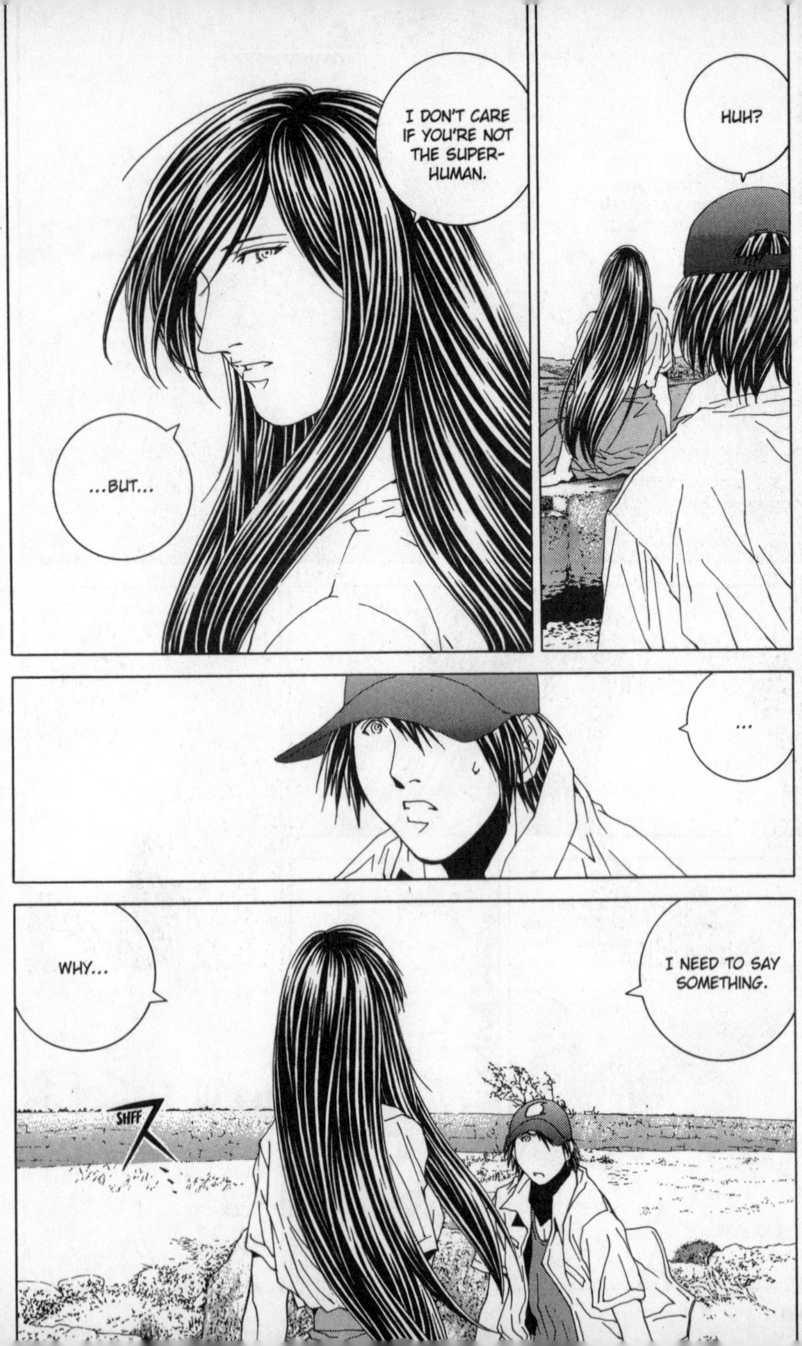
HUH?
I DON'T CARE IF YOU'RE NOT THE SUPER-HUMAN.
...BUT...
...
I NEED TO SAY SOMETHING.
WHY...
SHFF

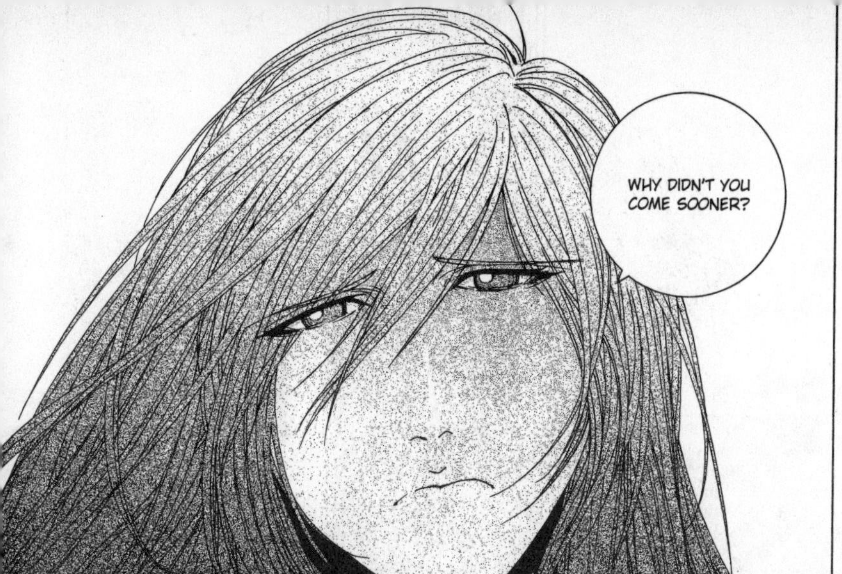
WHY DIDN'T YOU COME SOONER?
I WANTED YOU TO RESCUE ME SOONER.

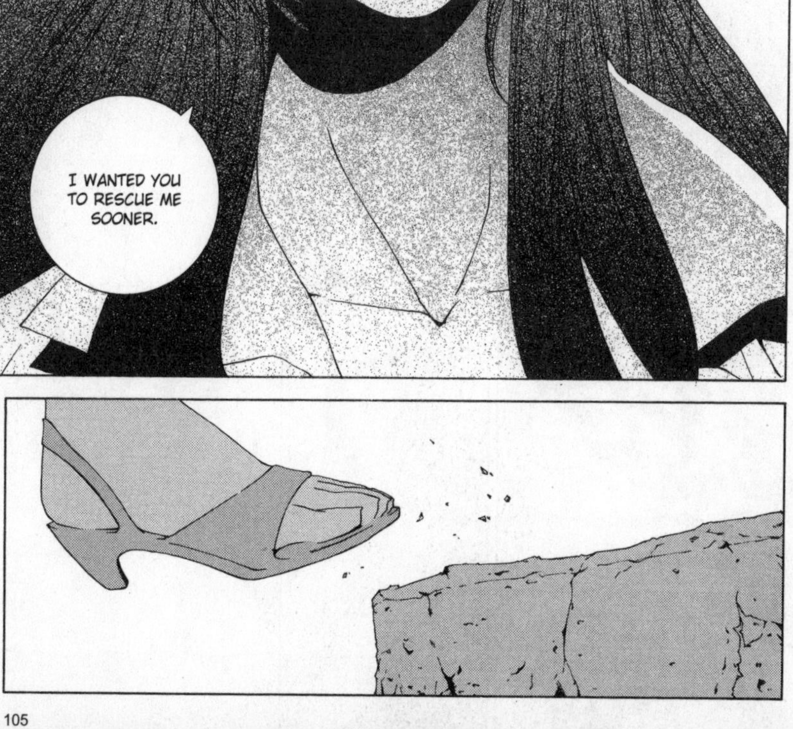

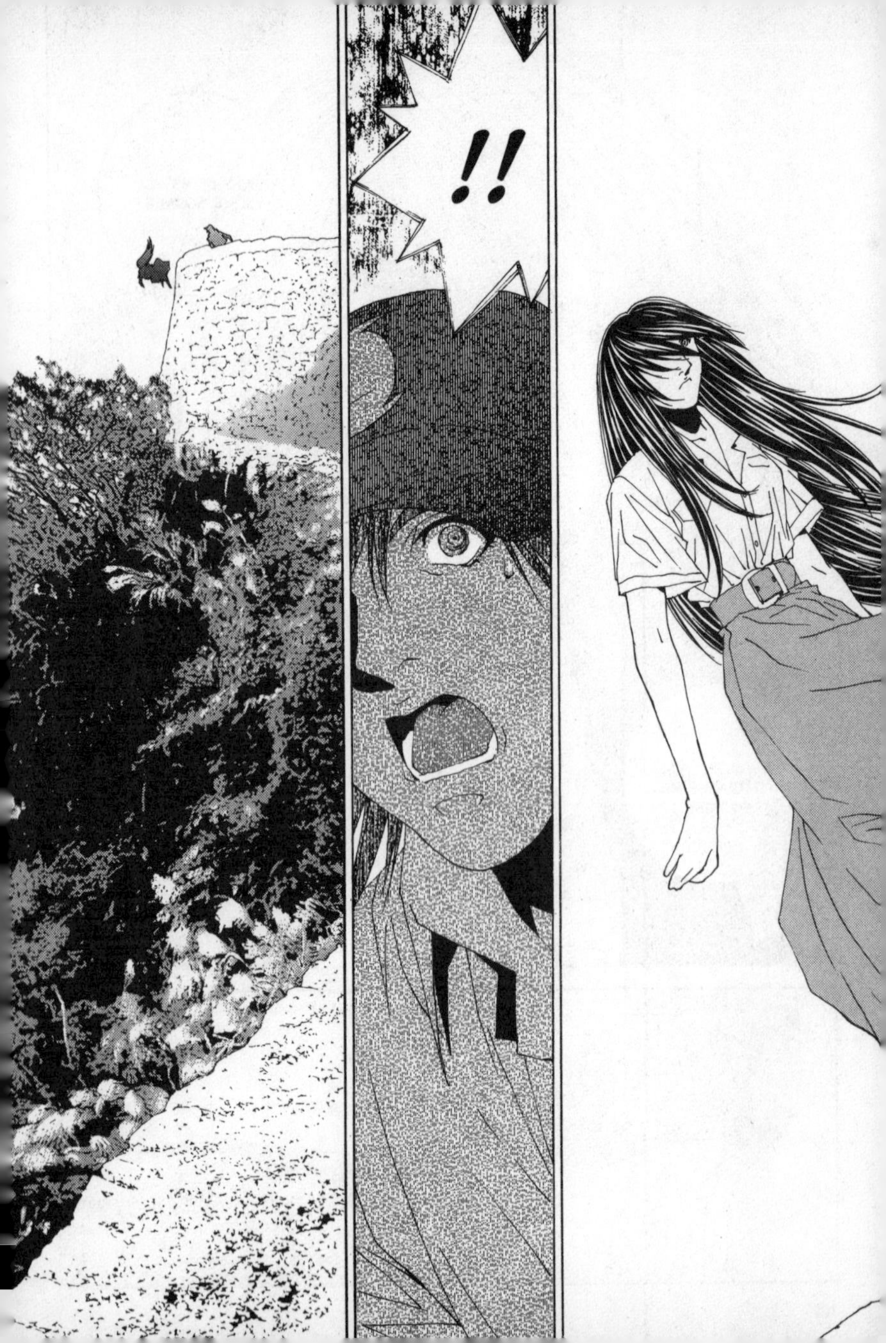
!!

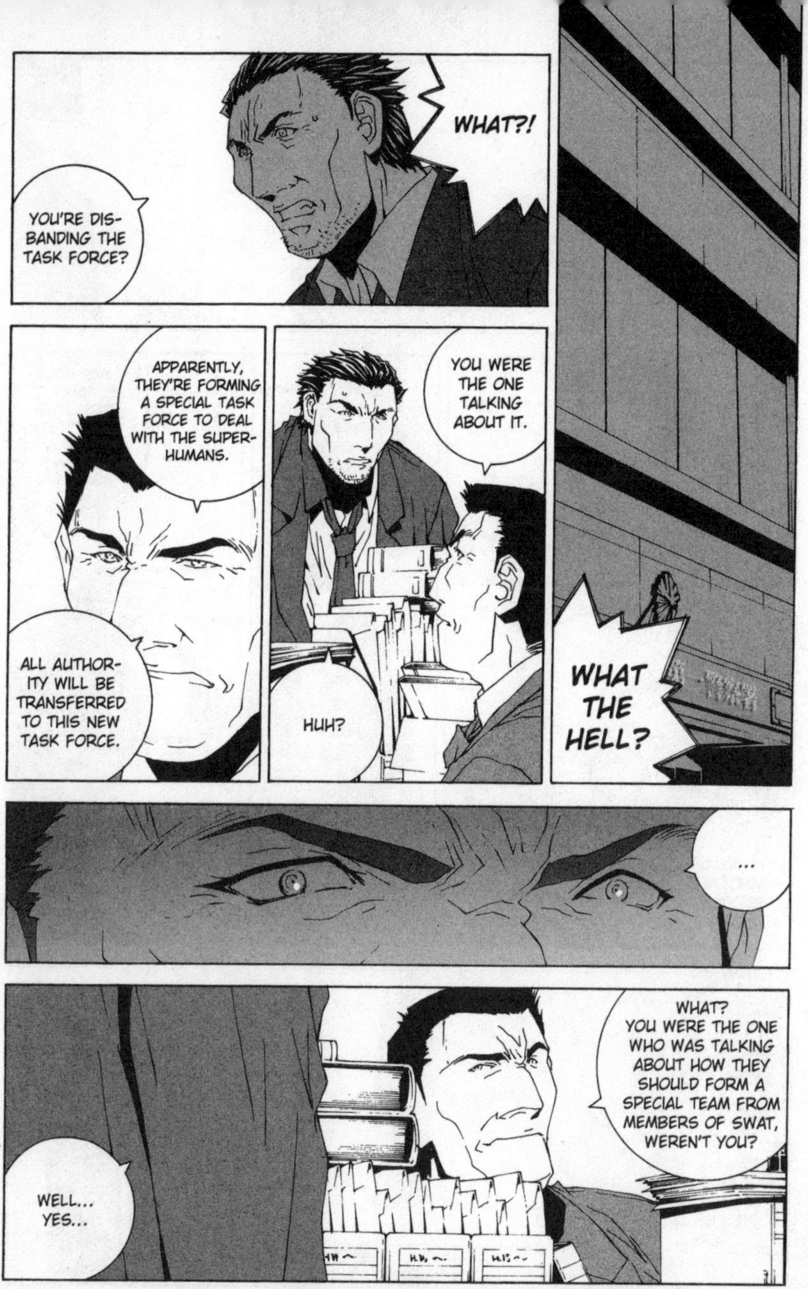
WHAT THE HELL?
WHAT?!
YOU'RE DIS-BANDING THE TASK FORCE?
YOU WERE THE ONE TALKING ABOUT IT.
HUH?
APPARENTLY, THEY'RE FORMING A SPECIAL TASK FORCE TO DEAL WITH THE SUPER-HUMANS.
ALL AUTHOR-ITY WILL BE TRANSFERRED TO THIS NEW TASK FORCE.
...
WHAT? YOU WERE THE ONE WHO WAS TALKING ABOUT HOW THEY SHOULD FORM A SPECIAL TEAM FROM MEMBERS OF SWAT, WEREN'T YOU?
WELL... YES...

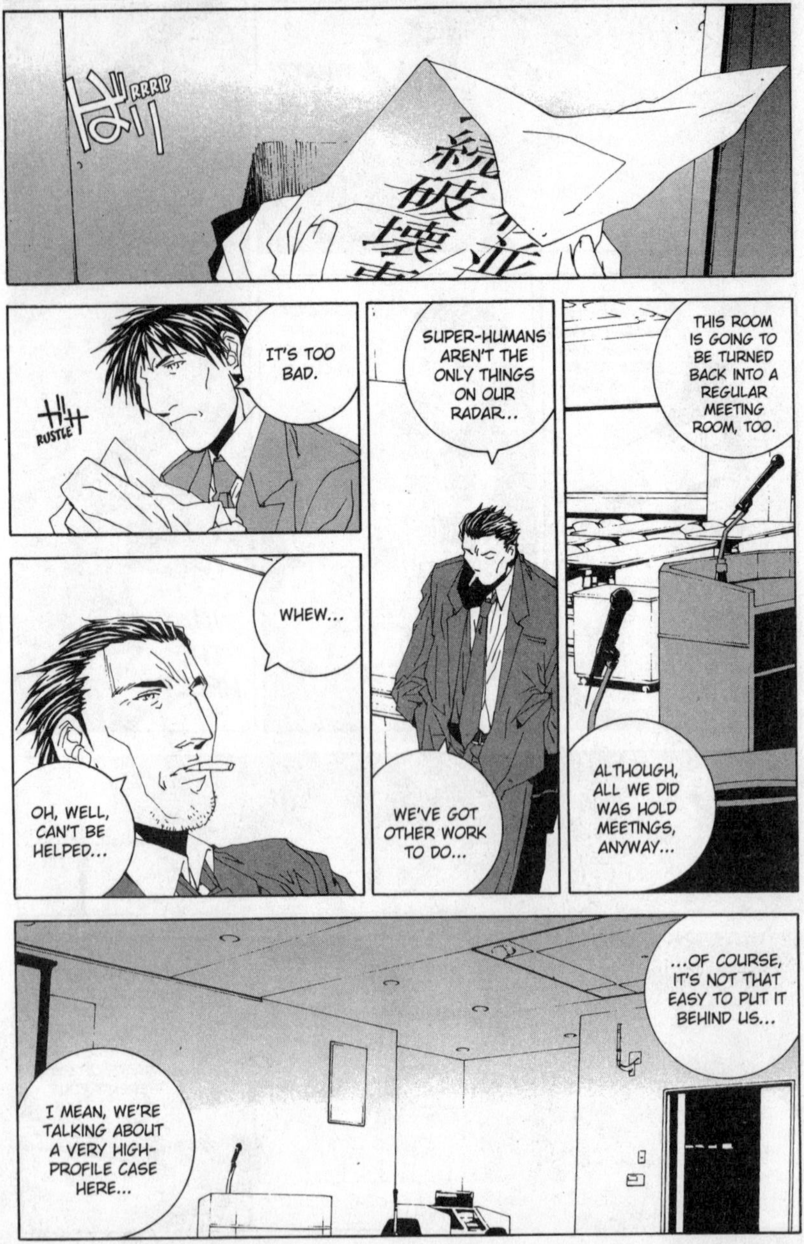
ばり RRRIP
THIS ROOM IS GOING TO BE TURNED BACK INTO A REGULAR MEETING ROOM, TOO.
ALTHOUGH, ALL WE DID WAS HOLD MEETINGS, ANYWAY...
SUPER-HUMANS AREN'T THE ONLY THINGS ON OUR RADAR...
WE'VE GOT OTHER WORK TO DO...
IT'S TOO BAD.
ガサ RUSTLE
WHEW...
OH, WELL, CAN'T BE HELPED...
...OF COURSE, IT'S NOT THAT EASY TO PUT IT BEHIND US...
I MEAN, WE'RE TALKING ABOUT A VERY HIGH-PROFILE CASE HERE...

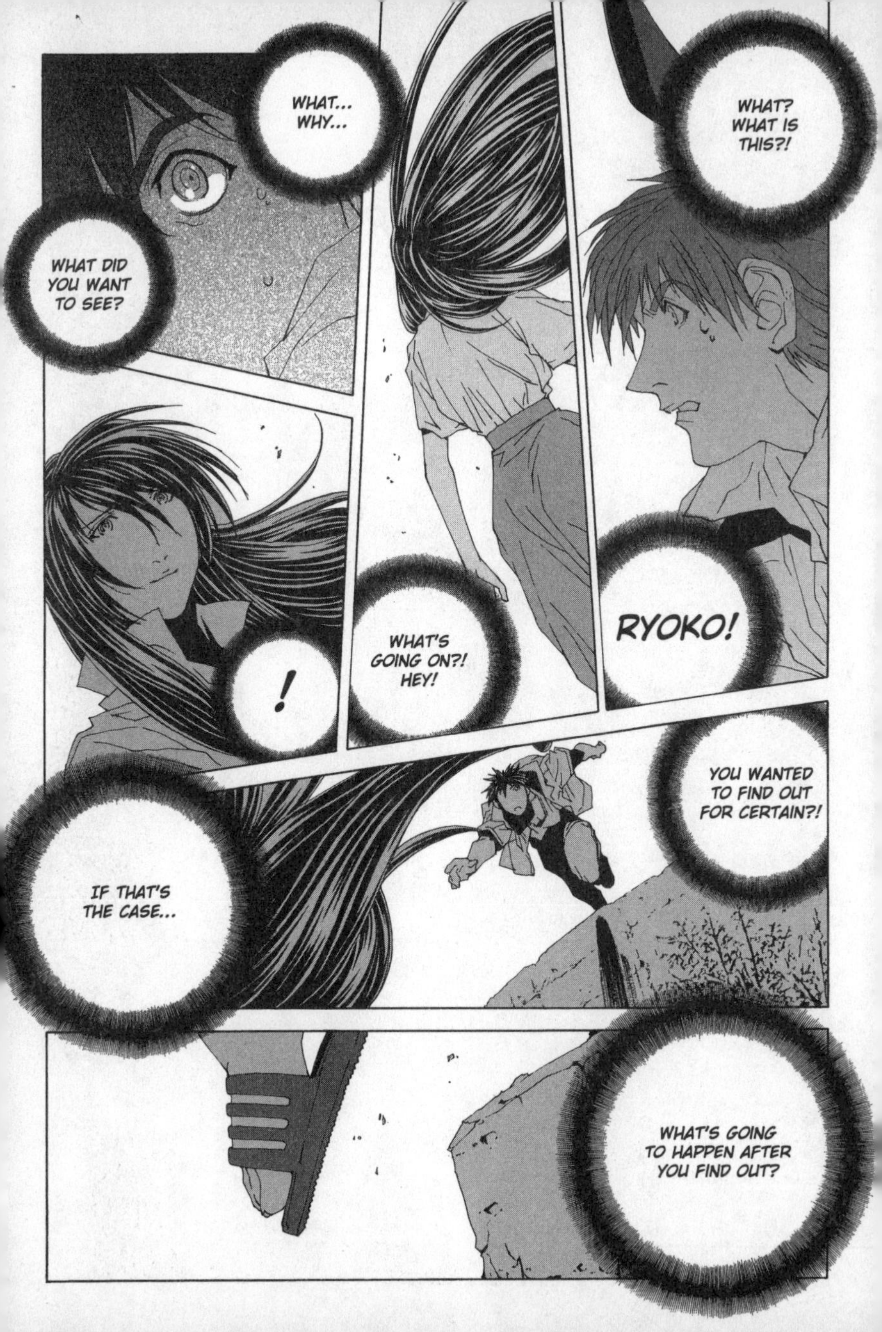
WHAT? WHAT IS THIS?!
RYOKO!
WHAT'S GOING ON?! HEY!
WHAT... WHY...
WHAT DID YOU WANT TO SEE?
!
YOU WANTED TO FIND OUT FOR CERTAIN?!
IF THAT'S THE CASE...
WHAT'S GOING TO HAPPEN AFTER YOU FIND OUT?

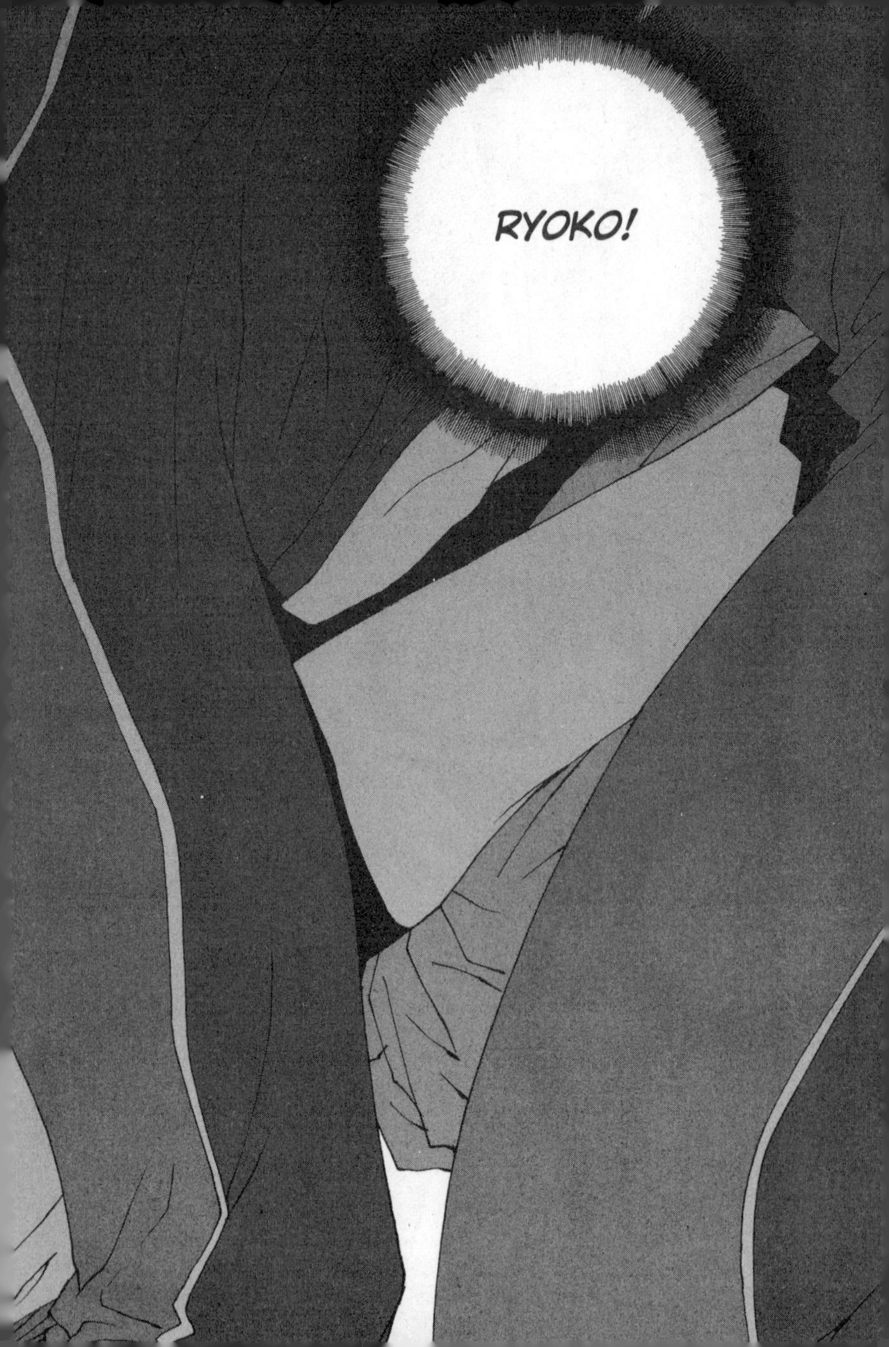
RYOKO!

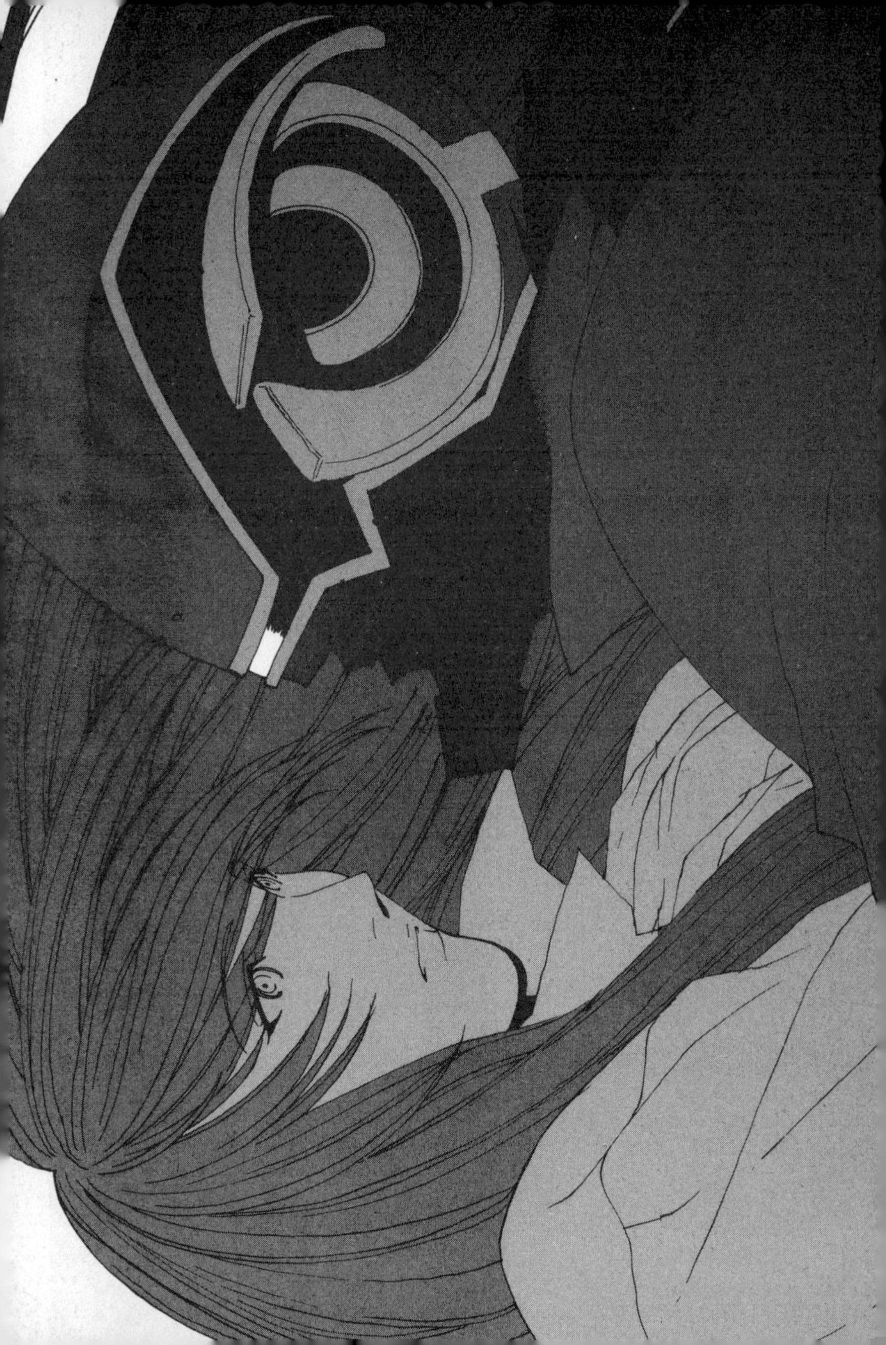

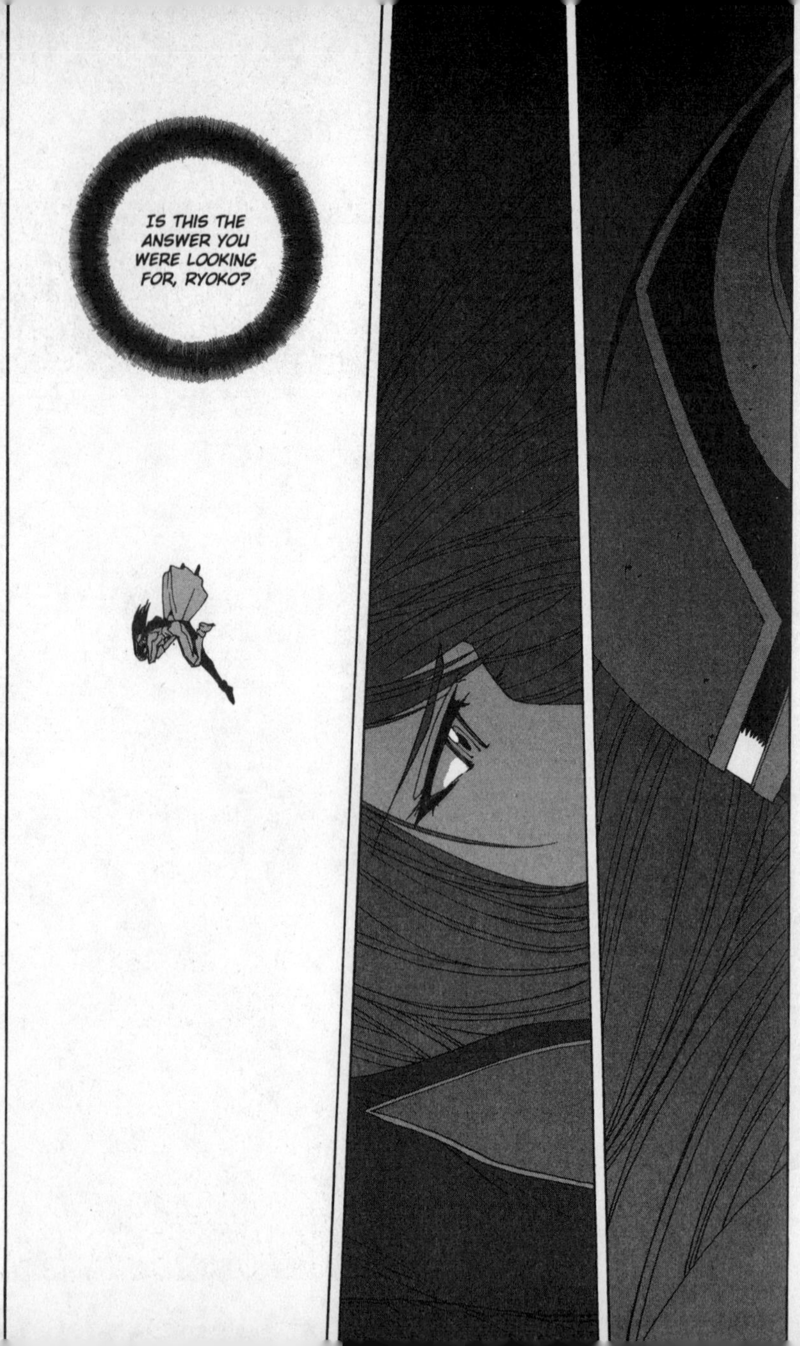
IS THIS THE ANSWER YOU WERE LOOKING FOR, RYOKO?

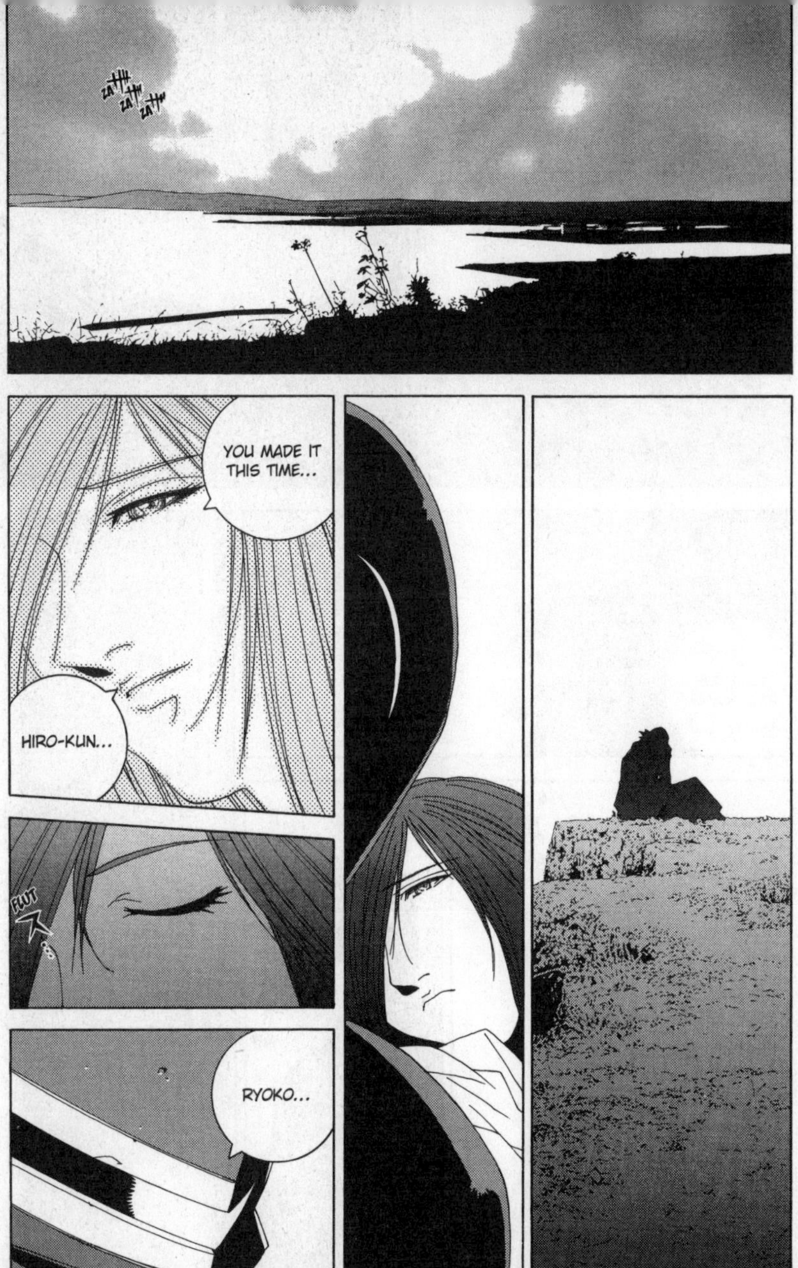
ZA
ZA
ZA
YOU MADE IT THIS TIME...
HIRO-KUN...
FLUT
RYOKO...

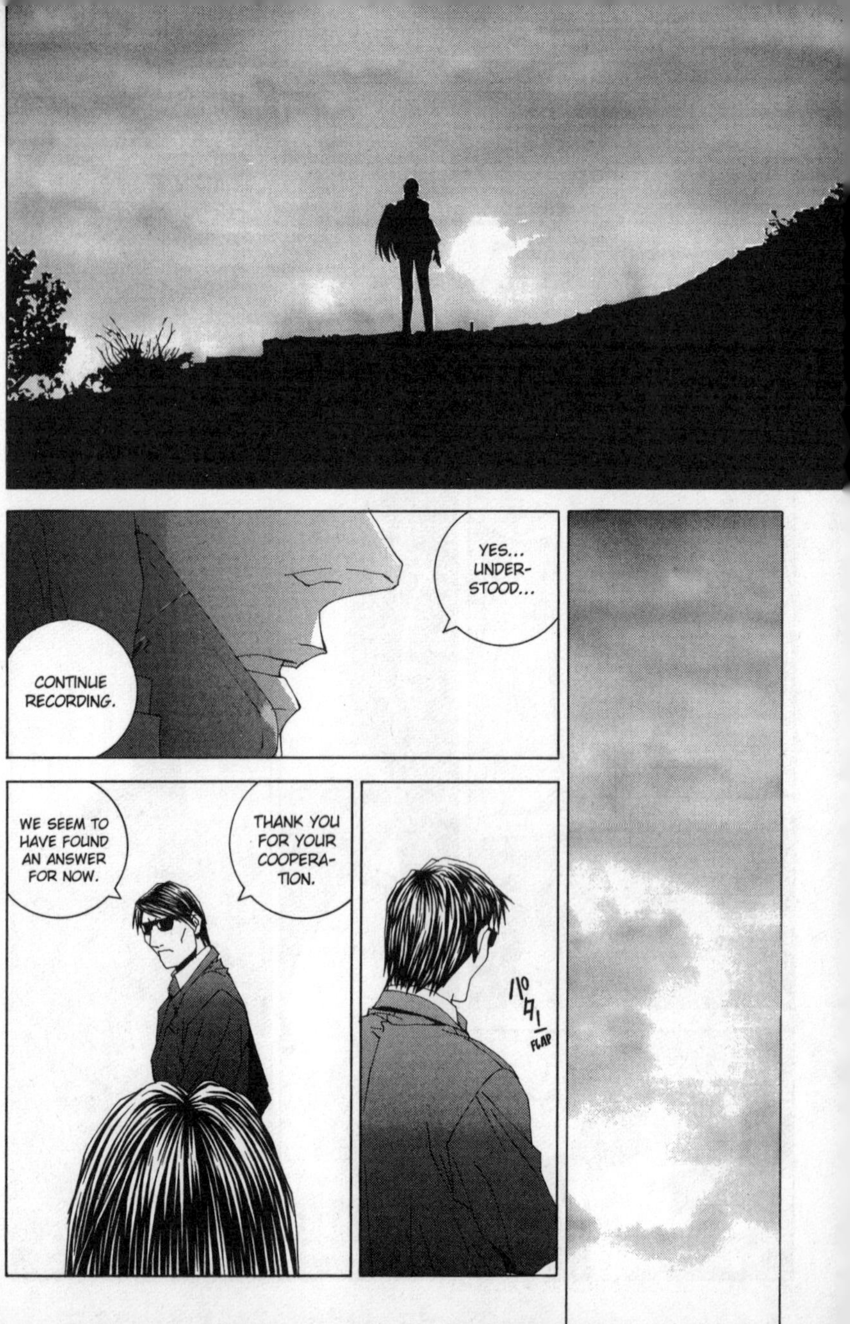
YES... UNDER-STOOD...
CONTINUE RECORDING.
FLAP
THANK YOU FOR YOUR COOPERA-TION.
WE SEEM TO HAVE FOUND AN ANSWER FOR NOW.

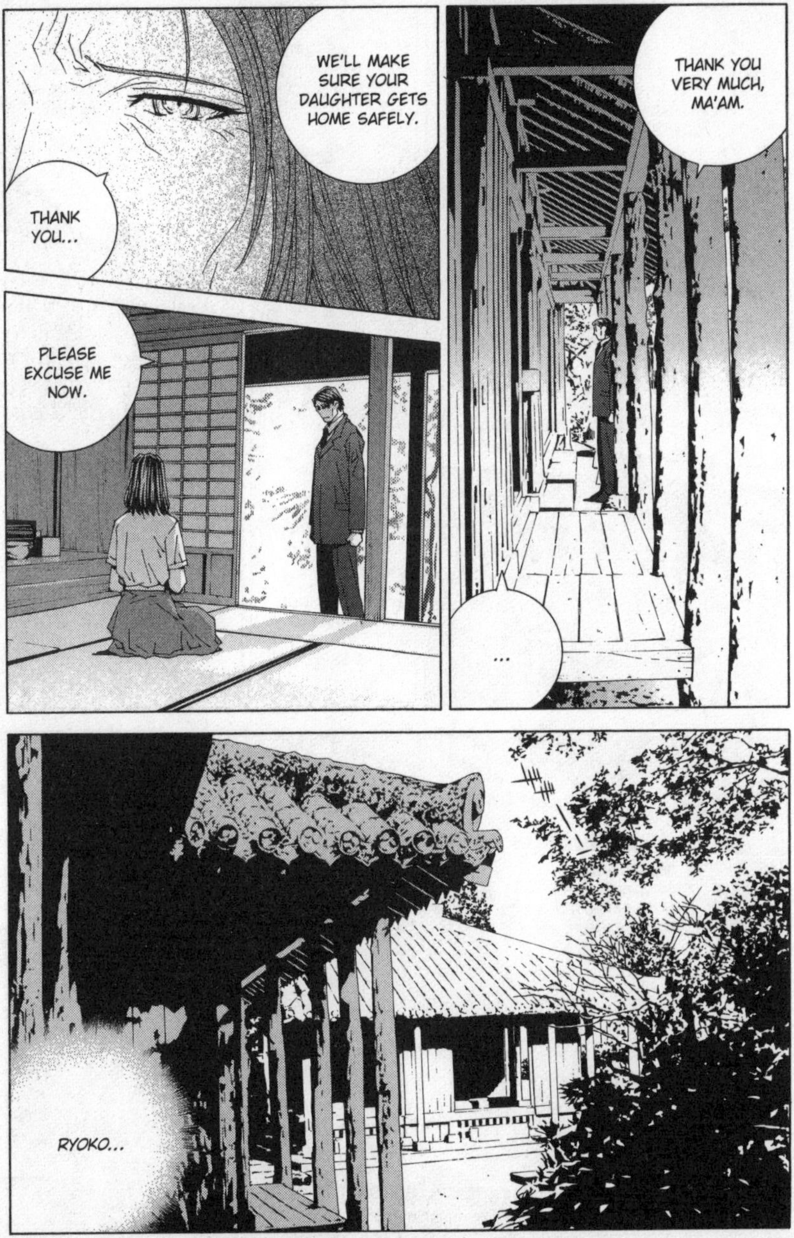
THANK YOU VERY MUCH, MA'AM.
...
WE'LL MAKE SURE YOUR DAUGHTER GETS HOME SAFELY.
THANK YOU...
PLEASE EXCUSE ME NOW.
RYOKO...

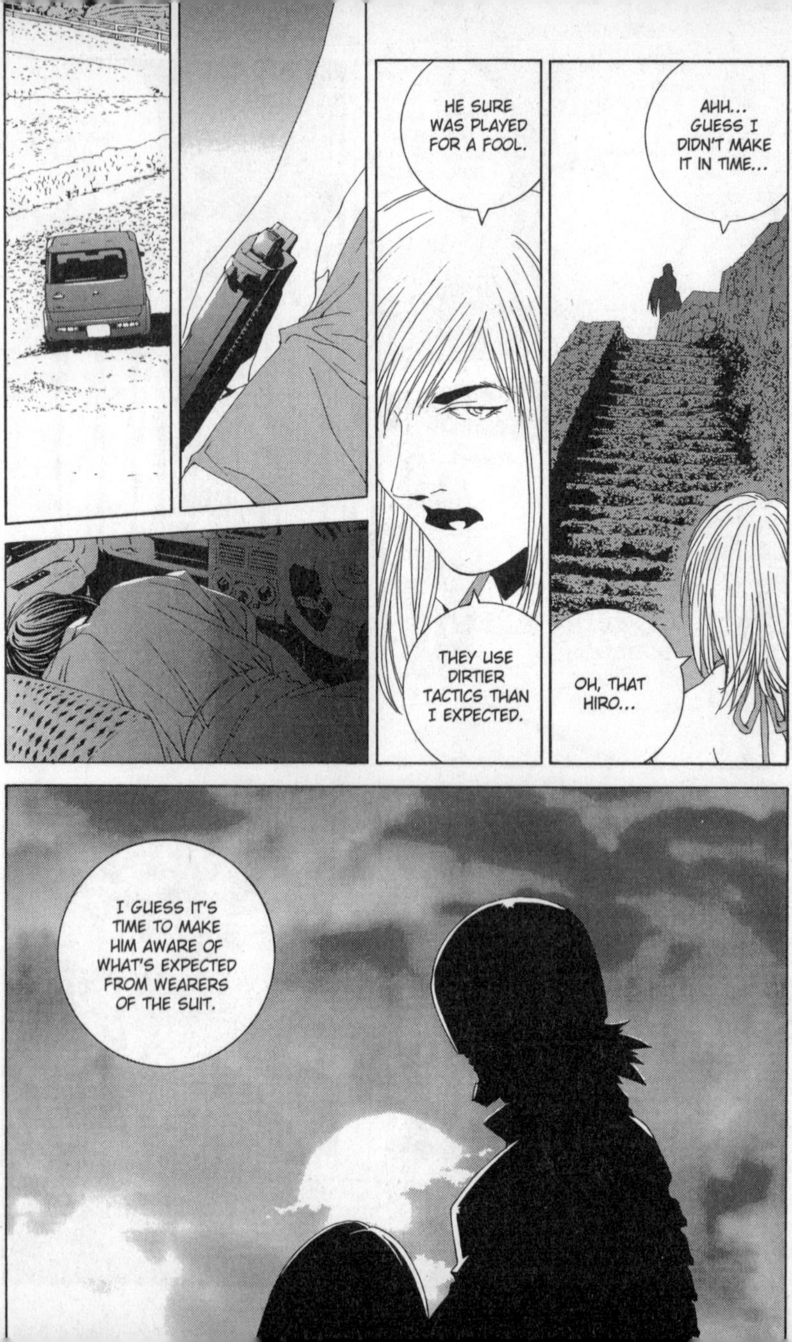
AHH... GUESS I DIDN'T MAKE IT IN TIME...
OH, THAT HIRO...
HE SURE WAS PLAYED FOR A FOOL.
THEY USE DIRTIER TACTICS THAN I EXPECTED.
I GUESS IT'S TIME TO MAKE HIM AWARE OF WHAT'S EXPECTED FROM WEARERS OF THE SUIT.

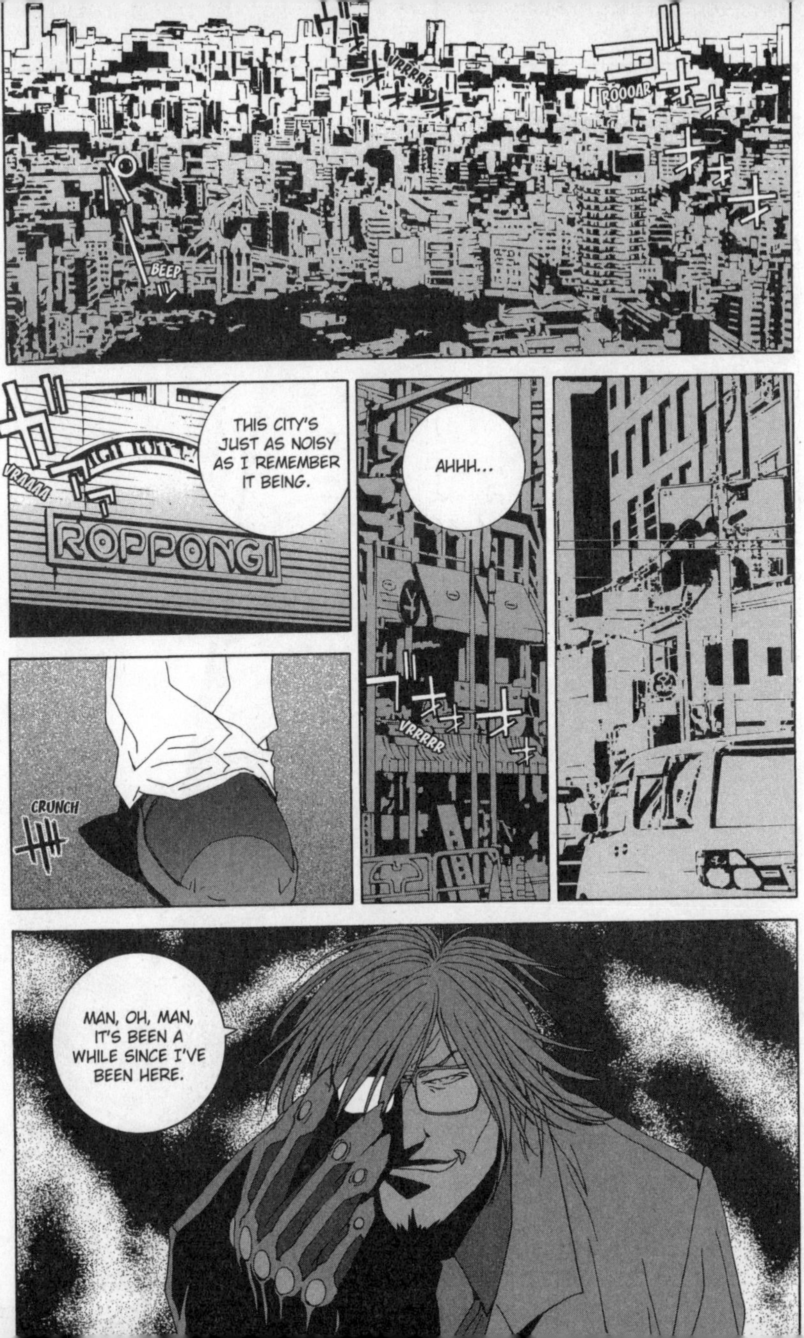

ROOOAR
VRRRRR
BEEP
AHHH...
VRRRRR
THIS CITY'S JUST AS NOISY AS I REMEMBER IT BEING.
VRAAAA
ROPPONGI
CRUNCH
MAN, OH, MAN, IT'S BEEN A WHILE SINCE I'VE BEEN HERE.

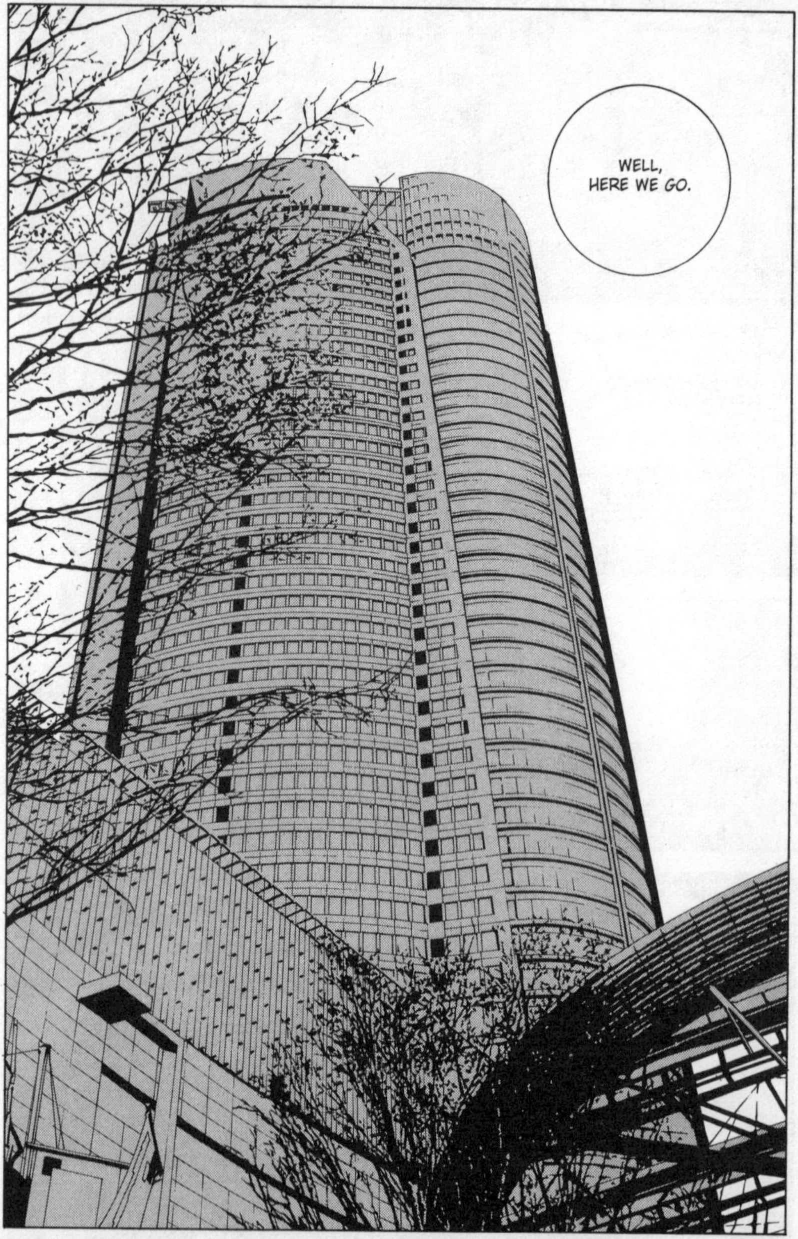
WELL,
HERE WE GO.

JUSTICE:24 JUNK GENOCIDE

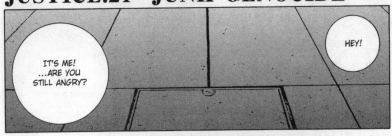

HEY!
IT'S ME! ...ARE YOU STILL ANGRY?
COME ON, GET OVER IT!
ANYWAY... DID YOU READ MY E-MAIL?
THAT'S RIGHT, TEN MINUTES! TEN MINUTES IS ALL I NEED.
IT SHOULD BE A PIECE OF CAKE FOR YOU, RIGHT? I'M COUNTING ON YOU!
WHAT THE HELL ARE YOU GOING TO DO?!
CLAK
CLAK
DON'T TELL ME YOU'RE GOING TO DESTROY THAT ENTIRE BUILDING...
HEY, HEY, COME ON, DON'T LUMP ME IN WITH THAT BLACK JUNK.
A BUNCH OF GUYS I USED TO WORK WITH STARTED UP THEIR OWN COMPANY.

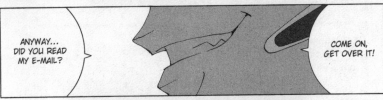

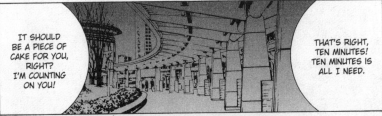

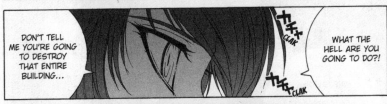

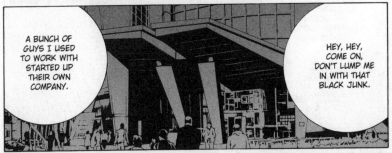

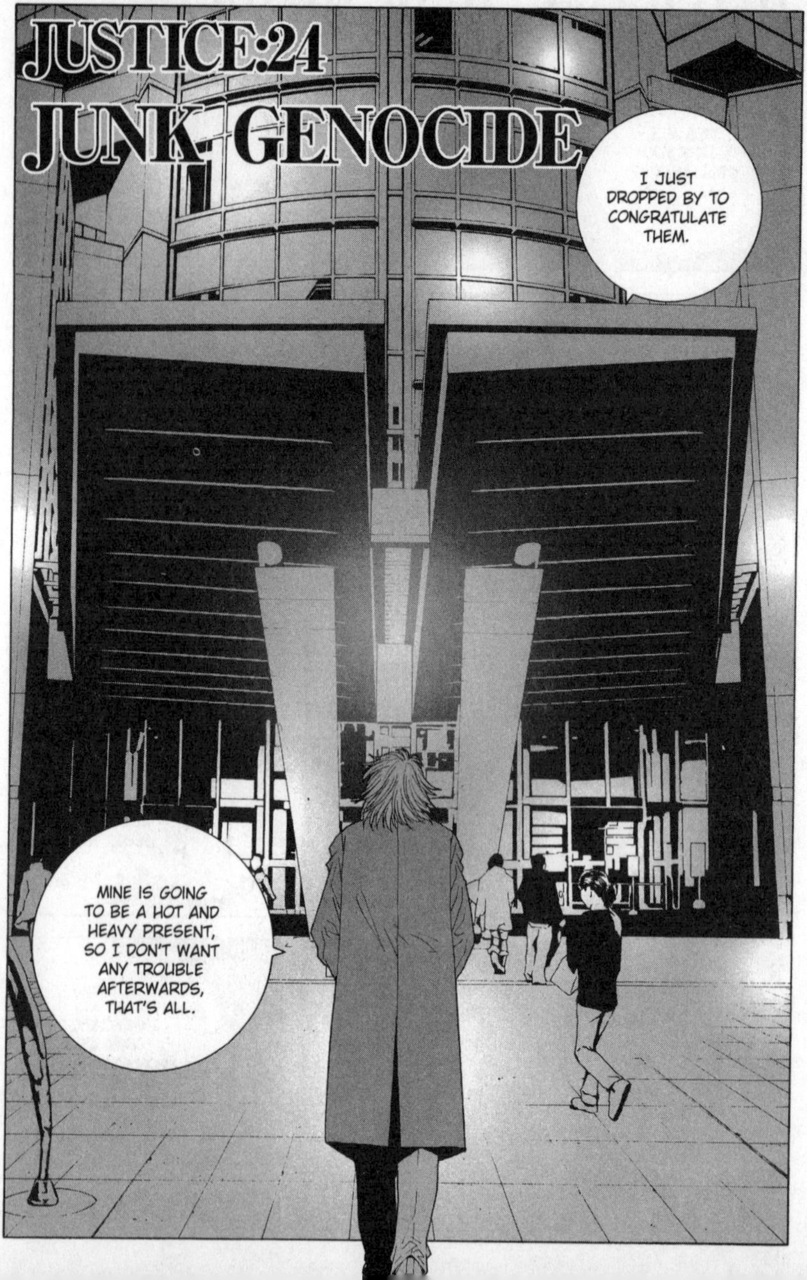
JUSTICE:24
JUNK GENOCIDE
I JUST DROPPED BY TO CONGRATULATE THEM.
MINE IS GOING TO BE A HOT AND HEAVY PRESENT, SO I DON'T WANT ANY TROUBLE AFTERWARDS, THAT'S ALL.

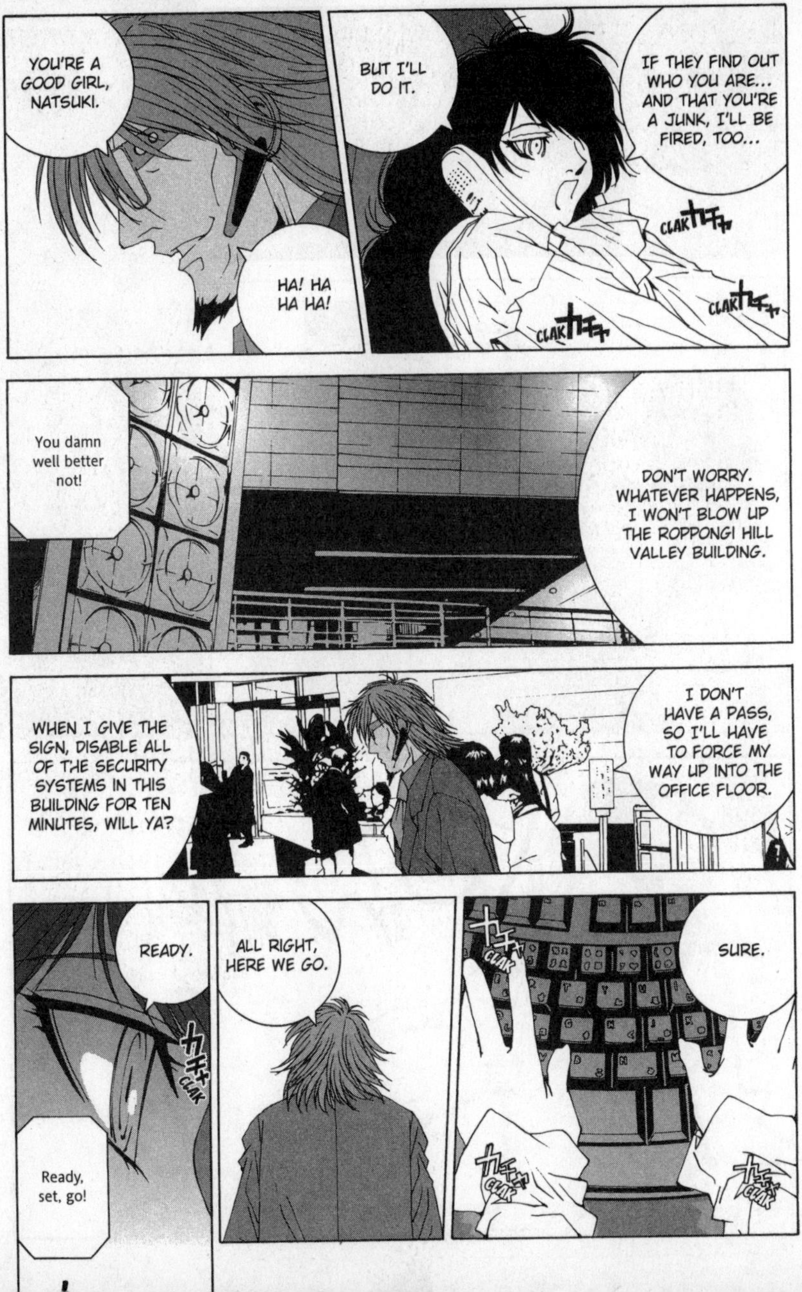

IF THEY FIND OUT WHO YOU ARE... AND THAT YOU'RE A JUNK, I'LL BE FIRED, TOO...
CLAK
CLAK
CLAK
BUT I'LL DO IT.
YOU'RE A GOOD GIRL, NATSUKI.
HA! HA HA HA!
DON'T WORRY. WHATEVER HAPPENS, I WON'T BLOW UP THE ROPPONGI HILL VALLEY BUILDING.
You damn well better not!
I DON'T HAVE A PASS, SO I'LL HAVE TO FORCE MY WAY UP INTO THE OFFICE FLOOR.
WHEN I GIVE THE SIGN, DISABLE ALL OF THE SECURITY SYSTEMS IN THIS BUILDING FOR TEN MINUTES, WILL YA?
SURE.
CLAK
CLAK
CLAK
ALL RIGHT, HERE WE GO.
READY.
CLAK
Ready, set, go!

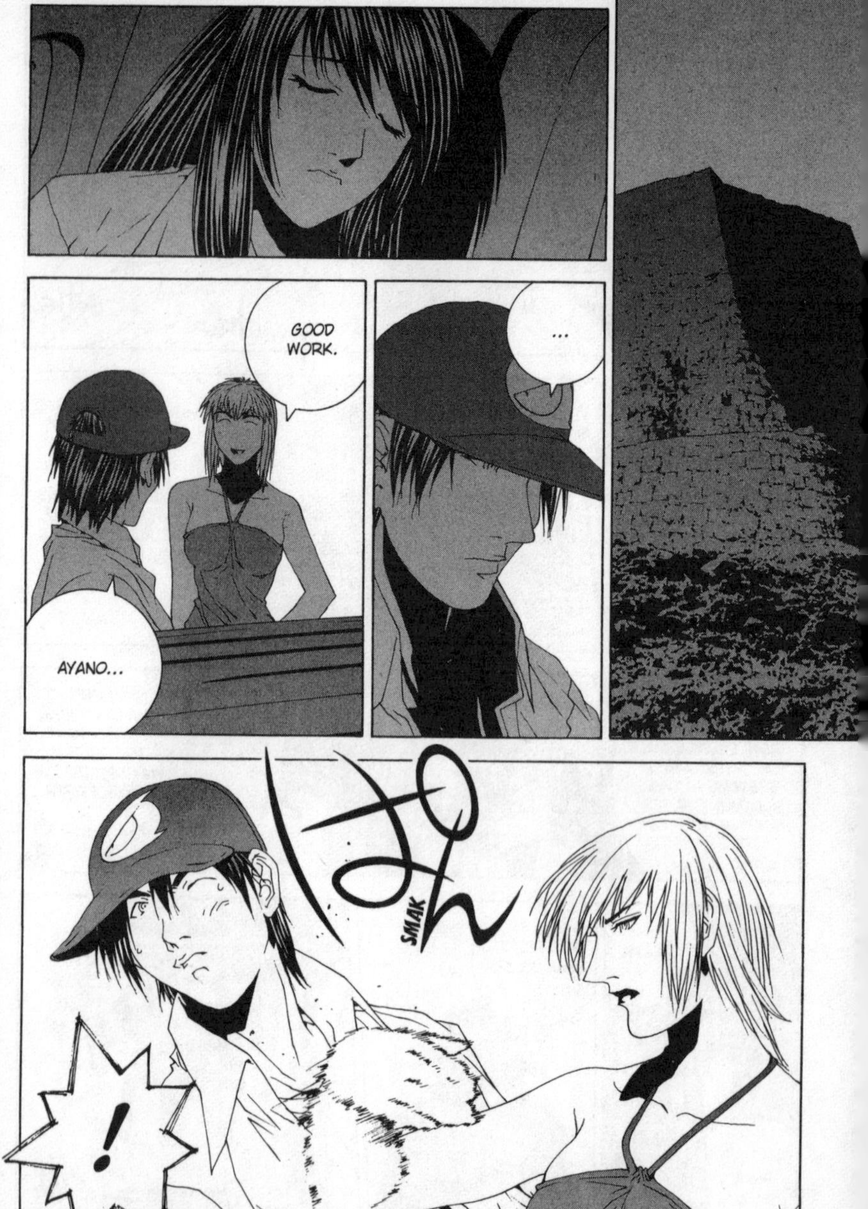
...
GOOD WORK.
AYANO...
SMAK
!

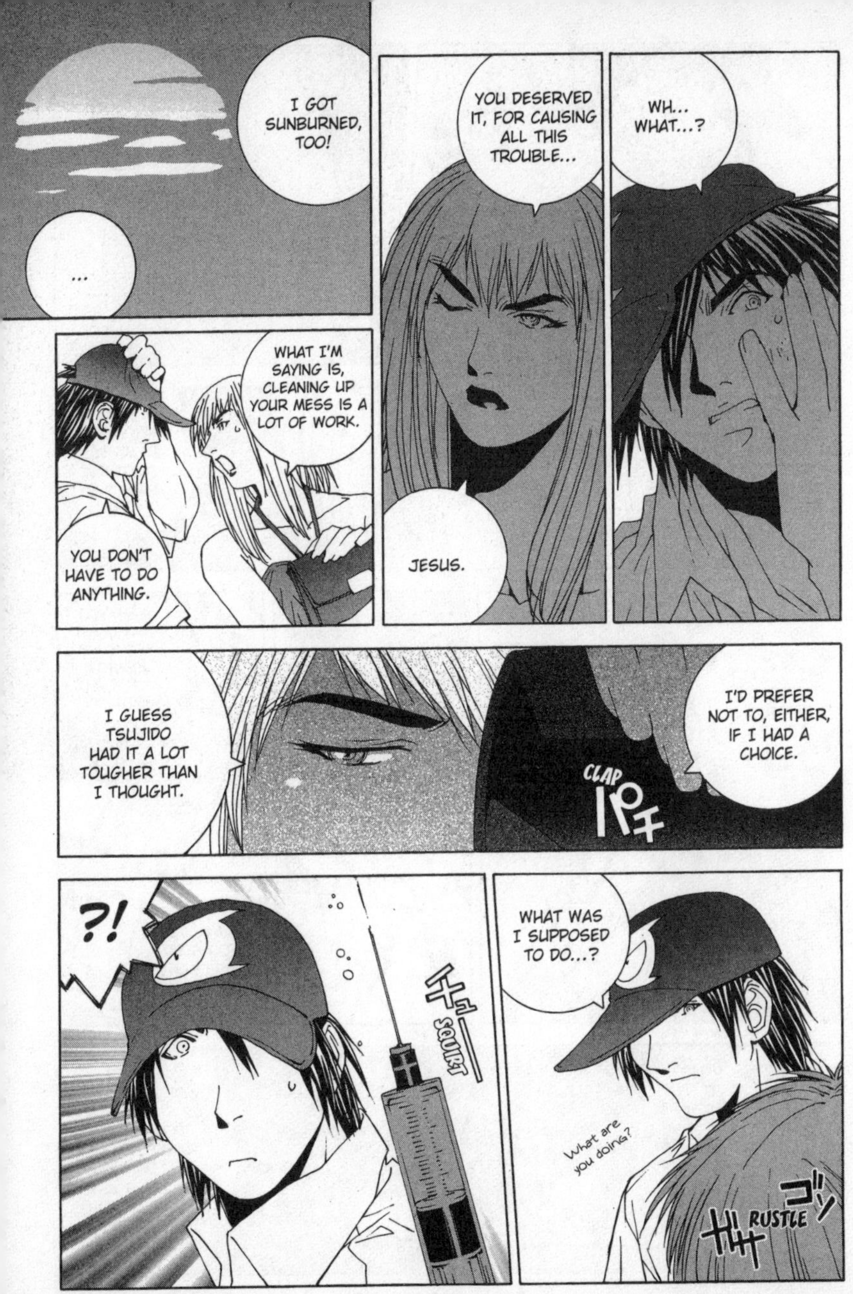
WH... WHAT...?
YOU DESERVED IT, FOR CAUSING ALL THIS TROUBLE...
JESUS.
I GOT SUNBURNED, TOO!
...
WHAT I'M SAYING IS, CLEANING UP YOUR MESS IS A LOT OF WORK.
YOU DON'T HAVE TO DO ANYTHING.
I'D PREFER NOT TO, EITHER, IF I HAD A CHOICE.
CLAP
I GUESS TSUJIDO HAD IT A LOT TOUGHER THAN I THOUGHT.
WHAT WAS I SUPPOSED TO DO...?
What are you doing?
RUSTLE
?!
SQUIRT

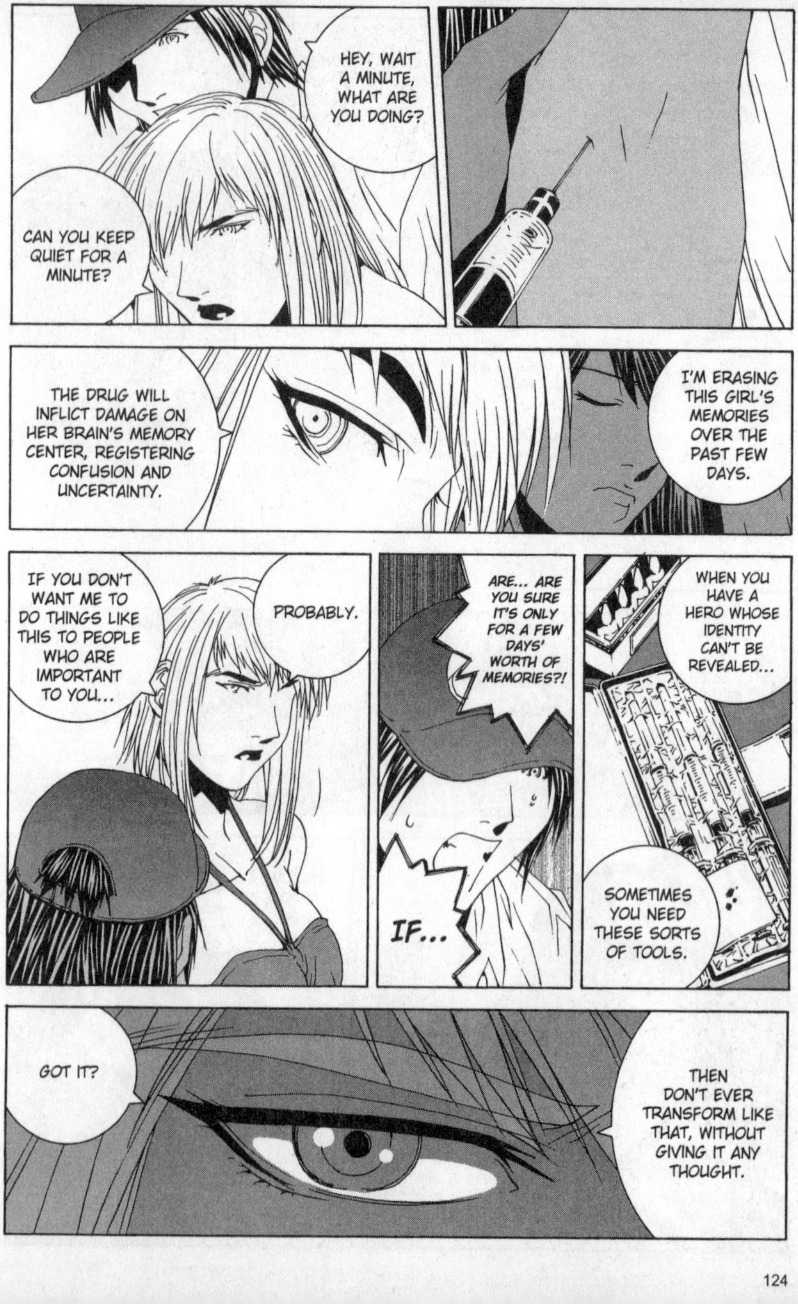
HEY, WAIT A MINUTE, WHAT ARE YOU DOING?
CAN YOU KEEP QUIET FOR A MINUTE?
I'M ERASING THIS GIRL'S MEMORIES OVER THE PAST FEW DAYS.
THE DRUG WILL INFLICT DAMAGE ON HER BRAIN'S MEMORY CENTER, REGISTERING CONFUSION AND UNCERTAINTY.
WHEN YOU HAVE A HERO WHOSE IDENTITY CAN'T BE REVEALED...
SOMETIMES YOU NEED THESE SORTS OF TOOLS.
ARE... ARE YOU SURE IT'S ONLY FOR A FEW DAYS' WORTH OF MEMORIES?!
IF...
PROBABLY.
IF YOU DON'T WANT ME TO DO THINGS LIKE THIS TO PEOPLE WHO ARE IMPORTANT TO YOU...
THEN DON'T EVER TRANSFORM LIKE THAT, WITHOUT GIVING IT ANY THOUGHT.
GOT IT?

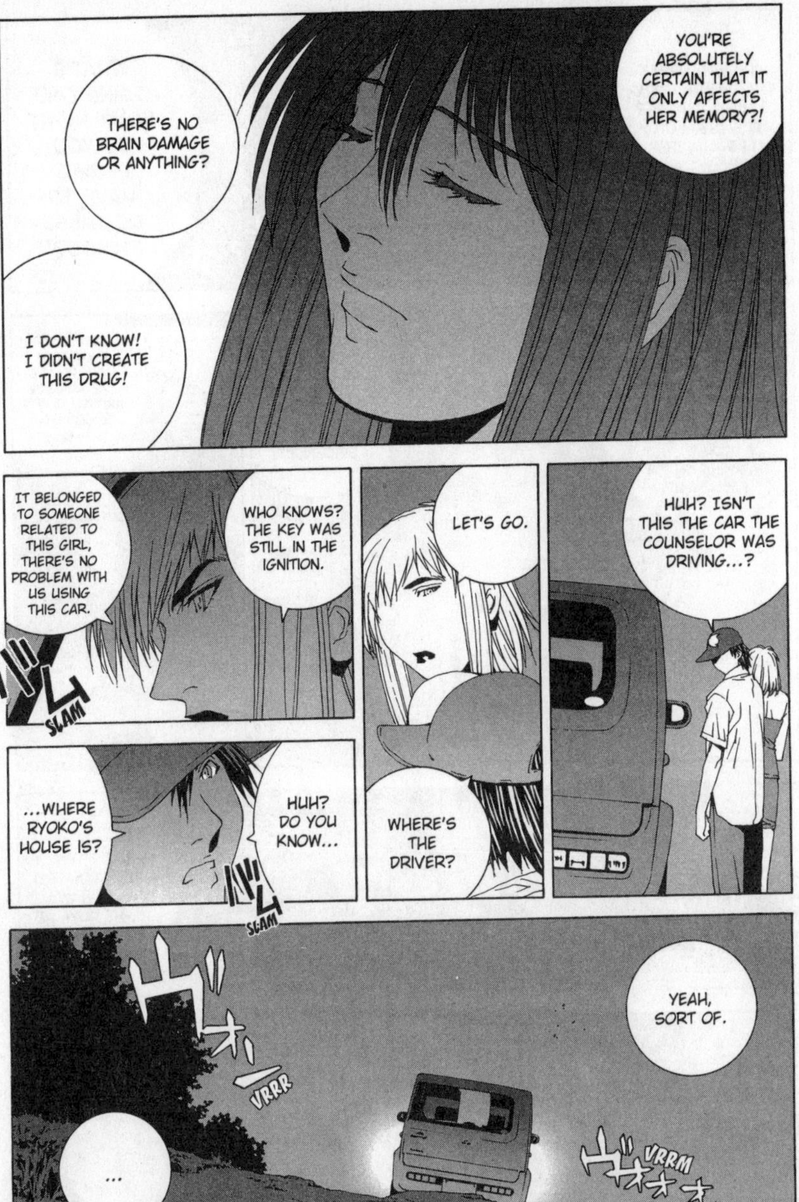
YOU'RE ABSOLUTELY CERTAIN THAT IT ONLY AFFECTS HER MEMORY?!
THERE'S NO BRAIN DAMAGE OR ANYTHING?
I DON'T KNOW! I DIDN'T CREATE THIS DRUG!
HUH? ISN'T THIS THE CAR THE COUNSELOR WAS DRIVING...?
LET'S GO.
WHERE'S THE DRIVER?
WHO KNOWS? THE KEY WAS STILL IN THE IGNITION.
IT BELONGED TO SOMEONE RELATED TO THIS GIRL, THERE'S NO PROBLEM WITH US USING THIS CAR.
SLAM
HUH? DO YOU KNOW...
...WHERE RYOKO'S HOUSE IS?
SLAM
YEAH, SORT OF.
VRRM
VRRR
...

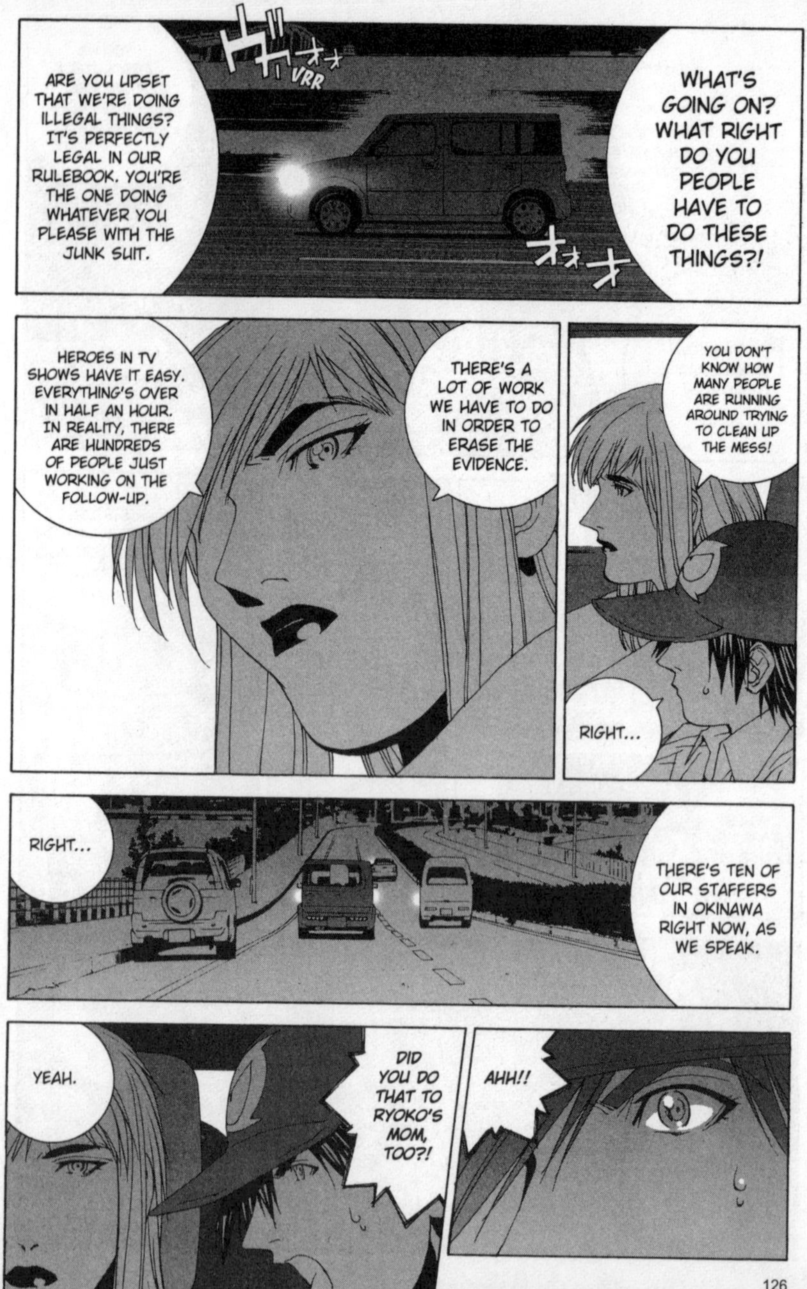
VRR
WHAT'S GOING ON? WHAT RIGHT DO YOU PEOPLE HAVE TO DO THESE THINGS?!
ARE YOU UPSET THAT WE'RE DOING ILLEGAL THINGS? IT'S PERFECTLY LEGAL IN OUR RULEBOOK. YOU'RE THE ONE DOING WHATEVER YOU PLEASE WITH THE JUNK SUIT.
YOU DON'T KNOW HOW MANY PEOPLE ARE RUNNING AROUND TRYING TO CLEAN UP THE MESS!
RIGHT...
THERE'S A LOT OF WORK WE HAVE TO DO IN ORDER TO ERASE THE EVIDENCE.
HEROES IN TV SHOWS HAVE IT EASY. EVERYTHING'S OVER IN HALF AN HOUR. IN REALITY, THERE ARE HUNDREDS OF PEOPLE JUST WORKING ON THE FOLLOW-UP.
THERE'S TEN OF OUR STAFFERS IN OKINAWA RIGHT NOW, AS WE SPEAK.
RIGHT...
AHH!!
DID YOU DO THAT TO RYOKO'S MOM, TOO?!
YEAH.

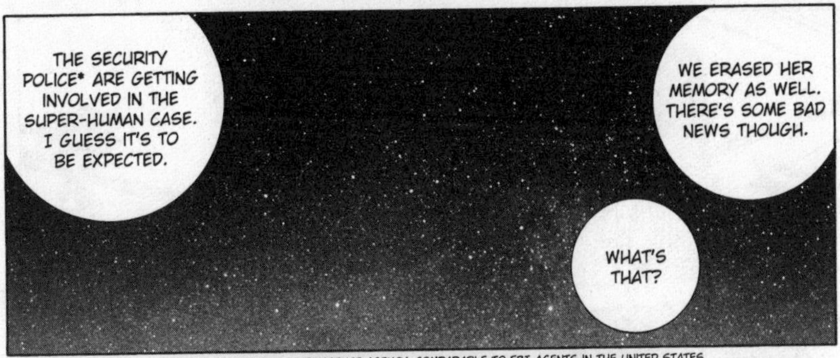
WE ERASED HER MEMORY AS WELL. THERE'S SOME BAD NEWS THOUGH.
WHAT'S THAT?
THE SECURITY POLICE* ARE GETTING INVOLVED IN THE SUPER-HUMAN CASE. I GUESS IT'S TO BE EXPECTED.

*OFFICERS WHO WORK IN THE PUBLIC SECURITY INTELLIGENCE AGENCY, COMPARABLE TO FBI AGENTS IN THE UNITED STATES

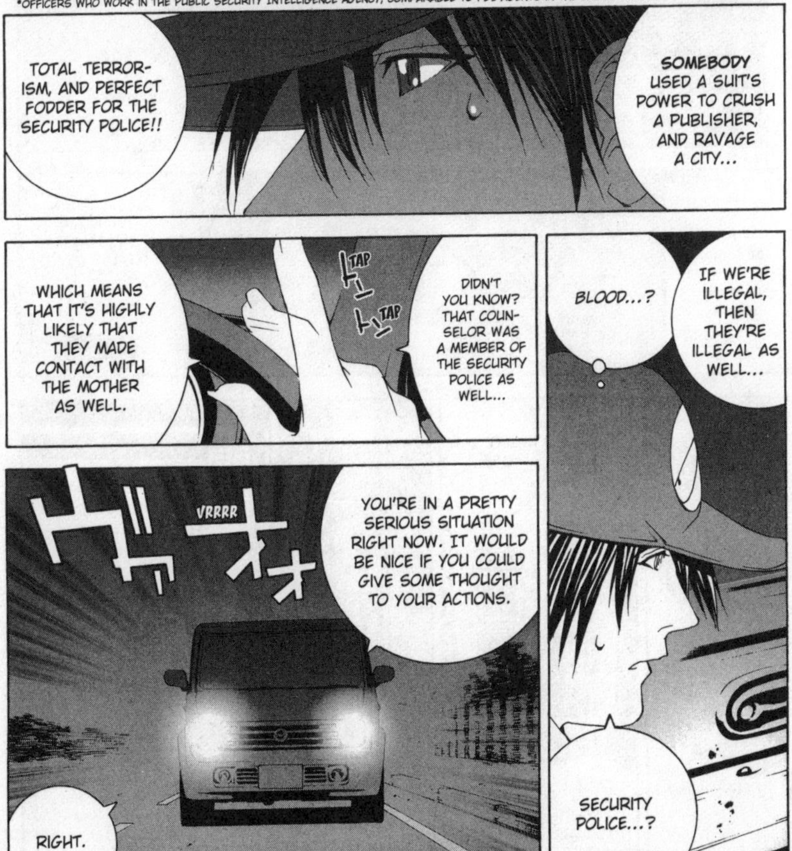
SOMEBODY USED A SUIT'S POWER TO CRUSH A PUBLISHER, AND RAVAGE A CITY...
TOTAL TERRORISM, AND PERFECT FODDER FOR THE SECURITY POLICE!!
IF WE'RE ILLEGAL, THEN THEY'RE ILLEGAL AS WELL...
BLOOD...?
SECURITY POLICE...?
DIDN'T YOU KNOW? THAT COUNSELOR WAS A MEMBER OF THE SECURITY POLICE AS WELL...
TAP
TAP
WHICH MEANS THAT IT'S HIGHLY LIKELY THAT THEY MADE CONTACT WITH THE MOTHER AS WELL.
YOU'RE IN A PRETTY SERIOUS SITUATION RIGHT NOW. IT WOULD BE NICE IF YOU COULD GIVE SOME THOUGHT TO YOUR ACTIONS.
VRRRR
RIGHT.

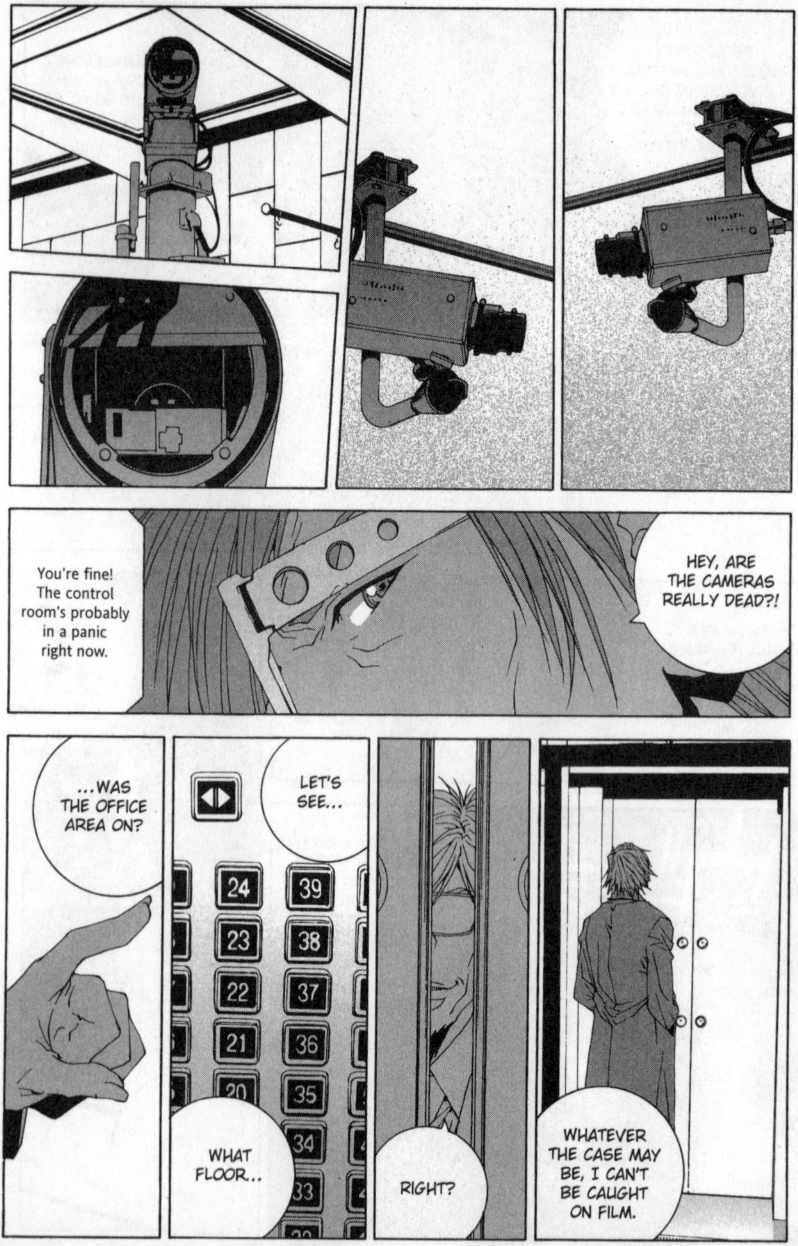
HEY, ARE THE CAMERAS REALLY DEAD?!
You're fine! The control room's probably in a panic right now.
WHATEVER THE CASE MAY BE, I CAN'T BE CAUGHT ON FILM.
RIGHT?
LET'S SEE...
WHAT FLOOR...
...WAS THE OFFICE AREA ON?

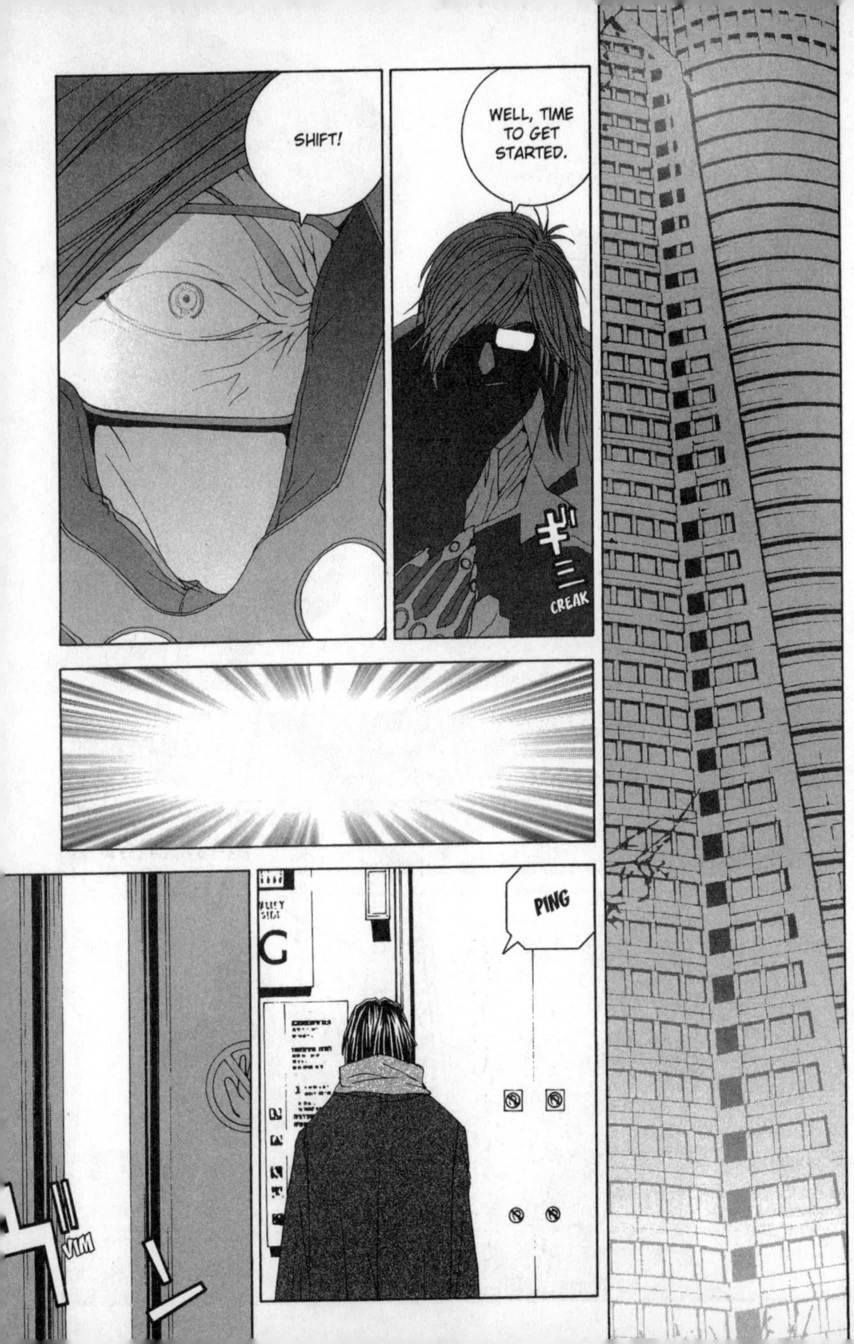
WELL, TIME TO GET STARTED.
CREAK
SHIFT!
PING
VIM

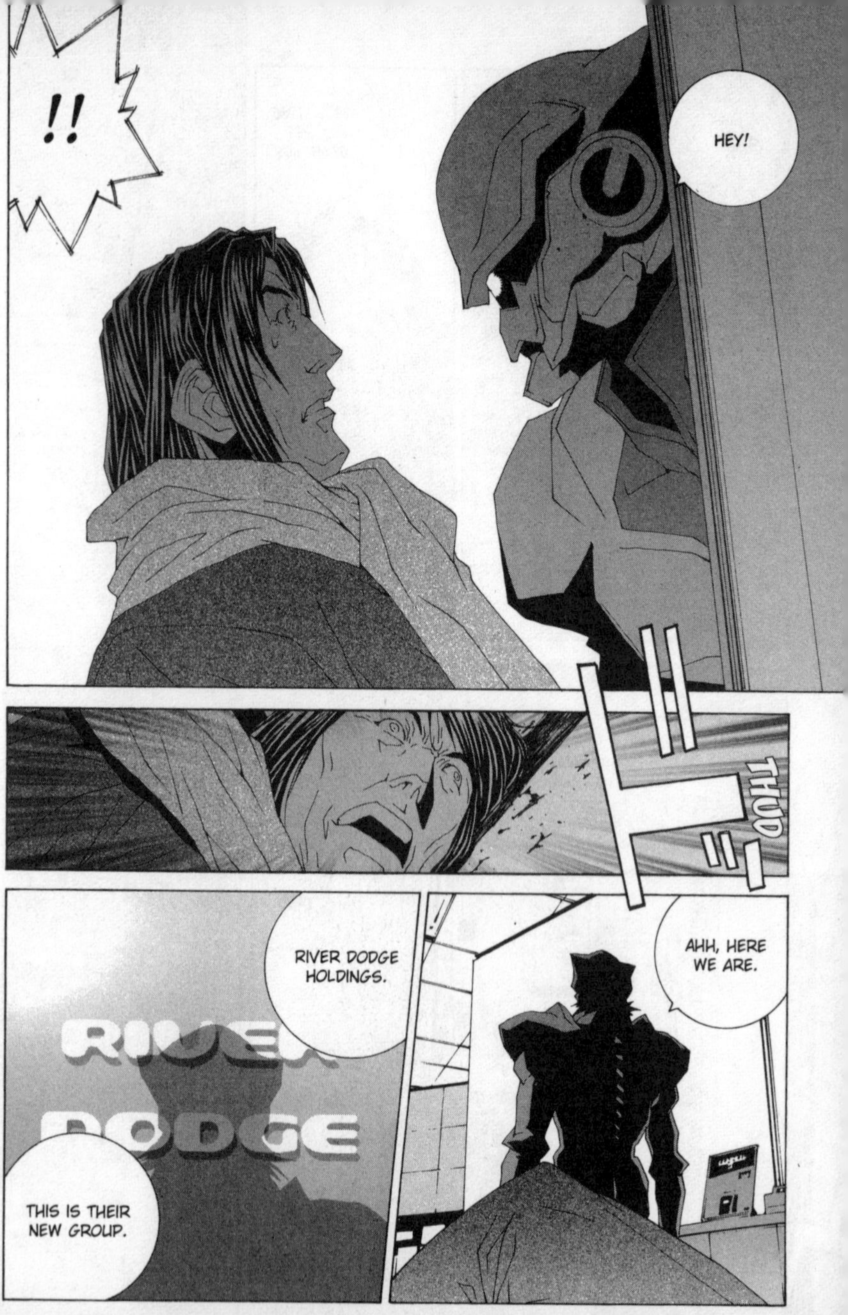
HEY!
!!
THUD
AHH, HERE WE ARE.
RIVER DODGE HOLDINGS.
DODGE
THIS IS THEIR NEW GROUP.

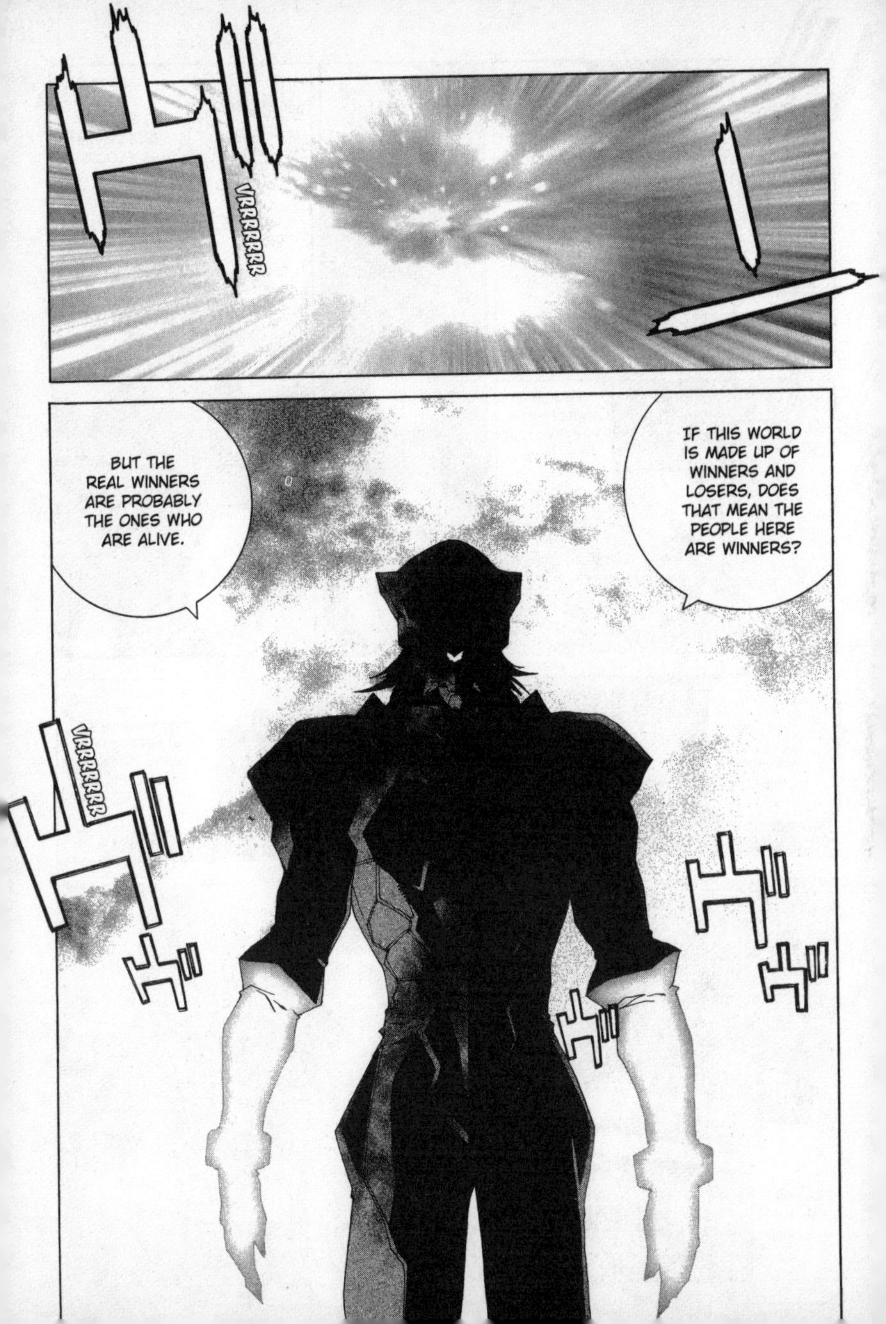
VRRRRRRR
IF THIS WORLD IS MADE UP OF WINNERS AND LOSERS, DOES THAT MEAN THE PEOPLE HERE ARE WINNERS?
BUT THE REAL WINNERS ARE PROBABLY THE ONES WHO ARE ALIVE.
VRRRRRRR

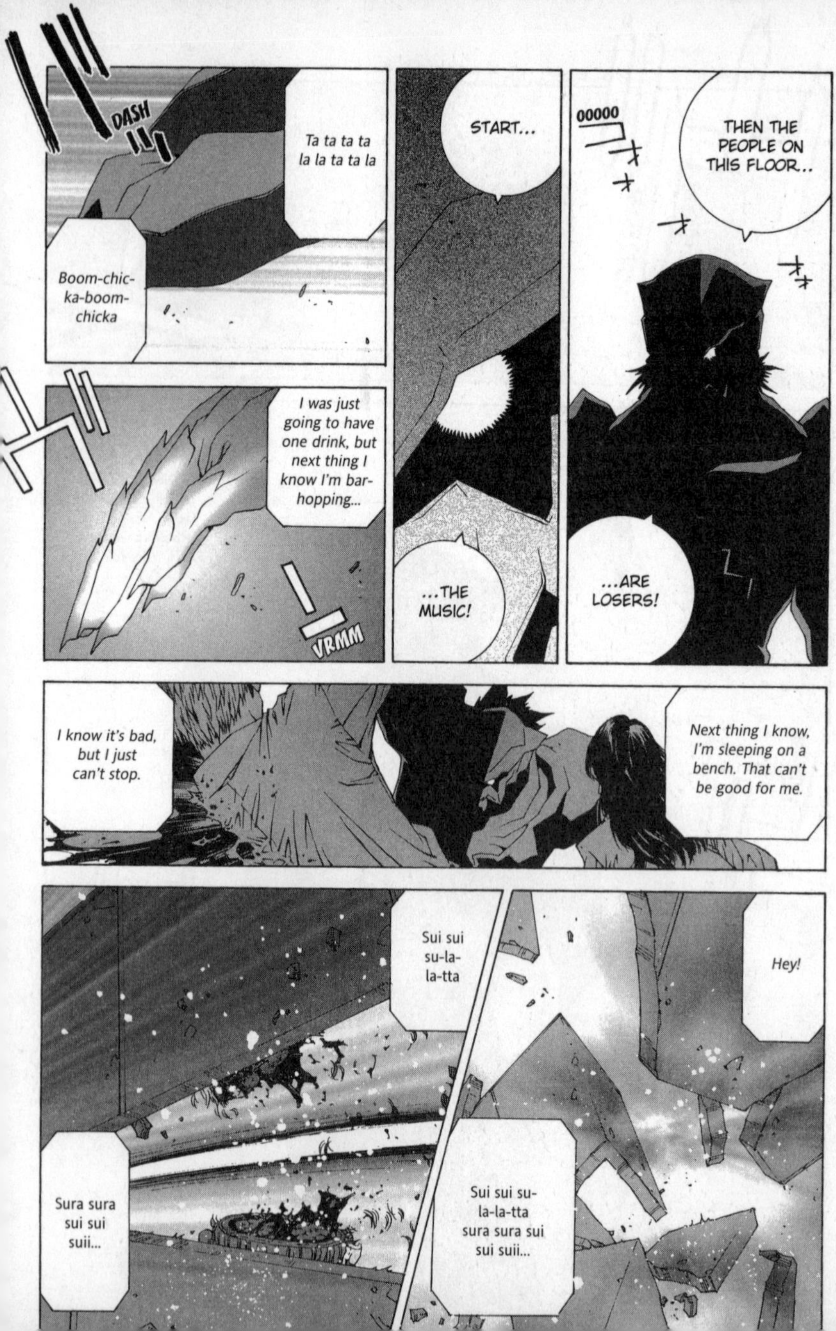
OOOOO
THEN THE PEOPLE ON THIS FLOOR...
...ARE LOSERS!
START...
...THE MUSIC!
DASH
Ta ta ta ta la la ta ta la
Boom-chic-ka-boom-chicka
I was just going to have one drink, but next thing I know I'm bar-hopping...
VRMM
Next thing I know, I'm sleeping on a bench. That can't be good for me.
I know it's bad, but I just can't stop.
Hey!
Sui sui su-la-la-tta
Sui sui su-la-la-tta sura sura sui sui suii...
Sura sura sui sui suii...

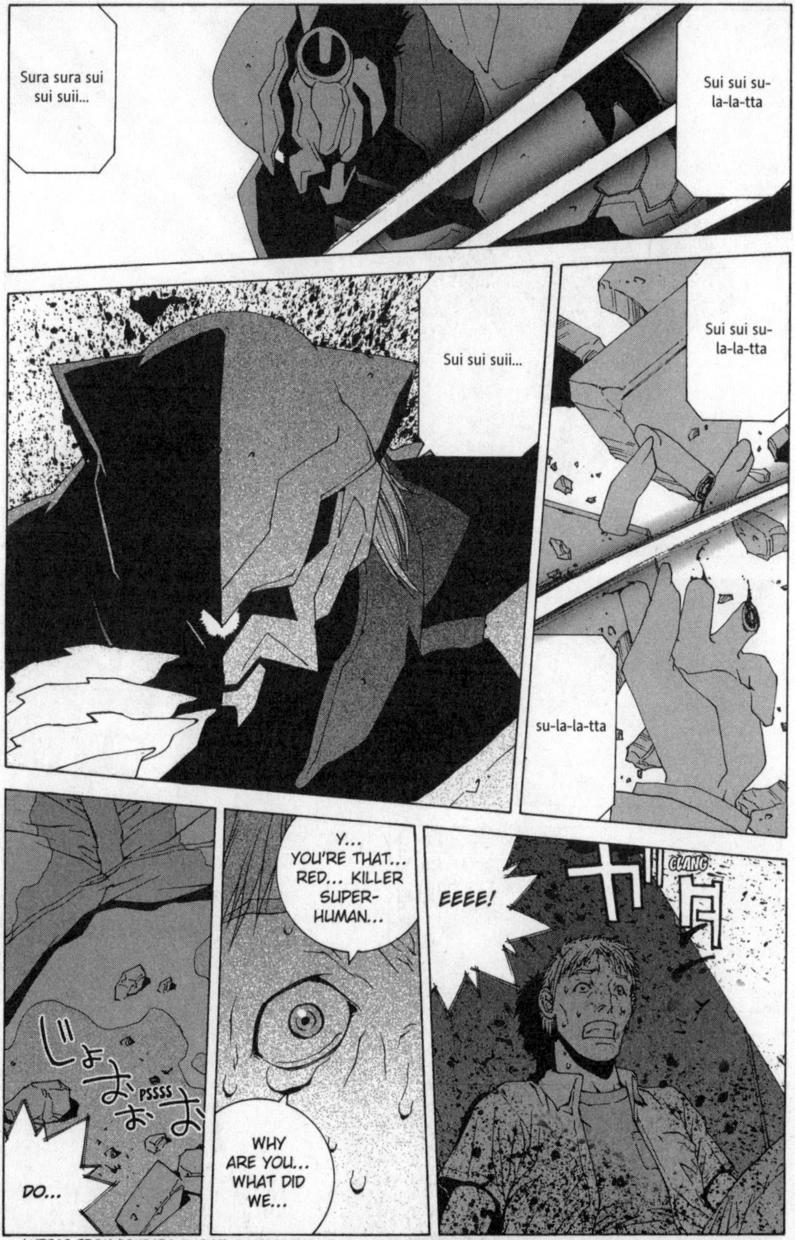

Sui sui su-la-la-tta
Sura sura sui sui suii...
Sui sui su-la-la-tta
su-la-la-tta
Sui sui suii...
CLANG
EEEE!
Y... YOU'RE THAT... RED... KILLER SUPER-HUMAN...
WHY ARE YOU... WHAT DID WE...
PSSSS
DO...

LYRICS FROM "SUDARA BUSHI" BY HITOSHI UEKI. LYRCS BY YUKIO AOSHIMA, COMPOSED BY HIROAKI HAGIWARA

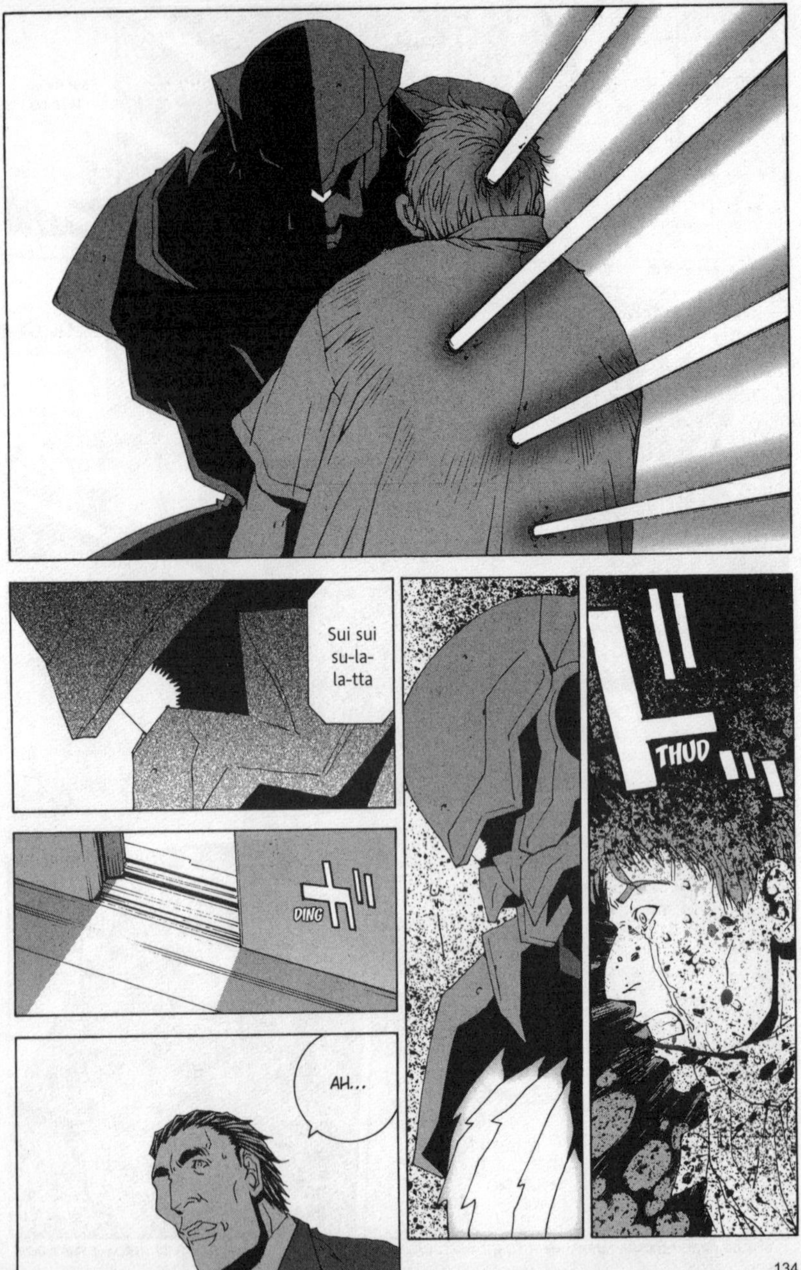
THUD
Sui sui su-la-la-tta
DING
AH...

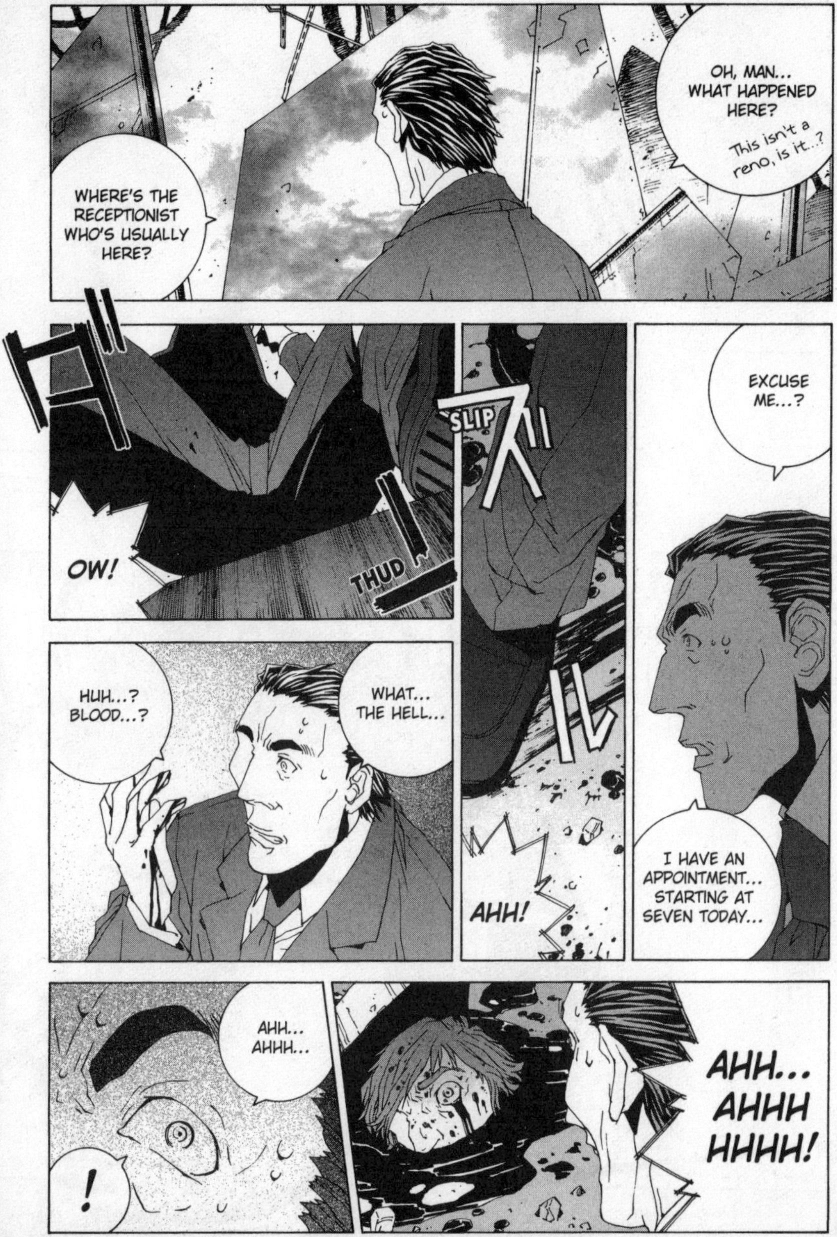
OH, MAN... WHAT HAPPENED HERE?
This isn't a reno, is it...?
WHERE'S THE RECEPTIONIST WHO'S USUALLY HERE?
EXCUSE ME...?
I HAVE AN APPOINTMENT... STARTING AT SEVEN TODAY...
SLIP
AHH!
OW!
THUD
WHAT... THE HELL...
HUH...? BLOOD...?
AHH... AHHH HHHH!
AHH... AHHH...
!

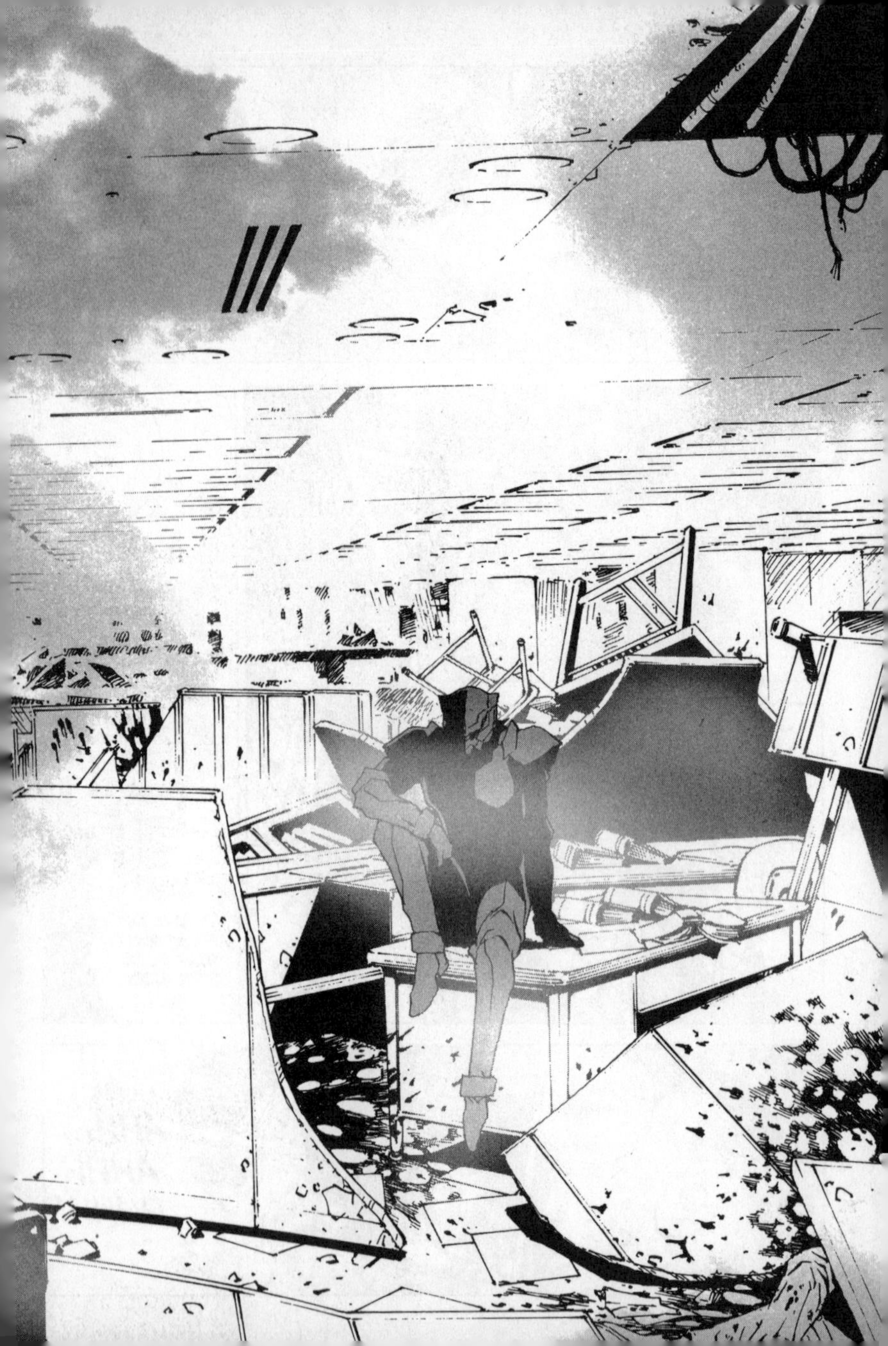

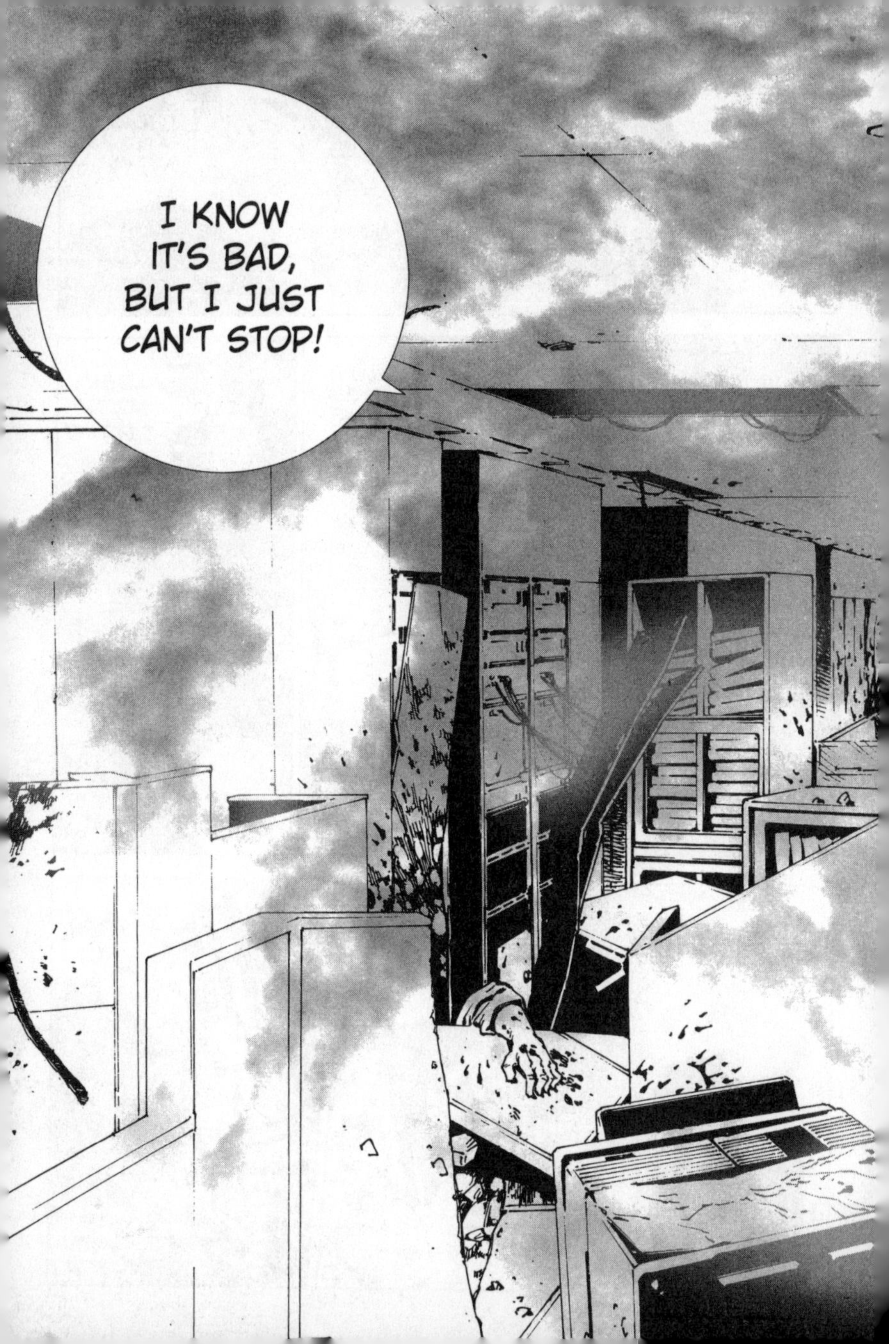
I KNOW IT'S BAD, BUT I JUST CAN'T STOP!

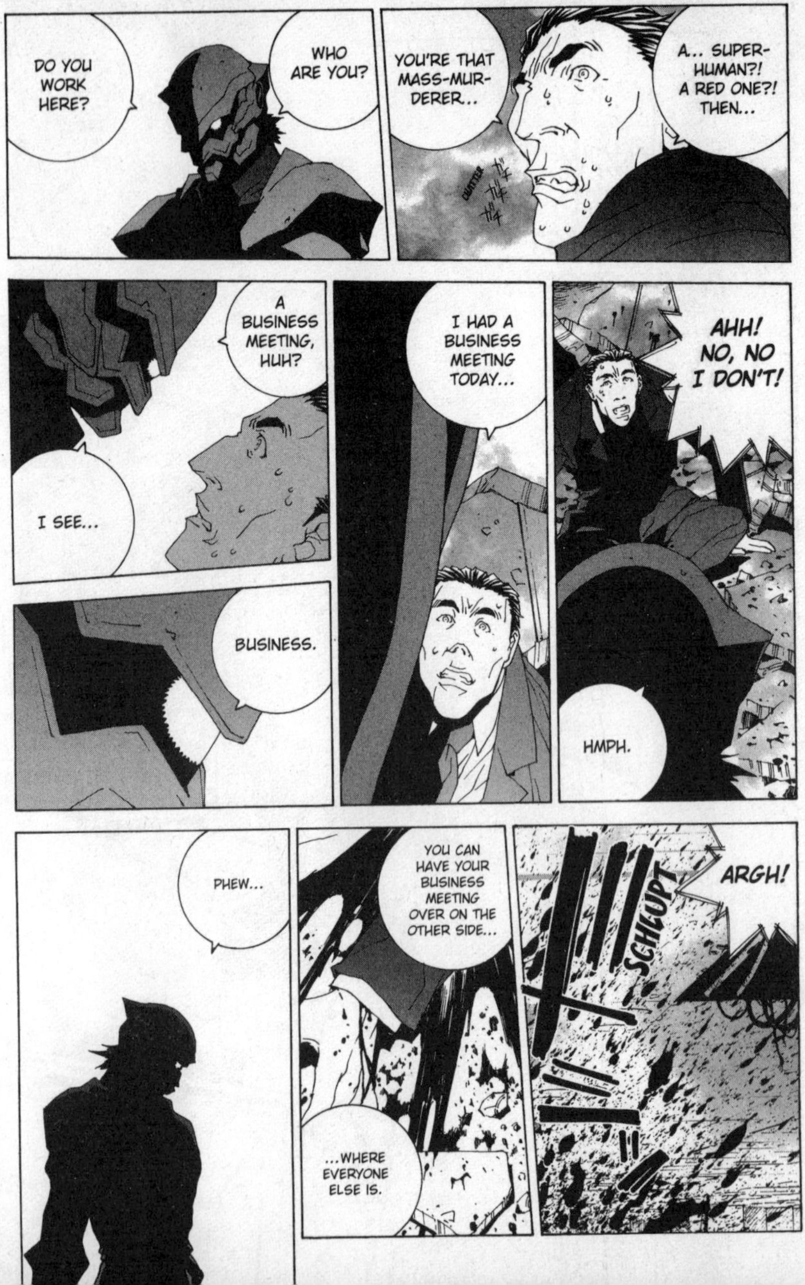
A... SUPER-HUMAN?! A RED ONE?! THEN...
YOU'RE THAT MASS-MURDERER...
CLATTER
WHO ARE YOU?
DO YOU WORK HERE?
AHH! NO, NO I DON'T!
HMPH.
I HAD A BUSINESS MEETING TODAY...
A BUSINESS MEETING, HUH?
I SEE...
BUSINESS.
ARGH!
SCHLUPT
YOU CAN HAVE YOUR BUSINESS MEETING OVER ON THE OTHER SIDE...
...WHERE EVERYONE ELSE IS.
PHEW...

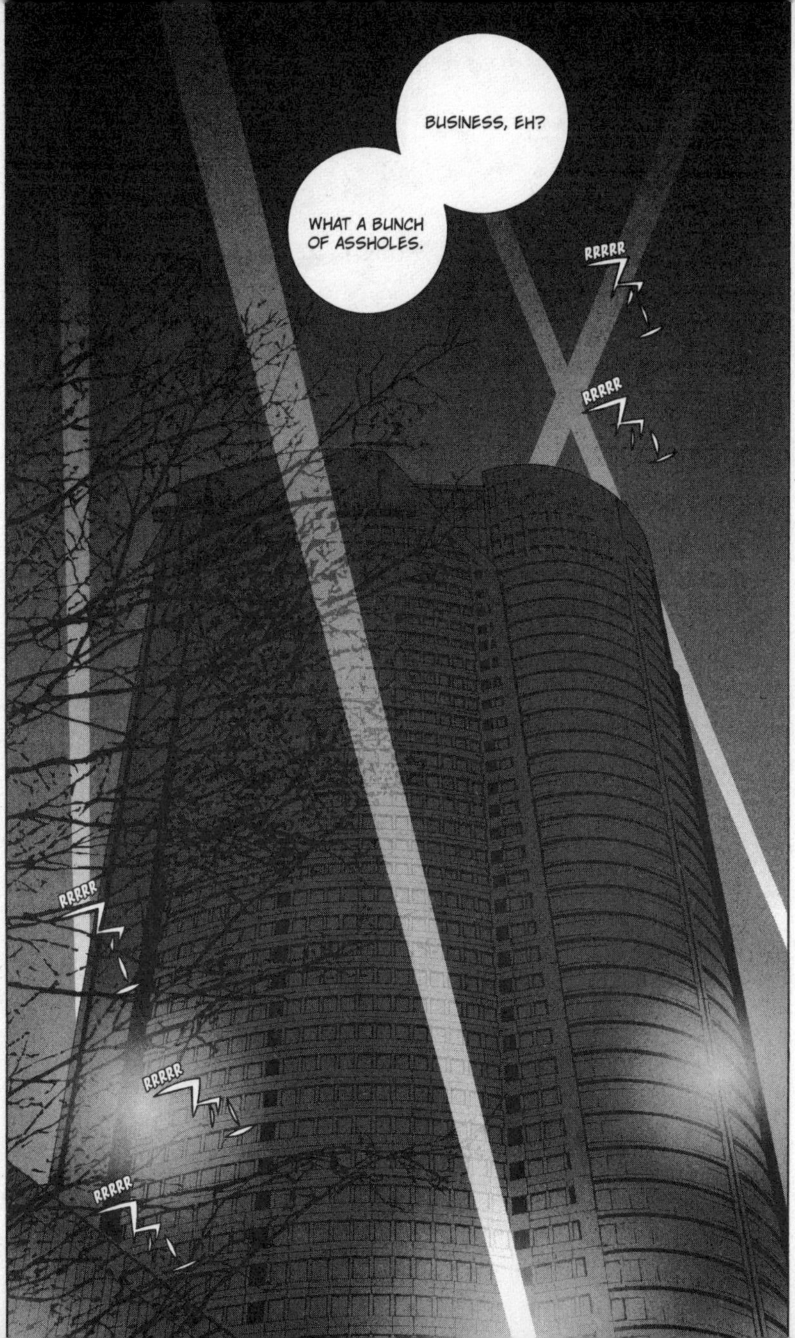
BUSINESS, EH?
WHAT A BUNCH OF ASSHOLES.
RRRRR
RRRRR
RRRRR
RRRRR
RRRRR

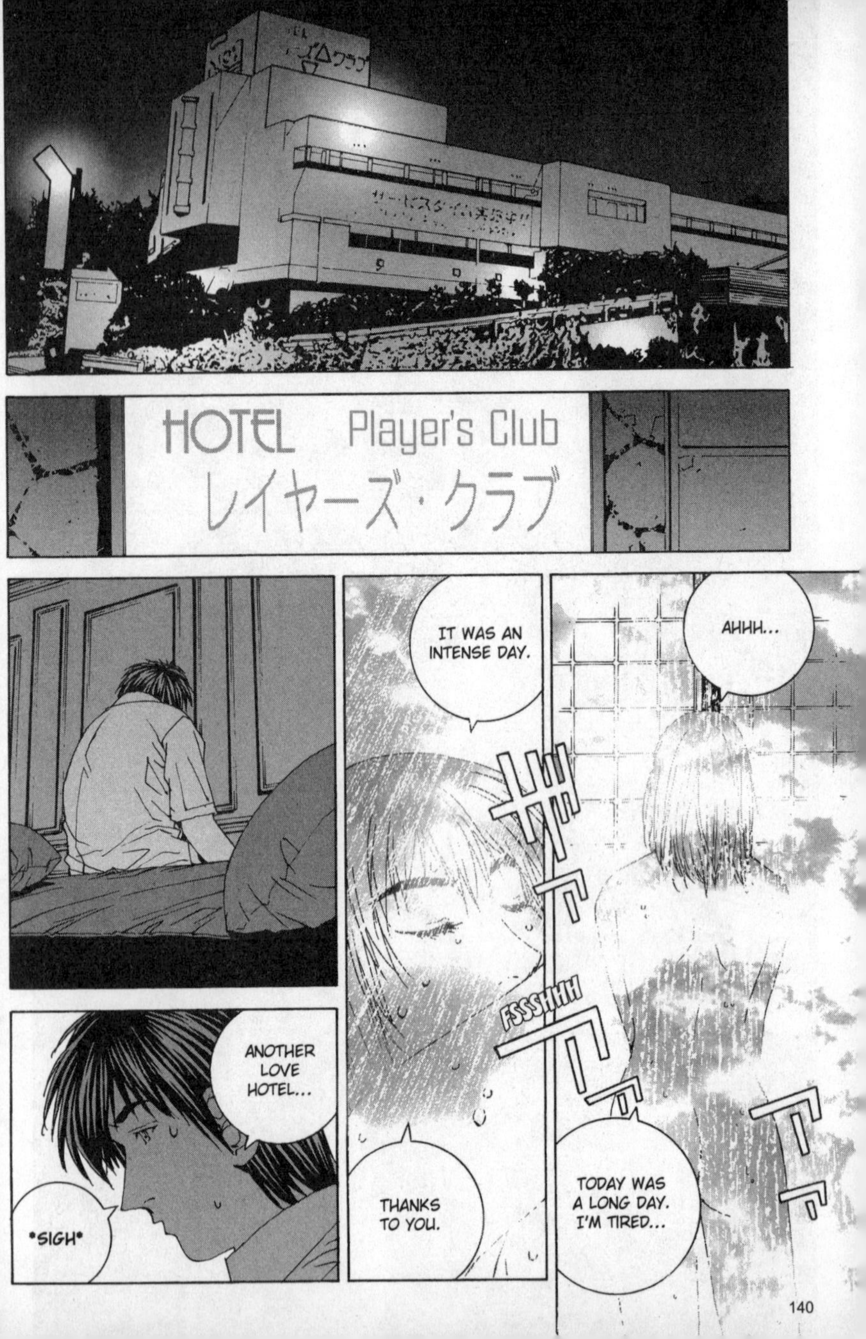
HOTEL Player's Club
レイヤーズ・クラブ
AHHH...
FSSSHHH
TODAY WAS A LONG DAY. I'M TIRED...
IT WAS AN INTENSE DAY.
THANKS TO YOU.
ANOTHER LOVE HOTEL...
SIGH

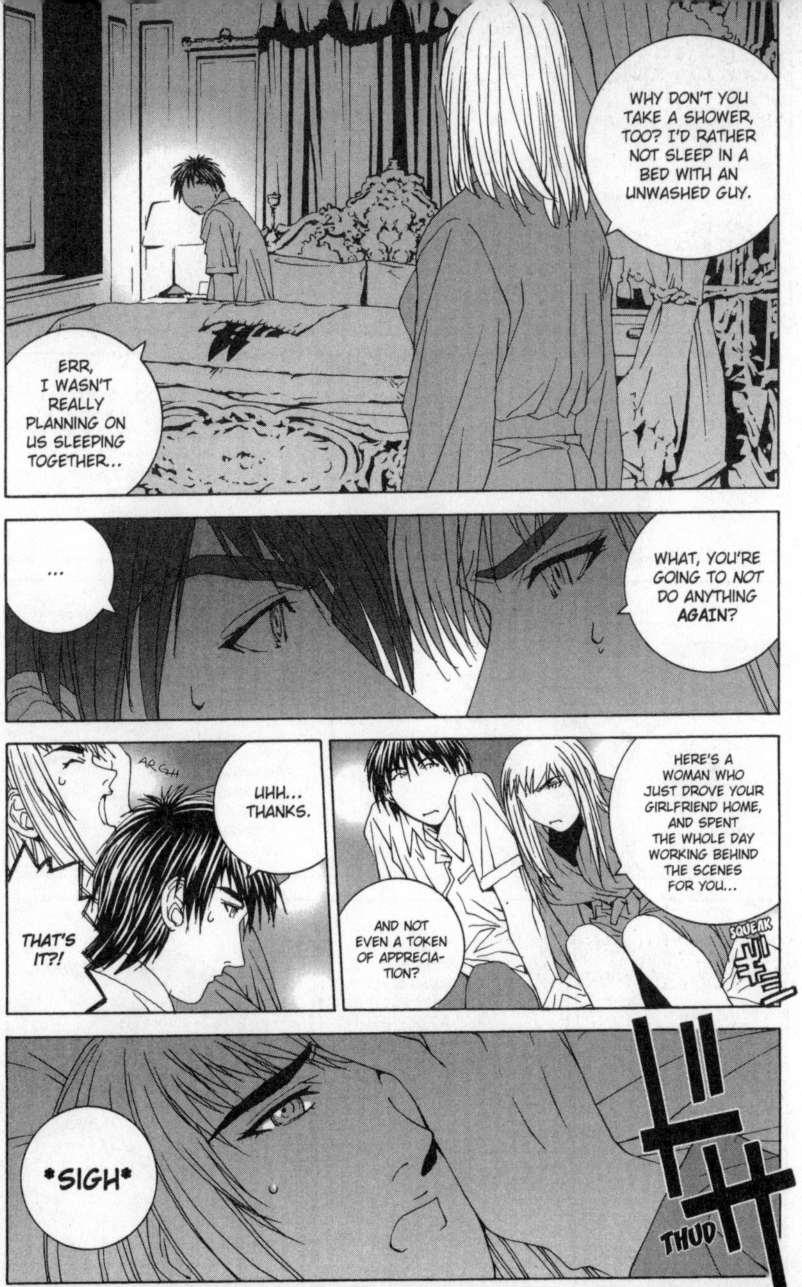
WHY DON'T YOU TAKE A SHOWER, TOO? I'D RATHER NOT SLEEP IN A BED WITH AN UNWASHED GUY.
ERR, I WASN'T REALLY PLANNING ON US SLEEPING TOGETHER...
WHAT, YOU'RE GOING TO NOT DO ANYTHING AGAIN?
...
HERE'S A WOMAN WHO JUST DROVE YOUR GIRLFRIEND HOME, AND SPENT THE WHOLE DAY WORKING BEHIND THE SCENES FOR YOU...
AND NOT EVEN A TOKEN OF APPRECIA-TION?
SQUEAK
UHH... THANKS.
ARGH
THAT'S IT?!
THUD
SIGH

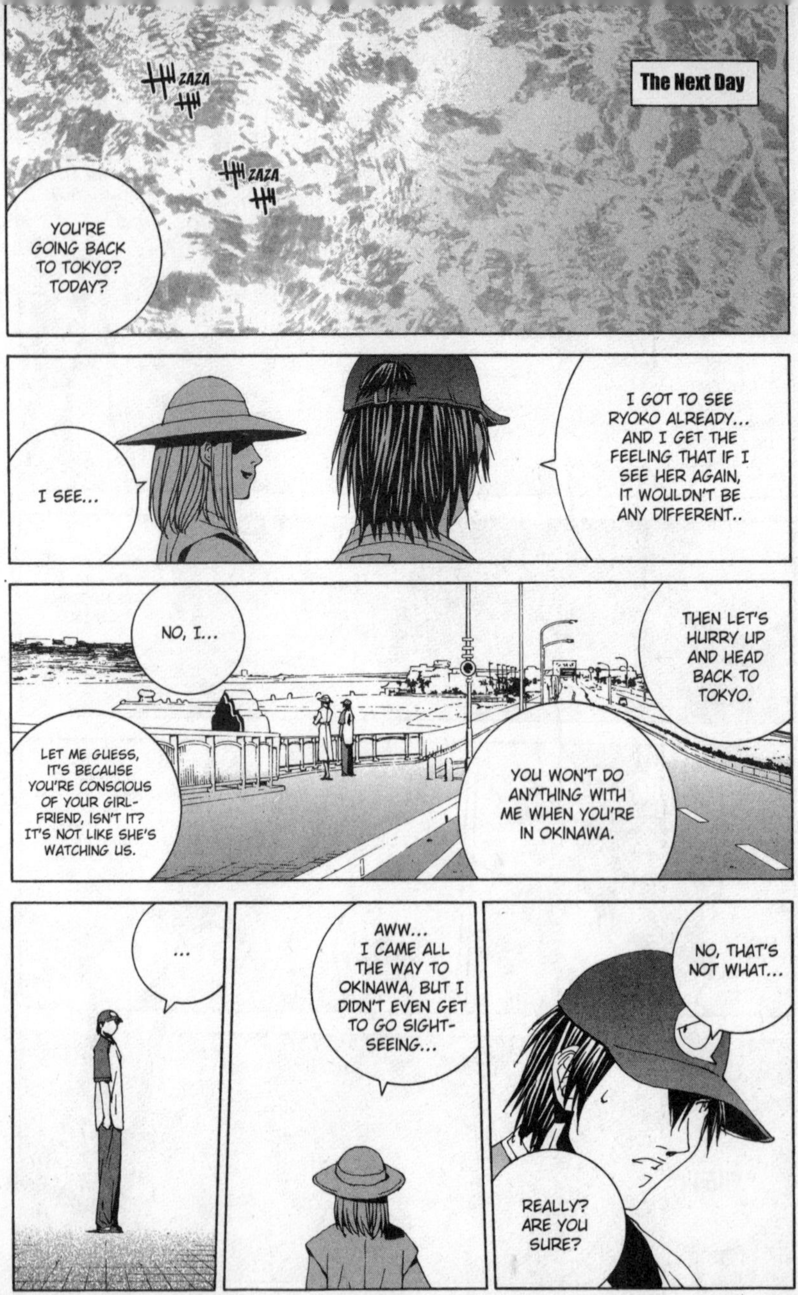
The Next Day
ZAZA
ZAZA
YOU'RE GOING BACK TO TOKYO? TODAY?
I GOT TO SEE RYOKO ALREADY... AND I GET THE FEELING THAT IF I SEE HER AGAIN, IT WOULDN'T BE ANY DIFFERENT..
I SEE...
THEN LET'S HURRY UP AND HEAD BACK TO TOKYO.
NO, I...
YOU WON'T DO ANYTHING WITH ME WHEN YOU'RE IN OKINAWA.
LET ME GUESS, IT'S BECAUSE YOU'RE CONSCIOUS OF YOUR GIRL-FRIEND, ISN'T IT? IT'S NOT LIKE SHE'S WATCHING US.
NO, THAT'S NOT WHAT...
REALLY? ARE YOU SURE?
AWW... I CAME ALL THE WAY TO OKINAWA, BUT I DIDN'T EVEN GET TO GO SIGHT-SEEING...
...

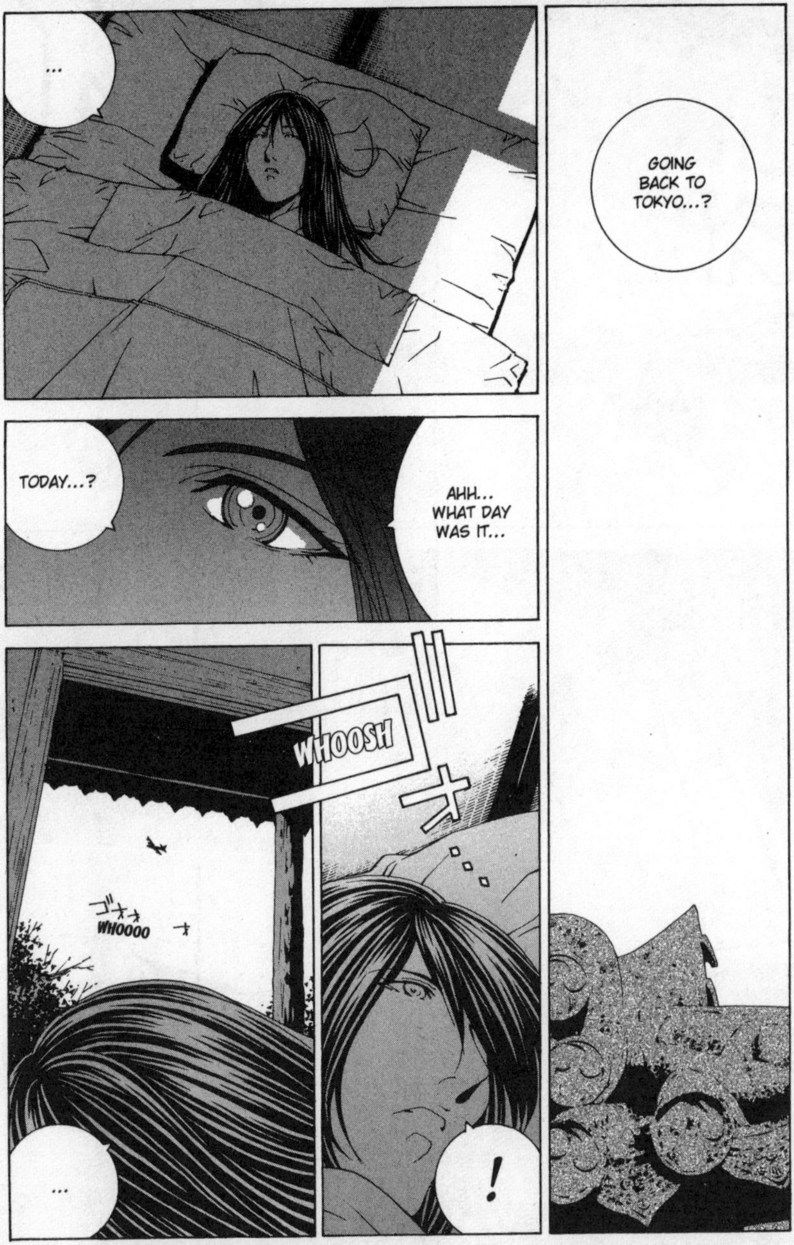
GOING BACK TO TOKYO...?
...
AHH... WHAT DAY WAS IT...
TODAY...?
WHOOSH
!
WHOOOO
...

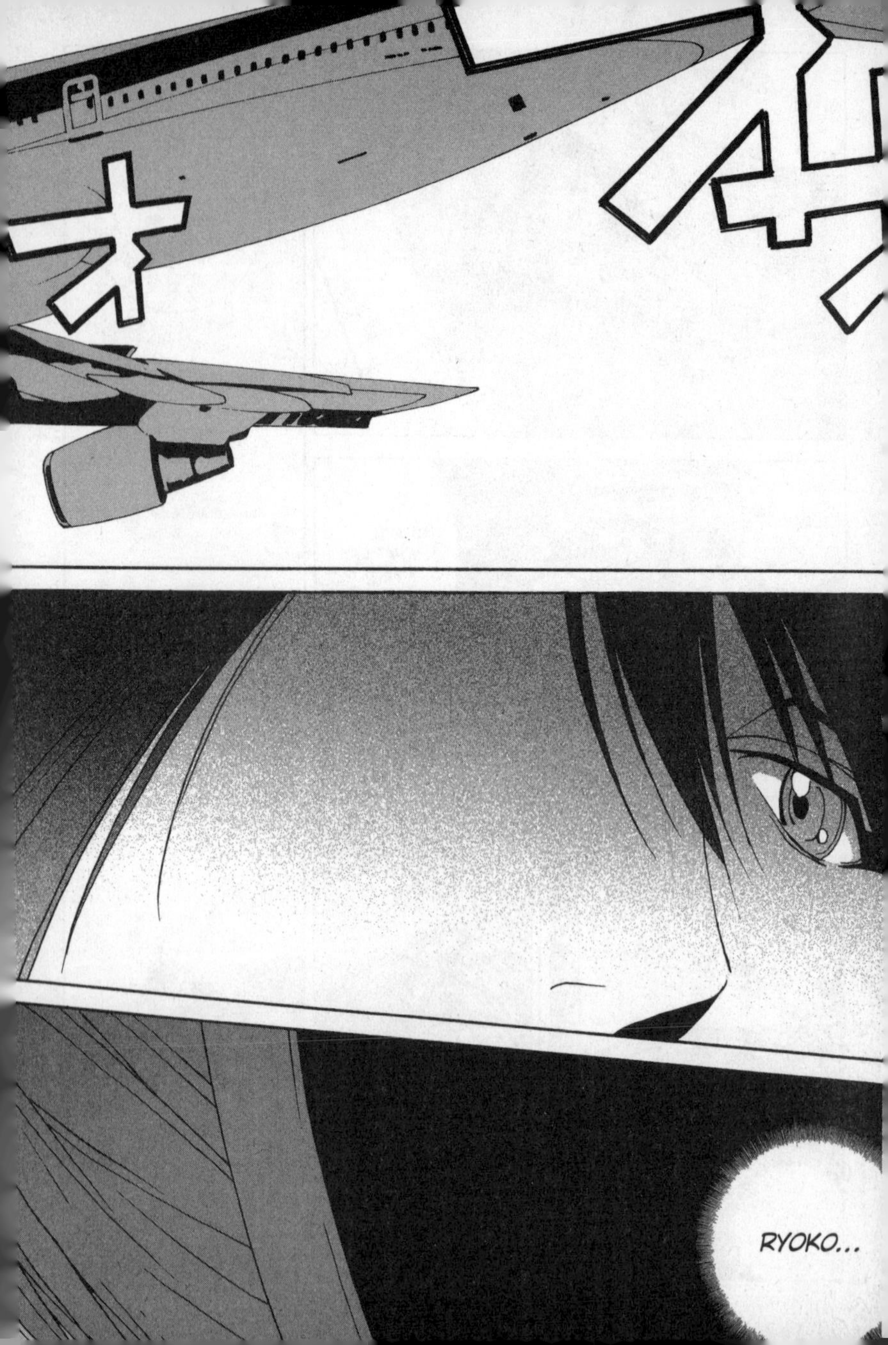
RYOKO...

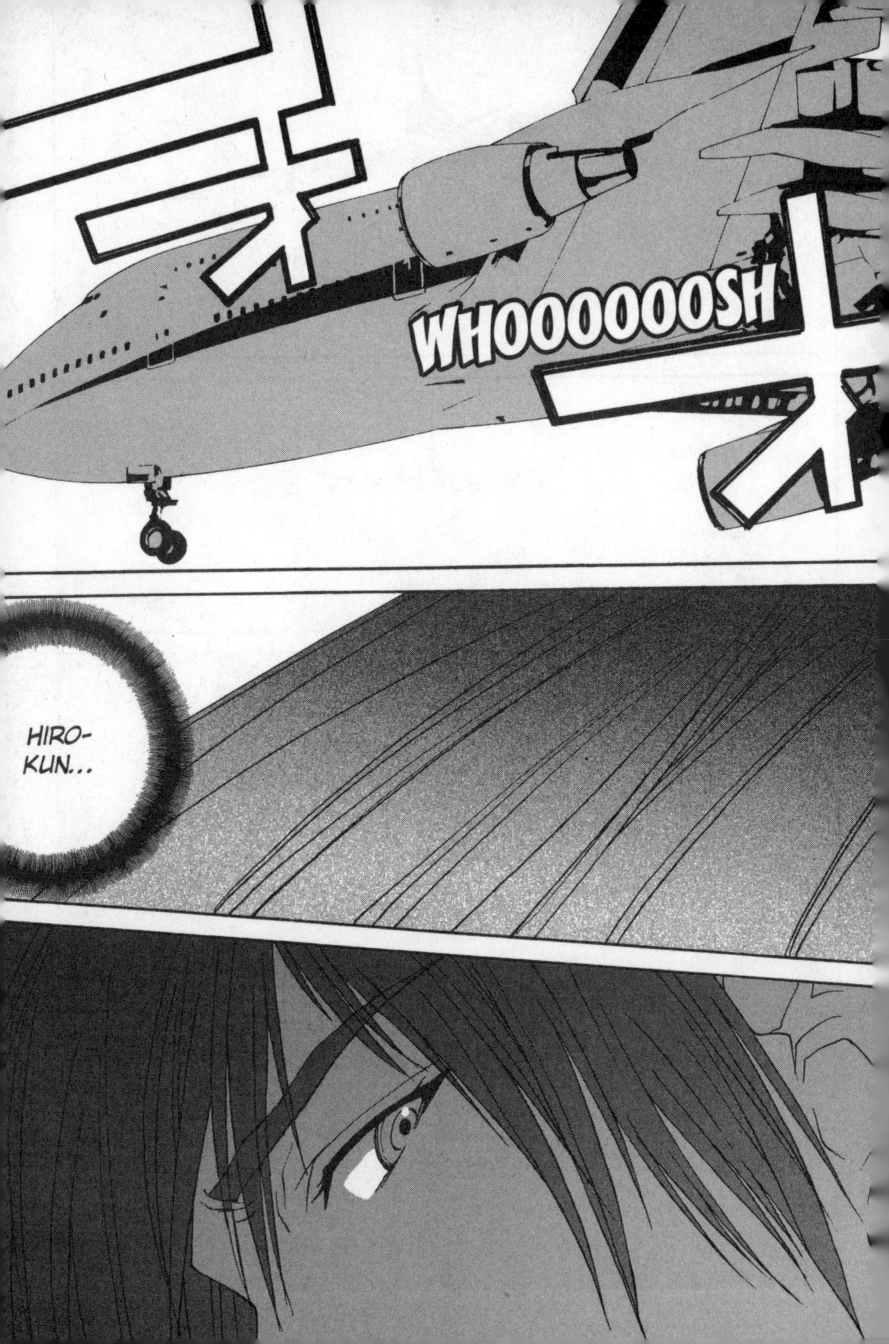
WHOOOOOOSH
HIRO-KUN...

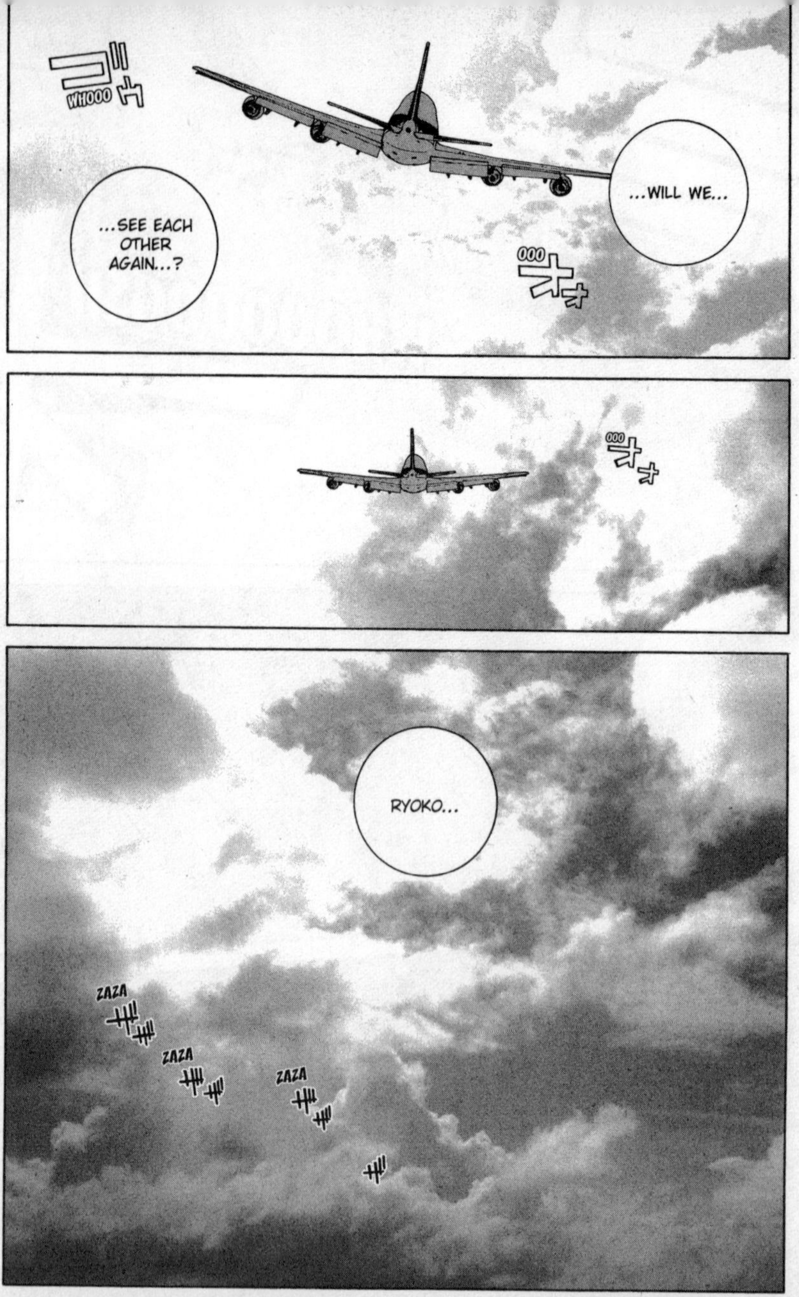
WHOOO
...WILL WE...
...SEE EACH OTHER AGAIN...?
OOO
OOO
RYOKO...
ZAZA
ZAZA
ZAZA

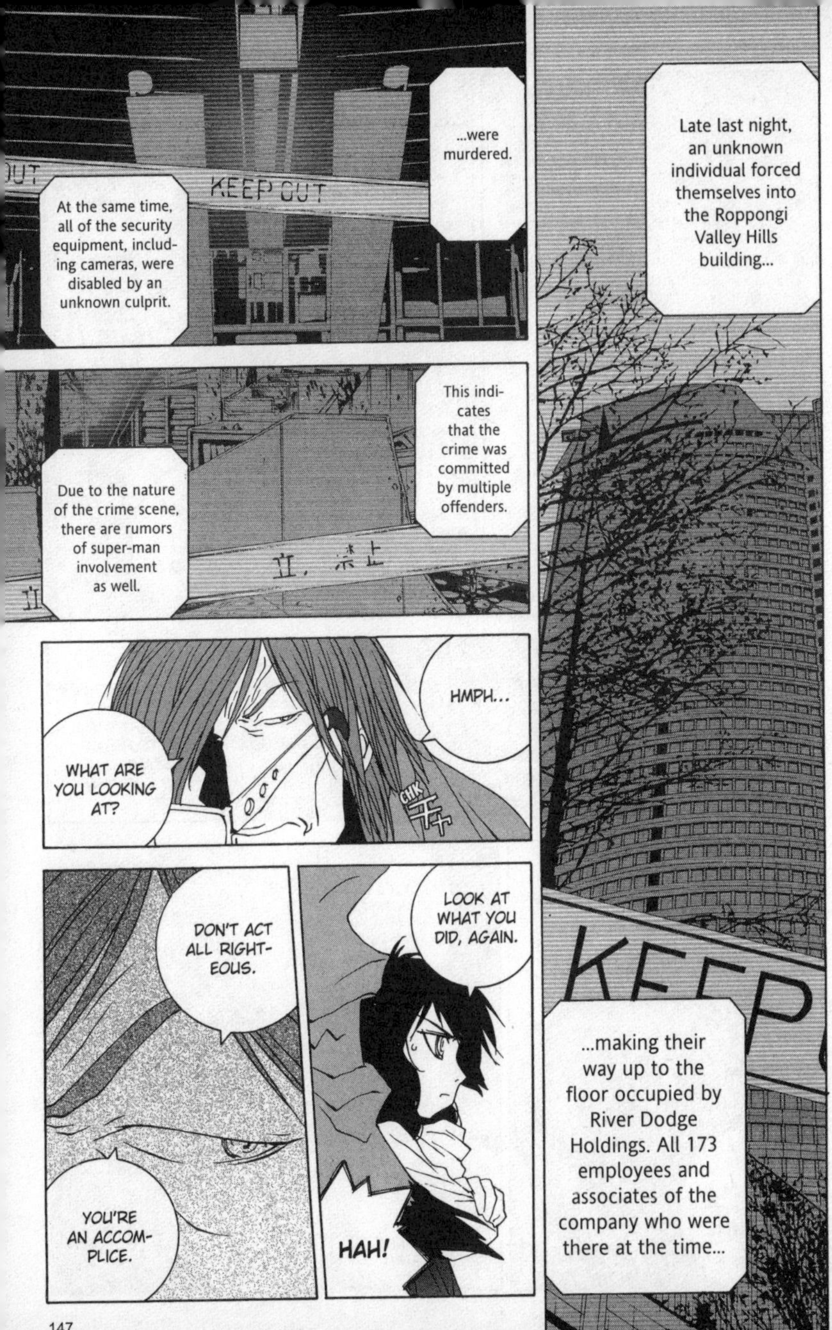
Late last night, an unknown individual forced themselves into the Roppongi Valley Hills building...
KEEP
...making their way up to the floor occupied by River Dodge Holdings. All 173 employees and associates of the company who were there at the time...
...were murdered.
KEEP OUT
At the same time, all of the security equipment, including cameras, were disabled by an unknown culprit.
This indicates that the crime was committed by multiple offenders.
Due to the nature of the crime scene, there are rumors of super-man involvement as well.
HMPH...
CHK
WHAT ARE YOU LOOKING AT?
LOOK AT WHAT YOU DID, AGAIN.
HAH!
DON'T ACT ALL RIGHTEOUS.
YOU'RE AN ACCOMPLICE.

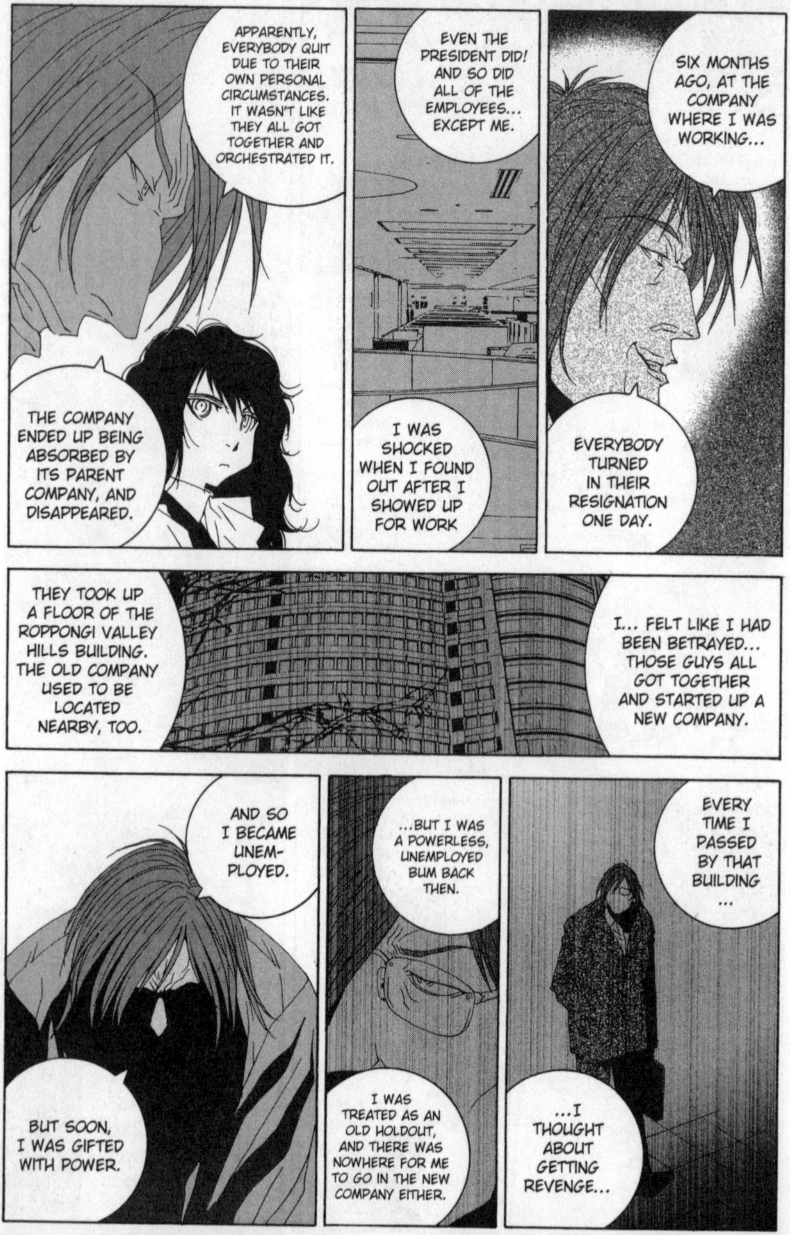
SIX MONTHS AGO, AT THE COMPANY WHERE I WAS WORKING...
EVERYBODY TURNED IN THEIR RESIGNATION ONE DAY.
EVEN THE PRESIDENT DID! AND SO DID ALL OF THE EMPLOYEES... EXCEPT ME.
I WAS SHOCKED WHEN I FOUND OUT AFTER I SHOWED UP FOR WORK
APPARENTLY, EVERYBODY QUIT DUE TO THEIR OWN PERSONAL CIRCUMSTANCES. IT WASN'T LIKE THEY ALL GOT TOGETHER AND ORCHESTRATED IT.
THE COMPANY ENDED UP BEING ABSORBED BY ITS PARENT COMPANY, AND DISAPPEARED.
I... FELT LIKE I HAD BEEN BETRAYED... THOSE GUYS ALL GOT TOGETHER AND STARTED UP A NEW COMPANY.
THEY TOOK UP A FLOOR OF THE ROPPONGI VALLEY HILLS BUILDING. THE OLD COMPANY USED TO BE LOCATED NEARBY, TOO.
EVERY TIME I PASSED BY THAT BUILDING ...
...I THOUGHT ABOUT GETTING REVENGE...
...BUT I WAS A POWERLESS, UNEMPLOYED BUM BACK THEN.
I WAS TREATED AS AN OLD HOLDOUT, AND THERE WAS NOWHERE FOR ME TO GO IN THE NEW COMPANY EITHER.
AND SO I BECAME UNEMPLOYED.
BUT SOON, I WAS GIFTED WITH POWER.

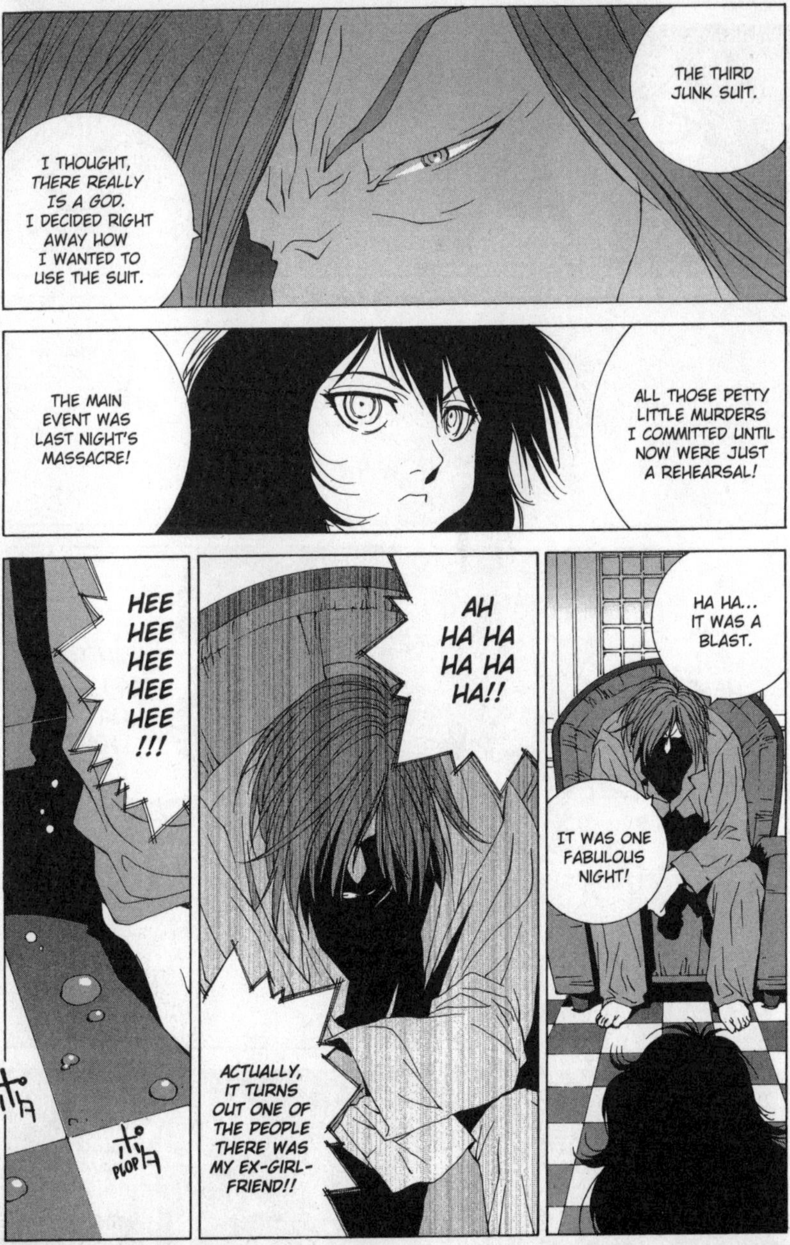
THE THIRD JUNK SUIT.
I THOUGHT, THERE REALLY IS A GOD. I DECIDED RIGHT AWAY HOW I WANTED TO USE THE SUIT.
ALL THOSE PETTY LITTLE MURDERS I COMMITTED UNTIL NOW WERE JUST A REHEARSAL!
THE MAIN EVENT WAS LAST NIGHT'S MASSACRE!
HA HA... IT WAS A BLAST.
IT WAS ONE FABULOUS NIGHT!
AH HA HA HA HA HA!!
ACTUALLY, IT TURNS OUT ONE OF THE PEOPLE THERE WAS MY EX-GIRL-FRIEND!!
HEE HEE HEE HEE HEE !!!
PLOP
PLOP

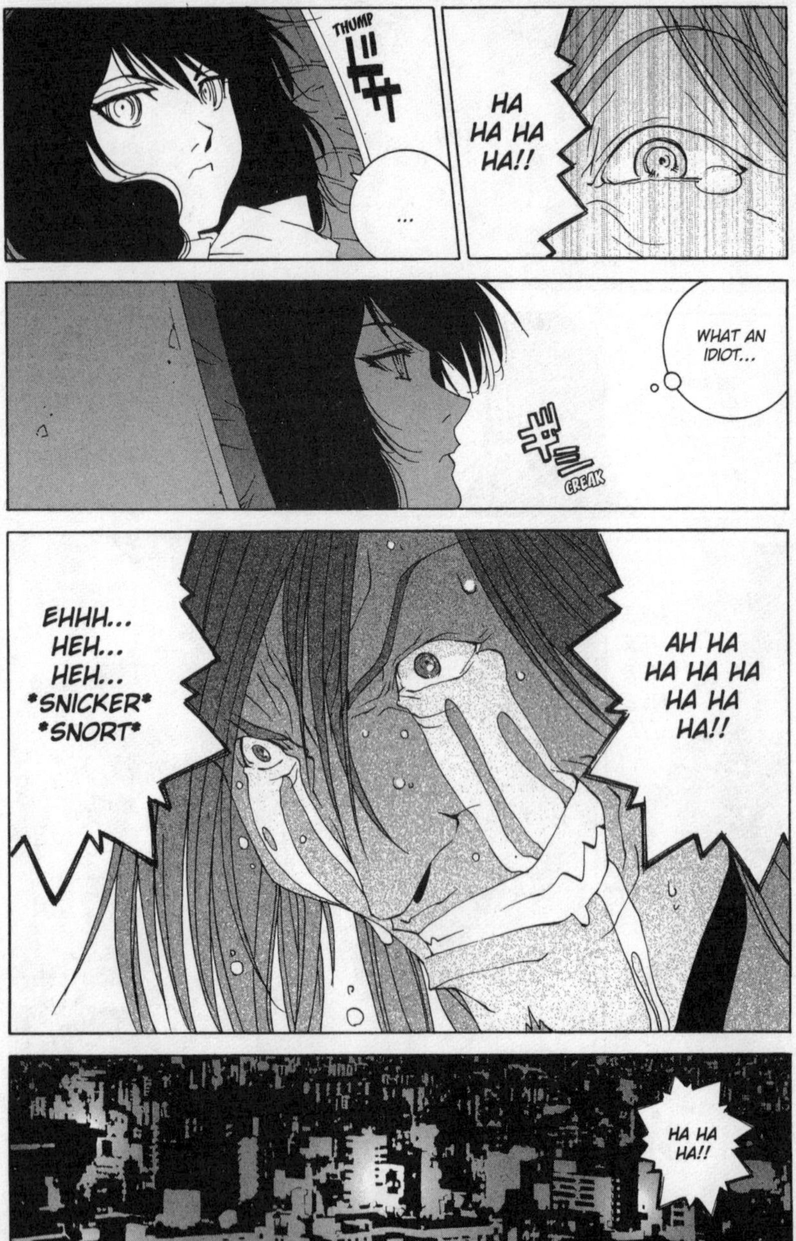
HA HA HA HA!!
THUMP
...
WHAT AN IDIOT...
CREAK
AH HA HA HA HA HA HA HA!!
EHHH... HEH... HEH... *SNICKER* *SNORT*
HA HA HA!!

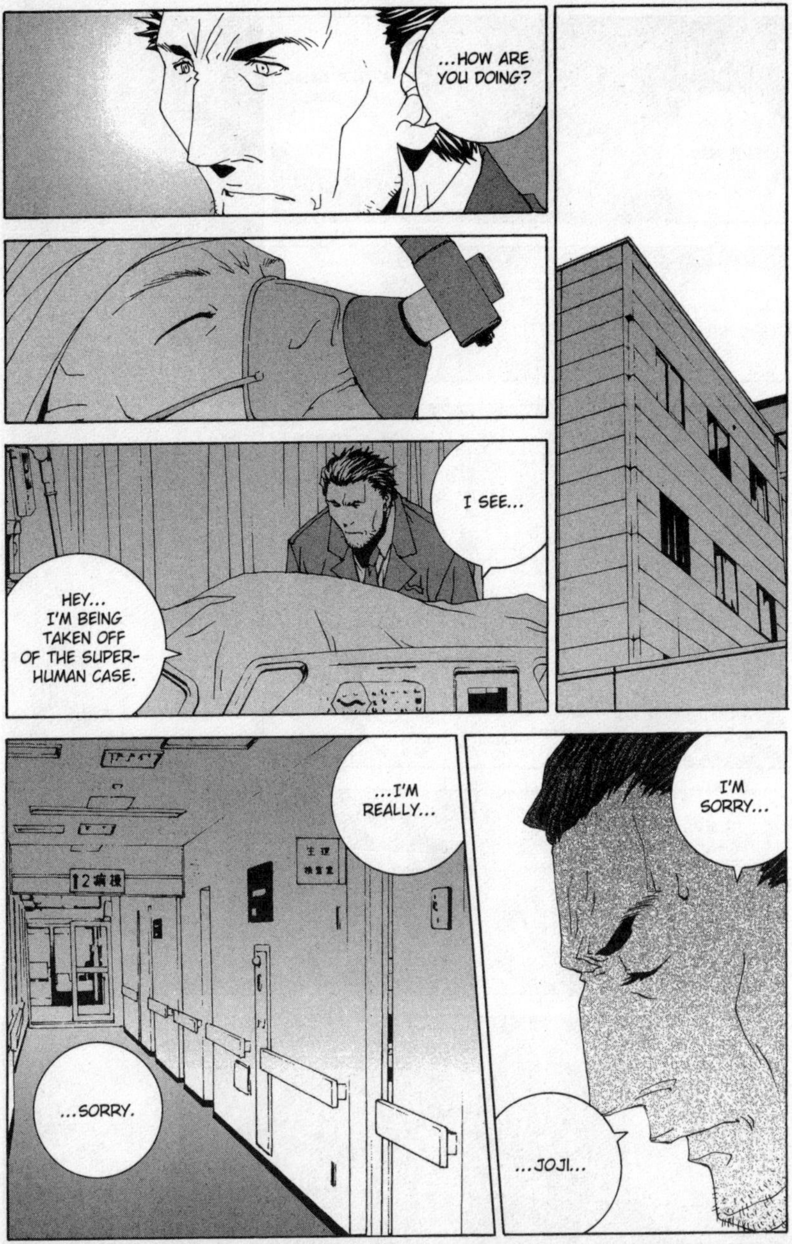
...HOW ARE YOU DOING?
I SEE...
HEY... I'M BEING TAKEN OFF OF THE SUPER-HUMAN CASE.
I'M SORRY...
...JOJI...
...I'M REALLY...
...SORRY.

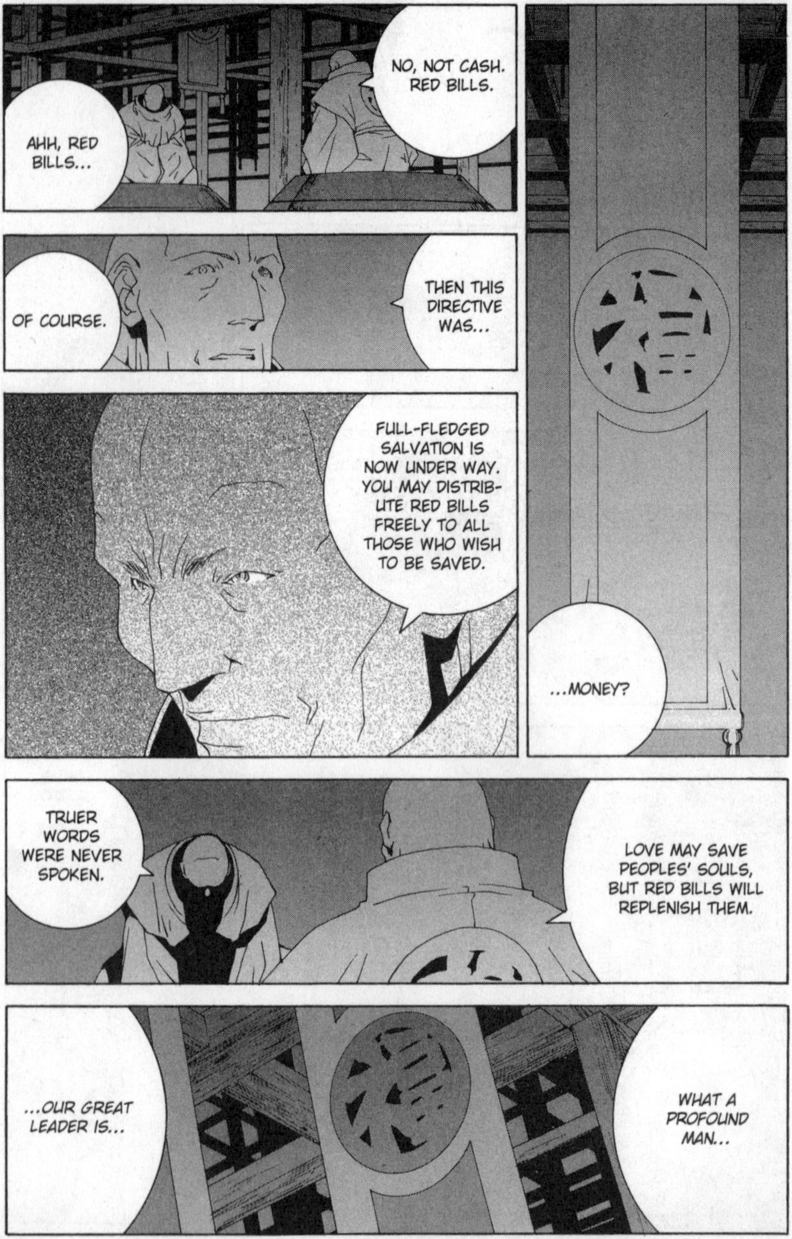

...MONEY?
NO, NOT CASH. RED BILLS.
AHH, RED BILLS...
THEN THIS DIRECTIVE WAS...
OF COURSE.
FULL-FLEDGED SALVATION IS NOW UNDER WAY. YOU MAY DISTRIBUTE RED BILLS FREELY TO ALL THOSE WHO WISH TO BE SAVED.
LOVE MAY SAVE PEOPLES' SOULS, BUT RED BILLS WILL REPLENISH THEM.
TRUER WORDS WERE NEVER SPOKEN.
WHAT A PROFOUND MAN...
...OUR GREAT LEADER IS...

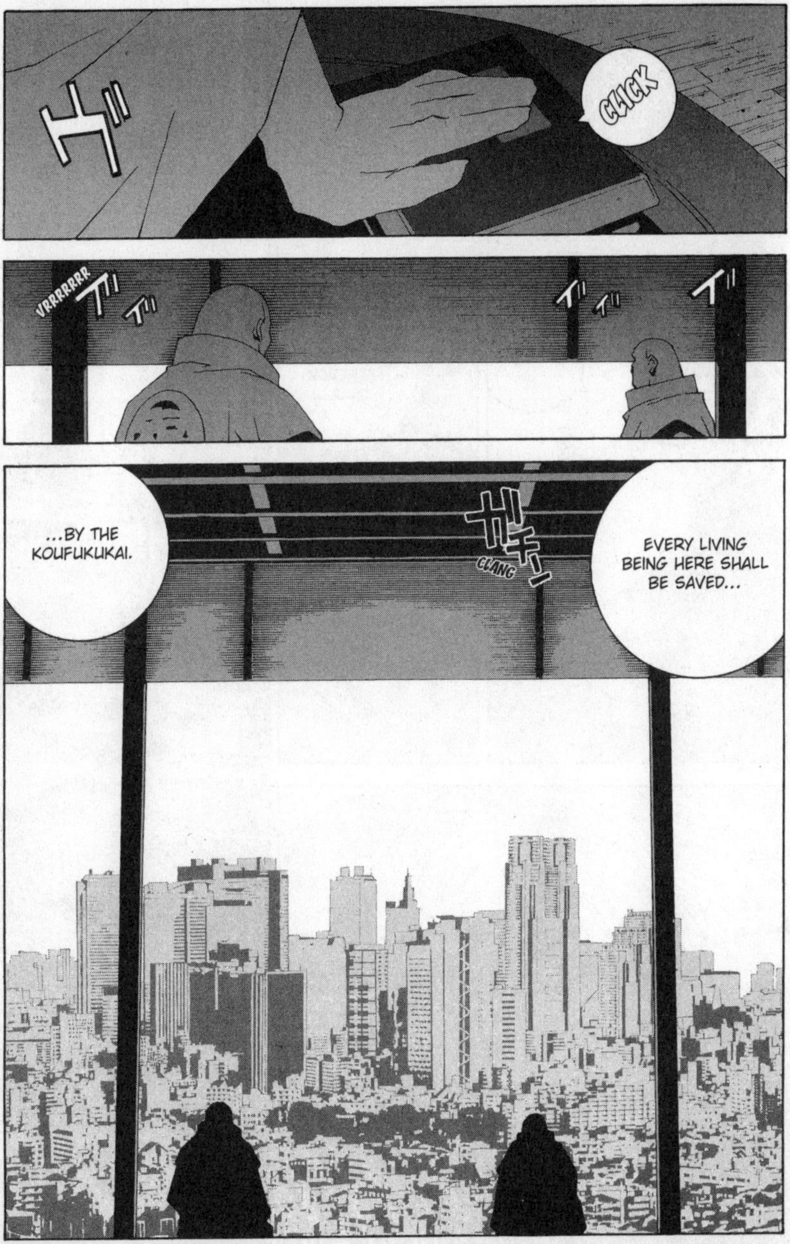
CLICK
VRRRRRRR
EVERY LIVING BEING HERE SHALL BE SAVED...
CLANG
...BY THE KOUFUKUKAI.

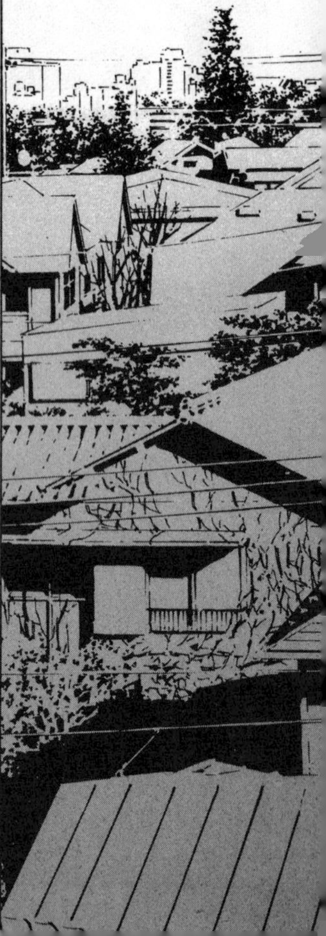

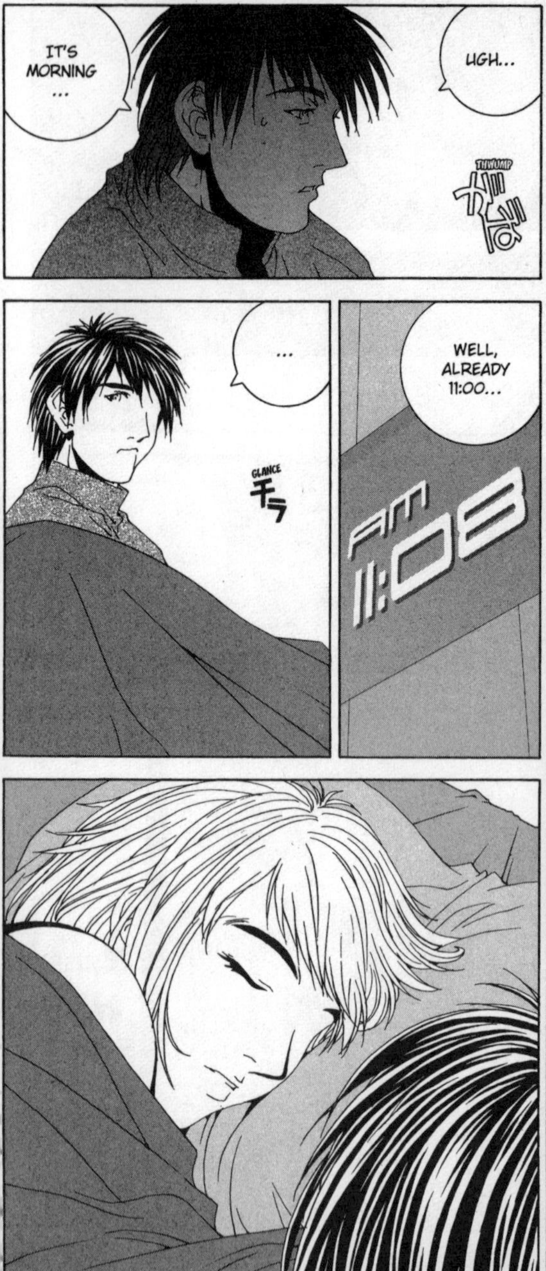
UGH...
THWUMP
がば
IT'S MORNING ...
WELL, ALREADY 11:00...
AM 11:08
...
GLANCE
チラ

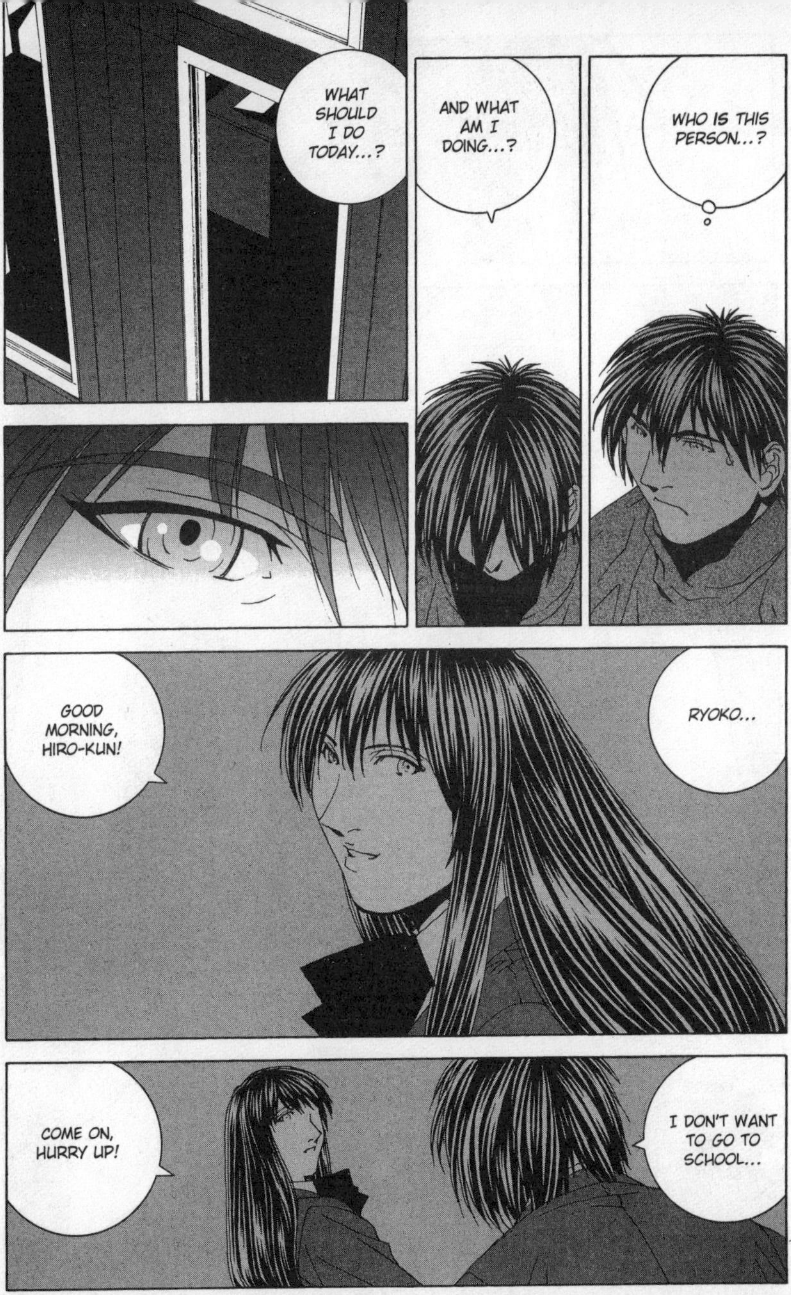
WHO IS THIS PERSON...?
AND WHAT AM I DOING...?
WHAT SHOULD I DO TODAY...?
RYOKO...
GOOD MORNING, HIRO-KUN!
I DON'T WANT TO GO TO SCHOOL...
COME ON, HURRY UP!

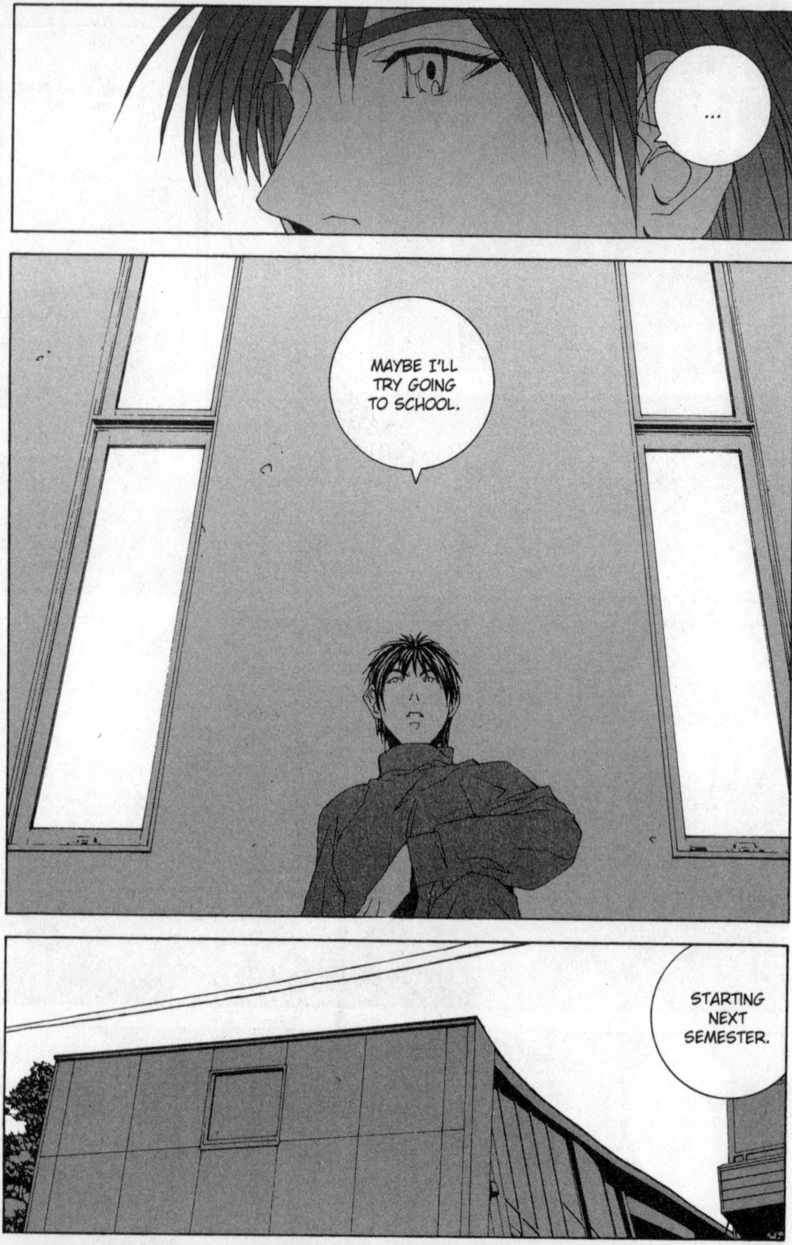
...
MAYBE I'LL TRY GOING TO SCHOOL.
STARTING NEXT SEMESTER.

JUSTICE:25 JUNK DAILY LIFE

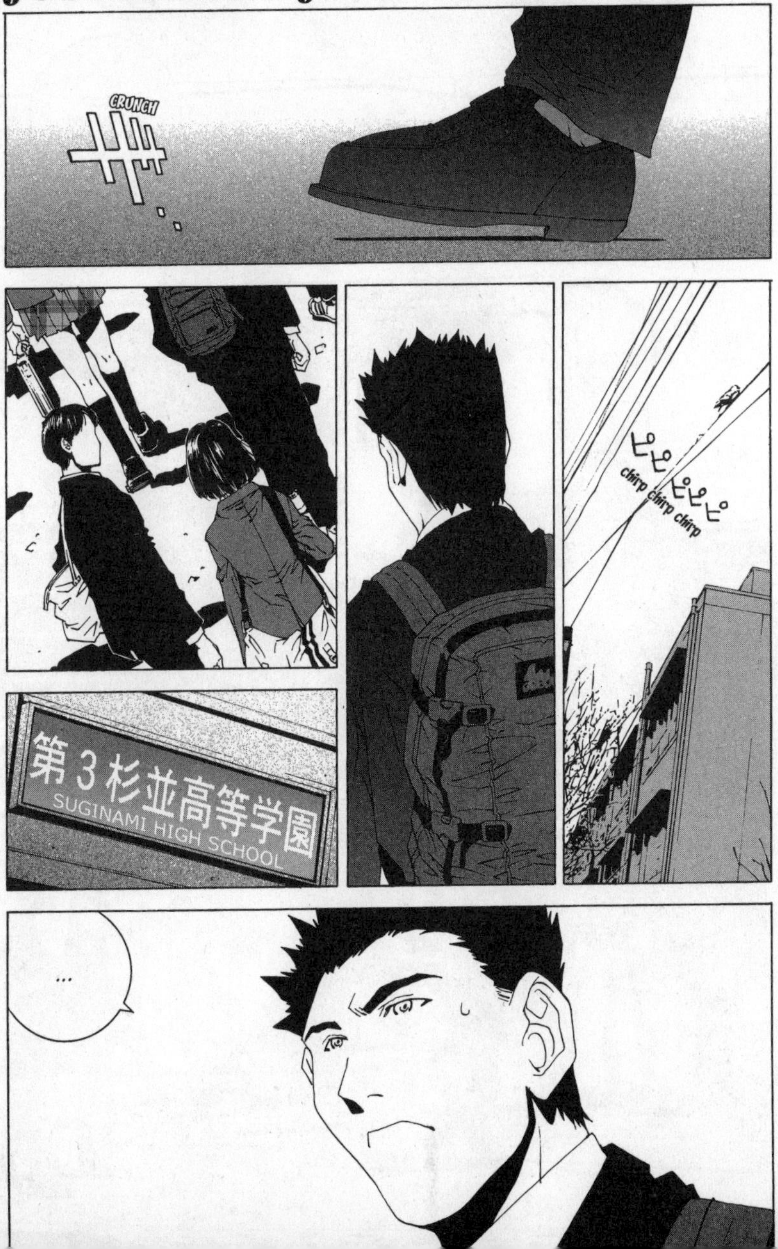
CRUNCH
ピピ ピピピ
chirp chirp chirp
第3杉並高等学園
SUGINAMI HIGH SCHOOL
...

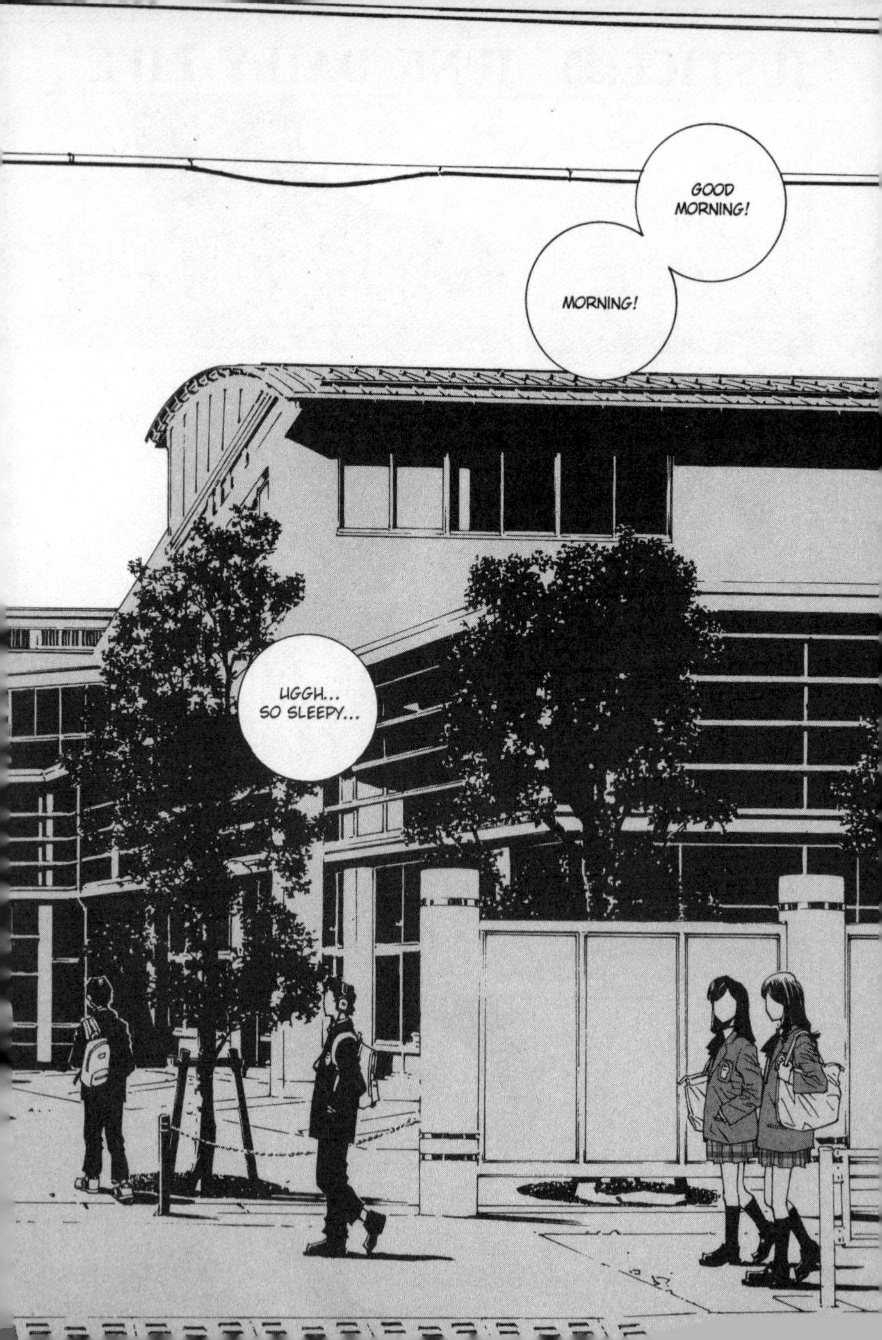
GOOD MORNING!
MORNING!
UGGH... SO SLEEPY...

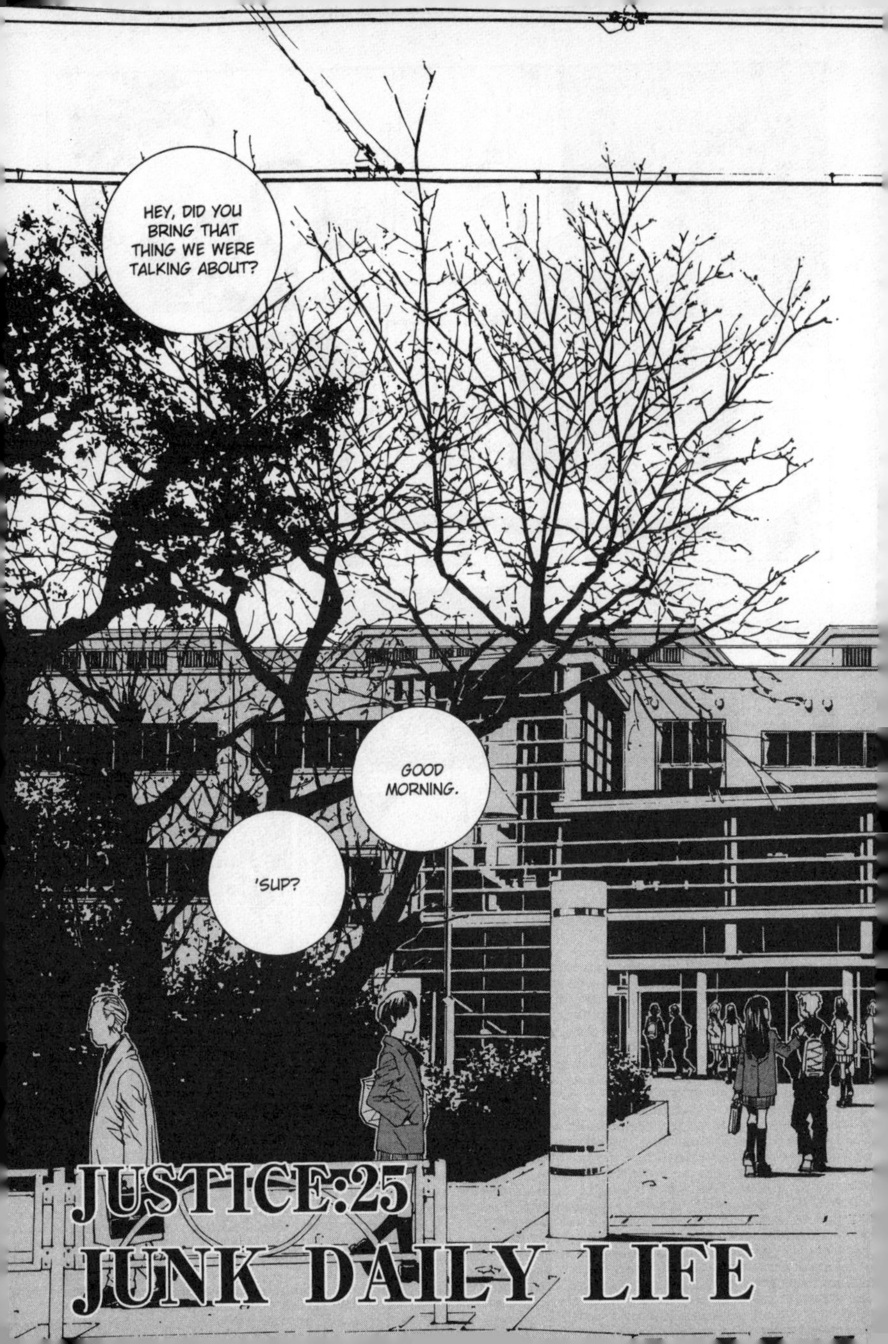
HEY, DID YOU BRING THAT THING WE WERE TALKING ABOUT?
GOOD MORNING.
'SUP?
JUSTICE:25
JUNK DAILY LIFE

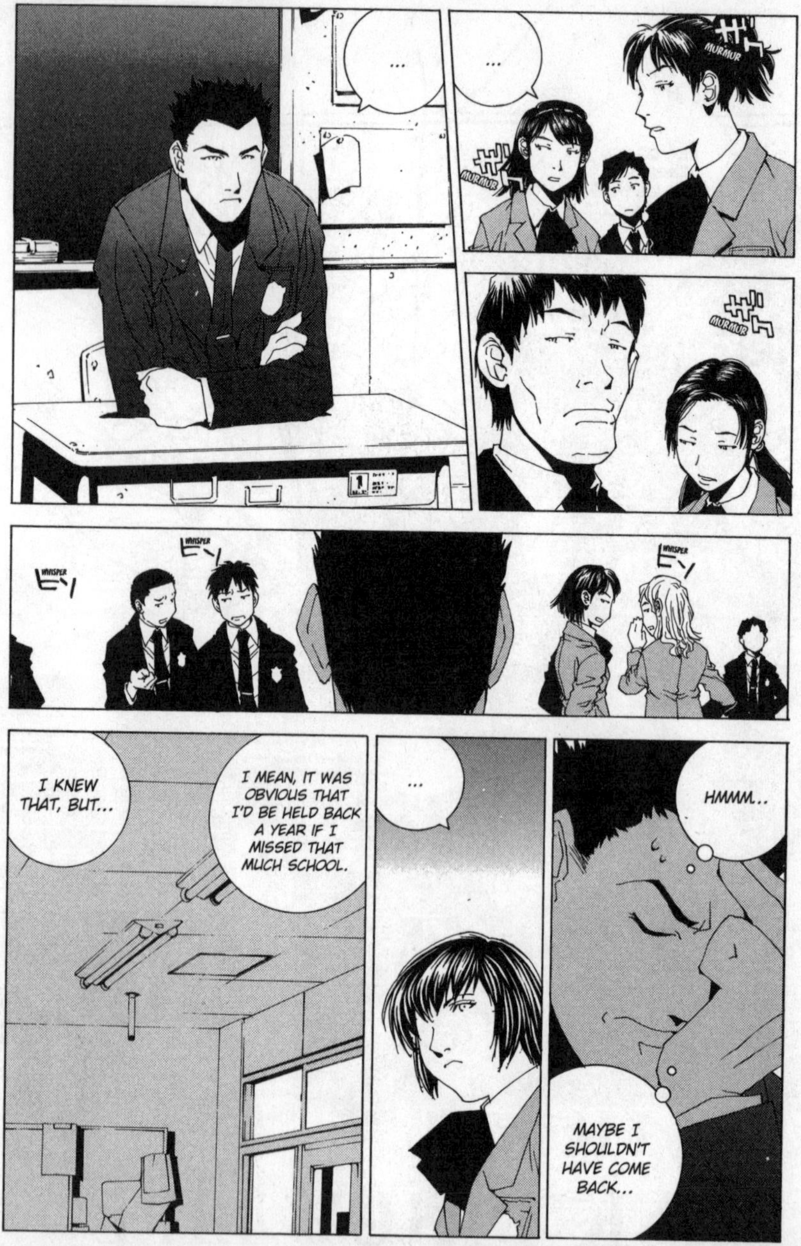
MURMUR
...
MURMUR
MURMUR
...
WHISPER
WHISPER
WHISPER
HMMM...
MAYBE I SHOULDN'T HAVE COME BACK...
...
I MEAN, IT WAS OBVIOUS THAT I'D BE HELD BACK A YEAR IF I MISSED THAT MUCH SCHOOL.
I KNEW THAT, BUT...

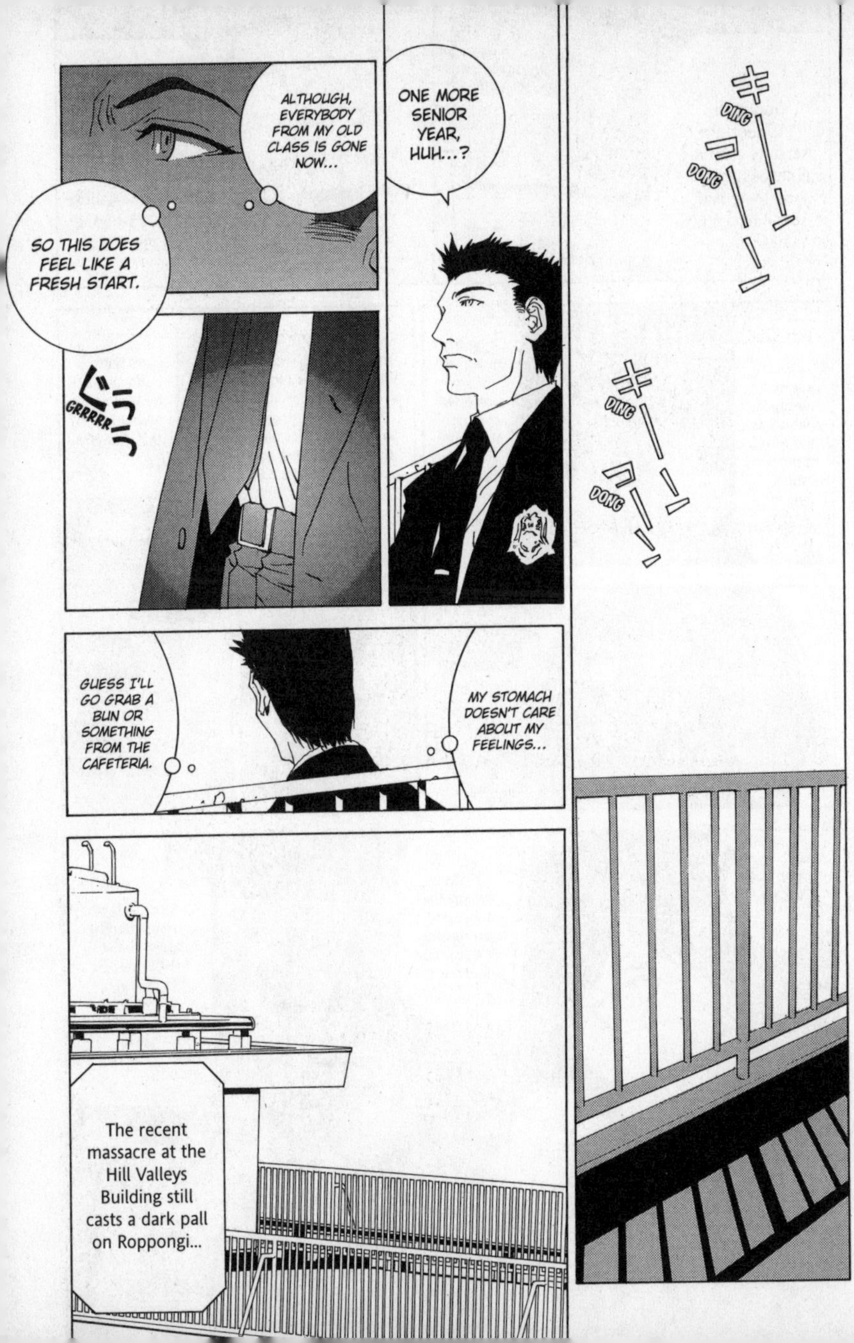
DING
DONG
DING
DONG
ONE MORE SENIOR YEAR, HUH...?
ALTHOUGH, EVERYBODY FROM MY OLD CLASS IS GONE NOW...
SO THIS DOES FEEL LIKE A FRESH START.
GRRRRR
MY STOMACH DOESN'T CARE ABOUT MY FEELINGS...
GUESS I'LL GO GRAB A BUN OR SOMETHING FROM THE CAFETERIA.
The recent massacre at the Hill Valleys Building still casts a dark pall on Roppongi...

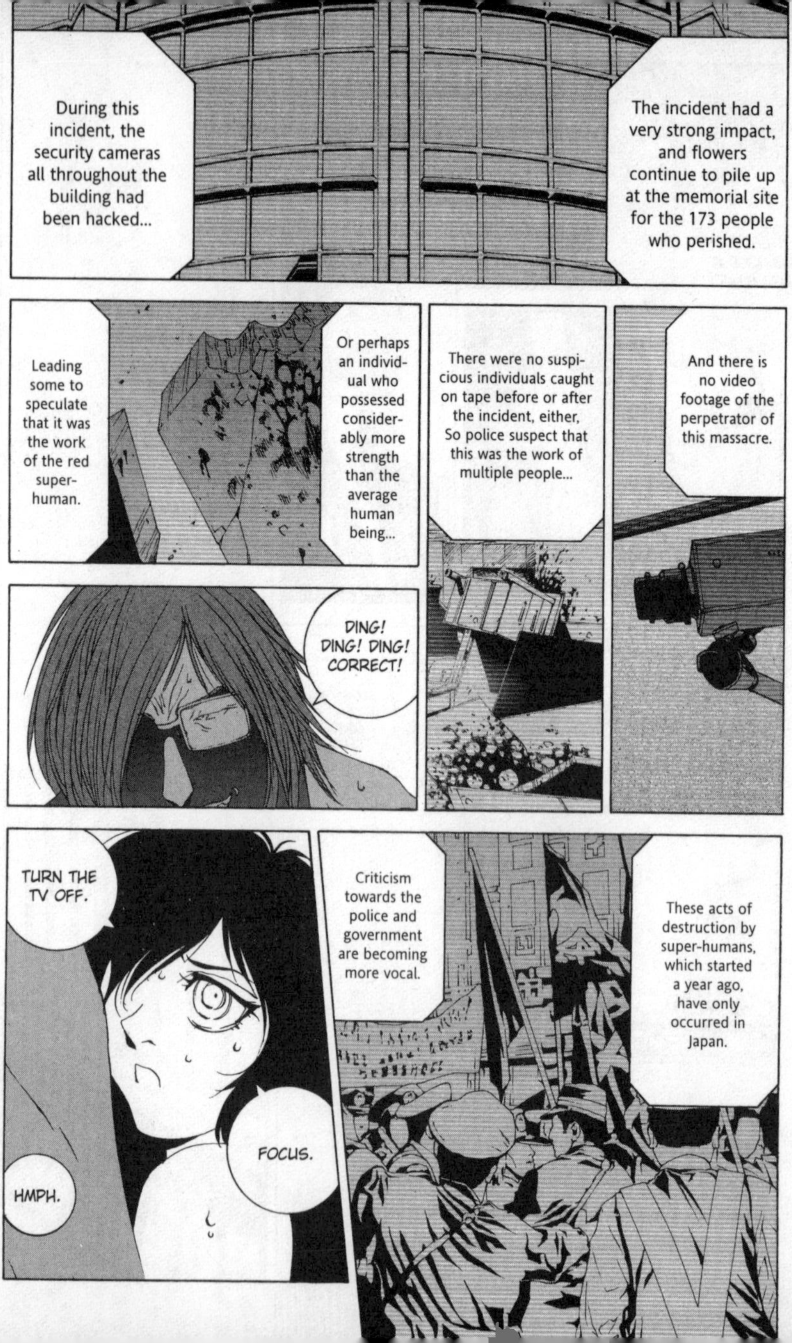
The incident had a very strong impact, and flowers continue to pile up at the memorial site for the 173 people who perished.
During this incident, the security cameras all throughout the building had been hacked...
And there is no video footage of the perpetrator of this massacre.
There were no suspicious individuals caught on tape before or after the incident, either, So police suspect that this was the work of multiple people...
Or perhaps an individual who possessed considerably more strength than the average human being...
Leading some to speculate that it was the work of the red super-human.
DING! DING! DING! CORRECT!
These acts of destruction by super-humans, which started a year ago, have only occurred in Japan.
Criticism towards the police and government are becoming more vocal.
TURN THE TV OFF.
FOCUS.
HMPH.

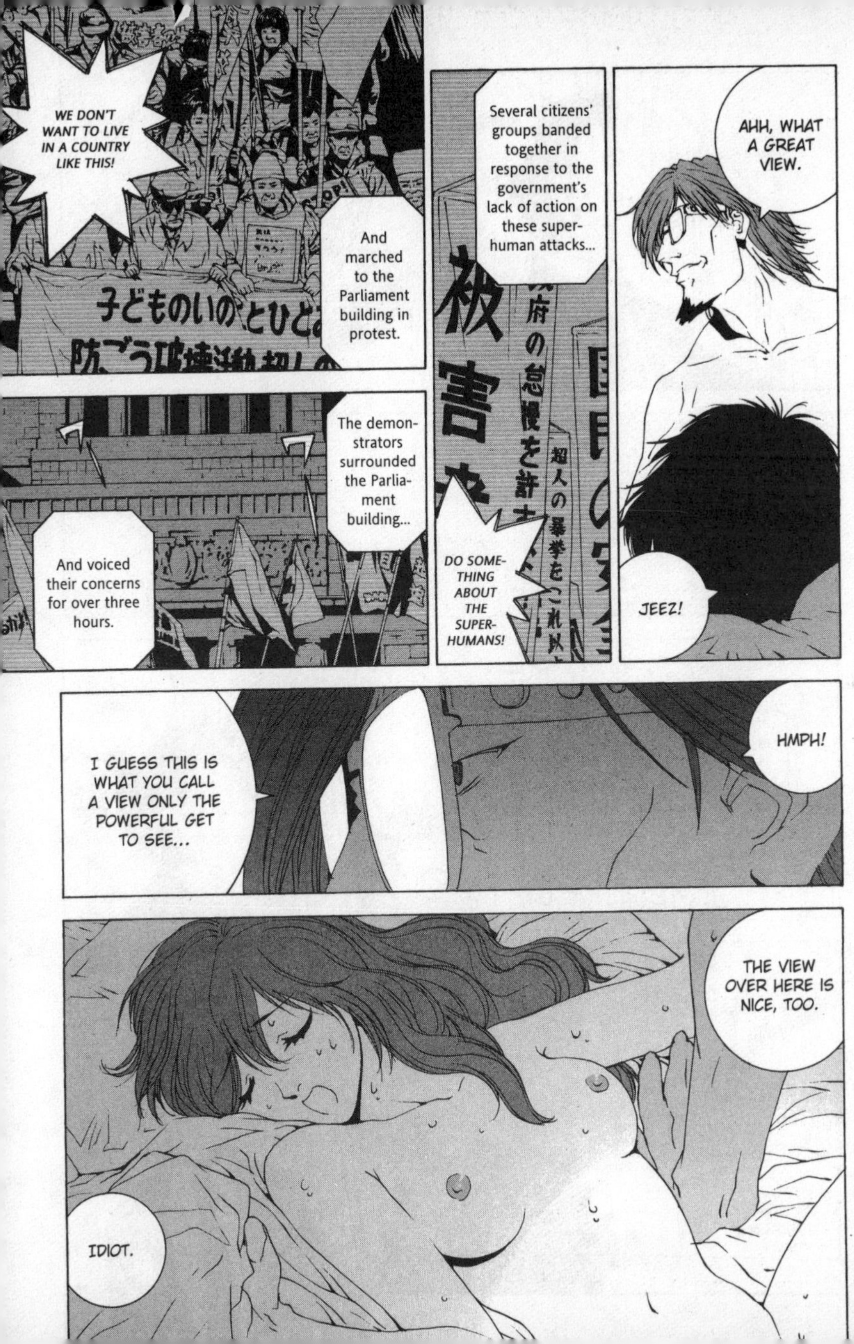
AHH, WHAT A GREAT VIEW.
JEEZ!
Several citizens' groups banded together in response to the government's lack of action on these super-human attacks...
DO SOME-THING ABOUT THE SUPER-HUMANS!
And marched to the Parliament building in protest.
WE DON'T WANT TO LIVE IN A COUNTRY LIKE THIS!
The demon-strators surrounded the Parlia-ment building...
And voiced their concerns for over three hours.
HMPH!
I GUESS THIS IS WHAT YOU CALL A VIEW ONLY THE POWERFUL GET TO SEE...
THE VIEW OVER HERE IS NICE, TOO.
IDIOT.

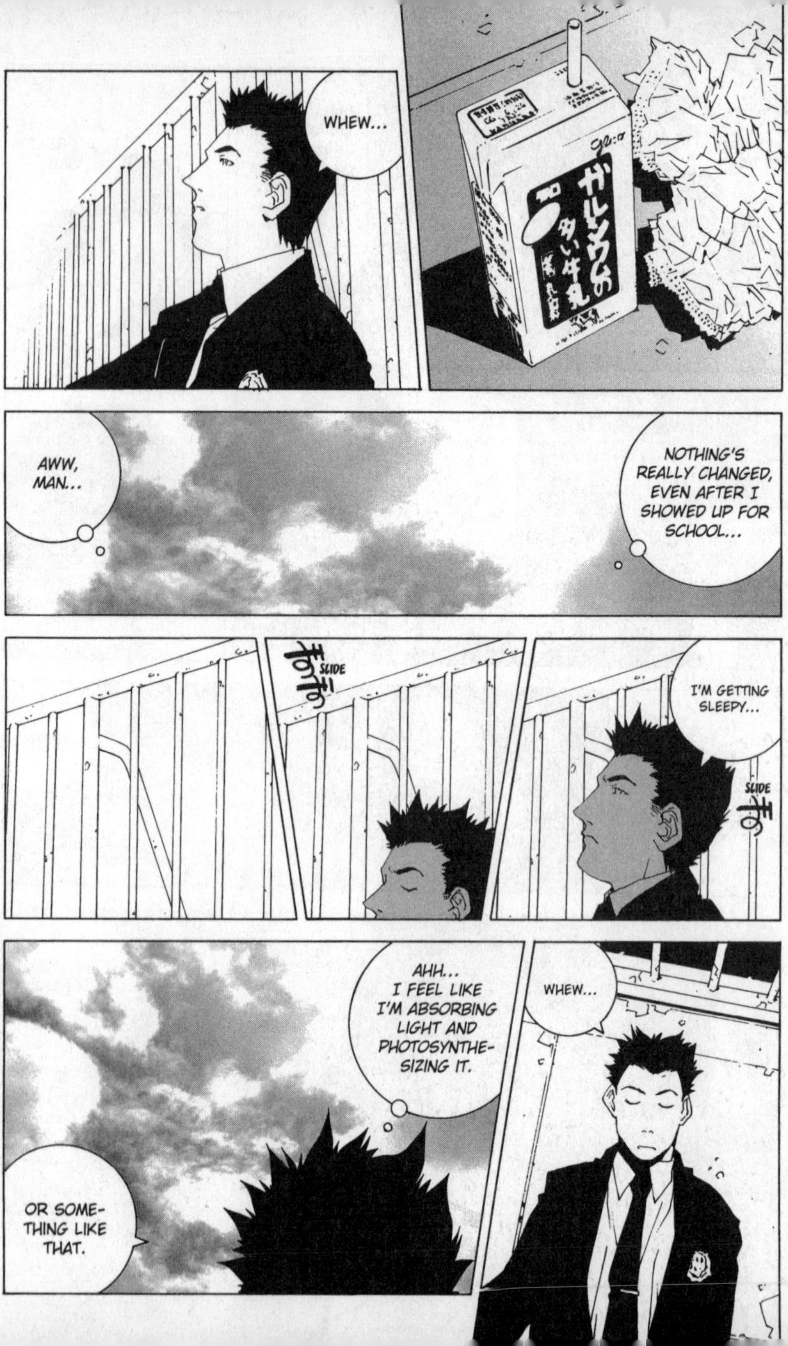
WHEW...
NOTHING'S REALLY CHANGED, EVEN AFTER I SHOWED UP FOR SCHOOL...
AWW, MAN...
I'M GETTING SLEEPY...
SLIDE
SLIDE
WHEW...
AHH... I FEEL LIKE I'M ABSORBING LIGHT AND PHOTOSYNTHE-SIZING IT.
OR SOME-THING LIKE THAT.

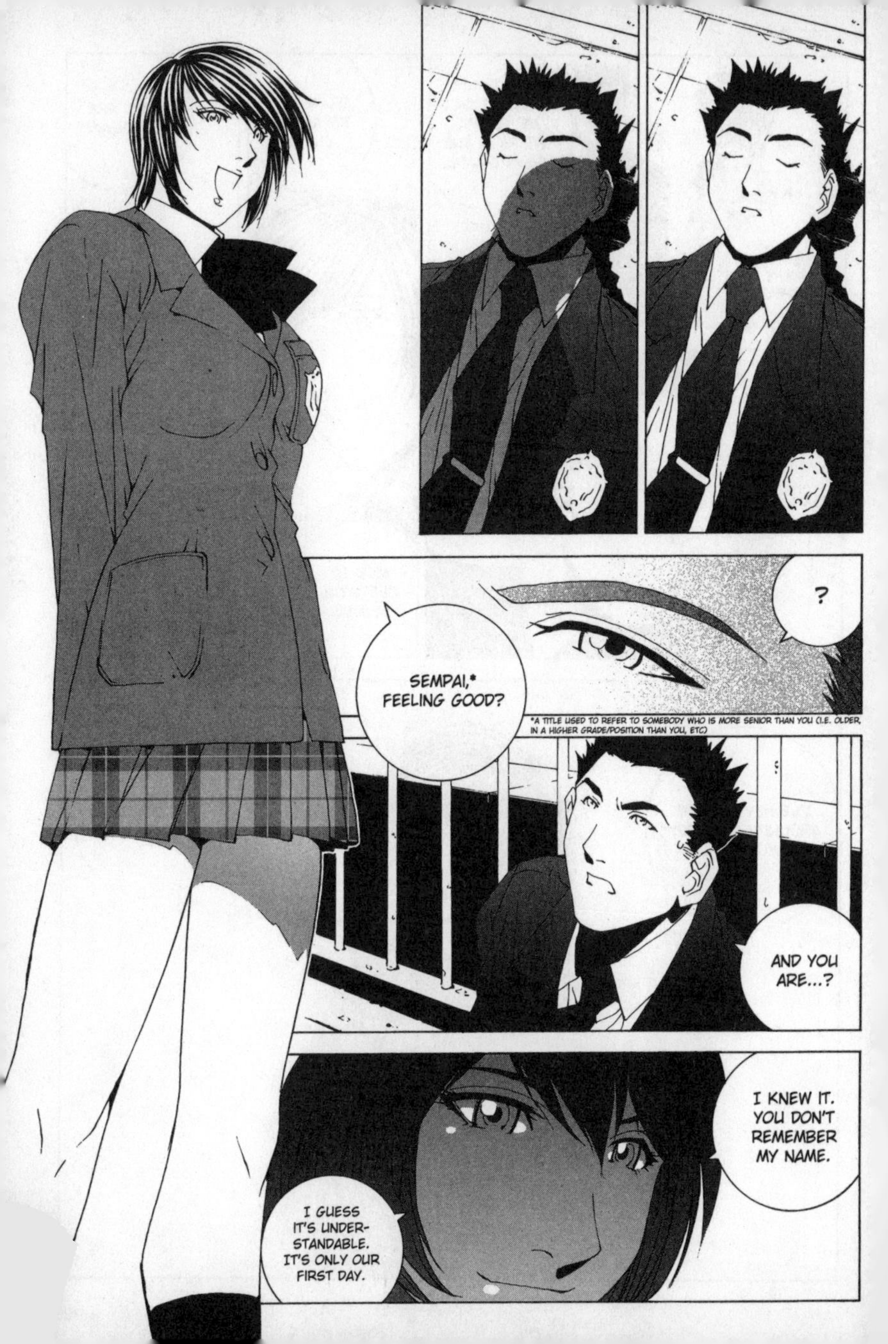
SEMPAI,* FEELING GOOD?
?
*A TITLE USED TO REFER TO SOMEBODY WHO IS MORE SENIOR THAN YOU (I.E. OLDER, IN A HIGHER GRADE/POSITION THAN YOU, ETC)
AND YOU ARE...?
I KNEW IT. YOU DON'T REMEMBER MY NAME.
I GUESS IT'S UNDER-STANDABLE. IT'S ONLY OUR FIRST DAY.

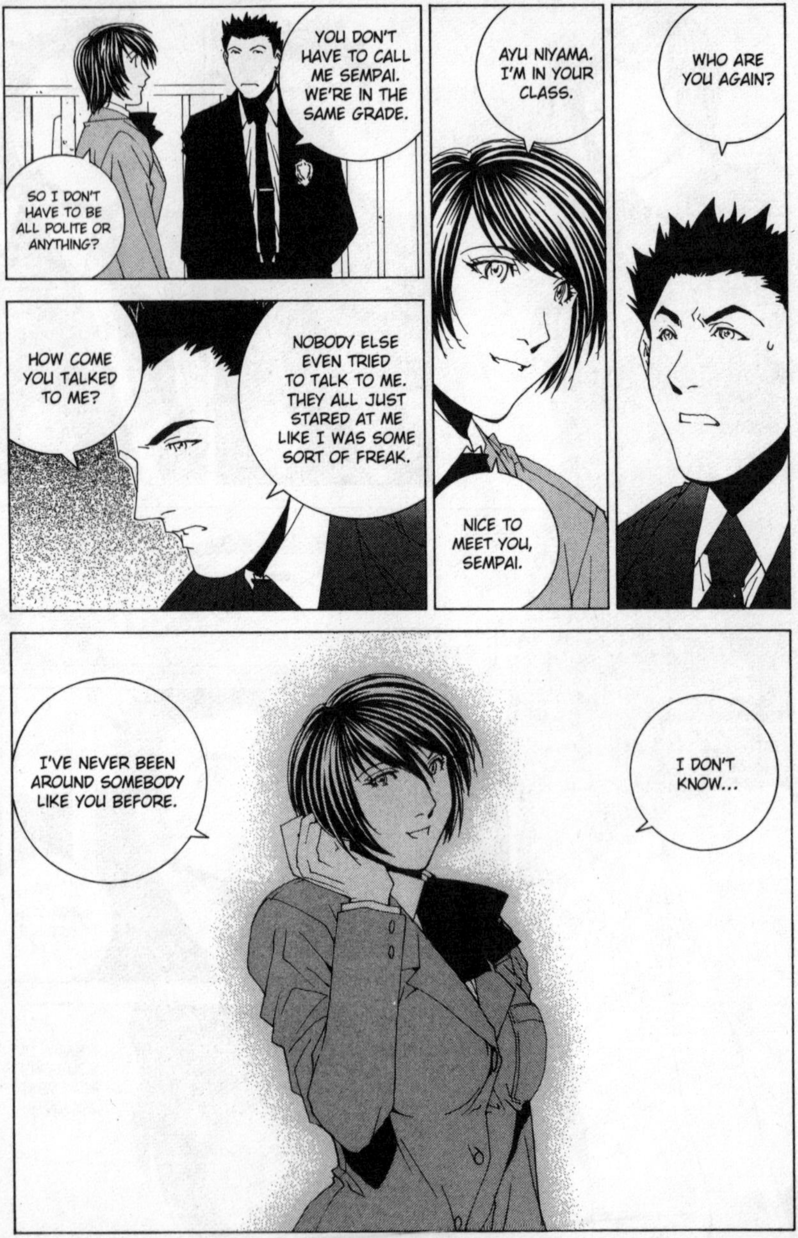
WHO ARE YOU AGAIN?
AYU NIYAMA. I'M IN YOUR CLASS.
NICE TO MEET YOU, SEMPAI.
YOU DON'T HAVE TO CALL ME SEMPAI. WE'RE IN THE SAME GRADE.
SO I DON'T HAVE TO BE ALL POLITE OR ANYTHING?
NOBODY ELSE EVEN TRIED TO TALK TO ME. THEY ALL JUST STARED AT ME LIKE I WAS SOME SORT OF FREAK.
HOW COME YOU TALKED TO ME?
I DON'T KNOW...
I'VE NEVER BEEN AROUND SOMEBODY LIKE YOU BEFORE.

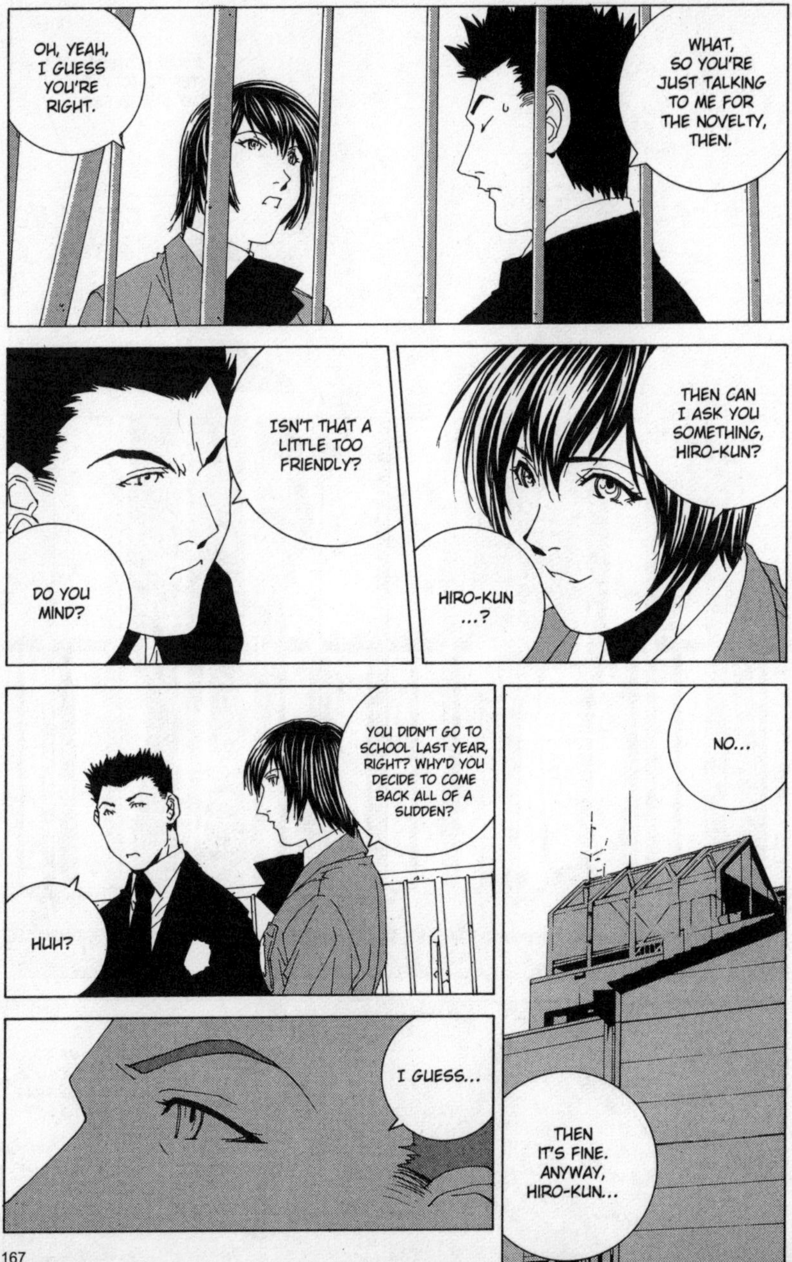
WHAT, SO YOU'RE JUST TALKING TO ME FOR THE NOVELTY, THEN.
OH, YEAH, I GUESS YOU'RE RIGHT.
THEN CAN I ASK YOU SOMETHING, HIRO-KUN?
HIRO-KUN ...?
ISN'T THAT A LITTLE TOO FRIENDLY?
DO YOU MIND?
NO...
THEN IT'S FINE. ANYWAY, HIRO-KUN...
YOU DIDN'T GO TO SCHOOL LAST YEAR, RIGHT? WHY'D YOU DECIDE TO COME BACK ALL OF A SUDDEN?
HUH?
I GUESS...

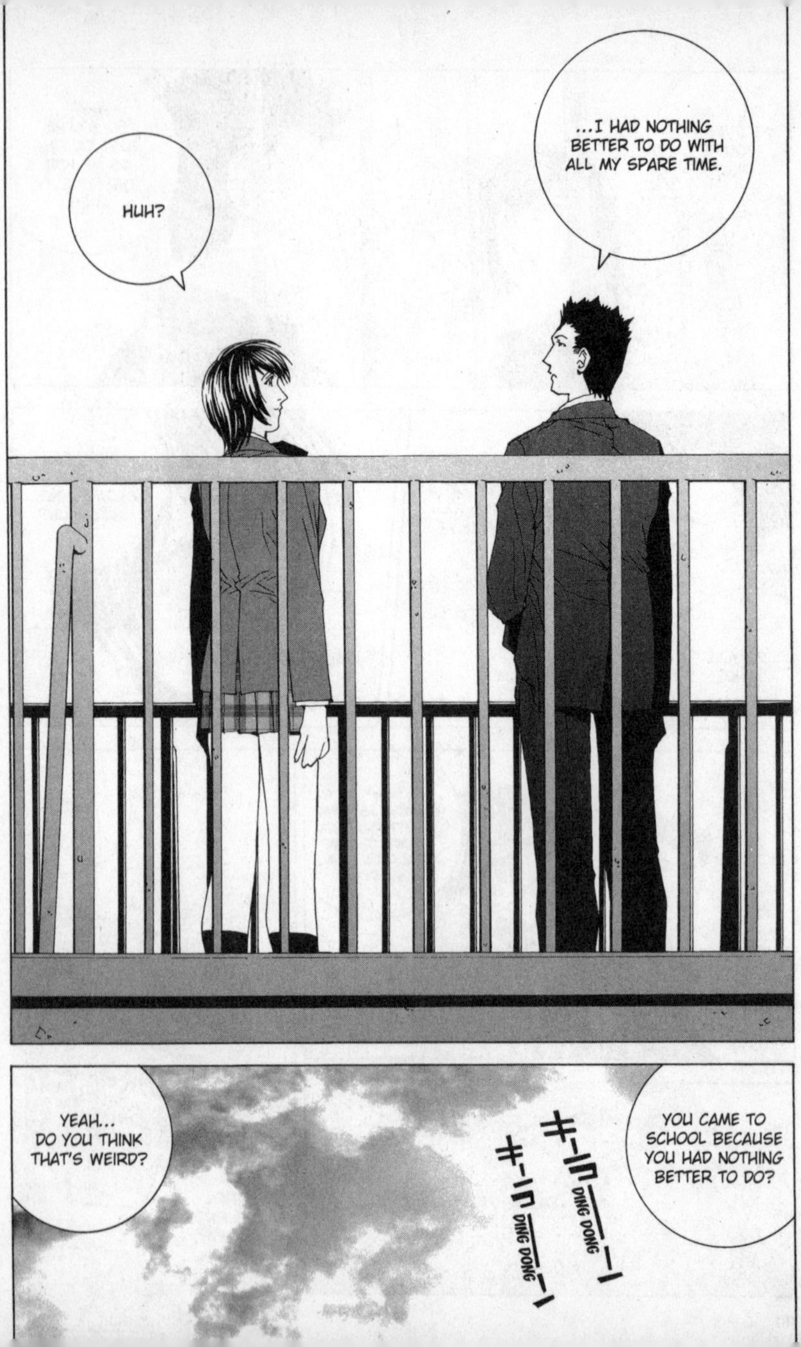
...I HAD NOTHING BETTER TO DO WITH ALL MY SPARE TIME.
HUH?
YOU CAME TO SCHOOL BECAUSE YOU HAD NOTHING BETTER TO DO?
DING DONG
DING DONG
YEAH... DO YOU THINK THAT'S WEIRD?

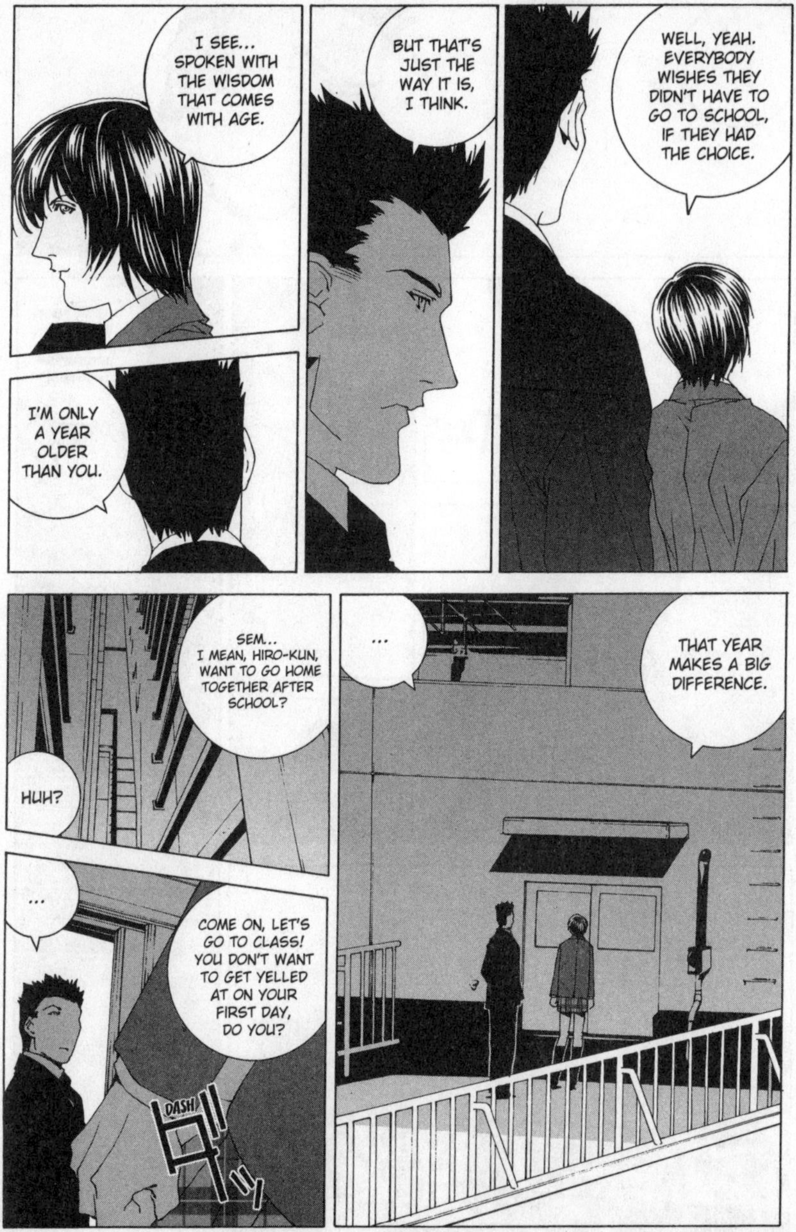
WELL, YEAH. EVERYBODY WISHES THEY DIDN'T HAVE TO GO TO SCHOOL, IF THEY HAD THE CHOICE.
BUT THAT'S JUST THE WAY IT IS, I THINK.
I SEE... SPOKEN WITH THE WISDOM THAT COMES WITH AGE.
I'M ONLY A YEAR OLDER THAN YOU.
THAT YEAR MAKES A BIG DIFFERENCE.
...
SEM... I MEAN, HIRO-KUN, WANT TO GO HOME TOGETHER AFTER SCHOOL?
HUH?
...
COME ON, LET'S GO TO CLASS! YOU DON'T WANT TO GET YELLED AT ON YOUR FIRST DAY, DO YOU?
DASH

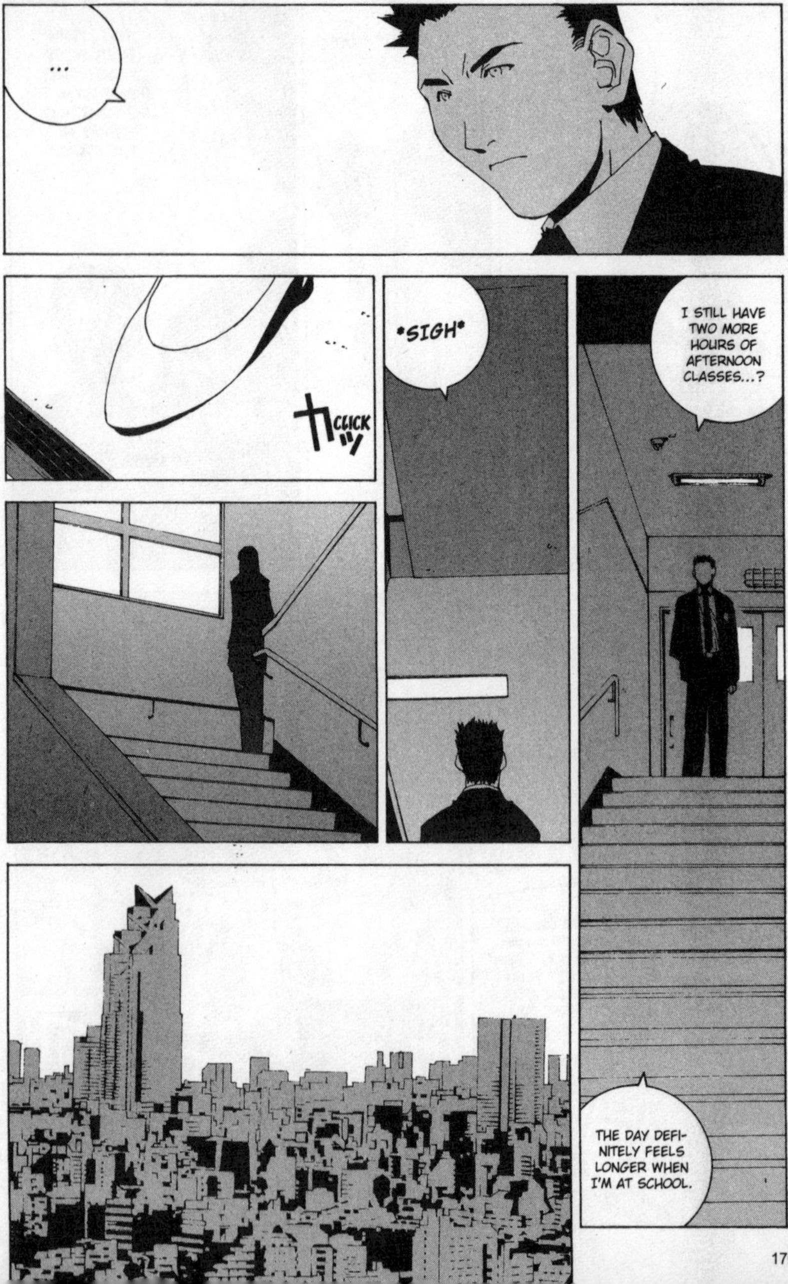
...
I STILL HAVE TWO MORE HOURS OF AFTERNOON CLASSES...?
THE DAY DEFI-NITELY FEELS LONGER WHEN I'M AT SCHOOL.
SIGH
カッ CLICK

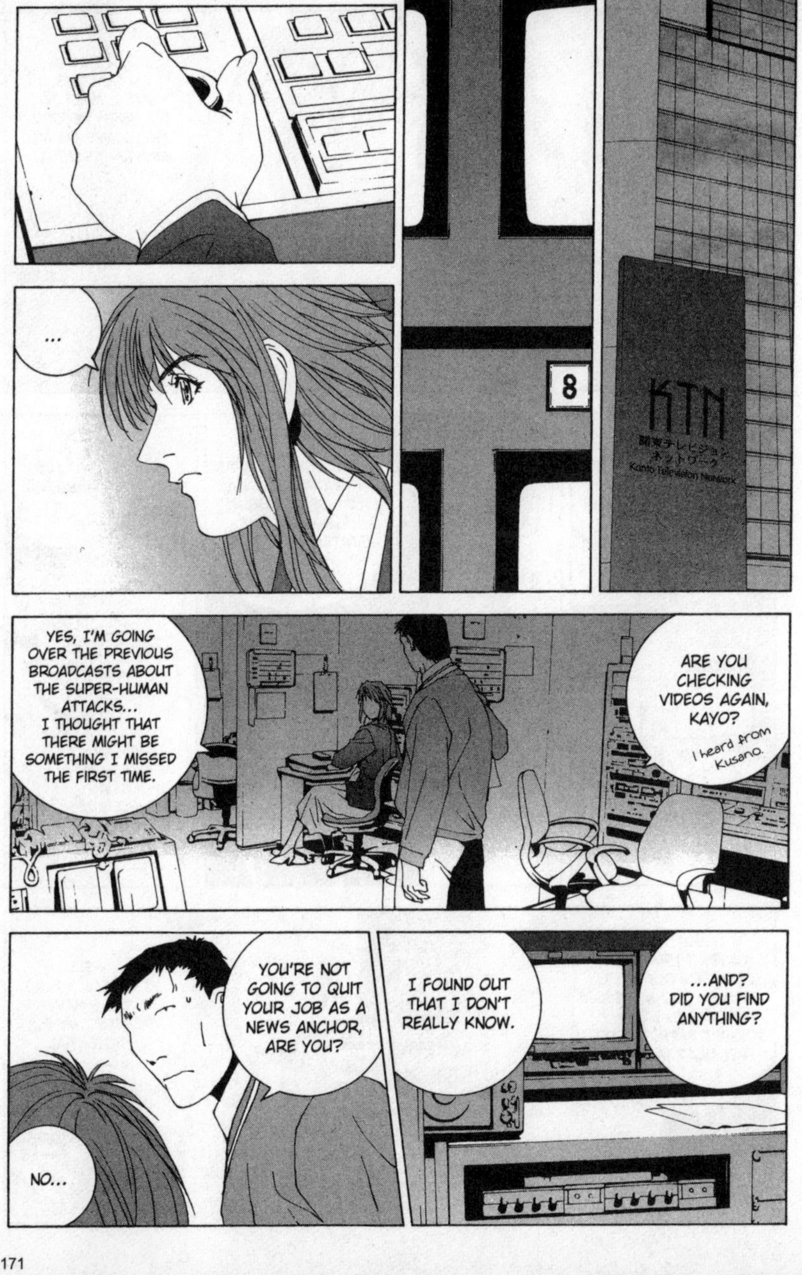
KTN
関東テレビジョン
ネットワーク
Kanto Television Network
8
...
ARE YOU CHECKING VIDEOS AGAIN, KAYO?
I heard from Kusano.
YES, I'M GOING OVER THE PREVIOUS BROADCASTS ABOUT THE SUPER-HUMAN ATTACKS... I THOUGHT THAT THERE MIGHT BE SOMETHING I MISSED THE FIRST TIME.
...AND? DID YOU FIND ANYTHING?
I FOUND OUT THAT I DON'T REALLY KNOW.
YOU'RE NOT GOING TO QUIT YOUR JOB AS A NEWS ANCHOR, ARE YOU?
NO...

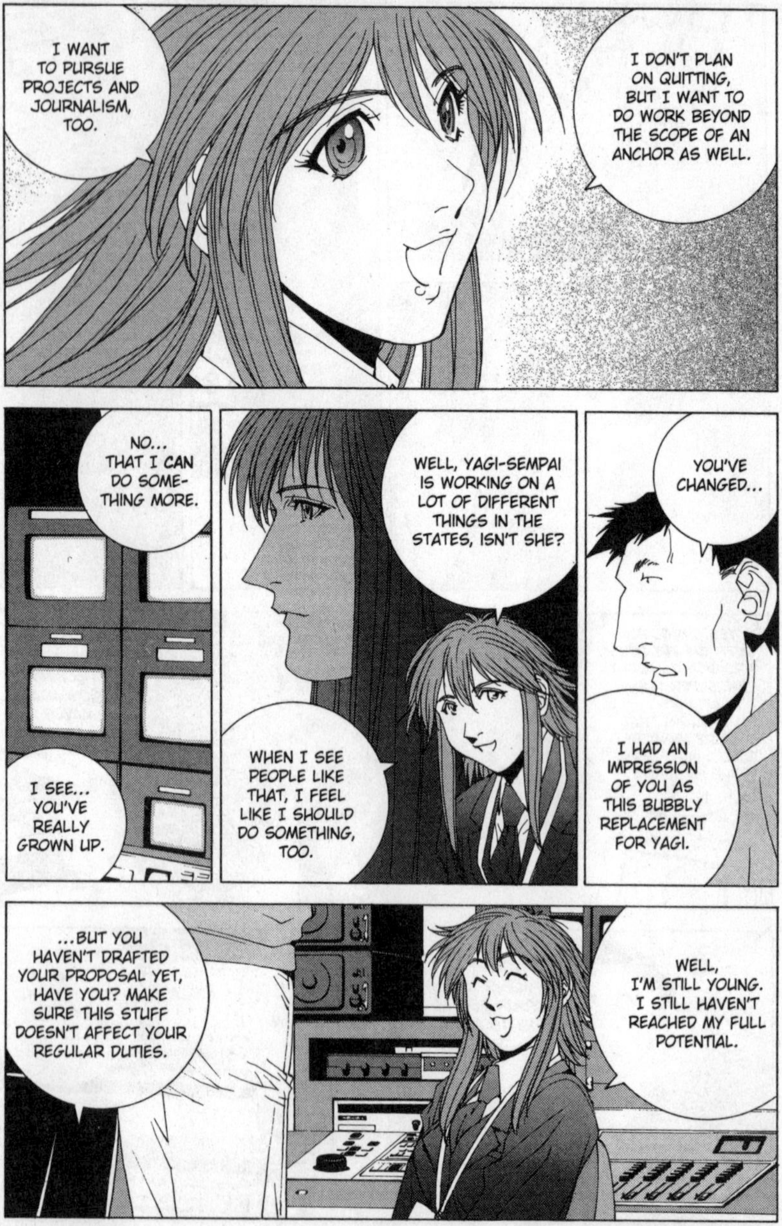

I DON'T PLAN ON QUITTING, BUT I WANT TO DO WORK BEYOND THE SCOPE OF AN ANCHOR AS WELL.
I WANT TO PURSUE PROJECTS AND JOURNALISM, TOO.
YOU'VE CHANGED...
I HAD AN IMPRESSION OF YOU AS THIS BUBBLY REPLACEMENT FOR YAGI.
WELL, YAGI-SEMPAI IS WORKING ON A LOT OF DIFFERENT THINGS IN THE STATES, ISN'T SHE?
WHEN I SEE PEOPLE LIKE THAT, I FEEL LIKE I SHOULD DO SOMETHING, TOO.
NO... THAT I CAN DO SOME-THING MORE.
I SEE... YOU'VE REALLY GROWN UP.
WELL, I'M STILL YOUNG. I STILL HAVEN'T REACHED MY FULL POTENTIAL.
...BUT YOU HAVEN'T DRAFTED YOUR PROPOSAL YET, HAVE YOU? MAKE SURE THIS STUFF DOESN'T AFFECT YOUR REGULAR DUTIES.

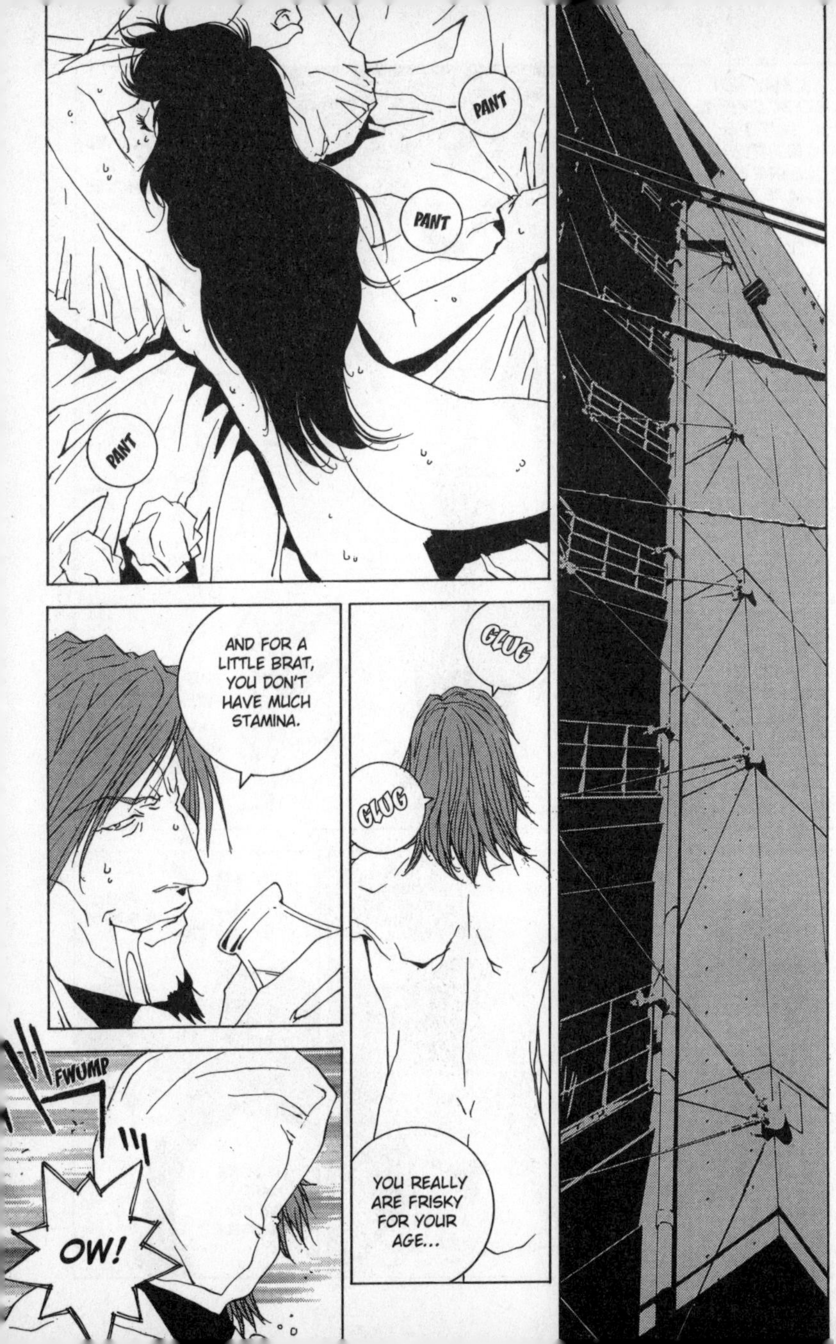
PANT
PANT
PANT
GLUG
GLUG
YOU REALLY ARE FRISKY FOR YOUR AGE...
AND FOR A LITTLE BRAT, YOU DON'T HAVE MUCH STAMINA.
FWUMP
OW!

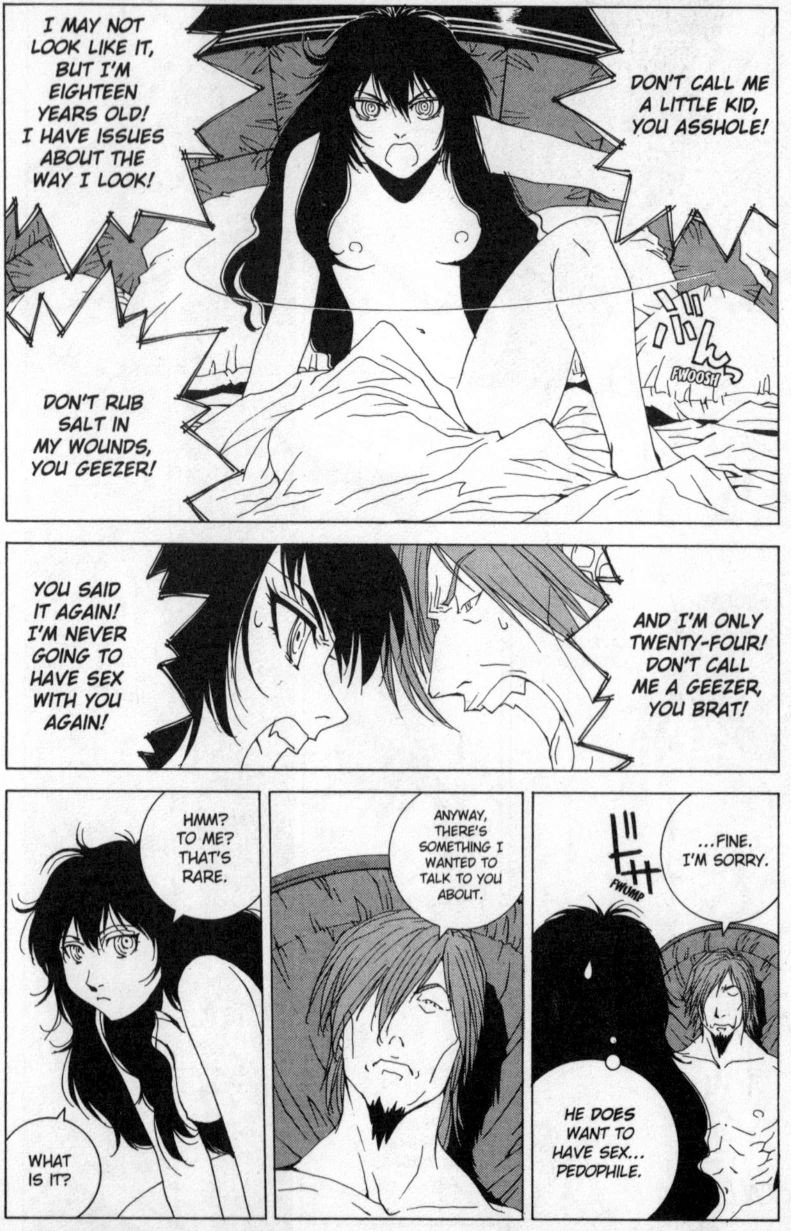
DON'T CALL ME A LITTLE KID, YOU ASSHOLE!
I MAY NOT LOOK LIKE IT, BUT I'M EIGHTEEN YEARS OLD! I HAVE ISSUES ABOUT THE WAY I LOOK!
FWOOSH
DON'T RUB SALT IN MY WOUNDS, YOU GEEZER!
AND I'M ONLY TWENTY-FOUR! DON'T CALL ME A GEEZER, YOU BRAT!
YOU SAID IT AGAIN! I'M NEVER GOING TO HAVE SEX WITH YOU AGAIN!
FWUMP
...FINE. I'M SORRY.
HE DOES WANT TO HAVE SEX... PEDOPHILE.
ANYWAY, THERE'S SOMETHING I WANTED TO TALK TO YOU ABOUT.
HMM? TO ME? THAT'S RARE.
WHAT IS IT?

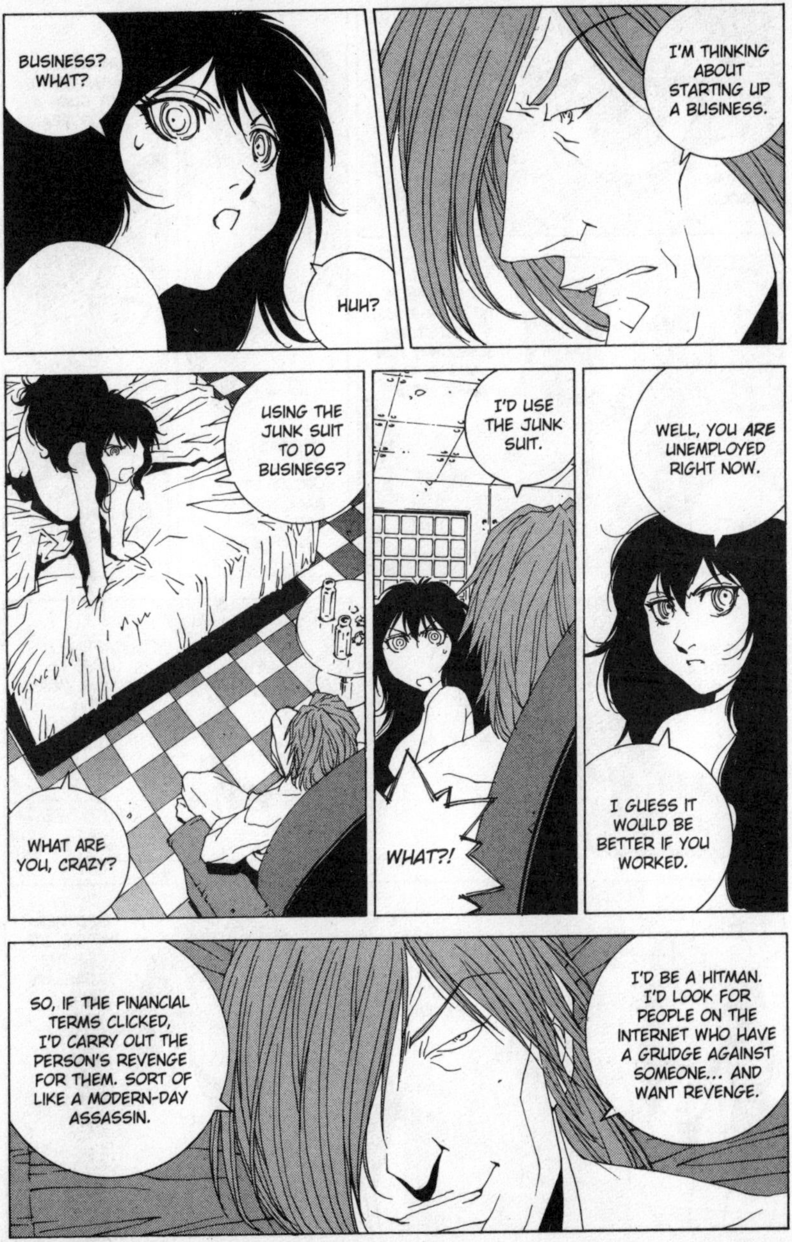
I'M THINKING ABOUT STARTING UP A BUSINESS.
BUSINESS? WHAT?
HUH?
WELL, YOU *ARE* UNEMPLOYED RIGHT NOW.
I GUESS IT WOULD BE BETTER IF YOU WORKED.
I'D USE THE JUNK SUIT.
WHAT?!
USING THE JUNK SUIT TO DO BUSINESS?
WHAT ARE YOU, CRAZY?
I'D BE A HITMAN. I'D LOOK FOR PEOPLE ON THE INTERNET WHO HAVE A GRUDGE AGAINST SOMEONE... AND WANT REVENGE.
SO, IF THE FINANCIAL TERMS CLICKED, I'D CARRY OUT THE PERSON'S REVENGE FOR THEM. SORT OF LIKE A MODERN-DAY ASSASSIN.

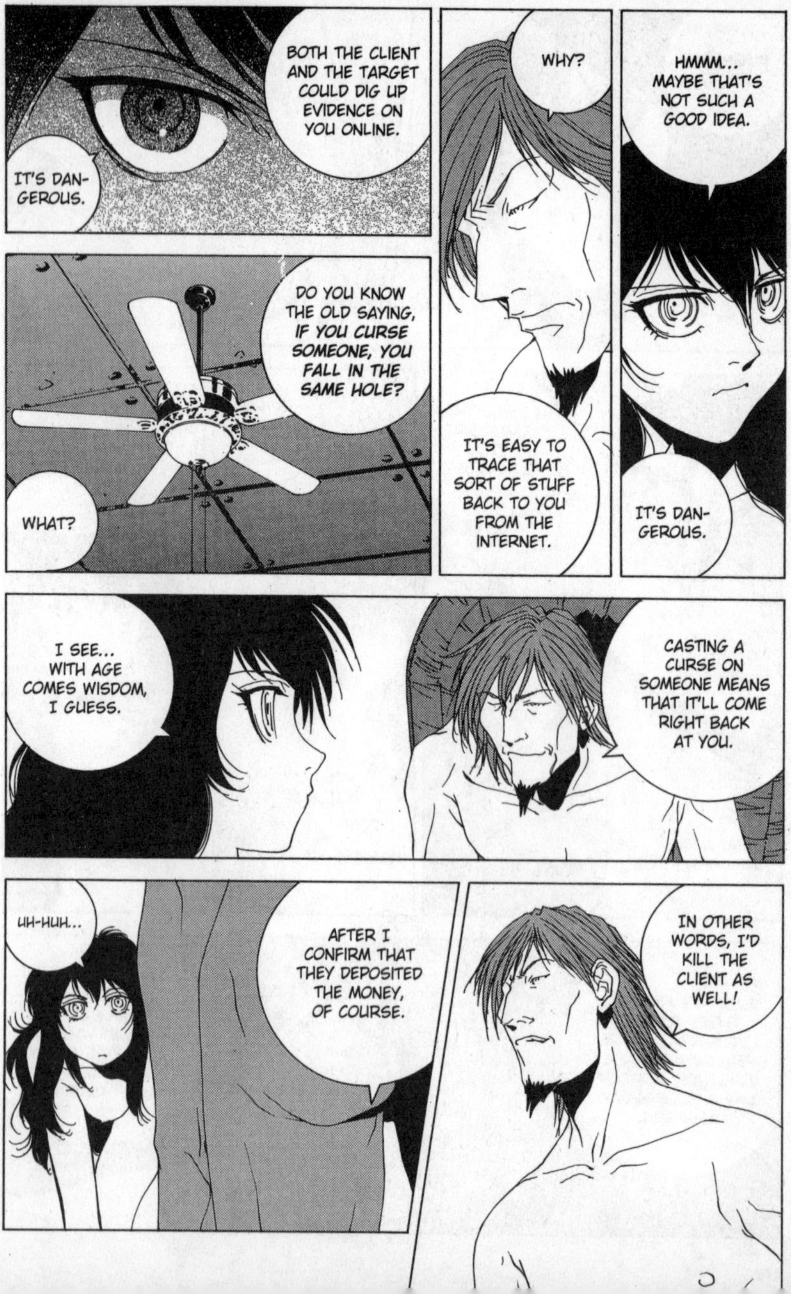
HMMM... MAYBE THAT'S NOT SUCH A GOOD IDEA.
IT'S DANGEROUS.
WHY?
IT'S EASY TO TRACE THAT SORT OF STUFF BACK TO YOU FROM THE INTERNET.
BOTH THE CLIENT AND THE TARGET COULD DIG UP EVIDENCE ON YOU ONLINE.
IT'S DANGEROUS.
DO YOU KNOW THE OLD SAYING, *IF YOU CURSE SOMEONE, YOU FALL IN THE SAME HOLE?*
WHAT?
CASTING A CURSE ON SOMEONE MEANS THAT IT'LL COME RIGHT BACK AT YOU.
I SEE... WITH AGE COMES WISDOM, I GUESS.
IN OTHER WORDS, I'D KILL THE CLIENT AS WELL!
AFTER I CONFIRM THAT THEY DEPOSITED THE MONEY, OF COURSE.
UH-HUH...

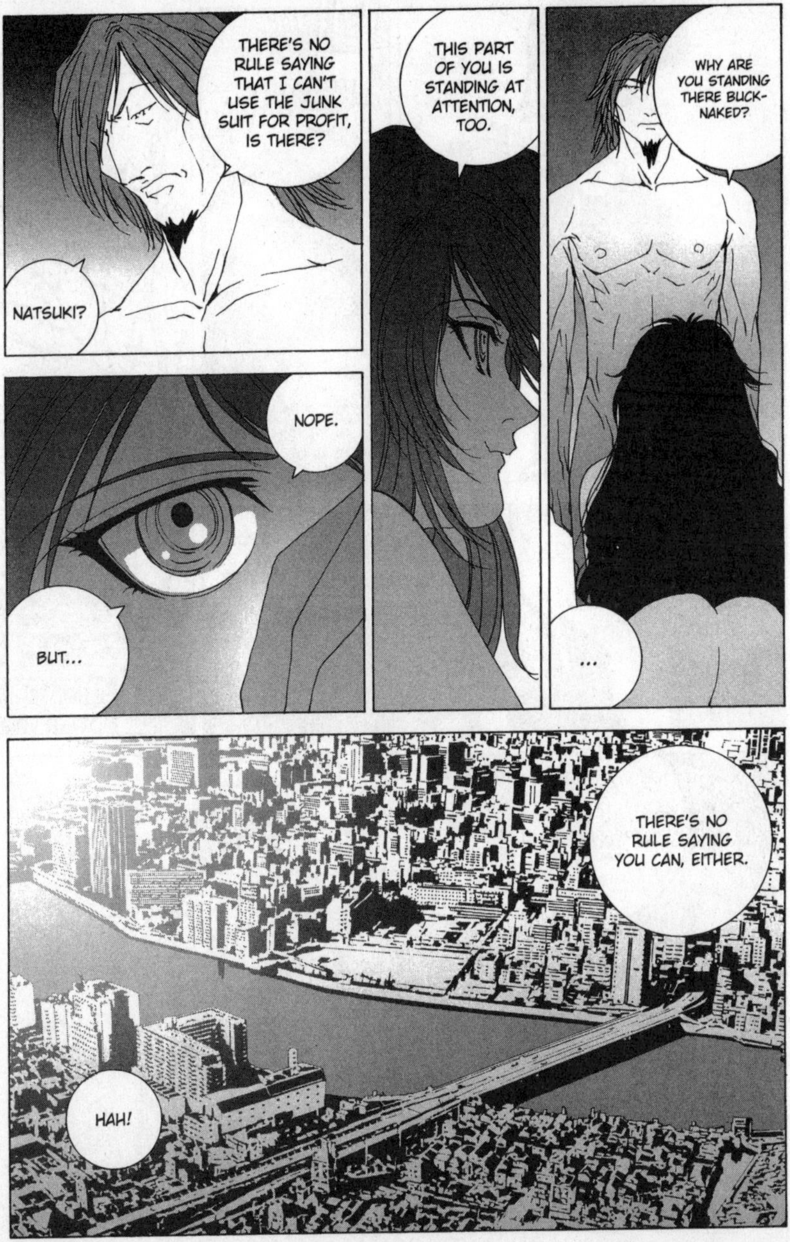
WHY ARE YOU STANDING THERE BUCK-NAKED?
...
THIS PART OF YOU IS STANDING AT ATTENTION, TOO.
THERE'S NO RULE SAYING THAT I CAN'T USE THE JUNK SUIT FOR PROFIT, IS THERE?
NATSUKI?
NOPE.
BUT...
THERE'S NO RULE SAYING YOU CAN, EITHER.
HAH!

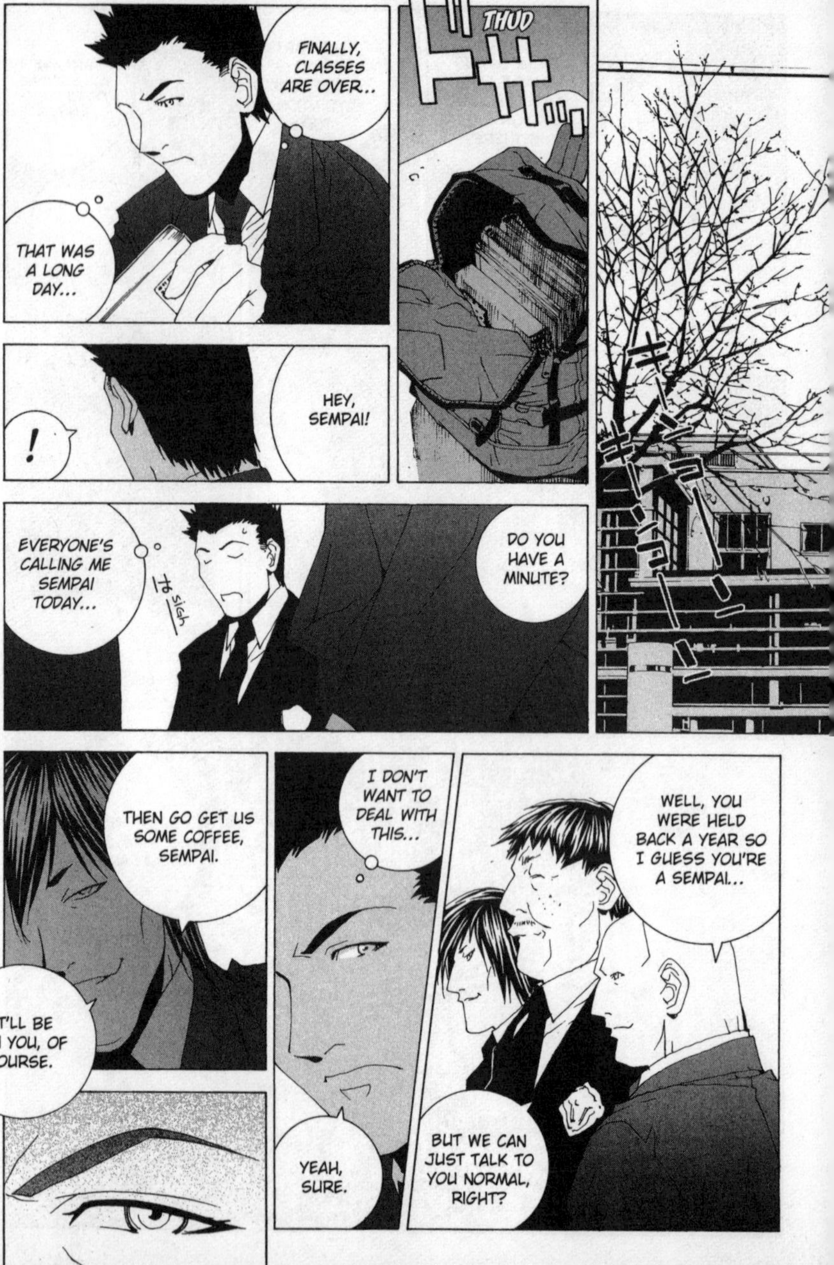
THUD
FINALLY, CLASSES ARE OVER..
THAT WAS A LONG DAY...
HEY, SEMPAI!
!
DO YOU HAVE A MINUTE?
EVERYONE'S CALLING ME SEMPAI TODAY...
sigh
WELL, YOU WERE HELD BACK A YEAR SO I GUESS YOU'RE A SEMPAI...
BUT WE CAN JUST TALK TO YOU NORMAL, RIGHT?
I DON'T WANT TO DEAL WITH THIS...
YEAH, SURE.
THEN GO GET US SOME COFFEE, SEMPAI.
IT'LL BE ON YOU, OF COURSE.

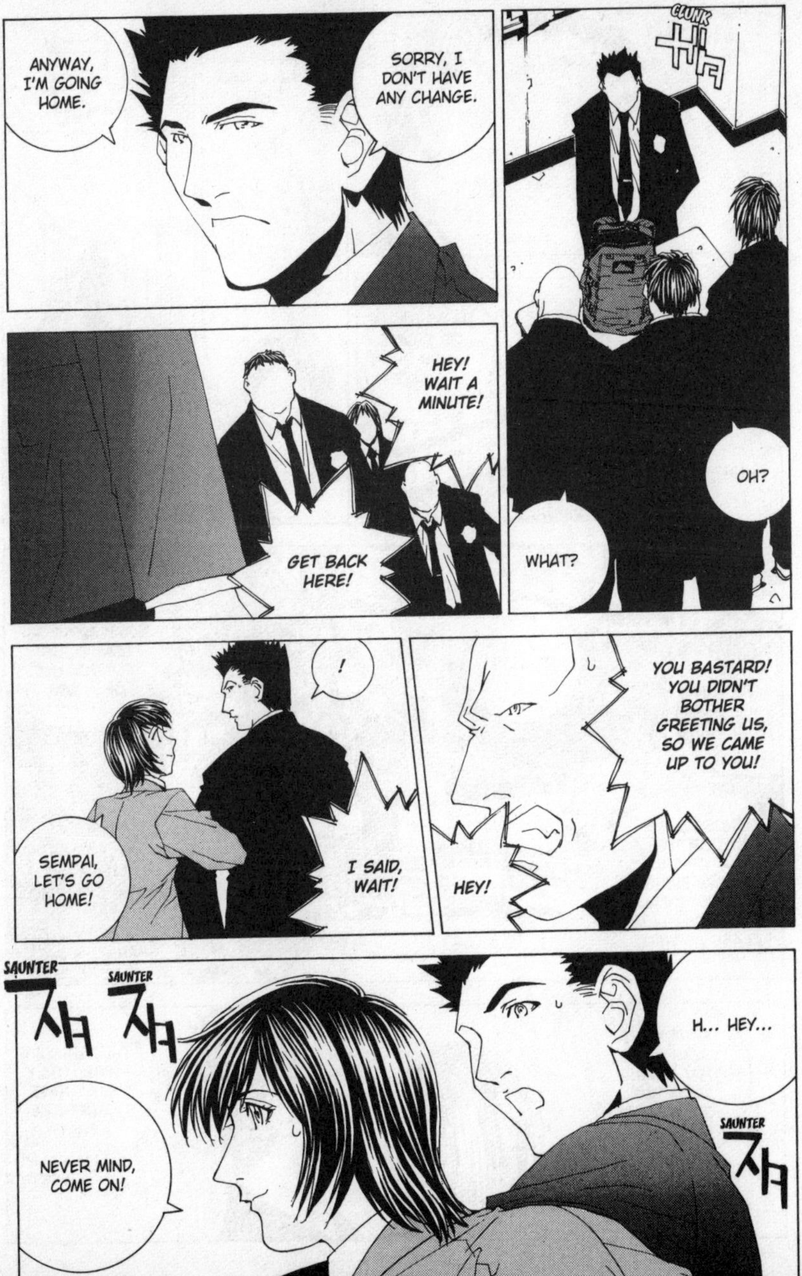
CLUNK
OH?
WHAT?
SORRY, I DON'T HAVE ANY CHANGE.
ANYWAY, I'M GOING HOME.
HEY! WAIT A MINUTE!
GET BACK HERE!
YOU BASTARD! YOU DIDN'T BOTHER GREETING US, SO WE CAME UP TO YOU!
HEY!
!
I SAID, WAIT!
SEMPAI, LET'S GO HOME!
H... HEY...
SAUNTER
SAUNTER
SAUNTER
NEVER MIND, COME ON!

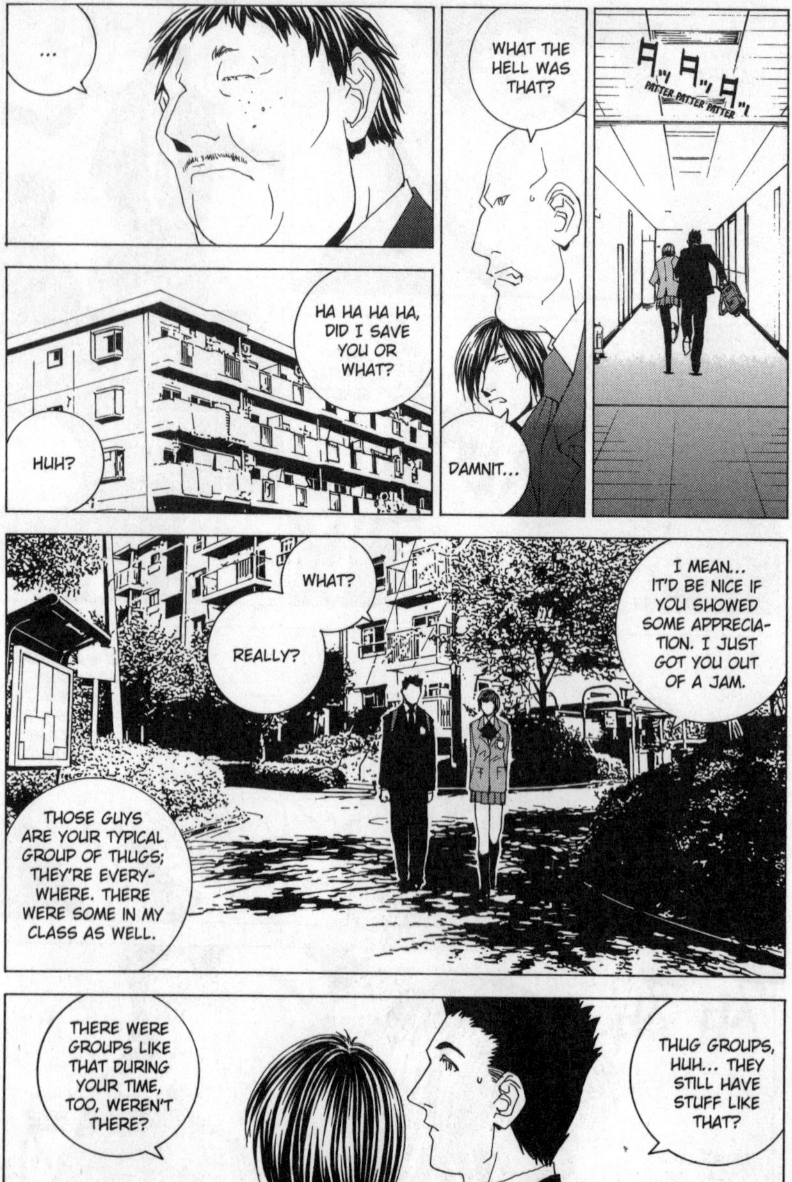
PATTER PATTER PATTER
WHAT THE HELL WAS THAT?
DAMNIT...
...
HA HA HA HA, DID I SAVE YOU OR WHAT?
HUH?
I MEAN... IT'D BE NICE IF YOU SHOWED SOME APPRECIA-TION. I JUST GOT YOU OUT OF A JAM.
WHAT?
REALLY?
THOSE GUYS ARE YOUR TYPICAL GROUP OF THUGS; THEY'RE EVERY-WHERE. THERE WERE SOME IN MY CLASS AS WELL.
THUG GROUPS, HUH... THEY STILL HAVE STUFF LIKE THAT?
THERE WERE GROUPS LIKE THAT DURING YOUR TIME, TOO, WEREN'T THERE?

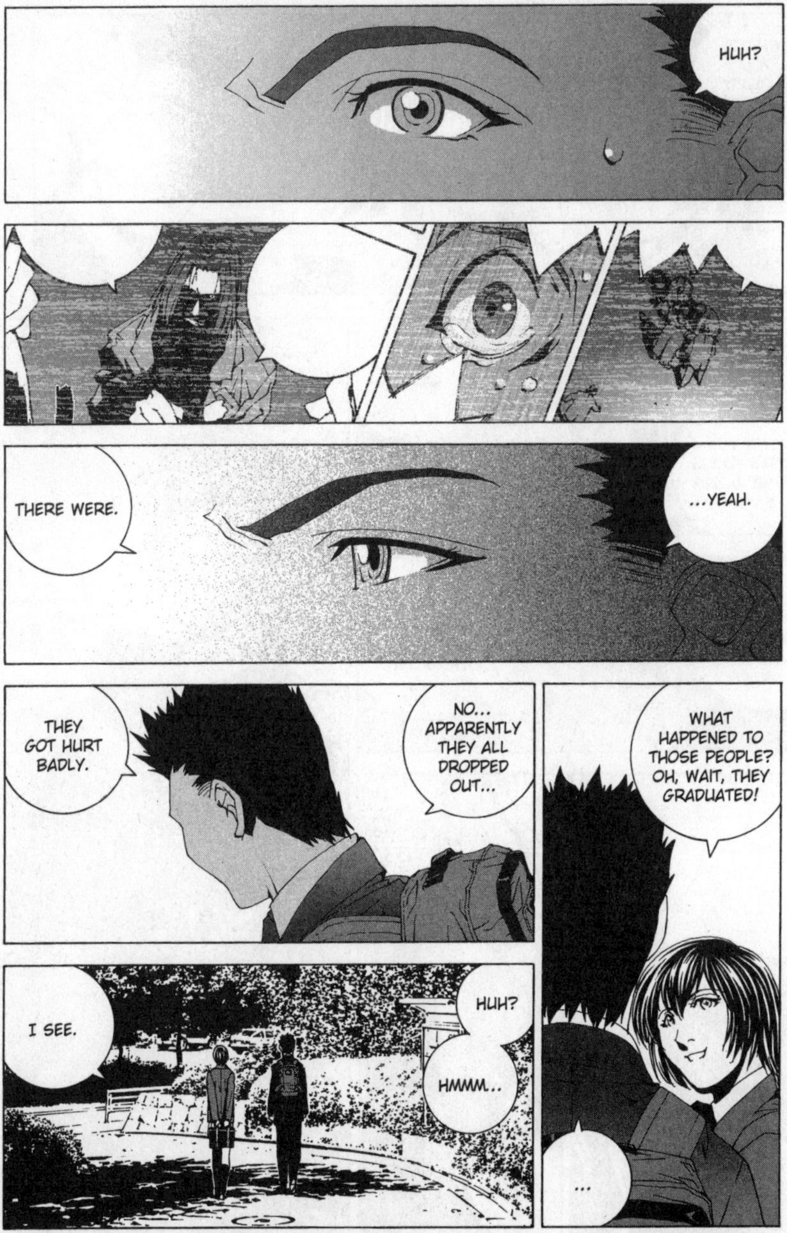
HUH?
...YEAH.
THERE WERE.
WHAT HAPPENED TO THOSE PEOPLE? OH, WAIT, THEY GRADUATED!
...
NO... APPARENTLY THEY ALL DROPPED OUT...
THEY GOT HURT BADLY.
HUH?
HMMM...
I SEE.

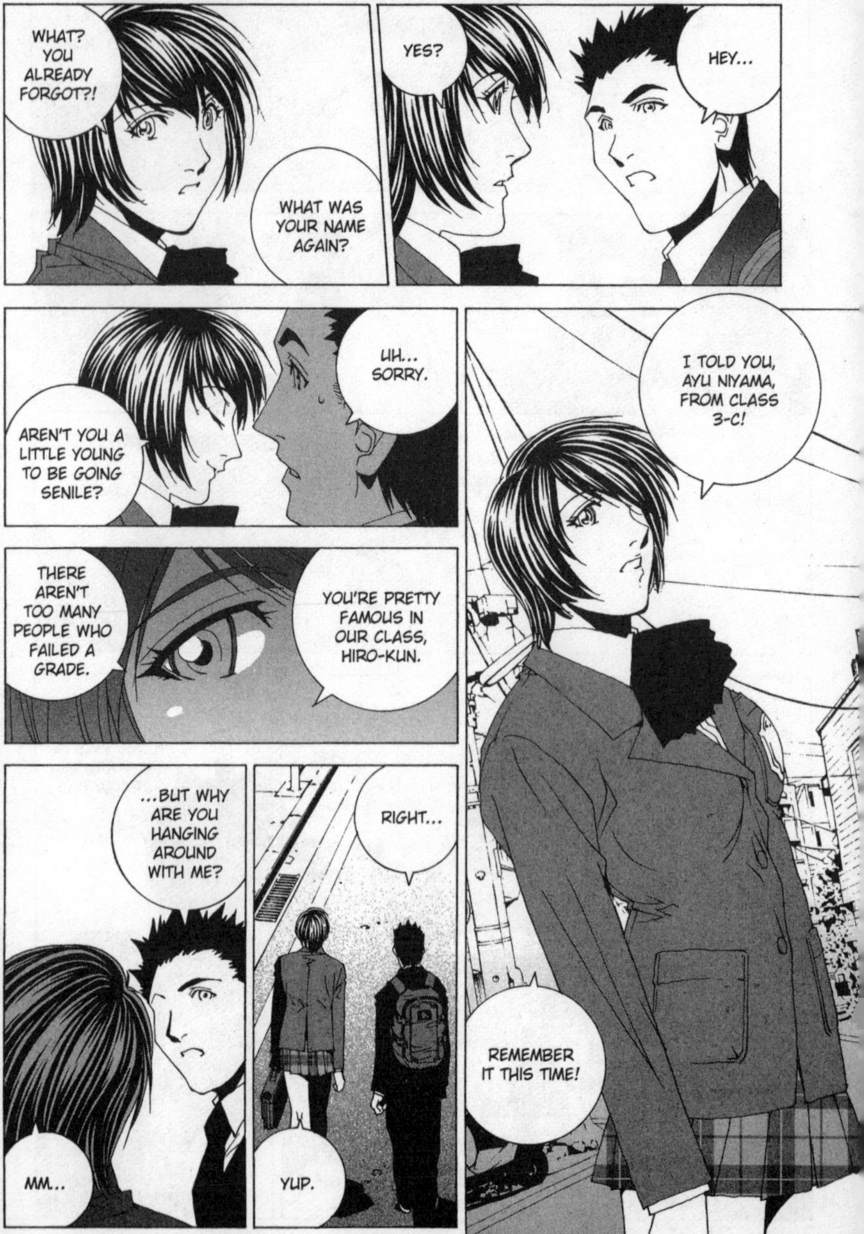
HEY...
YES?
WHAT WAS YOUR NAME AGAIN?
WHAT? YOU ALREADY FORGOT?!
I TOLD YOU, AYU NIYAMA, FROM CLASS 3-C!
REMEMBER IT THIS TIME!
UH... SORRY.
AREN'T YOU A LITTLE YOUNG TO BE GOING SENILE?
YOU'RE PRETTY FAMOUS IN OUR CLASS, HIRO-KUN.
THERE AREN'T TOO MANY PEOPLE WHO FAILED A GRADE.
RIGHT...
YUP.
...BUT WHY ARE YOU HANGING AROUND WITH ME?
MM...

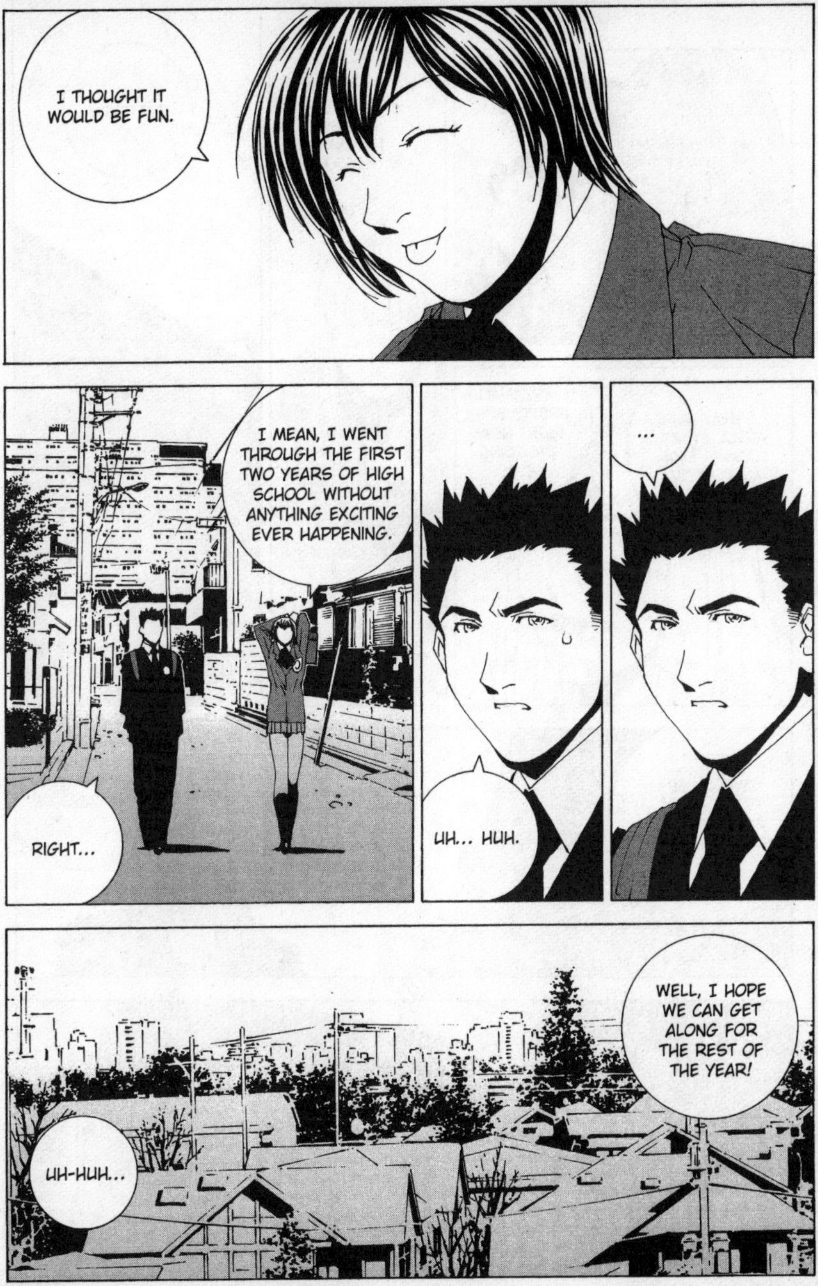
I THOUGHT IT WOULD BE FUN.
...
UH... HUH.
I MEAN, I WENT THROUGH THE FIRST TWO YEARS OF HIGH SCHOOL WITHOUT ANYTHING EXCITING EVER HAPPENING.
RIGHT...
WELL, I HOPE WE CAN GET ALONG FOR THE REST OF THE YEAR!
UH-HUH...

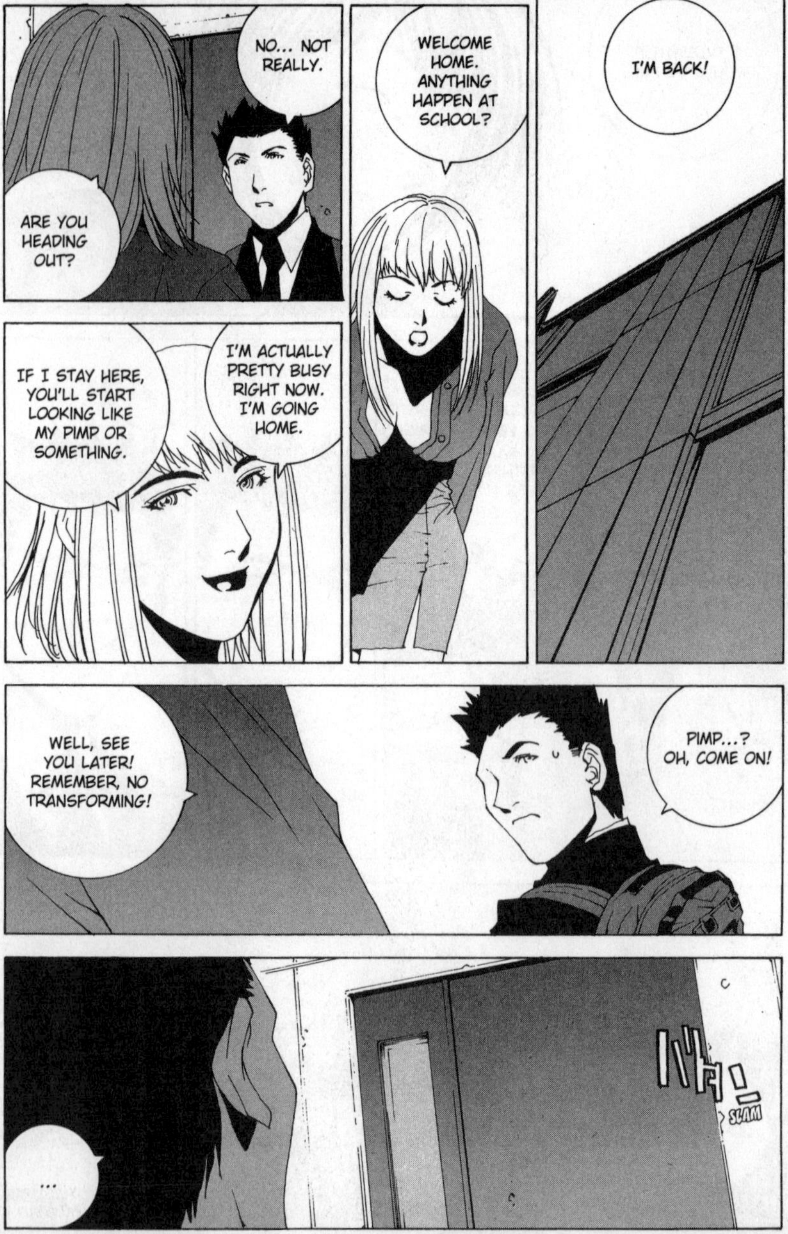
I'M BACK!
WELCOME HOME. ANYTHING HAPPEN AT SCHOOL?
NO... NOT REALLY.
ARE YOU HEADING OUT?
I'M ACTUALLY PRETTY BUSY RIGHT NOW. I'M GOING HOME.
IF I STAY HERE, YOU'LL START LOOKING LIKE MY PIMP OR SOMETHING.
PIMP...? OH, COME ON!
WELL, SEE YOU LATER! REMEMBER, NO TRANSFORMING!
SLAM
...

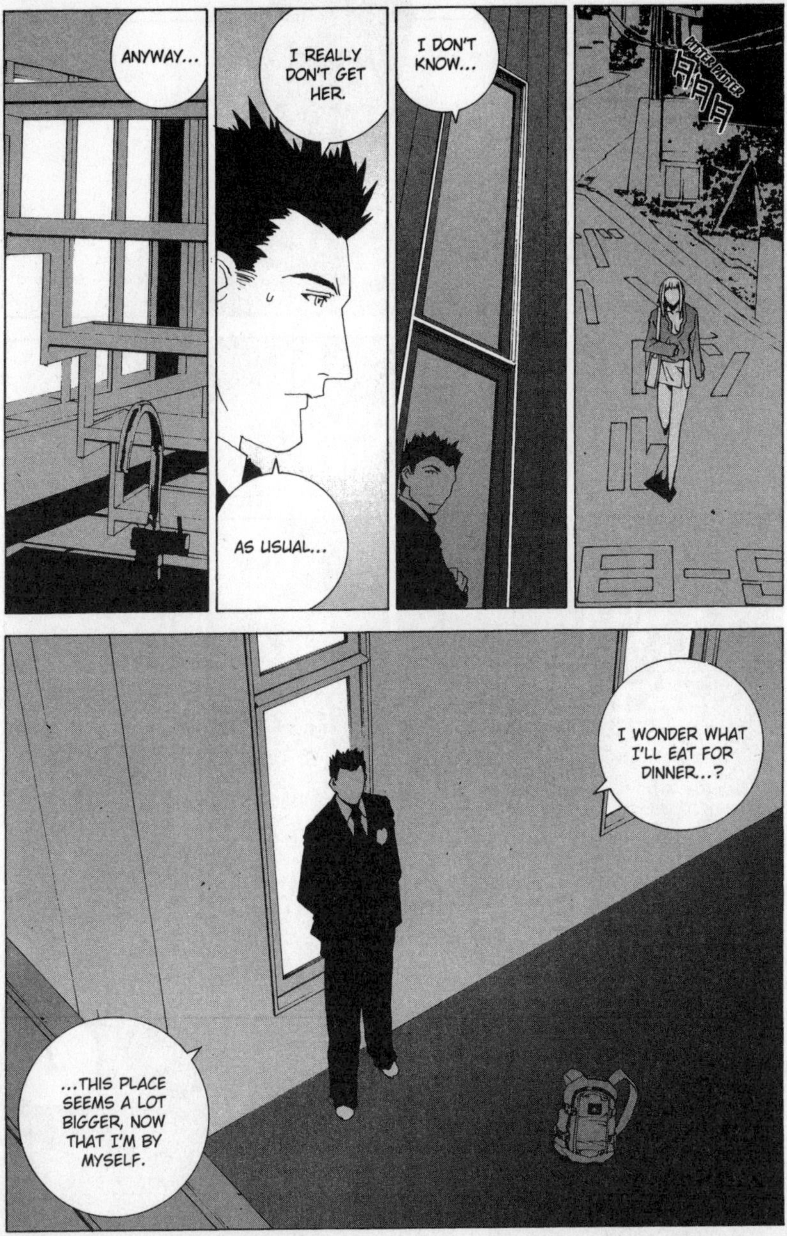
PATTER PATTER
I DON'T KNOW...
I REALLY DON'T GET HER.
AS USUAL...
ANYWAY...
I WONDER WHAT I'LL EAT FOR DINNER..?
...THIS PLACE SEEMS A LOT BIGGER, NOW THAT I'M BY MYSELF.

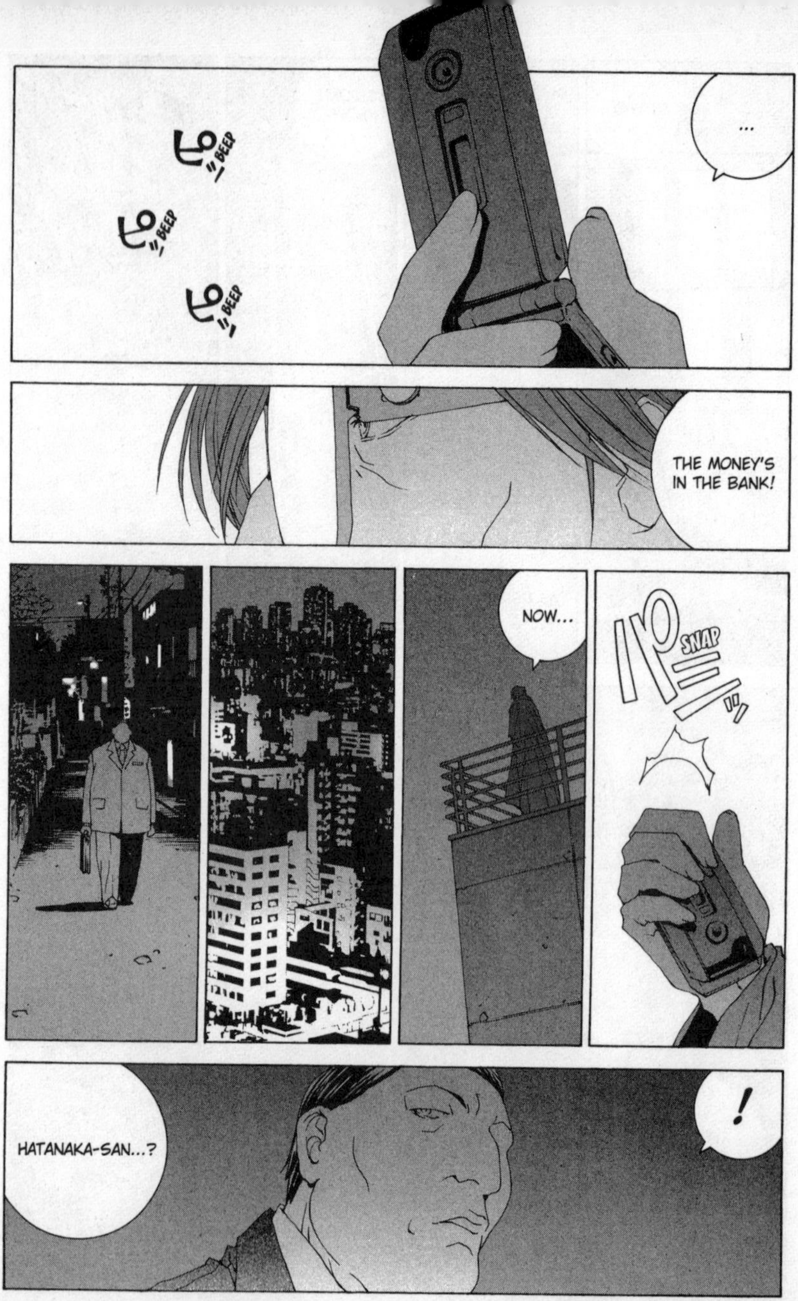
...
BEEP
BEEP
BEEP
THE MONEY'S IN THE BANK!
SNAP
NOW...
!
HATANAKA-SAN...?

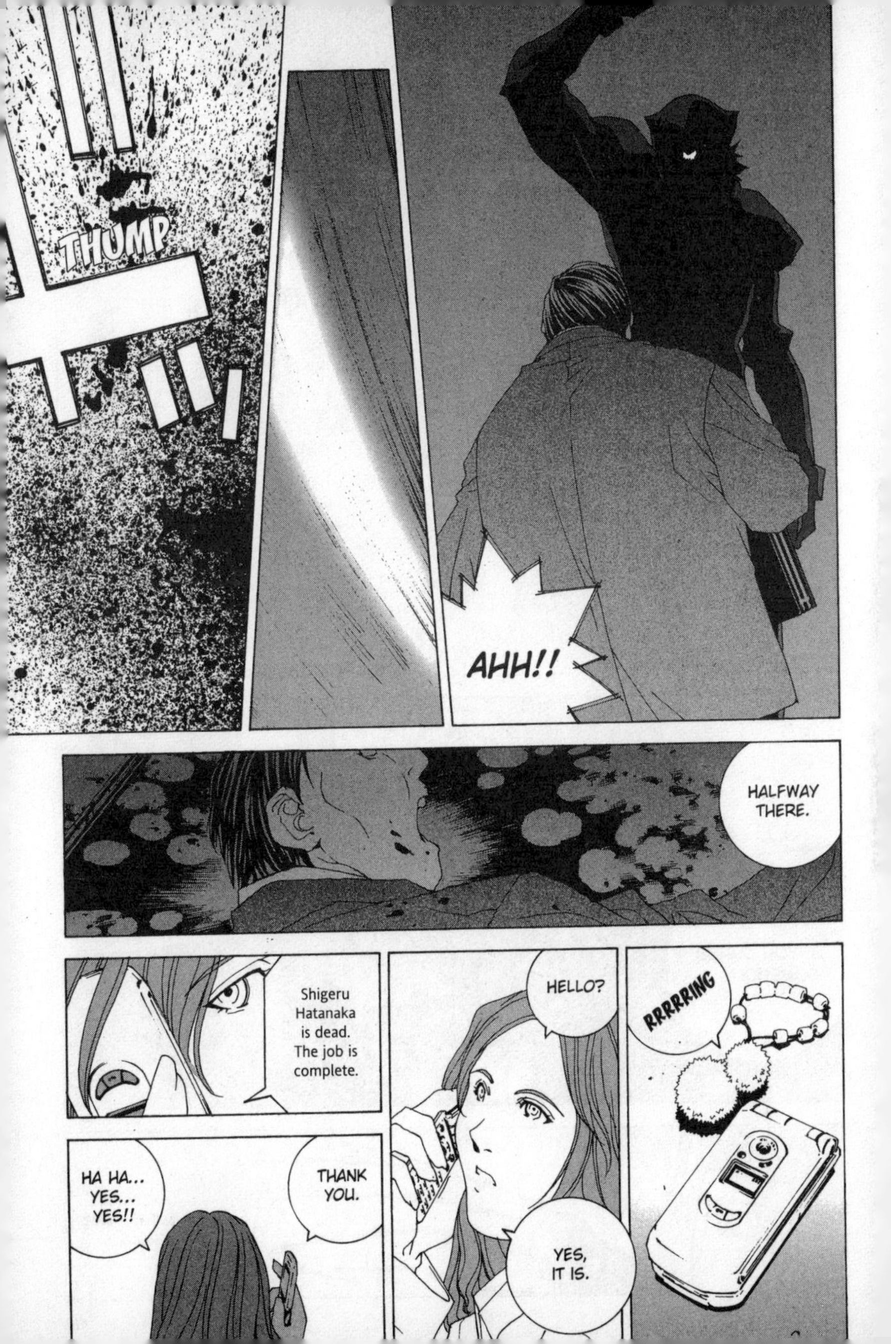
AHH!!
THUMP
HALFWAY THERE.
RRRRRING
HELLO?
YES, IT IS.
Shigeru Hatanaka is dead. The job is complete.
THANK YOU.
HA HA... YES... YES!!

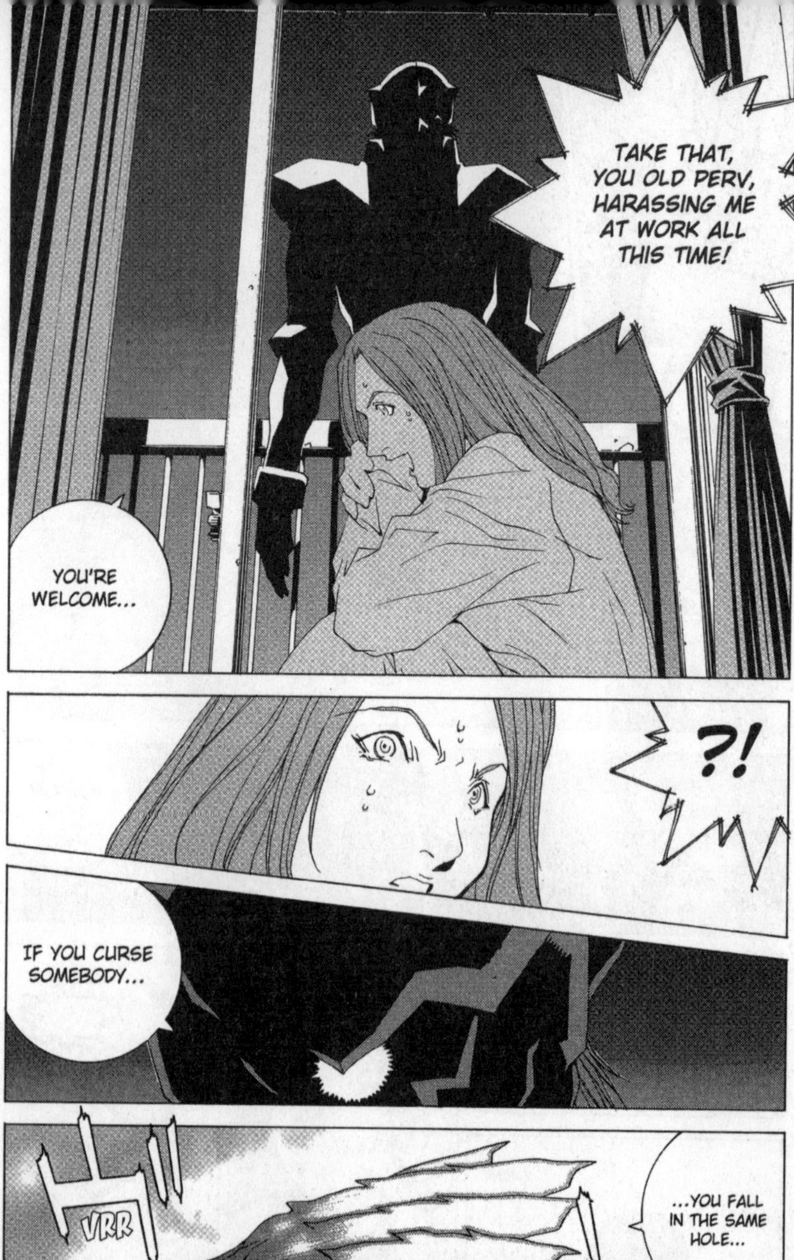
TAKE THAT, YOU OLD PERV, HARASSING ME AT WORK ALL THIS TIME!
YOU'RE WELCOME...
?!
IF YOU CURSE SOMEBODY...
...YOU FALL IN THE SAME HOLE...
VRR

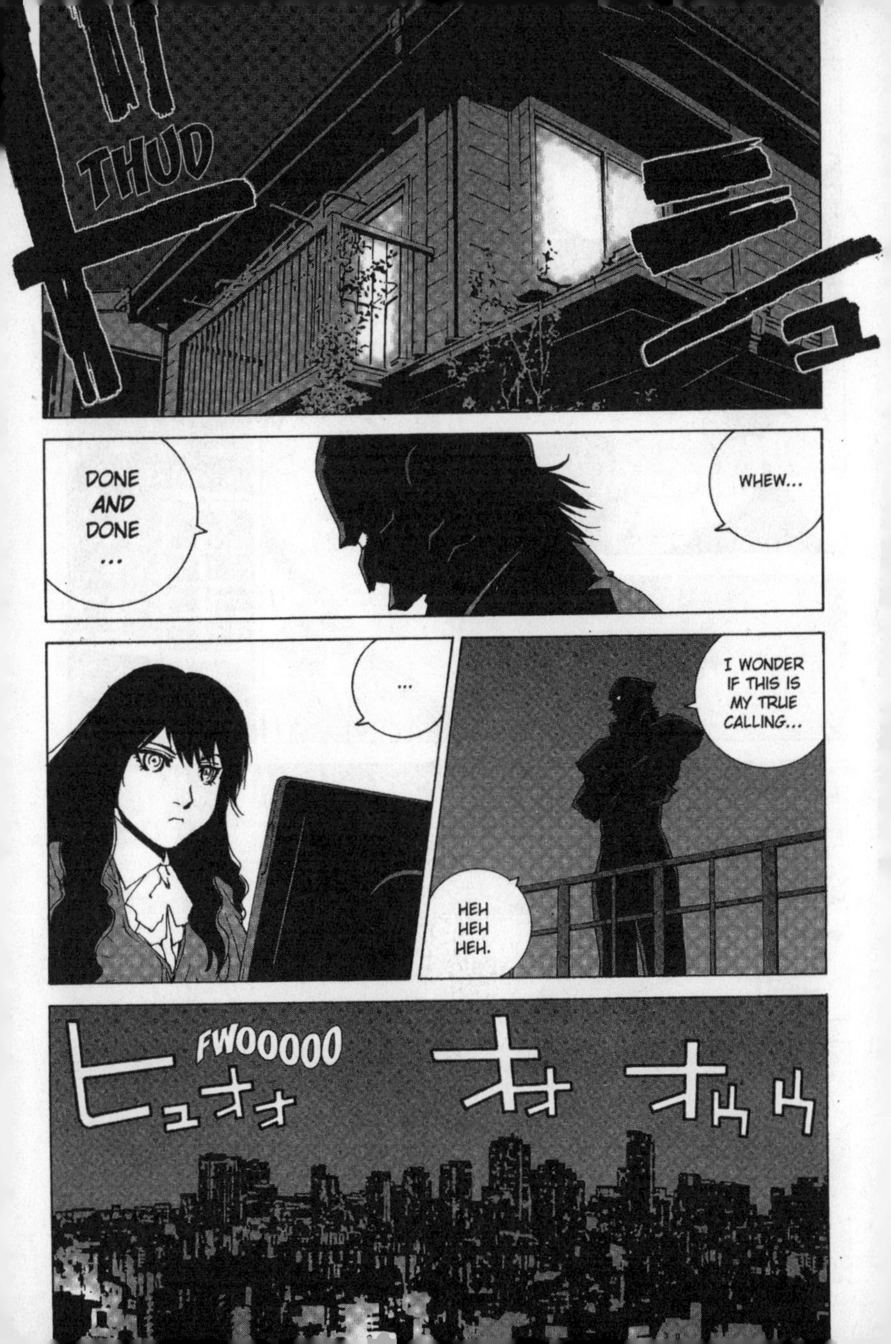
THUD
WHEW...
DONE AND DONE ...
I WONDER IF THIS IS MY TRUE CALLING...
HEH HEH HEH.
...
FWOOOOO

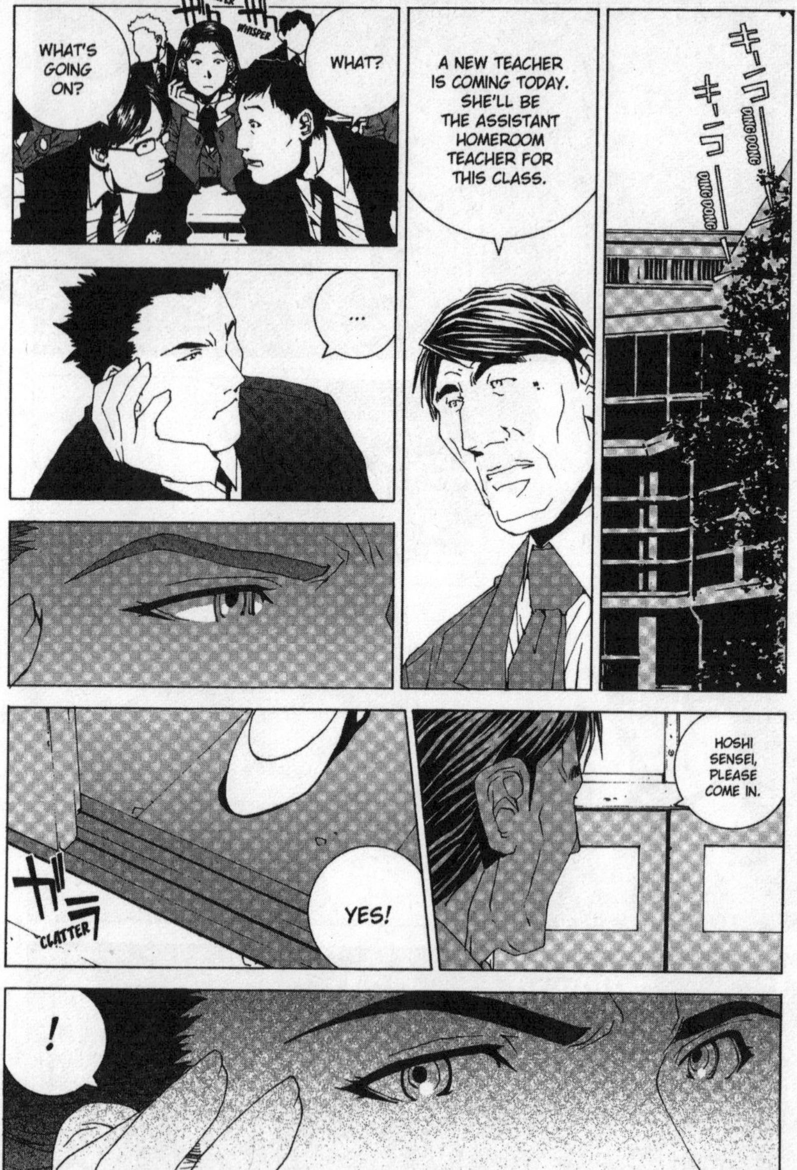

キーンコーン
DING DONG
キーンコーン
DING DONG
A NEW TEACHER IS COMING TODAY. SHE'LL BE THE ASSISTANT HOMEROOM TEACHER FOR THIS CLASS.
WHAT?
WHISPER
WHISPER
WHAT'S GOING ON?
...
HOSHI SENSEI, PLEASE COME IN.
YES!
CLATTER
!

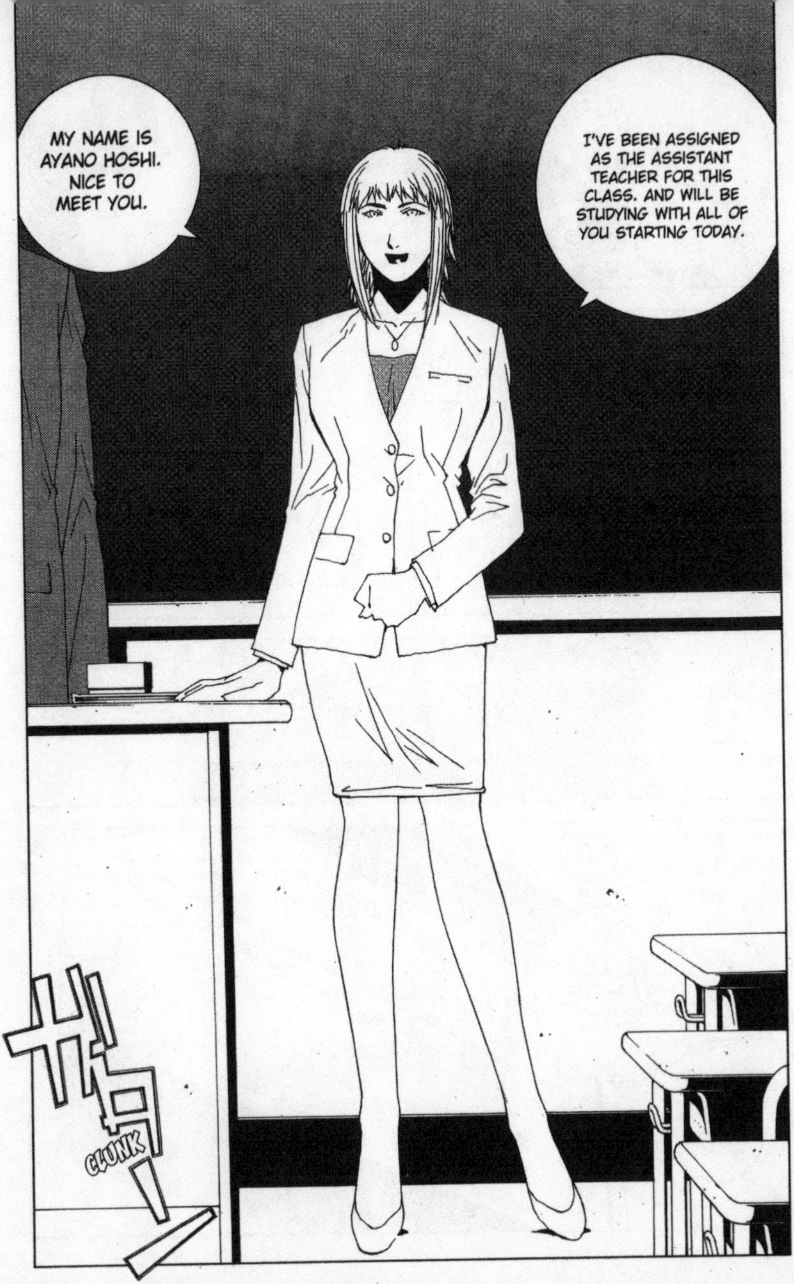
I'VE BEEN ASSIGNED AS THE ASSISTANT TEACHER FOR THIS CLASS. AND WILL BE STUDYING WITH ALL OF YOU STARTING TODAY.
MY NAME IS AYANO HOSHI. NICE TO MEET YOU.
CLUNK

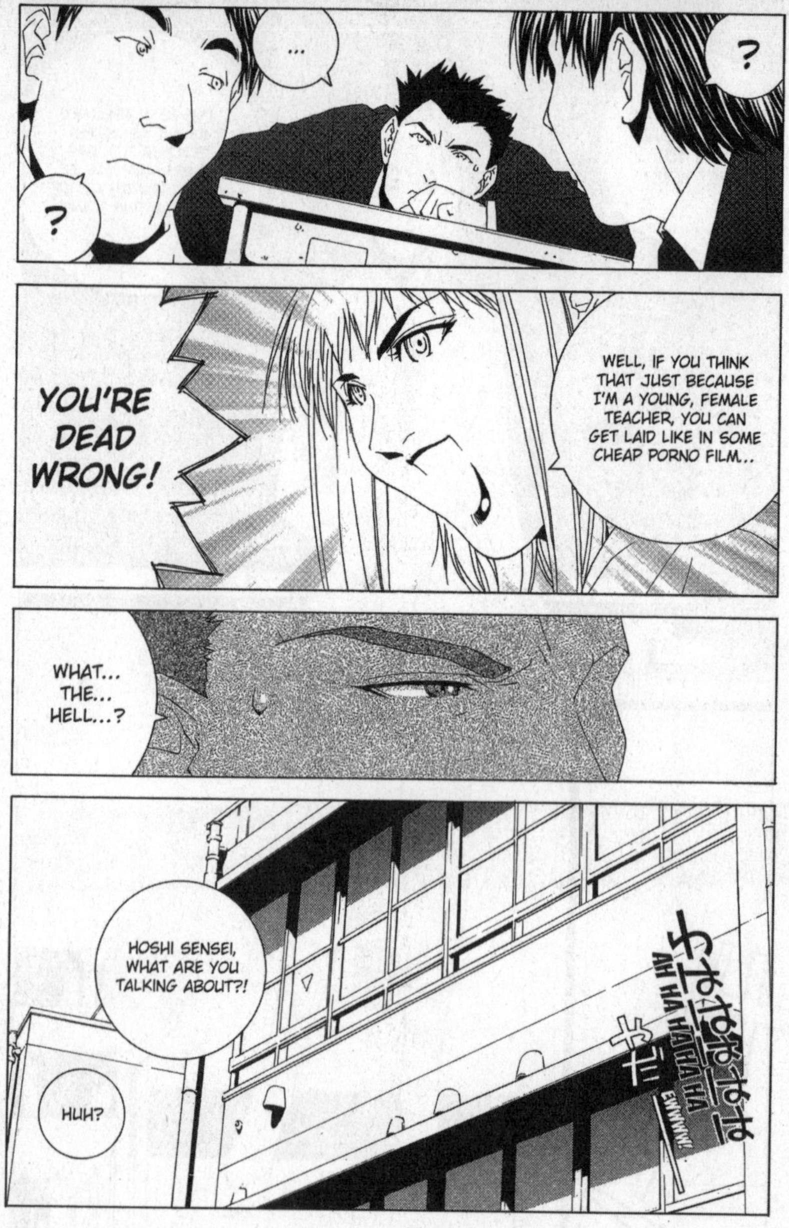
?
...
?
WELL, IF YOU THINK THAT JUST BECAUSE I'M A YOUNG, FEMALE TEACHER, YOU CAN GET LAID LIKE IN SOME CHEAP PORNO FILM...
YOU'RE DEAD WRONG!
WHAT... THE... HELL...?
AH HA HA HA HA HA
EWWWW!
HOSHI SENSEI, WHAT ARE YOU TALKING ABOUT?!
HUH?

STAFF LIST

art and directed by
KIA ASAMIYA

junk suit design by
YUTAKA IZUBUCHI

art assistant
NAOKI HYODOH

NOBUAKI TAKANO

JUN KANEKO

TAKESHI OHNISHI

editor
HONKI SUZU

NORIFUMI OSHINO

ATSUSHI ITO

book designed by
NORIKO IWASHITA

produced by
CHAMPION RED editorial department

special thanks to
ALL READERS

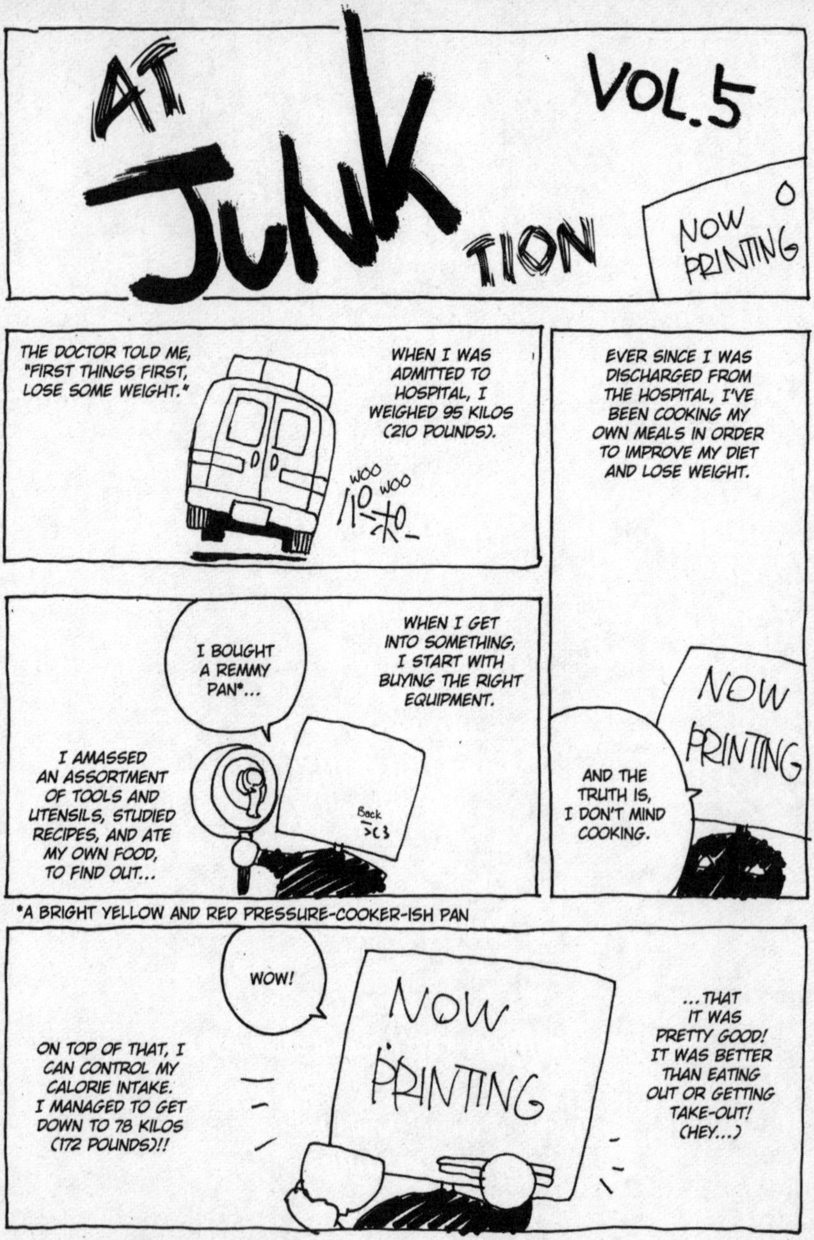
VOL.5
NOW PRINTING
AT JUNK TION
EVER SINCE I WAS DISCHARGED FROM THE HOSPITAL, I'VE BEEN COOKING MY OWN MEALS IN ORDER TO IMPROVE MY DIET AND LOSE WEIGHT.
NOW PRINTING
AND THE TRUTH IS, I DON'T MIND COOKING.
WHEN I WAS ADMITTED TO HOSPITAL, I WEIGHED 95 KILOS (210 POUNDS).
WOO WOO
THE DOCTOR TOLD ME, "FIRST THINGS FIRST, LOSE SOME WEIGHT."
WHEN I GET INTO SOMETHING, I START WITH BUYING THE RIGHT EQUIPMENT.
I BOUGHT A REMMY PAN*...
Back
I AMASSED AN ASSORTMENT OF TOOLS AND UTENSILS, STUDIED RECIPES, AND ATE MY OWN FOOD, TO FIND OUT...
*A BRIGHT YELLOW AND RED PRESSURE-COOKER-ISH PAN
...THAT IT WAS PRETTY GOOD! IT WAS BETTER THAN EATING OUT OR GETTING TAKE-OUT! (HEY...)
NOW PRINTING
WOW!
ON TOP OF THAT, I CAN CONTROL MY CALORIE INTAKE. I MANAGED TO GET DOWN TO 78 KILOS (172 POUNDS)!!

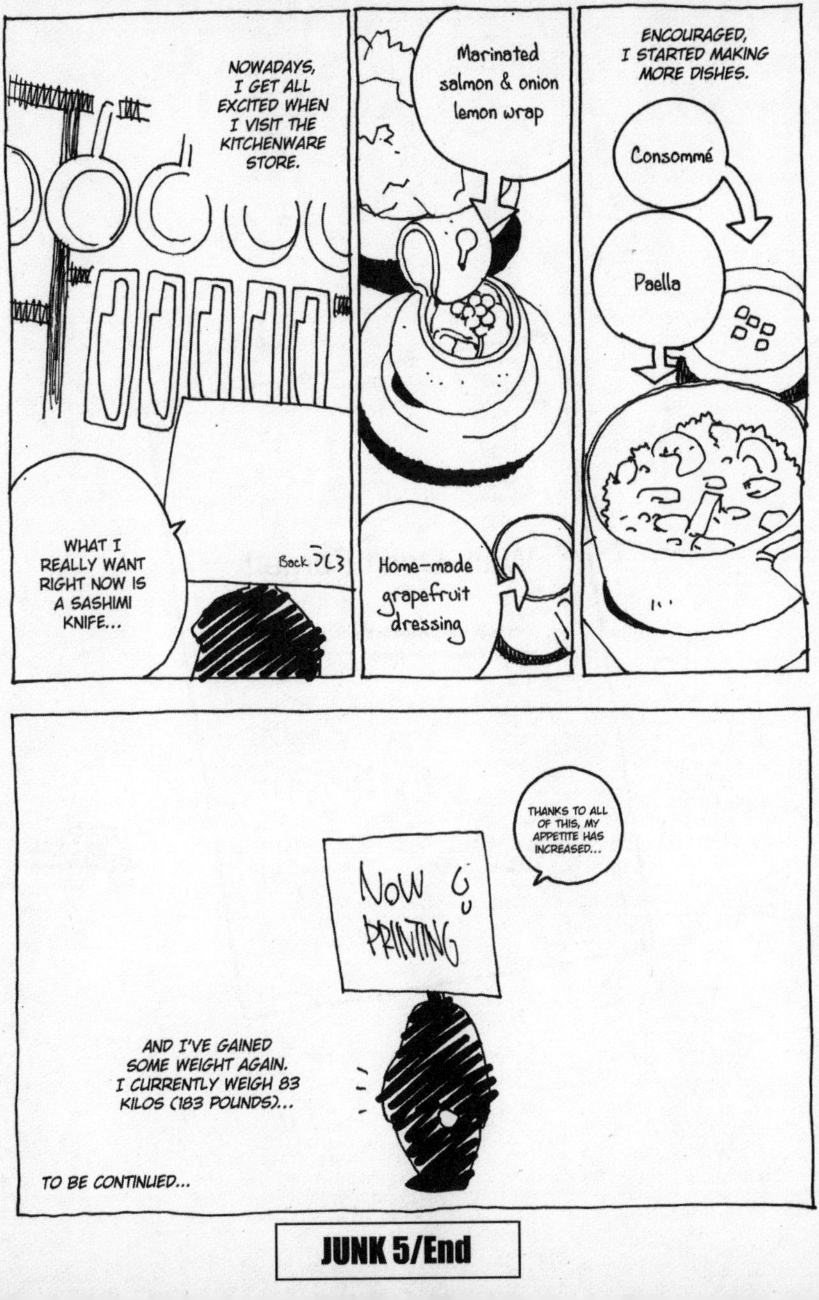
ENCOURAGED, I STARTED MAKING MORE DISHES.
Consommé
Paella
Marinated salmon & onion lemon wrap
Home-made grapefruit dressing
NOWADAYS, I GET ALL EXCITED WHEN I VISIT THE KITCHENWARE STORE.
Back うしろ
WHAT I REALLY WANT RIGHT NOW IS A SASHIMI KNIFE...
THANKS TO ALL OF THIS, MY APPETITE HAS INCREASED...
NOW PRINTING
AND I'VE GAINED SOME WEIGHT AGAIN. I CURRENTLY WEIGH 83 KILOS (183 POUNDS)...
TO BE CONTINUED...

JUNK 5/End

Wait, Don't Forget!

This book was printed in the original/Asian format. Please read panels from right to left.